Praise for *Preventing Prejudice*

Preventing Prejudice: A Guide for Counselors, Educators, and Parents is a unique and refreshing book that tackles two of the most interrelated and problematic issues in our society: prejudice and racism. The first edition was unanimously acclaimed as a major contribution to the field, and this second edition is destined to be a classic. It represents one of the most clear, concise, and honest looks at the origins, manifestations, dynamics, and psychological costs of prejudice and racism written thus far. One of its major strengths is the authors' ability to relate these topics to everyday life; to speak directly to counselors, educators, and parents in meaningful ways; to ground their concepts in the research and theories of the day; and to give an uplifting message about what can be done to combat these two evils. Toward this end they provide specific suggestions and exercises that can be used by readers to combat their own biases and to help others as well. Educators who wish to help their students begin the process of confronting their own biases, parents who desire to help their children become multicultural citizens of the world, and counselors who wish to become culturally competent will find much in this book. This is truly a superb book that makes a major contribution to the field and should be read by everyone.

—Derald Wing Sue, Ph.D.
Professor of Counseling and Clinical Psychology
Teachers College, Columbia University

The distance between aspiring toward human affirmation on one hand and legitimate change in the social climate of America on the other is paved with the road called rhetoric. Like a forbidden relationship, rhetoric promises much but delivers very little.

Politicians, educators, mental health professionals, and even parents use rhetoric because it protects our fragile sensibilities and disguises our prejudices, biases, and fears about issues of race, gender, class, sexual orientation, disability, and religion.

Preventing Prejudice: A Guide for Counselors, Educators, and Parents (2nd ed.) helps to close the gap between those two extremes and equips us all with a valuable and precious tool for confronting the many prejudices we often find difficult to engage, let alone admit to ourselves.

Beyond rhetoric, this text is an authentic expression and plea that challenges each of us to build alliances across demographic boundaries in order to fight an insidious social disease. Drs. Ponterotto, Utsey, and Pedersen succeed in dislodging us from our comfortable categories of intellectual, emotional, behavioral, and spiritual apathy and invite us to transcend the amount of social disappointment and despair and strive toward a more hopeful and optimistic future.

—Thomas A. Parham, Ph.D.
Distinguished Psychologist
Association of Black Psychologists

Preventing Prejudice is a critical resource book for educators, counselors, and parents who want to learn more about how to handle prejudice and should be required reading for all of us who work with diverse populations. I was thrilled to see the second edition and was most impressed with the authors' blend of scholarship and practical applications. It is a powerful book that helps us see that we can make a difference in fighting prejudice. The authors have significantly expanded on the excellent first edition in a practical and nonjudgmental way, and, most importantly, provide a concrete and proactive approach to reducing prejudice. The authors hope that by providing individuals with more knowledge and an opportunity to practice prejudice reduction, we can indeed combat prejudice in its many forms. That hope is realized by this excellent book.

—Nadya A. Fouad, Ph.D.
Professor, Department of Educational Psychology
University of Wisconsin–Milwaukee

From the Foreword

Preventing Prejudice is based in theory and research. It is also based in practice and experience, and it is informed by the people it is meant to reach. What do people really think, or know, or feel? Are you racist *because* you are White? Are you immune from racism if you are gay? Doesn't embracing your ethnic or racial group make you prone to bias against other groups? Isn't advocating racial identity, therefore, a threat to the very sensitive awareness of others advocated here? Are you better or worse off psychologically if you belong to multiple racial categories? Is there a personality type that supersedes and triumphs over it all? *Preventing Prejudice* addresses these questions and issues and many more with direct, clear, and cogent ideas and instruction. Readers will not just know the answer; they will know what to do about it.

Cultural diversity and multiculturalism are not just slogans; they are reality and promise. The first edition of *Preventing Prejudice* was a bold and important effort to address these complex problems. Its success was heralded when the Gustavus Myers Center for the Study of Human Rights in North America presented it with the prestigious award for "Outstanding Book on the Subject of Human Rights in North America." Ponterotto, Utsey, and Pedersen took this outstanding work and expanded and improved on it. The result is a testament to their dedication and a significant contribution to solving the problem of the 21st century: the problem of the culture line.

—James M. Jones, Ph.D.
Professor of Psychology
University of Delaware

Preventing Prejudice: A Guide for Counselors, Educators, and Parents (2nd ed.) is a must-read for anyone who is interested in better understanding what he or she can do to address the complex forms of prejudice, racism, and other types of cultural oppression that continue to exist in our contemporary society. Ponterotto, Utsey, and Pedersen have truly produced a masterpiece that highlights many practical strategies counselors, educators, and parents can use to foster a greater level of social justice and mental health in our 21st-century culturally and racially-diverse society. If I had to recommend one book for counselors, educators, and parents to read this year that addresses these issues, this would be it!

—Michael D'Andrea
Professor, Department of Counselor Education
University of Hawai'i
Executive Director of the National Institute for Multicultural Counseling

An impressive, deliberate, and problem-oriented second edition. Prejudice has no boundaries and spares no one. *Preventing Prejudice* offers hope and resources to all of us—counselors, educators, and parents. We are all agents of change.

—Patricia Arredondo, Ed.D.
Associate Vice President and Senior Advisor for Academic Initiatives
Arizona State University
President, American Counseling Association

I did not think it was possible, but the second edition of *Preventing Prejudice* is even better than the first! The authors have blessed us with a volume filled with relevant information about the causes and consequences of prejudice and discrimination, along with proactive strategies for reducing and ameliorating prejudice. Individuals who are serious about preventing and eradicating prejudice must not only read this book but should also ensure that it is a treasured work in their collections! The second edition of *Preventing Prejudice* is destined to be on everyone's all-time top ten list of books in the area of prejudice reduction and social justice action.

—Madonna G. Constantine, Ph.D.
Professor and Chair, Department of Counseling and Clinical Psychology
Teachers College, Columbia University

This expanded and updated version of *Preventing Prejudice* provides a wealth of information about the causes, manifestations, and correlates of prejudice as well as practical suggestions for activities aimed at reducing or preventing prejudice. Integrating evidence from a wide variety of sources, it is a valuable resource for both researchers and educators.

—Jean S. Phinney, Ph.D.
Professor of Psychology
California State University, Los Angeles

This important book is as much about promoting human potential and dignity as it is about preventing prejudice. The ideas presented by Ponterotto, Utsey, and Pedersen have implications for the welfare of all oppressed, disenfranchised, and marginalized people. While laying a sound conceptual and research foundation, the authors provide practical exercises and reader-friendliness for a variety of constituents.

—Charles R. Ridley, Ph.D.
Professor, Counseling Psychology
Indiana University

At a time in the field when everyone clamors to be included in the discussion about diversity and multiculturalism, Ponterotto, Utsey, and Pedersen bring us back to our historical roots in this book. They remind us that to participate in the discourse, discerning the nature of prejudice and racism and its psychological effects on ethnic and racial groups is at our core. And, if we fail in our appreciation of this concept, our ability to prevent prejudice becomes suspect.

—Donald B. Pope-Davis, Ph.D.
Professor, Department of Psychology
University of Notre Dame

Ponterotto and Pedersen's original book was a primer embraced by professionals and parents alike. It was a call to action, pressing the reader to DO SOMETHING to effect change. The second edition, with Utsey as a powerful third voice, is truly a new book. The field has grown, the literature has exploded, yet racial and cultural prejudice still flourish. This new book expands our awareness of the problem. The section on the history and consequences of prejudice is thought-provoking. The introduction of the multicultural personality builds on literature from several fields. Finally, the authors prompt the reader to apply this newfound knowledge with age-specific exercises. With this exciting edition in hand, there is no excuse to not DO SOMETHING to reduce or prevent prejudice.

—Sharon H. Bowman, Ph.D.
Professor and Chair, Department of Counseling Psychology and Guidance Services
Ball State University

More than a decade after the publication of the first edition of *Preventing Prejudice,* Drs. Ponterotto, Utsey, and Pedersen give a much-needed fresh look at the complexities of prejudice that continue to plague our society. Their book highlights hands-on remedies for counselors, educators, and parents. The text provides outstanding activities and instruction on creating contexts for change. This book is a MUST-READ!

—Lisa A. Suzuki, Ph.D.
Department of Applied Psychology
New York University

Readers of the first edition will welcome this extensively revised and expanded volume, especially the attention given to the multicultural personality. While retaining its foundation in racial and ethnic identity development, this work equips teachers, counselors, and parents with practical skills to be deliberate and intentional in preventing prejudice. Readers with particular interest in biracial, multiracial, and gay and lesbian identity development will find this book especially helpful in addressing concerns relevant to those populations. The section on Instruments and Resources for Prejudice Prevention Work is particularly useful for professionals working in the area of prejudice prevention.

—Don. C. Locke, Ed.D.
Distinguished Professor Emeritus
North Carolina State University

Preventing Prejudice is a tour de force in understanding the harmful effects of prejudice and racism on intergroup relations. Thoroughly researched and comprehensive in scope, this book offers state-of-the-art information on the causes and consequences of racial prejudice. The authors move beyond analysis to offer practical solutions for reducing prejudice. One of the book's unique contributions to the multicultural literature lies in the authors' ability to simultaneously address both professional audiences (e.g., educators and counselors) and lay audiences (e.g., parents). Without a doubt this book is one of the most important resources that social justice and human rights advocates can own. *Preventing Prejudice* should be required reading for all counselors, educators, and mental health professionals.

—Kevin O. Cokley, Ph.D.
Department of Educational, School, and Counseling Psychology, and Black Studies
University of Missouri

The second edition of *Preventing Prejudice: A Guide for Counselors, Educators, and Parents* is a critical reference for those conducting research and training aimed at understanding, reducing, and ultimately preventing prejudice. Ponterotto, Utsey, and Pedersen provide a careful review of history, definitions, theory, research, and application issues. They also add to the focus on racial and ethnic identity development by integrating theoretical and empirical developments on biracial, multiracial, and lesbian and gay identity development. Furthermore, they provide conceptual definition, elaboration, and operationalization of the concept of multicultural personality. An important and unique feature of the text is its presentation of creative exercises aimed at increasing multicultural awareness and reducing prejudice in different age groups. In addition, the authors provide a rich range of resources for research and personal development, including books, professional organizations, popular movies, and films, as well as selected instruments to measure critical constructs in the study and prevention of prejudice. The broad scholarly scope and applicability of this text is truly impressive.

—Bonnie Moradi, Ph.D.
Department of Psychology
University of Florida

Drs. Ponterotto, Utsey, and Pedersen have put together a book that has the potential to make an important impact in our world. Creating a dramatic improvement over the award-winning first edition, the authors have written a comprehensive book on prejudice prevention based on current theories and research in psychology and education. Remarkably, although reflecting the highest degrees of scholarship, this book offers easy access to a wide range of audiences including counselors, educators, administrators, and teachers. Indeed, this book is a must-read for anyone who is interested in reducing prejudice and all types of -isms (e.g., racism, heterosexism, and sexism) in our world.

—Bryan S. K. Kim, Ph.D.
Associate Professor, Department of Counseling, Clinical, and School Psychology
University of California, Santa Barbara

Preventing Prejudice is a must-read for anyone dealing with racism and monoculturalism in today's society. Theoretically based with relevant and masterful practical application, the book provides teachers, parents, researchers, and practitioners with the necessary tools to understand and fight prejudice. I especially like the applications for parents working with their children on issues of racism and prejudice.

—Daniel T. Sciarra, Ph.D.
Chairperson, Department of Counseling, Research,
Special Education, and Rehabilitation
Hofstra University

In our culturally diverse society, educational and helping service professionals have a need to understand the complex nature of prejudice and what may contribute to the prevention or maintenance of such beliefs. This book provides invaluable information on the historical and theoretical context for the development of prejudice and offers key insights to help professionals understand counselor, educator, and parental roles in the prevention of prejudice. Furthermore, professionals will find the descriptive information on exercises, measures, and other resources (e.g., books, videos/films, organizations) to be essential tools in their efforts to educate and sensitize others about the varied ways in which prejudice affects our lives.

—Alan W. Burkard, Ph.D.
Department of Counseling and Educational Psychology
Marquette University

This book is an essential reference for people working in the fields of multiculturalism, counseling, and education. The model of prejudice that this book uses reflects the most recent scholarship on the psychological impact of race and racism. This perspective considers prejudice not as an abhorrent isolated act or tendency but as an expression of an individual's level of racial identity in the context of societal racism. This holistic point of view locates the individual within cultural and societal systems of which he or she is a part. Individual prejudice and societal racism are considered together, as are the cost of both to people of color and to Whites (the latter is frequently ignored).

One especially valuable feature of this new edition is the emphasis on parents and educators. It opens the book to new audiences, particularly teachers and parents who have tremendous influence on the formation of the next generation. It gives added teeth to the word "preventing" in the title. To the extent that anti-racism education can be made a regular feature of elementary and high school curricula, this book may help a student address very serious issues before they become entrenched in his or her personality. So often, anti-prejudice training is remedial; this book is extraordinary because it truly focuses on prevention.

In academia, we frequently lament the gap between theory, research, and practice. These authors suggest that the ideas put forward are in fact amenable to practical application and empirical validation and, in each case, they provide the means to do so.

—George V. Gushue, Ph.D.
Department of Counseling and Clinical Psychology
Teachers College, Columbia University

Preventing Prejudice: A Guide for Counselors, Educators, and Parents (2nd ed.) is a courageous landmark book in which nationally and internationally known authors have taken on a daunting challenge to combat the hydra of prejudice that raises its ugly head in insidious ways in many painful -isms. In this definitive and monumental textbook on prejudice, Ponterotto, Utsey, and Pedersen have reaffirmed their commitment to enhance their manifesto of social justice, racial equities, and human rights through proactive approaches.

At the cusp of the new millennium, when problems of color and culture lines are still causing a pervasive and destructive American dilemma resulting in interracial hate, fears, violence, and abuse, this book is a much-needed and welcome addition to the field of helping professions. Through their tour de force of prejudice and quintessential concepts of multicultural scholarship, these authors have created a compendium of tools and a constellation of practical and concrete strategies that are designed to intervene and prevent the scourge of prejudice.

In *Preventing Prejudice: A Guide for Counselors, Educators, and Parents* (2nd ed.), the authors have presented their new ideas on how to combat and prevent prejudice through a most impressive, persuasive, and systematic manner, written with rare lucidity, grace, and stunning clarity. They also demonstrate tremendous depth, perception, and insight into the issues relating to prejudice.

This second edition has been expanded to include many new constructs of paramount importance from the multicultural personality, leading models of identity development, and African-centered psychology. *Preventing Prejudice* reflects a happy blending of didactic and experiential exercises. Inclusiveness and comprehensiveness are the hallmarks of this book. It is rich in detail, and in many ways it is original, profound, and provocative; it is destined to become one of the classic books and shining stars in the galaxy of multicultural counseling. This is a superb, comprehensive, and indispensable book both for the novice and the experienced mental health professional. It will become a desk reference for many clinicians working with multicultural populations that provides fascinating insights and enlarges their understanding about the hydra of prejudice.

—Daya Singh Sandhu, Ed.D.
Professor, Department of Educational and Counseling Psychology
University of Louisville, Kentucky

Preventing Prejudice

SECOND EDITION

MULTICULTURAL ASPECTS OF COUNSELING AND PSYCHOTHERAPY SERIES

VOLUMES IN THIS SERIES

Preventing Prejudice

A Guide for Counselors, Educators, and Parents

SECOND EDITION

Joseph G. Ponterotto
Fordham University

Shawn O. Utsey
Virginia Commonwealth University

Paul B. Pedersen
Syracuse University (Emeritus); University of Hawai'i (Visiting)

Multicultural Aspects of Counseling and Psychotherapy Series 2

SAGE Publications
Thousand Oaks ▪ London ▪ New Delhi

For information:

Sage Publications, Inc.
2455 Teller Road
Thousand Oaks, California 91320
E-mail: order@sagepub.com

Sage Publications Ltd.
1 Oliver's Yard
55 City Road
London EC1Y 1SP
United Kingdom

Sage Publications India Pvt. Ltd.
B-42, Panchsheel Enclave
Post Box 4109
New Delhi 110 017 India

Printed in the United States of America

Library of Congress Cataloging-in-Publication Data

Ponterotto, Joseph G.
Preventing prejudice : a guide for counselors, educators, and parents / Joseph G. Ponterotto, Shawn O. Utsey, Paul B. Pedersen.—2nd ed.
     p. cm.— (Multicultural aspects of counseling and psychotherapy series; 2)
Includes bibliographical references and index.
ISBN 0-7619-2818-9 (pbk.)
     1. Prejudices—United States. 2. Prejudices in children—United States.
3. Cross-cultural counseling—United States. I. Utsey, Shawn O. II. Pedersen,
Paul, 1936– III. Title. IV. Multicultural aspects of counseling and psychotherapy; 2.
BF575.P9P64 2006
303.3'850973—dc22   2005028326

This book is printed on acid-free paper.

06   07   08   09   10   9   8   7   6   5   4   3   2   1

Acquisitions Editor:	Kassie Graves
Editorial Assistant:	Veronica Novak
Production Editor:	Laureen A. Shea
Copy Editor:	Catherine M. Chilton
Typesetter:	C&M Digitals (P) Ltd.
Proofreader:	Teresa Herlinger
Indexer:	Michael Ferreira
Cover Designer:	Janet Foulger

Contents

Foreword

W. E. B. DuBois famously observed that the problem of the 20th century was the problem of the *color* line. White was on top and Black on the bottom, framed by discrimination, dislike, and disadvantage. As we inch into the 21st century, the problem of the *culture* line looms large.

The problem of the color line is that in the United States, we have for centuries and, in spite of our lofty democratic and egalitarian ideals and principles, systematically denigrated and disenfranchised groups of people who are different from the Anglo Americans who claim this society and culture. As I have offered in *Prejudice and Racism* (Jones, 1997), race-based denigration is woven into the fabric of our culture, has infiltrated and even authorized the structure and functions of our institutions, and seeps inexorably into the mental and emotional life of individual citizens—not just White citizens, but all of us.

In some ways, the color line problem was simple. The basis for social categorization was visible, but the assumptions of the underlying "inadequacy" of group members and the irrational fear and loathing of Whites clearly exposed bigots and racists for what they were. Deep-seated racial antipathy was exposed by Myrdal (1944) in *An American Dilemma* and challenged directly by the *Brown v. Board of Education* (1954) decision declaring racial segregation in schools unconstitutional. Resistance to progress was overcome, in part, by the will of the people, mostly Black but of various hues, culminating in the civil rights advances of the 1960s. However, to paraphrase Mark Twain, reports of the death of bigotry and bias were greatly exaggerated.

Disingenuously borrowing from Martin Luther King's "I have a dream" speech, and focusing exclusively on color, affirmative efforts to dismantle racial apartheid were scuttled by a "colorblind" ethos. Couched in principles of fairness and equality and wrapped in the Constitution's 14th Amendment and Title VI of the Civil Rights Act, color was declared an illegitimate basis for social decision making. Problem solved!?

Our mental and emotional life is still wrought with disgust and disease. If the foundation for this is not color, then what is it? "It's the *culture*, stupid," to paraphrase James Carville's brilliant strategy for President Clinton's election in 1992. Culture is a way of life, a design for living that is driven by beliefs, values, practices, symbols, and ways of being. If we multiply each of these dimensions by the numerous different cultural groups that have evolved in or immigrated to the United States, we have a multifaceted problem with complex and intertwining methods required to address them. Where to begin? *Preventing Prejudice* is an excellent place to start.

In the first edition of *Preventing Prejudice* in 1993, Ponterotto and Pedersen took the problem of the destructive nature of prejudice and racism and wrote a book that attempted to grapple with it head on. Thirteen years later, they return, with help from Shawn Utsey, a larger focus, and a grander mission. Clearly the authors want to make a difference, to help people help themselves and others to make a better society. As counseling psychologists, they use the tools of their profession and speak to the practitioners who are on the front line. They also speak directly to teachers and educators and, importantly, to parents and their children.

How exactly can you "prevent" prejudice? It seems to follow from the pervasive human tendency to categorize people into groups and treat groups "like us" better than groups that are "different" from us. If it is "hardwired" in this way, how can you prevent it from happening? In fact, the authors acknowledge this problem. Still, we *hate* others as a result of our prejudices, and we *hurt* them correspondingly. The authors argue that reducing hate and making hurting others unacceptable will have a net effect of reducing the manifestation, if not the fact, of prejudice. That is the intention of the authors. It is a sanguine, sincere, and salutary goal.

The authors have strong opinions and beliefs about threats to mental well-being and ways to protect and enhance it. They are driven by a fundamental belief in the decency and humanity of all of our citizens. Their approach is informed by the theoretical and empirical knowledge that this fundamental belief is not commonly shared. Professionals whose job it is to help others may well be under the influence of cultural dynamics that undermine their intention. Racial and ethnic bias is in the air we breathe, and it infects us all. *Preventing Prejudice* strives mightily to create behavioral and psychological antibodies to defend against the invasion of bias and bigotry, however subtle, however unintentional—and it succeeds.

With specific exercises and "attention paid," *Preventing Prejudice* addresses the premise that people are often unaware of their biases and thus need to become more sensitive to the existence of these biases and how they might be expressed, an idea supported with ample research. Historically, explicit attitudes about race, ethnicity, and gender were taken at face value. Negative attitudes were prevalent and, it was thought, gave rise to negative acts. As attitudes shifted in a more positive direction, however, there was nevertheless continuing evidence of hate crimes, bigotry, and violence, as well as more subtle forms of discrimination. What people *said* was not always consistent with what they *did.*

A method for detecting "implicit attitudes" enabled researchers to identify antipathies that respondents' self-censorship disguised in their measurement. The associations between negative sentiment and social categories were muted when mental control gave rise to "appropriate" verbalizations. However, when these associations were tapped in uncontrollable ways, the antipathy "leaked," and the scope of the problem was seen to be much wider and deeper than had been thought. Now we find brain functions validating the implicit measures of bias, which takes us back to the idea that change is not going to be easy.

An antidote to the "benign neglect" of the 1960s and the ostrichlike approach to bias promulgated under the colorblind strategy is much needed. That approach must confront prejudice, not ignore it; it must acknowledge it and not pretend it does not exist. The *Preventing Prejudice* approach does just that. Its approach is broad and relevant—children, adolescents, young adults, adults, teachers, educators, parents, all racial and ethnic groups, genders and sexual orientations, and various combinations among them are featured. The authors tell you why and how prejudice occurs, with what effect, and what you can do about it. As social psychology colleague Bill McGuire once said, "if you have a pretzel-shaped world, you need a pretzel-shaped theory to explain it."

Preventing Prejudice takes this pretzel-shaped world of prejudice head on in Part IV, Chapters 11–14. Each chapter contains four exercises appropriate to its focus: elementary and middle school, high school, college, and the community. The exercises educate young children about the symbols of our culture and why they might mean different things to people from different backgrounds. Stereotypes are examined in high school, debates are held in the college exercises, and "cultural grids" allow adults to examine how, as cultural psychologists argue, "culture and psyche make each other up." Readers, classrooms, administrative units, teachers, and parents are guided through the tough work of preventing prejudice with interesting, educational, and meaningful activities. The book is a wonderful teaching tool and provides myriad opportunities to learn.

Part V provides additional resources for the detection of prejudice, the culture-based competence to overcome it, the stress that it occasions, and, after the manner of Maslow, the apex of the *Preventing Prejudice* hierarchy: the multicultural personality. Assessment instruments and their use are presented and explained in Chapter 15. Chapter 16 provides interesting and relevant resources, including organizations, books, films, videos, and popular movies and, again, instructs the reader how to work with them. You are never left alone with ideas or issues; the authors stay with you and help you through it.

Preventing Prejudice is based in theory and research. It is also based in practice and experience, and it is informed by the people it is meant to reach. What do people really think, or know, or feel? Are you racist *because* you are White? Are you immune from racism if you are gay? Doesn't embracing your ethnic or racial group make you prone to bias against other groups? Isn't advocating racial identity, therefore, a threat to the very sensitive awareness of others advocated here? Are you better or worse off psychologically if you belong to multiple racial categories? Is there a personality type that supersedes and triumphs over it all? *Preventing Prejudice* addresses these questions and issues and many more with direct, clear, and cogent ideas and instruction. Readers will not just know the answer; they will know what to do about it.

Cultural diversity and multiculturalism are not just slogans; they are reality and promise. The first edition of *Preventing Prejudice* was a bold and important effort to address these complex problems. Its success was heralded when the Gustavus Myers Center for the Study of Human Rights in North America presented it with the prestigious award for "Outstanding Book on the Subject of Human Rights in North America." Ponterotto, Utsey, and Pedersen took this outstanding work and expanded and improved on it. The result is a testament to their dedication and a significant contribution to solving the problem of the 21st century: the problem of the culture line.

—James M. Jones
Lewes, Delaware

Preface

We are pleased to present to you the second edition of *Preventing Prejudice: A Guide for Counselors, Educators, and Parents.* This new and much expanded edition comes 13 years after the inaugural edition. When the first edition was published in 1993, we knew the book focused on a topic critical to all of us, and we were confident that it presented new and fresh perspectives on understanding and fighting prejudice. However, we did not expect the strong positive reception the book received from many professional and lay quarters. We were honored that the first edition won an international book award for "Outstanding Book on the Subject of Human Rights in North America," given out by the prestigious Gustavus Myers Center for the Study of Human Rights in North America. We were also delighted when the book quickly became an often-referenced scholarly source on the study of prejudice and racism and was selected as required reading by many professors of psychology and education in graduate programs throughout North America.

Much time has passed since the first edition was published, and although the problems of prejudice and racism remain as prevalent today as they did over a decade ago, there have been many new developments and advances in research on the topic in that decade. Clearly it was time for a fully up-to-date and expanded work in this critical subject area. This new and expanded edition of *Preventing Prejudice* aims to update the reader on these latest advances in the field.

Among the most significant revisions and updates presented in this second edition are the following:

1. Dr. Shawn O. Utsey, Professor in Psychology at Virginia Commonwealth University, has joined Joseph G. Ponterotto and Paul B. Pedersen (the authors of the first edition) as a coauthor of this second edition. Dr. Utsey is Executive Editor of the *Journal of Black Psychology* and a world authority on the study of racism in the United States. As a renowned scholar, teacher, and clinician, and as a Black man in America, Dr. Utsey

draws on both his professional and personal experiences in his written voice reflected throughout the book.

2. Soon after the first edition was published in 1993, the original coauthors began national tours, discussing the book in universities, schools, and communities. One point that struck us, particularly when visiting K–12 schools, was that the parents of the students, as well as the counselors, educators, and administrators, resonated with the book's contents. Although the first edition was aimed at professional counselors and educators, parents nationwide, representing a myriad of occupations and education levels, were also reading the book.

Therefore, in this second edition, we have expanded coverage to provide even more material of particular relevance to parents. In addition to including a full chapter that is solely devoted to parents, we have integrated parent-relevant material throughout the book. Also, as in the first edition, we have worked diligently to write this book using clear, crisp, and jargon-free language. Our expanded focus and coverage is reflected in the book's new title, where *parents* clearly play a central role.

3. One of the unique aspects of the original edition was that it was the first book to comprehensively link prejudice levels to stages of racial and ethnic identity development. It also clearly demonstrated the links between racial and ethnic identity development and psychological health. One major development that took place in the last decade was important theorizing and research on the study of biracial, multiracial, and lesbian and gay identity development. These topics were totally neglected in the first edition but assume a critical focus in this second edition. As United States society experiences a rapid demographic growth of biracial and multiracial families, and as the lesbian and gay population continues to face oppression and harassment at every turn, it was important that these topics be added to the second edition.

4. One reason the first edition was so embraced by many segments of society was that in addition to the authors' positions being firmly planted in theory and research, they provided examples of detailed exercises and activities that readers could use to increase multicultural awareness and sensitivity and reduce prejudice in themselves and others. This second edition has expanded the applied exercise content to four full chapters, covering children of all ages, adolescents, young adults, and adults in general.

5. Also particularly valued in the first edition was our review of measures and instruments that could be used by teachers, counselors, psychologists, managers, supervisors, and administrators to measure multicultural sensitivity and prejudice. In this new edition, we have expanded coverage of such measures, and we also include four featured measures in the appendixes. These measures will be of particular value to those conducting research or evaluating intervention programs in the topical area.

6. This new edition introduces the reader to a relatively new construct in the field of psychology—the multicultural personality. The multicultural personality builds off of and extends work on racial and ethnic identity development, as well as integrating theory and research in social psychology, organizational psychology, feminist psychology, and African-centered psychology. The multicultural personality is hypothesized to correlate with both life success in increasingly culturally diverse environments (such as the United States) and with quality of life in general.

7. The contents of the book have been significantly expanded and fully updated. Most of the chapters are completely new and original, and the remainder has been revised to incorporate the most recent theory and research on the varied topics. In a way, calling this book a "second edition" is a misnomer, as the contents constitute such a dramatic update and revision. This is clearly a new book.

Organization of the Book

This new edition is generally organized similarly to the first edition, except that it moves from four parts to five parts and from 11 chapters to 16 chapters. Part I, "Prejudice and Racism: Prevalence and Consequences," introduces the topics of prejudice and racism, provides key definitions and discusses debates common to the field, reviews important historical perspectives on the topic, and discusses in depth the causes of racism, as well as the consequences of prejudicial attitudes and racist behavior to both the targets and perpetrators of racism. We emphasize at the outset that all Americans need to be more involved in fighting the myriad forms and expressions of prejudice. Particularly, we believe that White Americans need to be more involved in fighting racism, that heterosexuals need to be more vocal in fighting antigay discrimination, and that men need to be more involved in stopping the oppression of women. *The targets of prejudice are not the problem; the oppressors themselves are the problem.*

Part II, "Racial, Biracial, Multiracial, and Lesbian and Gay Identity Development and the Multicultural Personality," reviews leading models of identity development across various segments of society. Given the correlation between identity development and both prejudice levels and psychological health, this section provides the key theoretical anchor for the whole book. The latest theory and research on identity development models for African Americans, Asian Americans, Hispanics, Whites, biracial and multiracial persons, and lesbians and gays is summarized. Research linking different stages of identity development to prejudice dispositions and psychological health is reviewed. As noted above, the latest work on multicultural personality development is summarized. For any professional or citizen hoping to intervene in the fight against racism and oppression toward any number of targeted groups, the information provided in this section is essential.

Part III, "Proactive Roles in Reducing Prejudice," moves to more applied perspectives on the topic. This section outlines the particular roles that counselors, teachers, and parents can play in proactively addressing prejudicial attitudes in their clients, students, and children. Complementing the applied perspective of Part III is the exercise-packed Part IV of *Preventing Prejudice*, "Practical Exercises for Multicultural Awareness and Prejudice Reduction." This section includes exercises for children, adolescents, and adults on multicultural awareness and prejudice reduction. We have used these exercises in many contexts and have found them to be highly effective in raising multicultural awareness and in stimulating extensive discussion on the selected topics.

The final section of the book is Part V, "Instruments and Resources for Prejudice Prevention Work." This section reviews leading and innovative paper-and-pencil assessments of prejudice, racism, homophobia, multicultural competence for counselors and teachers, the stressful effects of racism, and components of the multicultural personality. These measures can be used in research, training, and program evaluation at all levels. This section also reviews books, professional organizations, popular movies, and films that will be useful for those interested in self-development and training in the multicultural awareness area. Four particular instruments are featured, with complete copies and scoring directions presented in the book's appendixes.

Who Should Read This Book?

Well, we would like everyone to read this book! However, it is particularly geared to those of us who are educators, counselors, administrators, or parents. Professionals who do training and consulting in diversity will find this book to be a rich resource. Teachers and professors at all levels will find this book informative, and the book is suggested as required reading for undergraduate and graduate courses in multicultural education, racism and prejudice, multicultural counseling, human development, and cross-cultural psychology. Clinicians in counseling, psychology, social work, psychiatry, and general medicine will find the book's contents helpful for better understanding their clients and patients with regard to identity issues, struggles, and strengths. Given the empirical connection between higher stages of identity development and the multicultural personality to indexes of psychological health and well-being, the theory and research summarized in this book are important to any health professional.

—Joseph G. Ponterotto, Shawn O. Utsey, and Paul B. Pedersen
New York City

Acknowledgments

Writing a book is a major undertaking, and we would not have been successful without the support of many individuals. A few of these individuals are noted in the Dedication; others we will thank here.

First, we want to thank our families, both nuclear and extended, for their love and support throughout the past few years as we worked diligently on this book.

A special thanks goes to Dr. Arthur Pomponio, our Sage editor, who supported us every step of the way. His enthusiasm, emotional and material support, vision, patience, and general warmth of personality made the writing process as enjoyable as it can be. We also want to thank all of the Sage staff for their coordinated and cooperative efforts in helping us produce and market this award-winning book, particularly Laureen Shea, Veronica Novak, Anna Clifford, Carmel Withers, and Tim MacPhee. We are especially grateful to Kate Chilton, who did a marvelous job copyediting the entire text. We believe Sage has risen to be the world market leader in publishing scholarly books in multicultural psychology, and we are honored that they have chosen to publish this second edition.

We were also honored when James M. Jones agreed to write the Foreword to this second edition. Dr. Jones is a pioneer in American psychology and a world-renowned authority on the study of racism. His voice, which opens this book, sets an important tone for the chapters that follow. James, to us, is also a warm, funny, loving, and fascinating person, and we are so pleased that he is part of this book. James, thank you!

To the distinguished national scholars who regularly used the first edition of this book and provided extensive feedback on our proposal for the new edition, Dr. Michael D'Andrea of the University of Hawai'i; Dr. George Gushue of Teachers College, Columbia University; and Dr. Danielle Martines of Montclair State University, thank you!

We also gratefully acknowledge the support of our colleagues and students at our respective universities. We particularly thank our many students over the years, who now number in the thousands, for their enthusiasm, vision, challenges, and hard work. They are and will always be a significant source of inspiration for us.

Part I

Prejudice and Racism

Prevalence and Consequences

Part I of *Preventing Prejudice* includes three introductory chapters that serve to define prejudice and racism, review important historical perspectives on the origins and development of prejudice, and highlight the consequences of racist behavior to both the targets and perpetrators of racism and prejudice. Collectively, these three chapters provide a firm foundation that will allow the reader to digest and integrate the remaining parts of the book.

Chapter 1, "Understanding Prejudice and Racism," defines important constructs used throughout the book, explores the nature and development of prejudice in people, and discusses the particular responsibility White Americans have in fighting racism in themselves and in society. Chapter 2, "Some Historical Background on the Origins and Evolution of Racial Prejudice," provides a concise historical overview on the evolution of racism. This chapter reviews the roots of racism, starting from prehistoric times and moving through pre-Christian Europe, the scientific era, and modern-day racist behavior. Finally, Chapter 3, "Causes and Consequences of Racial Prejudice," focuses on White racism toward Blacks. The mechanisms of anti-Black racism are delineated, and the consequences of White racism for both African Americans and Whites are highlighted.

1

Understanding Prejudice and Racism

*Civilized men have gained notable mastery over energy, matter,
and inanimate nature generally, and are rapidly learning to
control physical suffering and premature death. But, by contrast, we appear to be living in the Stone Age so far as our han-
dling of human relationships is concerned.*

—Gordon W. Allport (1954, p. xiii)

It is fitting to begin Chapter 1 of this book with this quotation from Gordon
W. Allport, who in 1954 published *The Nature of Prejudice*, undoubtedly
one of the most important books of the 20th century. In the more than 50
years since the publication of this classic work, hundreds of articles, books,
films, and documentaries on the subject of prejudice and racism have
appeared. Unfortunately, despite a worldwide focus on the topic, prejudice
and racism remain as prevalent today as they did during Allport's lifetime
(1897–1967).

The Problem of Hate

As we put the final touches on this book (August 2005), the world appears
to be engulfed in violence and hatred. The seeds of this contempt toward one
another are often found in differences in nationality, ethnicity, race, religion,

or sexual orientation. We term this focused violence *ethnoviolence*, which is defined as "an act or attempted act which is motivated by group prejudice and intended to cause physical or psychological injury" (The Prejudice Institute, n.d.). Group-level violence rages in Iraq, Afghanistan, Israel, Northern Ireland, Spain, and parts of Africa, and individual acts of ethnoviolence are a daily occurrence in every part of the world.

The European Union's Monitoring Centre on Racism and Xenophobia[1] reports an alarming new wave of anti-Semitism in European Union countries (Ehrlich, n.d.). In fact, anti-Semitism seems to be on the rise worldwide (see Rosenbaum, 2004). With regard to the United States, since September 11, 2001 (9/11—a day of mass ethnoviolence, when terrorists simultaneously attacked multiple cities in the United States using hijacked American air carriers), there has been a marked increase of violence directed against Muslim Americans (Kobeisy, 2004; Willoughby, 2003), with the Council of American-Islamic Relations logging more than 700 acts of discrimination against Muslims in the United States (Ali, Liu, & Humedian, 2004).

Looking more generally at the incidence of ethnoviolence in the United States, The Prejudice Institute (n.d.), in their systematic and ongoing research program, reports a 20% to 25% rate of such incidents. This translates into one out of every four or five adult Americans being harassed, intimidated, or assaulted for reasons of group affiliation. The greatest percentage of ethnoviolent incidents, generally, is based on racial differences, and the greatest percentage of violent, brutal, physical assaults is based on sexual orientation (The Prejudice Institute, n.d.). The Southern Poverty Law Center's (SPLC's) most recent Intelligence Project report (March 2005) documented the existence of 762 hate groups and 468 hate Web sites active during 2004, numbers that were up slightly from the previous year.

As a microcosm of society at large, the college campus is a good place to look for rates of ethnoviolence. For the year 2001, the latest year where a complete data set is available, the FBI documented 286 hate crimes (note that *hate crime* is a specific form of ethnoviolence that has a legal definition and prosecutorial implications), although the U.S. Department of Education recorded 487 hate crimes. Both numbers are drastic underrepresentations, as many colleges throughout the nation and 20 specific U.S. states failed to report such crimes in 2001. Campus security experts estimate the number at roughly four times that which is reported to authorities (see Willoughby, 2003). Thus we can infer roughly 4 × 500 crimes, for a total of 2000 hate crimes committed on college campuses during 2001.

In most jurisdictions, the legal definition of *hate crime* focuses on attacks based on race, religion, and ethnicity but exclude gender as a target (The Prejudice Institute, n.d.). Thus emotional and physical violence toward women is not included in hate crime statistics. If we include violence toward women as a form of ethnoviolence and hate crime, we can see that the country is in a sorry state indeed, as abuse of women in various forms (assault, domestic violence, harassment, date rape, and so on) is endemic to the fabric of society (DePorto, 2003).

Purpose and Focus of This Book

Psychological and physical violence toward persons based on prejudice represents a world tragedy. We all have to be involved in fighting prejudice, whether it is focused on racial or ethnic minorities (racism); women (sexism); gay, lesbian, or bisexual persons (homophobia and heterosexism); the elderly (ageism); or some other point of difference. Albert Einstein once wrote, "The world is too dangerous to live in—not because of the people who do evil, but because of the people who sit and let it happen" (cited in Sue, 2003, p. 14). This book is a call for counselors, psychologists, educators, administrators, and parents to take a more proactive stand in fighting prejudice. To equip you to take this stand, the book provides a comprehensive explanation of the nature, origins, manifestations, and impact of prejudice on both those who are targeted by it and those who perpetuate it, whether overtly (directly) or covertly (indirectly).

The topics of prejudice and racism are broad and complex and necessitate a focus for in-depth coverage in one volume. In this book, as in our first edition of *Preventing Prejudice*, we focus more on racial and ethnic prejudice than on other forms of prejudice, such as that directed at women; gays, lesbians, and bisexuals; religious minorities; the elderly; the disabled; and so forth. Our focus is reflected in our own expertise and research over the last four decades. In addition to our general racial and ethnic focus, we also focus particularly on the nature of *White* racism, for reasons that will be made clear in this and subsequent chapters.

Prejudice and racism transcend national boundaries and can be found worldwide. Our focus in this text is on prejudice and racism as widespread phenomena in the United States. Notwithstanding this focus, research and literature from other countries will be incorporated into our discussions when a more international perspective helps to clarify a relevant concept or position.

This book is written for counselors, psychologists, educators, administrators, those in leadership positions, and, most important, parents, who are the first to inculcate racial, ethnic, and gender attitudes, as well as empathy skills, in the nation's youth.

Some Important Definitions

It is important to clarify and define key terms used throughout this book. This section on definitions examines the following terms: *race, ethnicity, culture, minority, majority,* and *racial and ethnic minority groups.*

Race

Race—this four-letter word has wreaked more havoc on people in the world than all the four-letter words banned by censors of the U.S. airwaves. Race divides human beings into categories that loom in our psyches. Racial differences create cavernous divides in our psychological understandings of who we are and who we should be. (Jones, 1997, p. 339)

James M. Jones, a social psychologist at the University of Delaware, is a world authority on the study of race and racism. His words, quoted here, capture well the social implications embedded in the popular term *race*. In this section, we briefly explore the definition of this term. Our presentation is brief and summative, and for more in-depth discussion we refer interested readers to Jones's (1997) *Prejudice and Racism*, a definitive book on the study of racism.

Perhaps the most popular definitions of race have had a biological and genetic basis. For example, *Merriam-Webster's Collegiate Dictionary* (2004) defines race in a number of different ways, including "a family, tribe, people, or nation belonging to the same stock," "a class or kind of people unified by shared interests, habits, or characteristics," and "a category of humankind that shares certain distinctive physical traits" (p. 1024). Krogman's (1945) definition is often cited in the literature and states that race refers to "a sub-group of people possessing a definite combination of physical characteristics, of genetic origin, the combination of which to varying degrees distinguishes the sub-group from other sub-groups of mankind" (p. 49).

Simpson and Yinger (1985) summarize commonly recognized physical characteristics that distinguish one race from another: skin pigmentation, nasal index and lip form, and the color distribution and texture of body hair. Commonly recognized racial types are Caucasoid (White Americans), Mongoloid (Asian Americans, Pacific Islanders, and Native Americans), and Negroid (Black Americans) (Atkinson, Morten, & Sue, 1998; Sue, 2003).

Despite the popularity of biologically based definitions of race, there are myriad problems with defining race in biological terms. First, there is a great deal of overlap between recognized racial types, and there are certainly more genetic similarities across all people than there are differences. As a species, humans are very much alike. The U.S. Department of Energy's groundbreaking Genome Project, which has successfully mapped the entire human genome sequence, has found that this genome sequence is 99.9% exactly the same in all human beings. Each human being has an estimated 30,000 genes, and if we all have 99.9% shared gene variance, that means we all match on 29,970 out of 30,000 genes (see Bonham, Warshauer-Baker, & Collins, 2005, and the U.S. Department of Energy Genome Programs Web site at http://www.ornl.gov/hgmis). Second, in addition to shared genetic similarity across all races, there are also myriad nongenetic differences (e.g., language, religion, customs, values) within any one racial category because of cultural differences. Researchers often comment that there are more differences within racial groups than between them (e.g., Atkinson, Morten, & Sue, 1998; Sue et al., 1998).

It is fair to say that at this point, many biologists have abandoned the notion of race as a useful classification construct.[2] In Jones's (1997) comprehensive treatise on race and racism, he quotes a distinguished panel of scientists, who state, "From a biological viewpoint the term race has become so encumbered with superfluous and contradictory meanings, erroneous concepts, and emotional reactions that it has almost completely lost its utility" (p. 345).

The most current scholarship on race indicates that the term is more of a socially constructed concept than a biologically legitimate one (Eberhardt, 2005; Smedley & Smedley, 2005). Despite its lack of biological validity, the term *race* is probably here to stay because of its implied social implications (Carter & Pieterse, 2005; Sue, 2003). In the United States, race is associated with social meaning that people cannot easily give up because they have been conditioned to use race to organize their thinking about people and the groups to which they belong (Jones, 1997). Jones cites numerous social or social constructionist definitions of *race*, including that by Omi and Winant (1986):

> Race is indeed a pre-eminently sociohistorical concept. Racial categories and the meaning of race are given concrete expression by the specific social relations and historical context in which they are embedded. Racial meanings have varied tremendously over time and between societies. (p. 60; cited in Jones, 1997, p. 348)

What people believe about race has profound social consequences as they come to accept as "social fact" the myriad stereotypes about a group of people based solely on their skin color, facial features, and so forth (see Carter & Pieterse, 2005; Helms & Cook, 1999). Clearly, in the United States, the concept of race has been used as a political pawn by the power-dominant group (i.e., White males) to maintain the oppression of minority groups (Sue, 2003). A good example of this oppression is in the association of intelligence with racial characteristics: Blacks and other racial and ethnic minority groups have been labeled as less intelligent than Whites (Anderson & Nickerson, 2005; Sue et al., 1998). We say more about this topic in Chapter 2.

We have noted the complexity of the concept of race and suggest that readers keep this in mind as they read subsequent chapters. For our present purposes, racial groups include White Americans, African Americans, Asian Americans and Pacific Islanders, and Native Americans. Hispanics can belong to any of the aforementioned groups. Although our classification system is rather simplistic and does nothing to solve the terminology dilemmas just reviewed, it does allow us to integrate past research on *race* into our current discussion.

Ethnicity

The terms *race* and *ethnicity* are often used interchangeably in U.S. society, but there are important distinctions between constructs. First, race has long included biological aspects, and second, the socially constructed nature of race has been more values laden than has ethnicity (Helms & Cook, 1999; Jones, 1997). Ethnicity can be considered a group classification of individuals who share a unique social and cultural heritage (e.g., language, customs, religion) passed on between generations (Rose, 1964). Our preferred definition and the one we rely on in this book is that presented by Yinger (1976), who defines *ethnic group* as

> A segment of the larger society whose members are thought, by themselves and/or others, to have a common origin and to share important segments of a common culture and who, in addition, participate in shared activities in which the common origin and culture are significant ingredients. (p. 200)

Using this definition, we can demonstrate the differentiation of the terms *race* and *ethnicity*. Using the Jewish people as an example, Jews, given their shared cultural, religious, and social heritage, are an ethnic group rather than a race. Understandably, Jewish people are represented among all racial groups, and yet they share a particular ethnic heritage.

Culture

The word *culture* has also been used interchangeably with the terms *race* and *ethnicity*. Once again, however, there are important distinctions between these terms. For example, the White American racial group is composed of many different ethnic groups, such as Irish, Polish, Jewish, Italian, and so on. Within these ethnic groups lie a diversity of cultures predicated on such factors as length of time living in the United States, socioeconomic status, religion, sexual orientation, geographic locale, and so on. Given this diversity between and within human groups, we prefer the broad definition of culture put forth by Linton (1945): "the configuration of learned behavior whose components and elements are shared and transmitted by the members of a particular society" (p. 32).

Minority

One of the most popular and controversial terms heard in everyday language today is *minority*. This term has direct relevance to our discussions throughout this book, and our usage of the term parallels the definition of *minority* presented by Wirth (1945):

A group of people who, because of physical or cultural characteristics, are singled out from others in the society in which they live for differential and unequal treatment, and who therefore regard themselves as objects of collective discrimination. . . . Minority status carries with it the exclusion from full participation in the life of the society. (p. 347)

A key component of Wirth's definition is the lack of economic, political, and social power and influence faced by certain groups in American society. It is important to note that the focus of this definition is *not* on numerical representation. For example, females in the United States constitute 51% of the total population (see U.S. Census Bureau, 2005) and therefore represent a numerical majority; however, by our definition, women are clearly a minority group, given the level of social, economic, and political power and influence they hold relative to men. Furthermore, when taking a global perspective, it is important to acknowledge that people of color are indeed the numerical majority relative to White persons, who represent the numerical minority.

Despite its popularity in the lexicon of the English language, the term *minority* is controversial. The term minority can imply "less than" in the minds of people, and persons of color do not see themselves as less than anyone. For some Americans of color, the term minority can be offensive (see Helms & Cook, 1999, and Sue et al., 1998). In our use of the term throughout this text, we rely on Wirth's (1945) conceptualization that it acknowledges a group singled out by the power-dominant group for unequal and oppressive treatment. In no way do we see any ethnic or racial group as "less than" any other in value.

Majority

To speak of a *minority group* implies by its very nature the existence of a contrasting group—the *majority group*. The majority group (sometimes referred to as the dominant or mainstream group) is that group that holds the balance of power, influence, and wealth in society. The majority group in the United States consists of the White population generally and, more specifically, White middle and upper class males (see Sue et al., 1998).

Derald Wing Sue (2003), in his recent groundbreaking contribution *Overcoming Our Racism: The Journey to Liberation*, presents evidence of White male power dominance in the United States when he notes that although White males only represent 33% of the total U.S. population, they hold approximately

- 80% of tenured faculty positions in colleges and universities
- 80% to 85% of seats in both the U.S. Senate and House of Representatives
- 92% of the Forbes 400 chief executive officer positions

- 90% of public school superintendencies
- 99.9% of professional athletic team ownerships
- 100% of U.S. presidencies (and vice presidencies) (p. 9)

Sue (2003) asks his readers: "Where are the persons of color? Where are the women?" (p. 9). Speaking to the point of White persons as the reference marker for immigrants, Gordon (1964) noted the following:

> If there is anything in American life that can be described as an overall American culture that serves as a reference point for immigrants and their children, it can be described . . . as the middle-class patterns of largely White Protestant Anglo-Saxon origins. (cited in Markides & Mindel, 1987, p. 14)

Our present usage of the term *majority group* incorporates not only White, Anglo Saxon Protestants but also White ethnic groups. A rationale for this grouping is provided by Ponterotto and Casas (1991), who note that although most White immigrant groups were confronted with prejudice and oppression when they first arrived in the United States, their experience in this country has been qualitatively different from the experiences of non-White people. These authors point out that because of their more Anglolike features (mainly their white skin), White ethnics were allowed eventually (sometimes by changing their last names to sound more Anglolike) to assimilate and become part of "mainstream" America. This was not the case, however, for people of color, who, because of their physical differences, have been blocked from fully participating in the "land of opportunity."

Our position that all White Americans, regardless of ethnic or cultural background, belong to the majority (or dominant) group is further supported by Pettigrew (1988), who speaks to the unique experience of Blacks in America:

> In a significant way, European immigrants over the past century and Blacks face opposite cultural problems. The new Europeans were seen as not "American" enough; the dominant pressure on them was to give up their strange and threatening ways and to assimilate. Blacks were Americans of lower caste; the pressure on them was to "stay in their place" and not attempt assimilation into mainstream culture of the privileged. (p. 24)

Racial and Ethnic Minority Groups

This book focuses on the differential power-influenced relationship between the majority group in the United States (i.e., White Americans) and racial and ethnic minority groups (i.e., African Americans, Hispanic Americans, Asian Americans and Pacific Islanders, and Native Americans).

For the purposes of accuracy and clarity, the term *racial or ethnic minority* group is the term that best captures this collective grouping. *Racial* incorporates the biological and heredity classifications; *ethnic* incorporates classifications of individuals who share a unique social and cultural heritage; and *minority* reflects the lower economic, political, and social status conferred on specific groups by the White majority (Ponterotto & Casas, 1991).

We want to again remind the reader that there are limitations in our selection of terminology and that other scholars prefer different terms. For example, two noted researchers in the field of multicultural counseling, Janet E. Helms and Donelda A. Cook, prefer the acronyms VREG (visible racial ethnic group) or ALANA (African, Latino(a), Asian and Pacific Islander, and Native American) to refer to racial and ethnic minority groups collectively (see discussion in Helms & Cook, 1999; Sue et al., 1998).

Understanding Prejudice

This book is about preventing prejudice. In reality, it is quite difficult to prevent prejudice, because as you will read shortly, prejudice occurs naturally in the human species. Certainly, however, the prevalence of negative ethnic prejudice can be reduced. In this section on understanding prejudice, we first define the term and then discuss the nature and expressions of prejudice.

Defining Prejudice

Allport (1954, 1979) provides a thorough and clear conceptualization of the term *prejudice*. Historically, the word prejudice stems from the Latin noun *praejudicium*, meaning a precedent or judgment based on previous decisions and experiences. According to Allport (1979), prejudice can be defined using a unipolar (negative) component, as in "thinking ill of others without sufficient warrant," or incorporating a bipolar (negative and positive) component, as in "a feeling, favorable or unfavorable, toward a person or thing, prior to, or not based on actual experience" (p. 6). Both of these definitions include an "attitude" component and a "belief" component. The attitude is either negative or positive and is tied to an overgeneralized or erroneous "belief."

Although prejudice can hold either a positive or negative valence, racial and ethnic prejudice in the United States has taken on primarily negative connotations (Allport, 1979). Our emphasis in this book is on prejudice as a negative phenomenon. Our usage of the term *prejudice* parallels Allport's (1979) often-cited definition for *negative ethnic prejudice:* "Ethnic prejudice is an antipathy based upon a faulty and inflexible generalization. It may be directed toward a group as a whole, or toward an individual because he is a member of that group" (p. 9).

This definition contains three key components worth specifying. First, prejudice is negative in nature and can be individually or group focused. Second, prejudice is based on faulty or unsubstantiated data. Third, prejudice is rooted in an inflexible generalization (Ponterotto, 1991). This last point is particularly important because the inflexible nature of a prejudice makes it highly resistant to evidence that would contradict it. For our purposes, prejudice includes internal beliefs and attitudes that are not necessarily expressed or acted on. Racism, on the other hand, as we discuss later, has an "action" or behavioral component.

The Nature of Prejudice

Allport (1979) argues convincingly that human beings have a natural propensity toward prejudice. Prejudicial views result quite easily from an interaction of three factors: our tendency toward ethnocentrism, our lack of meaningful intergroup contact, and our inclination to organize information into predeveloped categories.

Ethnocentrism

It is natural for people to cling to their own values and personal views and to hold them in high esteem. It is also common for people to prefer their own "in-group"—family, religious group, ethnic group—to "out-groups." Certainly, there are positive aspects to prejudice. People develop a sense of security and affiliation by identifying with a particular in-group. This can be seen in the teenager who joins a particular gang; a high school student who affiliates with a certain school clique, such as a tech-savvy group; or the high school or college athlete who associates almost exclusively with other athletes. Having a positive prejudice toward one's own in-group gives one a sense of belonging, identity, pride, and comfort.

Prejudice toward one's group can also serve as a survival mechanism. Groups that have been historically oppressed have had to rely on one another to cope with harsh and oppressive conditions. Consider the Jews throughout Europe in the late 1930s and early 1940s; they often could not trust non-Jewish neighbors and friends for fear they might report their identity and whereabouts to Nazi authorities. In the United States, Native Americans could not trust European settlers. Many promises (treaties) were made by White male settlers to the Native peoples of America, and most were broken (Ponterotto & Casas, 1991). A positive prejudice toward their own tribal group and a concomitant distrust of the European settlers constituted, therefore, a healthy and justified coping response. Similar scenarios with other American minority groups, such as African Americans in slavery and Japanese Americans in internment camps, also serve as relevant examples.

Often, however, and without sufficient warrant, people exaggerate the virtues of their own group. Allport (1979) uses the term "love prejudice" to refer to people's tendency to overgeneralize the virtues of their own values, family, and group. Love prejudice toward one's own group can lead to antagonism toward outside groups and thus serve as the foundation for ethnocentrism. Aboud (1987) defines ethnocentrism as "an exaggerated preference for one's group and concomitant dislike of other groups" (p. 49). Ethnocentrism serves as a building block for negative racial prejudice (Ponterotto, 1991).

Lack of Significant Intergroup Contact

Separation between human groups is common throughout the world. People often prefer their "own kind" as a matter of convenience. Allport (1979) asks, "with plenty of people at hand to choose from, why create for ourselves the trouble of adjusting to new languages, new foods, new cultures, or to people of a different educational level?" (p. 17). This preference to associate primarily with "like-minded" individuals leads to a form of cultural ignorance among many people. Without significant intercultural contact, people's perceptions of individuals representing other racial and ethnic groups is more often than not based on faulty information.

Here in the United States, we have what we term "the illusion of integration." This nation is becoming increasingly diverse culturally, yet clearly the level of meaningful intergroup contact and dialogue is not keeping pace with the rapid demographic shifts in process. The title of Beverly Daniel Tatum's (1997) popular book *"Why Are All the Black Kids Sitting Together in the Cafeteria?" And Other Conversations About Race* captures well the reality of true segregation within the illusion of integration. In high schools, colleges, workplaces, and cities, we see the continuation of racial and ethnic segregation in society. Segregation hinders the meaningful interracial contact that is necessary for increased racial harmony and a truly democratic society (Ehrlich, n.d.).

Relying on Ethnic Categorizations

As in-group preference and separatism among human groups is common, so, too, is the tendency to categorize and overgeneralize. To manage and cope with daily events in a highly technological, Internet-focused, stimuli-loaded environment, individuals must process and sort abundant amounts of information. To do so quickly and efficiently, people rely on predeveloped categorizations. Unfortunately, due to a lack of meaningful intergroup contact and knowledge, cognitive categorizations formed with regard to racial, ethnic, and religious groups are often based on stereotypical information. Stereotypes can be defined as "rigid and inaccurate preconceived notions that [one holds] about all people who are members of a particular group, whether it be defined along racial, religious, sexual, or other lines" (Sue, 2003, p. 25).

Therefore, by understanding the nature of ethnocentrism, separatism, and cognitive categorizations, it is easy to see how prevalent and natural prejudice is. Combating negative prejudice entails reducing ethnocentrism through the development of a healthy racial and ethnic identity, increasing levels of meaningful contact with different types of people, and developing critical thinking and decision-making skills. These topics are addressed at length in Parts III and IV of this book.

Expressions of Prejudice

One of Gordon Allport's many lasting contributions to psychology was to delineate clearly the various forms and escalating expressions of prejudice. Specifically, Allport (1979) presented a five-phase model of "acting out prejudice." His model presents expressions of prejudice on a continuum from least to most energetic. The five phases or levels are named *antilocution*, *avoidance*, *discrimination*, *physical attack*, and *extermination*.

Antilocution is the mildest form of prejudice and is characterized by prejudicial talk among like-minded individuals and the occasional stranger. This is a rather controlled expression of antagonism that is limited to small circles. As an example, a group of White neighbors may express fear that the neighborhood is becoming too integrated and not only will their property values go down, their children will be more likely to be exposed to aggressive peers. As another example, we turn to the high school setting. A group of White students sitting together at lunch comment negatively about a group of Asian American students who sit together, stating, "Look at those Asian Americans all sitting together at that table; they always do that at lunch; they are so antisocial."

Avoidance occurs when the individual moves beyond just talking about certain groups to conscious efforts to avoid individuals from these groups. The individual expressing avoidance behavior will tolerate inconvenience for the sake of avoidance. Thus, for example, instead of getting off at bus stop z and walking one block to work, this individual will get off at bus stop y and walk six blocks to work just to avoid the people around bus stop z. Back to our high school example: White students may avoid studying in a particular part of the school library where the Asian American or African American students commonly study. A third example would be a White family who moves out of their neighborhood because more and more minority families are moving in. It is important to emphasize that the inconvenience is self-directed, and the individual takes no directly harmful action against the group being avoided.

During the *discrimination* phase, the individual takes active steps to exclude or deny members of another group access to or participation in a desired activity. Discrimination practices in the past (and currently) have led to segregation in education, employment, politics, social privileges, and recreational opportunities (see D'Andrea & Daniels, 2001, and Jones, 1997, for specifics). Thus a White member of a cooperative housing board may vote against a Mexican American family attempting to secure housing in the co-op building. Families in a particular neighborhood may pressure the local real estate agent not to show houses to families of color. Qualified job candidates of color may be turned down in favor of less qualified White candidates. In the United States, discrimination based on race, gender, religion, ethnicity, age, and so forth is illegal; nonetheless, it happens every day.

The fourth phase in Allport's (1979) model of prejudice expression is *physical attack*. Under tense and emotionally laden conditions, or even under peer pressure, it does not take much for an individual to move quickly from the discrimination stage to physical confrontation. On any given day in any city newspaper, you are likely to read of race- or religious-based destruction of property or of an actual physical confrontation. From the high school grounds to the college campus to the city streets, we seem increasingly to hear of race- and religious-influenced confrontations and attacks (see The Prejudice Institute, n.d.; Willoughby, 2003).

Extermination marks the final phase of Allport's (1979) five-point continuum. As the term implies, extermination involves the systematic and planned destruction of a group of people based on their group membership. Allport cites lynchings, pogroms, massacres, and Hitlerian genocide as the ultimate expression of prejudice. Examples of attempted genocides fill an entire book (see Michael Mann's 2005 *The Dark Side of Democracy: Explaining Ethnic Cleansing*), and unfortunately, genocide is not just a human catastrophe of past generations. Most of our readers are familiar with the attempted Nazi destruction of the Jewish people, during which 6 million Jews were murdered. Most are familiar with the mass destruction of millions of African people during their forced enslavement. Many are also familiar with the story of the American Indians in the lower 48 states, whose population was reduced from as many as 9 million during the time of Christopher Columbus's invasion[3] to only 2 million today (Herring, 1999).

Fewer readers are likely to be aware of the similar destruction of the Native Hawai'ian people, who numbered between .4 and 1 million in 1778 when Captains James Cook and George Vancouver and their men invaded the island. By 1822, there were only 200,000 pure Hawai'ians left alive; by 1878, only 48,000; by 1922, only 24,000; and in 2003, only 5000 pure Hawai'ians remained alive[4] (Noyes, 2003). These Native peoples were murdered directly by White male settlers or died of various diseases brought over by the invaders that the Native peoples had no experience with and therefore no natural immunity to (see Trask, 1999).

As noted earlier, genocide is unfortunately not just a reality of the past. Recent ethnic-based mass destruction efforts in Eastern Europe (Bosnian Serbs versus Bosnian Muslims) and Rwanda (e.g., clashes between the Tutsis and Hutu) are relatively current events (see reviews in Mann, 2005; Jones, 1997). It is probable that by the time this book reaches publication, early in the year 2006, we will be reading of yet another attempt at ethnic destruction.

It is important to emphasize that individuals at one particular phase in Allport's sequence may never progress to the next. However, increased activity at any one level increases the likelihood that an individual will cross the boundary to the next. Allport (1979) provides a poignant example:

> It was Hitler's antilocution that led Germans to avoid their Jewish neighbors and erstwhile friends. This preparation made it easier to enact the Nurnberg laws of discrimination which, in turn, made the subsequent burning of synagogues and street attacks upon Jews seem natural. The final step in the macabre progression was the ovens at Auschwitz. (p. 15)

Understanding Racism

Racism continues to tear at the soul of America (Sue, 2003). Understanding the definition and impact of racism is critical to all citizens of this country, from parents to educators to politicians. This section defines racism, describes its manifestations, and points out those who need to be most involved in the fight against racism—White Americans.

Defining Racism

According to Dovidio and Gaertner (1986) the term *racism* became popular in the American lexicon after its use in the *Report of the National Advisory Commission on Civil Disorders* (National Advisory Commission on Civil Disorders, 1968). This well-known report cited racism by Whites as a factor in the disadvantaged plight of many Blacks in America. Since the publication of this report, numerous scholars have elaborated on the term racism. Jones (1972) defined racism broadly as follows: "[Racism] results from the transformation of race prejudice and/or ethnocentrism through the exercise of power against a racial group defined as inferior, by individuals and institutions with the intentional or unintentional support of the entire culture" (p. 117).

Jones delineates the complexity of racism by unpacking three forms of racism reflected in this more general definition. *Individual racism* is conceptualized as a person's race prejudice based on biological considerations and involving actual behavior that is discriminatory in nature. Specifically, Jones (1997) defines the *individual racist* as

> one who considers the black people as a group (or other human groups defined by essential racial characteristics) are inferior to whites because of physical (i.e., genotypical and phenotypical) traits. He or she further

believes that these physical traits are determinants of social behavior and of moral or intellectual qualities, and ultimately presumes that this inferiority is a legitimate basis for that group's inferior social treatment. An important consideration is that all judgments of superiority are based on the corresponding traits of white people as norms of comparison. (p. 417)

Jones specifies a second form of racism, *institutional racism*, which includes the intentional or unintentional manipulation or toleration of institutional policies (e.g., school admission criteria, taxes) that unfairly restrict the opportunities of targeted groups. Specifically, Jones (1997) defines *institutional racism* as

those established laws, customs, and practices which systematically reflect and produce racial inequalities in American society. If racist consequences accrue to institutional laws, customs, or practices, the institution is racist whether or not the individuals maintaining those practices have racist intentions. Institutional racism can be either overt or covert (corresponding to de jure and de facto, respectively) and either intentional or unintentional. (p. 438)

Jones's third form of racism is *cultural racism*, which is the more subtle form of racism and the most pervasive and insidious. This form of racism includes the individual and institutional expression of the superiority of one race's cultural heritage (and concomitant value system) over that of other races. Specifically, Jones (1997) defines *cultural racism* as comprising

the cumulative effects of a racialized worldview, based on belief in essential racial differences that favor the dominant racial group over others. These effects are suffused throughout the culture via institutional structures, ideological beliefs, and personal everyday actions of people in the culture, and these effects are passed on from generation to generation. (p. 472)

A more counseling- and education-focused discussion is provided by Ridley (1989, 1995, 2005). Ridley (1995) defines racism as "any behavior or pattern of behavior that tends to systematically deny access to opportunities or privileges to members of one racial group while perpetuating access to opportunities and privileges to members of another racial group" (p. 28). Ridley emphasizes the terms *behavior* and *systematic* in his definition. Behavior implies human action that is observable and measurable.

Ridley (1995, 2005) distinguishes between individual and institutional racism. His distinctions are similar to those outlined by Jones (1972, 1997) and reviewed a bit earlier in this chapter. Individual racism involves the harmful behavior of one person or a small group of individuals. Institutional racism involves the harmful effects endemic to institutional or social structures or social systems. These categories can be further broken down into smaller units of analysis based on whether the behavior is overt or covert and whether it is intentional or unintentional. Tables 1.1 and 1.2 (adapted and expanded from Ridley, 1995, 2005) present a matrix depicting these distinctions in the contexts of counseling and education.

Table 1.1   Varieties of Racism in Counseling

	Individual Racism	*Institutional Racism*
Overt		
Intentional	Counselor believes that racial and ethnic minorities are more challenging to work with and, on this basis, refuses to accept them as clients	Counseling agency openly denies services to racial and ethnic minority clientele
Covert		
Intentional	Counselor assigns a racial or ethnic minority client to a student intern because of social discomfort but claims to have a schedule overload	Counseling agency deliberately sets fees above the affordable range of most lower income and middle income minority families, thus effectively excluding them from counseling
Unintentional	Counselor misinterprets a minority client's lateness or lack of eye contact and a firm handshake as resistance to the counseling process	Counseling agency uses standardized psychological tests without considering the relevance and validity of test scores to culturally diverse clients

SOURCE: Reprinted and adapted from Ridley (1995, p. 37), with the permission of the publisher.

In examining these tables, the reader will note that overt acts of racism are always intentional—the intentionality is defined by the behavior. Covert racism, by contrast, can be intentional or unintentional. Tables 1.1 and 1.2 provide specific examples of each form of racism.

On a more general level, one operationalization of both institutional and cultural racism is in the intentional or unintentional imposition of the dominant White societal cultural value system onto others whose worldviews may be anchored in different value systems. Table 1.3 presents a comparison of the White middle and upper class value system with value systems

Table 1.2   Varieties of Racism in Education

	Individual Racism	*Institutional Racism*
Overt		
Intentional	An elementary school teacher believes minority students are less motivated and, therefore, intentionally assigns these students to the less desirable and challenging classroom activities	The administration of an elite private college believes minority students would ultimately detract from the school's "prestige" and therefore discourages its college recruiters from visiting high schools with large minority student enrollments
Covert		
Intentional	A high school assistant principal assigns a majority of African American students to the most disliked teachers because she or he believes these students cannot really be taught, anyway	An elite high school deliberately sets tuition fees above the affordable range of most lower and middle class minority families, thus effectively excluding them from the school
Unintentional	An elementary school teacher misinterprets a (recently immigrated) Mexican American student's nonassertiveness and lack of eye contact as an indication of the student's noninterest in school	A doctoral program in counseling psychology uses a high score on the Graduate Record Exam (GRE) as an admission cutoff score without considering cultural influences in standardized testing

SOURCE: Adapted from Ridley (1995, p. 37), with the permission of the publisher.

more common to certain subgroups (e.g., those less acculturated) of other racial and ethnic groups. Column 1 lists key values often associated with European-descended White American culture, while column 2 presents values often found in subgroups of Native American Indians, African Americans, Hispanics, and Asian Americans and Pacific Islanders. For example, institutional racism may be reflected in a high school or college that promotes and rewards *individualism* (e.g., individual assignments, tests, projects) over *collectivism* (e.g., working together in teams or groups in which members have equal power and share a common goal). Such an educational practice gives White middle class students an advantage over less-acculturated minority groups, such as Native American or Mexican American students (see Ponterotto & Casas, 1991, and Sue et al., 1998, for more discussion on value systems).

Table 1.3   Value Systems (Worldviews) in Human Behavior

European American Value System	*Non–European American Value Systems*
Dominant cultural value system; White middle and upper class value system	Systems common to segments of racial and ethnic minority groups
Individualism Individual is most important; self-expression, assertiveness, autonomy, and individuation valued; individual achievements and accomplishments highly prized; self-esteem important	**Collectivism** Group, family, tribe is most important; individual success and accomplishments are secondary to group or family achievement; family, group, or tribal esteem is primary
Competition Considered valuable and healthy; promoting competition to isolate individual successes deemed important	**Cooperation** Valued over individual competition in activities; working together in teams or groups with shared power and common goals deemed valuable
Nuclear family Parents and children considered the primary family unit; parents make decisions for children	**Extended family** Family includes grandparents, godparents, cousins, community elders, all of whom are central to family functioning; extended family is involved in decisions regarding children
Linear time Time is considered to be linear, limited, and a commodity that should not be wasted; sense of time urgency	**Circular time** Time is seen as circular and plentiful as day and seasonal cycles repeat; less time rigidity and urgency
Nonverbal behavior Example—Direct eye contact and firm handshakes seen as a sign of competence and confidence: During a job interview, it is best to look the interviewer in the eye and shake hands firmly	**Nonverbal behavior** Example—Firm handshakes and direct eye contact seen as aggressive and disrespectful: During a job interview it would be polite to look down when the interviewer addresses you and shake hands softly as a sign of respect for the interviewer's authority and status
Written tradition The written word or contract is preferred; "get it in writing"; quantitative research methods highly valued	**Oral tradition** Oral history and traditions seen as critical to family legacy and learning; spoken word highly valued; "my word is my bond"; qualitative research methods given equal weight with quantitative methods

European American Value System	Non–European American Value Systems
Future oriented	**Past oriented**
Past seen as disconnected from present and future; emphasis is on preparing for the future	Past seen as intimately connected to present and future; past history, legacy, and traditions anchor present and future plans and behavior
Spirituality-psychology disconnected	**Spirituality-psychology interconnected**
Spirituality is unrelated to psychological processes and functioning; individuals and groups are separate and not interconnected	Spiritual connectedness is an essential component of healthy psychological functioning; all individuals and groups are interconnected in a higher-order, spiritual way

SOURCES: Katz (1985), Ponterotto & Casas (1991), Sue et al. (1998).

As another example, we turn to the fifth value listed in Table 1.3, *nonverbal behavior*. If a corporate manager expects a firm handshake and eye-to-eye contact during a discussion with a colleague or subordinate, then employees who represent cultural value systems in which a firm handshake is considered aggressive and looking in the eyes of a superior is considered a sign of disrespect will be at a marked disadvantage when the manager needs to make decisions about career advancement and promotions.

In a final example, we will examine the value pair of *nuclear family* and *extended family*. If a teacher or counselor expects only the nuclear family to come in for a teacher-parent conference or a family counseling or therapy session and neglects to invite extended family, such as grandparents or godparents, many families adhering to traditional Native American and Hispanic worldviews may feel insulted.

The Prejudice-Racism Distinction

Our general usage of the term *racism* throughout this book parallels that of Ridley (1989, 1995, 2005). We are concerned with the effects and consequences of harmful behaviors directed toward certain racial and ethnic groups. Our conception of prejudice focuses on an attitude or belief that is negative and based on a faulty and inflexible generalization about a person because he or she is a member of a particular group. Race-based prejudice often leads to racist behaviors—but not always. A person can have race-based prejudice but not act on it (see Schutz & Six, 1996). Racism, on the other hand, involves intentional or unintentional actions that oppress others.

Who Can Be Racist?

The three authors of this book travel extensively, nationally and internationally. One question that is often posed to us by students, parents, community groups, politicians, and others is "Can anyone be racist, or is racism really the responsibility of White people?" Before we give you our response to this question, let us review some of the varied reactions of other racism researchers who study racism primarily in the United States.

James M. Jones, the social psychologist whose work we rely heavily on throughout this book, has a section in the second edition of his classic book, *Prejudice and Racism* (1997), titled "Whose Problem Is It Anyway?" In this brief section, Jones emphasizes that

> the problems posed by prejudice and racism belong to all of us. Problematizing one group or another is a hindrance to finding solutions to the discord wrought by prejudice and racism. By framing the issue in terms of the total cultural fabric, we see clearly that we cannot solve a problem this complex and ingrained in society by singling out a particular group—whether the group be white men, say, or Latina immigrants. (p. 531)

Charles R. Ridley (1995), a counseling psychologist and expert on racism, maintains that members of all racial groups can be racist, because racism is determined by the consequences of one's actions. He notes that minority groups can be racist against other minority groups, and in the few cases when a minority group has power over a White person, there can be anti-White racism. However, Ridley (1995) acknowledges that power (the ability to control) is needed to subjugate or oppress others, and given that the majority of power in the United States is in the hands of White people, they are the major perpetuators of racism.

The noted and pioneering counseling psychologist Derald Wing Sue has been the most direct at tackling the issue of who can be racist. Sue (2003) is careful to distinguish between *racial discrimination* ("acting on one's prejudice such as any action that differentially treats individuals or groups of color based on prejudice," p. 29) and racism ("any attitude, action, or institutional structure or any social policy that subordinates persons or groups because of their color. . . . it involves the power to carry out systematic discriminatory practices in a broad and continuing manner," p. 31). He notes that members of any racial group can harbor prejudice and manifest racial discrimination toward members of other racial groups. However, Sue (2003) believes that only White people can be racist, because racism "is a pervasive and systematic exercise of real power to deny minorities equal access and opportunity, while maintaining the benefits and advantages of White Americans" (p. 31). Thus, Sue believes that because White Americans control the institutions and social policies that enforce their own cultural values and norms, only Whites can be racist.

Racism Is a White Problem

Although the three renowned psychologists cited here differ to some degree in assigning the responsibility of racism to White people, a close reading of their books will show that they all agree that power in the United States is in the hands of White people, particularly White males, and given that power is central to the ability to exercise racism, racism is, de facto, chiefly and primarily the responsibility of Whites. Ridley (1995, 2005) and Sue (2003) are the most direct in tackling this question of responsibility for racism, and their differences in opinion stem in part from their definitions of racism. Ridley focused on defining racism through the consequences of action and believes that in certain contexts a group of minority members may hold power and thus possess the ability to act racist. Sue, on the other hand, emphasizes that racism involves the systematic exercise of power, a level of power that only Whites possess in the United States, and thus only Whites can exercise racism.

Our own view is a mixture of the positions of Ridley (1995, 2005) and Sue (2003). We use Jones's (1997) tripartite model of racism—individual, institutional, and cultural—as a context for our position. Individual racism, although usually the province of Whites, can be exhibited by members of any group in a context where they hold the power over another. Institutional racism is almost exclusively the province of Whites, as they run the majority of major institutions (government offices, corporations, universities, and so on) and possess the power to control others directly or indirectly. Finally, cultural racism is a function only of White society, given the predominant White "American" value system that dominates society (refer back to column 1 of Table 1.3). We do not see, for example, the Native American or Africentric value systems replacing the current dominant and empowered value system of the primarily White middle and upper class, and therefore we do not see that the responsibility for cultural racism can be placed upon anyone except White people.

Prevalence of Racism

We opened this chapter by emphasizing the significant prevalence of ethnoviolence throughout the world society. Now we address the prevalence of racism in the United States. In an often cited review focusing on White racism toward Blacks, Pettigrew (1981) found that roughly 15% of White adults are extremely racist, largely due to authoritarian personality needs. Approximately 60% of White adult Americans are conforming bigots, reflecting the racist ideology of the larger society. Finally, about 25% of White adults consistently support rights for Blacks and can be said to be antiracist in ideology and behavior.

These data are still quite disconcerting in that as late as the 1980s, only 25% of White people took an active stand against racism. Although only

15% of survey participants reviewed by Pettigrew were extremely racist, 60% of White Americans conformed to racist ideology in society. By not being part of the solution, this 60% was part of the problem (see discussions in Jones, 1997). Therefore, 75% of the White population, to some degree, promoted the status quo, which meant racial inequality. Pettigrew (1981) emphasized that White Americans increasingly rejected racial injustice in principle but remained reluctant to accept and act on measures necessary to eliminate the injustice.

The Pettigrew study is 25 years old. Is not the status and prevalence of White racism much improved in the year 2006? This question is somewhat debatable, and we address it further in the next chapter. Clearly the nature of racism has evolved over the past half century; "old-fashioned," overt racist views and actions have been replaced by "modern" racism and more subtle, yet equally insidious, forms of racist expression. Present-day racism researchers present convincing evidence that White racism is not only alive and well but thriving. Among these researchers are Derald Wing Sue of Teachers College, Columbia University, in New York and Michael D'Andrea and Judy Daniels at the University of Hawai'i. These researchers have been studying the incidence and manifestations of White racism for the past 20 years, using a variety of qualitative methods such as person-to person interviews, field study techniques, and participant observations in a wide variety of settings. The results of their work can be summarized in part through the following quotes. First, we quote directly from Sue (2003), who speaks to the critical responsibility of White citizens to be active in fighting racism:

> You do not have to be actively racist to contribute to the racism problem. Inaction, itself, is tacit agreement that racism is acceptable; and because White Americans enjoy the benefits, privileges, and opportunities of the oppressive system, they inevitably are racist by both commission and omission. As a result, it is my contention that White racism is truly a White problem and that it is the responsibility of my White brothers and sisters to be centrally involved in combating and ending racial oppression. (p. 99)

Next we quote from D'Andrea and Daniels (2001), who discuss the results of their 16-year study on racism, which sampled a broad spectrum of White Americans nationwide:

> It is very important to understand that most of the racism that exists in the United States is perpetuated by millions of well-meaning, liberal-thinking White persons who react with passive acceptance and apathy to the pervasive ways in which this problem continues to be embedded in our institutional structures. From the results of our extensive research in this area, we have concluded that most of the racism that continues to be perpetuated in the United States is, in fact, fueled by broad-based passive acceptance

the transformation of racial prejudice in modern times (see Table 2.1 for an outline of the history of prejudice). Finally, we discuss the implications of the longevity of racism in human history and the efforts of counselors, educators, and parents to reduce racial prejudice.

Table 2.1   Chronicle of Significant Historical Events in the Evolution of Racial Prejudice

Time Period	Events	Notes
Human migration out of Africa 100,000–40,000 BCE	Human migration out of Africa into Europe and Asia resulted in genetic adaptation to climatic changes	Evolution of a recessive gene for melanin expression in humans who migrated to Europe during glacial Ice Age. White skin adaptive for low level of ultraviolet radiation in Europe; dark skin a genetic threat for rickets and perceived potential extinction of White race
Prehistoric Era 50,000–10,000 BCE	Tribalism, survival of the fittest, competition for resources	Physical differences facilitated in-group–out-group distinctions in relation to sharing or hoarding resources in times of famine
Pre-Christian Era 10,000–2000 BCE	Blacks viewed positively in Greco-Roman societies	The Greeks borrowed a number of gods and goddesses from Egypt and other parts of Africa (Snowden, 1995)
Christian Era 0–1600 CE	Religious propaganda fuels anti-Black racial prejudice in Europe	Many historical records point to this time period as the beginning of modern-day racial prejudice
New World 1600–1900 CE	Importation of enslaved Africans, institutionalized race-based slavery, Jim Crow laws, racial violence	Institutionalized racism and racial prejudice function as instruments of exploitation and domination
Modern Era 1900–present	Scientific racism, modern racism, institutional racism	Science legitimizes racism in Europe and the United States; psychologists play a major role in perpetuation of scientific racism

NOTE: Some events may overlap between periods.

Prehistoric Roots of Racial Prejudice

Evolution and the Genetic Predisposition Toward Prejudice

Schaller, Park, and Faulkner (2003) posited that racism and prejudice are psychological responses to evolutionary pressures. Specifically, they asserted that the human capacity to experience *fear*, evolution of a *disease-avoidance mechanism*, and vigilance regarding *threat* of physical harm or bodily injury served important survival functions in evolutionary history. The human capacity for fear ensured that individuals would recognize environmental cues that would signal imminent danger. The disease-avoidance theory holds that a tendency on the part of early humans to avoid interpersonal contact with others who were potentially contagious had an adaptive function. Naturally, physiognomic markers and phenotypic features (e.g., skin color, facial features) would have been prime choices for connoting disease. Threat is likely the most basic of human survival mechanisms in that the ability to recognize threat would be directly related to harm-avoidance. According to Schaller et al. (2003), the evolutionary process resulted in the development of adaptive psychological responses (i.e., emotions, thoughts, and behaviors) that persist in contemporary human intergroup interactions. These once-adaptive psychological responses appear to have evolved into an innate predisposition toward racism and prejudice.

Some scholars have argued that the origins of racial prejudice can be explained by molecular biology, evolution, and genetics. For example, Hoyle and Wickramasinghe (1999) posited that contemporary race prejudice is rooted in the biological and genetic adaptation of humans to prehistoric climatic conditions. They argue, as do others (e.g., Bradley, 1991; Diop, 1981), that as humans migrated out of the tropical climate of Africa to colder climates in Europe and Asia, cellular-level physiological adaptations occurred as a function of a decline in ultraviolet radiation from the sun. For those who migrated toward the greyer skies and colder climate of Europe, there was a suppression of the gene responsible for the production of melanin. Melanin is the skin pigmentation that darkens the skin and protects it from the ultraviolet radiation of the sun. Melanin also regulates the amount of ultraviolet radiation that penetrates the skin, a process necessary for the production of vitamin D. Vitamin D is necessary for the absorption of calcium from food; a deficiency of this substance would potentially result in the development of rickets, a crippling disease characterized by severe bone deformities. As such, dark skin would have been nonadaptive in the colder climates of Europe and Asia, and white skin would have been nonadaptive in the tropics of Africa. Consequently, the white-skinned Nordic tribes living under the glacial Ice Age conditions of prehistoric Europe would have viewed the potential for interbreeding with the darker humans coming out of Africa as a threat to their genetic survival. Hoyle and Wickramasinghe (1999) conclude that under these circumstances, prohibitions against Black-White mating would have been a natural outcome, and racial prejudice would have evolved along with the social and cultural traditions of early humans.

Tribalism and Survival in Prehistoric Times

Human survival in prehistoric times often depended on the ability to secure resources in times of shortage. This was most effectively facilitated by encouraging in-group loyalty and out-group mistrust (Zarate, Garcia, Garza, & Hitlan, 2004). The *realistic group conflict theory* posits that contemporary prejudice is the result of competition between prehistoric ancestral groups for limited resources (Sherif, Harvey, White, Hood, & Sherif, 1961). As competition between groups (e.g., clans, tribes, or villages) for limited resources intensified, out-group discrimination emerged as a necessary and viable adaptive mechanism. The racial component of realistic group conflict is a natural extension of this phenomenon, given that members of the same clan (family), tribe, or village tended to share phenotypic features.

In prehistoric tribal societies, where survival depended on which group controlled the resources, interactions between groups often had lethal consequences. According to Schaller (2003), adopting negative and derogatory beliefs about a competing out-group gave the in-group a significant survival advantage. For example, propagating the notion that all members of a given clan, tribe, or village were flesh-eating cannibals was likely to result in the in-group's (and possibly allied groups') avoidance of not only the identified group but of other similar, potentially dangerous groups. The result of this struggle for individual and group survival, particularly where climatic conditions were harsh and resources scarce, was a genetic predisposition toward aggression and racial prejudice (Bradley, 1991).

Origins of Modern Racial Prejudice

Racial Prejudice in Pre-Christian Europe

The attitudes of Europeans toward Blacks in antiquity were surprisingly favorable. In fact, there is evidence that Blacks were held in high regard in Greco-Roman societies (Guthrie, 1998; Jahoda, 1999). For example, the fifth-century Greek historian Herodotus, expressing the general sentiment of the people of that era, stated that "the Ethiopians [i.e., "Negroes"] . . . are said to be the tallest and most attractive people in the world." Not only were there Olympian gods and goddesses who were portrayed as mulatto or Black, a number of artistic representations of historically significant figures in legend and tradition (e.g., the Queen of Sheba, St. Gregorius, and Prester

John) depicted them as Black Africans (Jordan, 1968). Moreover, Ethiopians (Blacks) were represented in the Roman armies, served as ambassadors in European courts, and were sought by Europeans to assist with their wars against Muslim enemies (Jahoda, 1999; Jordan, 1968).

By most accounts, anti-Black racism emerged in Europe at around the beginning of the Christian era. In fact, by the time the trans-Atlantic slave trade was burgeoning, at around the middle of the 17th century, a solid body of anti-Black literature already existed in Europe (Jahoda, 1999; Jordan, 1968). Several of Europe's most prolific writers were major contributors to the anti-Black racial sentiment that would later be used to justify the enslavement of Africans. For example, Diodorus, the famous Greek philosopher, stated that the inhabitants of Ethiopia were a depraved people who lived among wild beasts and feared the sun because of its unmerciful heat. Pliny, another Greek philosopher, in referring to the tribes of Africa, described monsterlike humans with animal-like features. Aristotle stated that the heat of the sun adversely affected the brains of Ethiopians, limiting their mental capacities. Ptolemy posited that the Ethiopians had acquired their black skin, woolly hair, and shrunken stature from being burnt by the sun (Jahoda, 1999).

Racial Prejudice in the New World

Pedersen (1994) and Miles (1989) maintain that racism was developed to rationalize world exploration by European powers in the 14th to 16th centuries. In fact, these authors assert that early colonialism was primarily racism against Islam. Europeans in the New World asserted that enslaving Africans was justified because Africans were a separate and subhuman species of humankind, best suited to serve as beasts of burden (Jahoda, 1999; Jordan, 1968). Furthermore, it was suggested that the Africans were a brutish and uncivilized lot of heathens who would in fact benefit from their servitude under the highly "civilized" and "cultured" White race (Thompson, 1977). These justifications for the forced servitude of Africans, though obviously flawed and irrational, would eventually become permanently incorporated into the psychological and social consciousness of White America (Jordan, 1968; Pinkney, 1993) and Black America (Akbar, 1984, 1996; Wilson, 1990).

Chattel Slavery

Historians (Bennett, 1966; Everett, 1991; Morgan, 1985; Pinkney, 1993; Stampp, 1956) generally agree on the unusual harshness and brutality of U.S. slavery. The first Africans to arrive in the New World around 1619 CE were not slaves but indentured servants who worked alongside their English and Irish brethren (Jordan, 1968; Stampp, 1956). When they had completed their term of service, they were free to go, like other indentured servants. Prior to chattel slavery, Africans were free to own land, enter into contracts, and hold indentured servants, both Black and White (Bennett, 1966). As the demand for labor grew, the indentured workforce could not keep pace with the demand. Gradually, Whites began to renege on the contracts and would frequently hold indentured servants past the agreed-on length of service. As a result, individuals were forced to flee their forced servitude. At some point, Whites realized that a race-based system of perpetual servitude would best serve their economic interest. The first enslaved Africans arrived in the New World around 1640, and as they say, the rest is history (Everett, 1991).

Under the institution of chattel slavery, all aspects of a slave's life were dictated according to the rigid social, psychological, and physical controls implemented by the slavocracy (Everett, 1991; Stampp, 1956). According to Stampp, the collective strategy for the maintenance of such absolute control was carried out by several methods. First, slaveholders had to establish and maintain strict discipline: The slave must willingly obey at all times. In addition, the slave needed to accept her or his personal inferiority and status in perpetual servitude as the natural order of things. To instill a sense of awe in the slave, slaveholders often demonstrated their enormous power and control over the slave to the degree that it produced a constant state of fear in the slave community (Bennett, 1966; Stampp, 1956). Finally, a most effective and lasting method of control was to instill in slaves a sense of general helplessness and complete dependence upon their masters for all of their needs (Akbar, 1984; Morgan, 1985).

Jim Crow Segregation

Although slavery officially ended at the conclusion of the Civil War in 1865, the status of Black people changed little over the next few decades (Bennett, 1966; Pinkney, 1993). For a brief moment in history, during the period of Reconstruction, some Blacks in a few areas enjoyed some privileges associated with being full participants in a free society (Bennett, 1966). However, shortly thereafter, the Union Army left, and almost immediately, "Black codes" were enacted to restrict the rights of African Americans and maintain White racial superiority in the former slave states (Everett, 1991; Pinkney, 1993). For the next eight decades or so, African Americans would exist under a system of racial apartheid unparalleled in the history of the world. Moreover, now that African Americans were no longer the valuable property of White plantation owners, they faced even greater threats to their personal safety (Everett, 1991).

Many of the myths developed and maintained about the innate inferiority and deficient moral character of African Americans to justify keeping them in bondage were now used to keep them from being full participants in American society. The racial codes were strictly enforced, often through the use of violence. Violence directed toward African Americans during this period was widespread; burning and lynching were common (Jordan, 1968; Stampp, 1956). Race became the dominant factor in the social, economic, and political structure of American society. Several major Supreme Court rulings served as the vehicle that officially relegated African Americans to a subordinate status in society. For example, In 1883, the court ruled that the Civil Rights Act of 1875, which made it a crime to deny any citizen equal access to public accommodations, was unconstitutional (Jones, 1997; Pinkney, 1993). Additionally, in the *Plessy v. Ferguson* case of 1896, the court ruled that racially segregated facilities mandated by law were not in violation of the Thirteenth and Fourteenth Amendments to the Constitution. The majority opinion of the court declared that the inherent racial inferiority of African Americans could not be undone by any provision of the U.S. Constitution (Pinkney, 1993).

Struggle for Civil Rights

During the first half of the 20th century, America would experience many changes, but the status of African Americans would remain relatively static. Although African Americans would engage in constant struggle for their civil and human rights and, in some cases, win major concessions to undo government-sponsored segregation, little could be done to change White America's perception of African Americans as being innately inferior and subhuman (Jones, 1997; Jordan, 1968). The tenets of White supremacy had become so ingrained in the consciousness of White America that it soon found expression in almost all aspects of American life (Jordan, 1968). By the time Jim Crow had been dismantled and African Americans were (in theory) entitled to equal protection under the law and access to public accommodations, racism and White supremacy had become a permanent fixture in the psychological, social, political, and economic landscape of American society.

Birth of Scientific Racism

The term *scientific racism* was coined by Stephen Jay Gould to describe the historical role of science in propagating the idea of White racial superiority (Guthrie, 1998). The exact birth date of scientific racism is difficult to pinpoint, but early attempts to classify man according to a hierarchical system of superior and inferior beings were certainly a start. Carl Von Linnaeus developed the first classificatory system of racial designations based on phenotypes, temperament, and customs (Guthrie, 1998; Jahoda, 1999). It is hardly surprising that Blacks were at the bottom of the hierarchy or that Whites occupied the superior position.

Darwinism

Charles Darwin, reportedly an antislavery proponent (Bergman, 2002), is probably the person most responsible for the perpetuation of scientific racism in Europe and the United States. His most famous work, *The Origin of Species by Means of Natural Selection, or the Preservation of Favored Races in the Struggle for Life*, is arguably the conceptual genesis for the doctrine of White racial superiority. Darwin has been credited with proposing a theory of evolution, but in actuality he is responsible for several related theories (Bergman, 2002). These theories are as follows: (a) evolution—organisms transform over time; (b) common descent—every group of organisms is descended from a common ancestor; (c) multiplication of species—species multiply by splitting or budding; (d) gradualism—evolution occurs through gradual change, not suddenly; (e) and natural selection—only the most adaptive organisms survive to reproduce.

Darwin's belief that certain races of man were superior and others inferior finds expression in *The Descent of Man*, where he states that "at some future period, not very distant as measured by centuries, the civilized races of man will almost certainly exterminate, and replace, the savage races throughout the world" (cited in Bergman, 2002). According to evolutionary theory, the more recently evolved races are superior to less evolved, more primitive races. Early anthropologists recognized three common racial classifications, as follows: Negroid, Mongoloid, and Caucasoid. Darwin and his predecessors believed that the Negroid race was the least evolved and the Mongoloid and Caucasoid the more highly evolved (Jahoda, 1999). Darwin's theory of evolution was instrumental in establishing a foundation from which scientific racism blossomed in the 19th and 20th centuries (Guthrie, 1998). The eugenics movement sprouted from Darwin's theory of evolution.

Eugenics

The eugenics movement had its beginnings in Europe during the early 20th century. Sir Francis Galton, the first cousin of Charles Darwin, coined the term *eugenics*, a Greek word meaning "good genes" (Guthrie, 1998). Eugenicists operated under the assumption that human traits, both physical (eye color, blood type, etc.) and mental (intelligence, personality, etc.), were hereditary. In his 1869 treatise *Hereditary Genius: Its Laws and Consequences,* Galton attempted to demonstrate that exceptional men beget other exceptional men. His desire was to create the perfect society by encouraging reproduction among the best and discouraging it among those considered less desirable (Guthrie, 1998; Thomas & Sillen, 1972). Galton was a proponent of White racial superiority, as he demonstrates in the following statement: "No more than there is equality between man and man of the same nation is there equality between race and race" (as cited in Guthrie, 1998, p. 43).

The eugenics movement enjoyed widespread popularity in the United States, where its racial element became a central component. Elaborate research programs were established to demonstrate the relationship between genotype and phenotype (Allen, 2001). Based on research that was said to establish a genetic link between criminality, feeblemindedness, other undesirable traits, and race-group membership, the Johnson-Reed Act of 1924 was passed by the House Committee on Immigration and Naturalization banning the immigration of individuals from Southern and Eastern Europe (Allen, 2001). In addition, more than 35 states enacted laws allowing for the forced sterilization of persons deemed genetically defective. By the time these laws had been repealed in most states, more than 60,000 people had been subjected to sterilization procedures. A similar eugenics program occurred in Nazi Germany around 1933 and resulted in the forced sterilization of more than 400,000 Jews.

Racism and Psychology

Historically, the proponents of White superiority and Black inferiority have garnered a great deal of support from the field of psychology. For example, Dr. Cartwright, a Louisiana physician in the antebellum South, coined the term *Drapetomania* (or "the flight from home madness"), which referred to slaves who escaped or otherwise attempted to run away (Stampp, 1956; Thomas & Sillen, 1972). He is also credited with the diagnosis of Dysaesthesia Aethiopica (or "insensibility of nerves"), a term used to describe slaves who caused problems for their overseers or failed to perform their duties (Stampp, 1956). Later, the eminent psychologist Carl Jung suggested that the "childlike" and "primitive" nature of the Negro could be explained by the fact that they had less brain matter than Whites (Guthrie, 1998). Another prominent psychologist, Arrah B. Evarts, published a paper titled *Dementia Praecox in the Colored Race,* in which he asserts that slavery aided Blacks in developing their full potential as a race (Thomas & Sillen, 1972). In addition, William McDougall, in his influential work *Introduction to Social Psychology,* asserted that Blacks are instinctively submissive.

White scholars have spent considerable time and energy gathering empirical evidence to support the notion of African Americans' innate intellectual inferiority. The development of complex statistical procedures and the advent of mental abilities testing converged to launch the pseudoscience of the intelligence quotient (IQ) and heritability. Alfred Binet and Theodore Simon developed the first cognitive abilities test intended to segregate retarded children for the purpose of school instruction (Guthrie, 1998). Lewis Terman, an American psychologist who later revised the Binet-Simon scales, was among the first to promote the hereditability of low intelligence in certain races (i.e., Native Americans, Mexicans, and Negroes) (Guthrie,

1998; Thomas & Sillen, 1972). According to Guthrie (1998), Terman provided the impetus for individuals such as Edward Thorndike, Robert Yerkes, William Shockley, Audrey Shuey, Arthur Jensen, Hans Eysenck, and others who would devote considerable attention to proving that Blacks are innately less intelligent than Whites.

Although many had carried the eugenics mantle of race and the hereditability of IQ, it was Jensen's 1969 paper on race and IQ, published in the *Harvard Educational Review,* that had the greatest influence on the modern eugenics movement. Jensen's thesis was simple: (a) Blacks score significantly lower than Whites on IQ tests; (b) this difference cannot be explained by environmental factors and is probably genetic; and (c) given the genetic, immutable nature of the IQ gap, compensatory education (e.g., Head Start) for disadvantaged Black children is of no consequence (Guthrie, 1998; Thomas & Sillen, 1972). A number of prominent scholars have challenged Jensen's claim that the Black-White IQ difference is genetically determined (e.g., Lee J. Cronbach of Stanford University, Martin Deutsch of New York University, Robert Sternberg of Yale). They have accused Jensen of distorting the literature, misrepresenting the hereditability data, and making arbitrary interpretations, all in an effort to attribute the Black-White IQ gap to hereditary factors (Guthrie, 1998). In spite of the refutation of Jensen's argument for the hereditability of the Black-White IQ gap by some of the most prominent scholars in the field of education, much damage has been done.

In 1994, Richard Herrnstein and Charles Murray published a book titled *The Bell Curve: Intelligence and Class Structure in American Life.* This text added little to Jensen's basic claim of a genetic basis for the Black-White IQ gap. What we do observe, however, are even more sophisticated techniques for misrepresenting the literature and distorting data; added to these are, again, arbitrary interpretations. As with Jensen's dubious scholarship, scholars in education and psychology have refuted the work of Herrnstein and Murray (Sternberg & Kaufman, 1998). The damage resulting from *Bell Curve* is difficult to measure but is probably more substantial than Jensen's article in the *Harvard Educational Review.* Unlike the Jensen article, *Bell Curve* was marketed to the general public. The level of public debate over the book provided a simplified version of scientific racism for consumption by a nonacademic public.

This long history of scientific racism has had several significant and lasting effects on American society: It validated many of the racist beliefs held by some Whites about the inferiority of African Americans; many African Americans have themselves internalized the notions promulgated by scientific racism relating to their own innate inferiority; and Whites could now deny any responsibility for the wretched condition of African Americans, pointing to their own innate incapability as the cause of their condition.

Evolution of Racial Prejudice

A number of researchers have reported a reduction in the expression of racial prejudice by Whites toward Blacks and other people of color (Jackson, Brown, & Kirby, 1998; Sears, 1998). However, other scholars suggest that negative attitudes toward Blacks and other people of color have not disappeared but are expressed differently in contemporary society (e.g., Bobo, Kleugel, & Smith, 1997; Carr, 1997; Hughes, 1999; Walker, 2001). From the 1800s to about the 1950s, expressions of racial prejudice were overt and oftentimes violent. During this time period, lynching, beatings, cross burnings, and legal segregation were typical expressions of racial animosity (Jones, 1997; Jordan, 1968). Table 2.2 defines the different expressions of racism discussed in detail here.

Out With the Old; in With the New

Dominative or Old-Fashioned Racism

Dominative (old-fashioned) racism refers to the more overt and hostile expression of racial animosity (Hughes, 1999; Walker, 2001). This is the type of racism that comes to mind most often when White Americans are asked to judge whether their actions are racist. The dominative racist believes that Blacks are inherently inferior and deserve unequal treatment (Kovel, 1970). They support the idea that racial segregation is necessary to maintain the purity of the White race. They do not hesitate in resorting to violence to make their point. There is general agreement among scholars in the area of racial prejudice that dominative racism has been in decline since the death of Jim Crow (legal segregation). However, in recent times we have witnessed a dramatic increase in the type of horrific racial violence common during Jim Crow. A few examples are (a) the dragging death of James Byrd in Jasper, Texas; (b) the fatal shooting (41 times) of Amadou Diallo by New York City police; (c) the beating and sodomy of Abner Louima, again by New York City police; and (d) several cases of the murder of unarmed Blacks at the hands of White mobs (e.g., Yusef Hawkins and Michael Griffin).

Symbolic, or Modern, Racism

Symbolic, or modern, racism emerged following the death of Jim Crow and dominative expressions of racial animosity. Theorists hold that in contrast to old-fashioned racism, symbolic racism did not result from any economic, social, political, or sexual threat posed by Blacks against White interests (Hughes, 1999). Instead, they argue, symbolic racism represents the belief by Whites that Blacks violate traditional American

Table 2.2   Various Types of Expressions of Racism

Type	Originating Authors	Distinguishing Features
Dominative (old-fashioned) racism	Allport, 1954; Jones, 1972	Overt expressions of racial hostility, expressed belief in White racial superiority, acting out of racist fantasies
Symbolic (modern) racism	McConahay, 1986; Sears, 1988	New form of anti-Black racial prejudice based on learned social values related to a Protestant ethic and anti-Black fear
Laissez-faire racism	Bobo et al., 1997	Based on changing economic and political realities of race in the United States; legitimizes persistent Black oppression in the United States
Ambivalent racism	Walker, 2001	Characterized by the coexistence of positive and negative racial attitudes toward Blacks
Aversive racism	Kovel, 1970	Belief in White racial superiority, but not expressed; when possible, contact with Blacks is avoided; despite aversion to Blacks, advocates egalitarian principles
Colorblind racism	Carr, 1997	Denies, distorts, or evades the reality of racism and oppression in U.S. society

values and are to blame for any social, economic, and political inequality they may experience.

White American values of individualism, self-reliance, obedience, discipline, and social morality are the cornerstone of symbolic racism (Bobo et al., 1997; Hughes, 1999). At its most basic level, symbolic racism is a mix of anti-Black affect and traditional American values (individualism, self-reliance, etc.). Whites who practice symbolic racism typically do not endorse the tenets associated with dominative or old-fashioned racism. McConahay (1982) used the term *modern racism* to describe a concept similar to symbolic racism. A major tenet of modern racism, according to McConahay, is that most Whites believe racism no longer exists in U.S. society and that Blacks are too demanding of privileges not afforded to others.

Laissez-Faire Racism

Laissez-faire racism is similar to symbolic racism in that it is more subtle than old-fashioned racism and emerged following its decline (Bobo et al., 1997). The distinction between laissez-faire racism and symbolic racism is that the former results from a complex and interdependent relationship between economics, politics, and race in the United States. Like symbolic racism, laissez-faire racism attributes the economic and political failures of Blacks to their own cultural inferiority (Bobo et al., 1997). A second component of laissez-faire racism is the denial by Whites that structural and institutional barriers to minority progress exist. Third, Whites who express laissez-faire racism are resistant to efforts that seek to remedy institutional and social inequality.

Ambivalent Racism

A number of scholars have maintained that concepts such as modern racism and laissez-faire racism do not capture the multidimensional complexity of racism. The term *ambivalent racism* was coined by Walker (2001) to describe the phenomena whereby it is possible, and even likely, that Whites hold contradictory attitudes toward minority groups. According to Walker, the coexistence of positive and negative racial attitudes toward Blacks, when they exist, is based on White American value systems that are in themselves contradictory. For example, the belief in humanitarian and egalitarian values would tend to support racial equality and social justice, just as the Protestant ethic of hard work, individual achievement, and self-reliance is potentially translated into anti-Black racial animosity. The enduring nature of anti-Black racial animosity has been attributed to ambivalent racism phenomena because of its strong connection to the cultural values of White America (i.e., individualism and egalitarianism), which are in themselves a contradiction.

Aversive Racism

Aversive racism is similar in many respects to ambivalent racism. The term was first coined by Joel Kovel (1970) to describe the changing nature of racism in the United States. According to Kovel, the aversive racist, consciously or subconsciously, buys into the racial superiority of Whites but does nothing to act on this belief. The term was later refined by Dovidio and Gaertner (1986), who stated that aversive racism is a

> subtle form of bias that is characteristic of many White Americans who possess strong egalitarian values and who believe that they are not prejudiced . . . but [who] may also possess negative racial feelings and beliefs that they are unaware of, or that they try to dissociate from their images of themselves as non-prejudiced. (p. 4)

This duality may result in a state of cognitive dissonance for Whites who publicly espouse a belief in racial equality but privately harbor a sense of fear, discomfort, uneasiness, and even disgust (Dovidio & Gaertner, 1998). The strong negative feelings harbored by aversive racists toward other racial groups causes them to avoid intimate contact with members of these groups whenever possible.

Colorblind Racism

Neville, Worthington, and Spanierman (2001) suggested that racism is beyond psychological attitudes held by individuals and groups and is embedded in social structures. The core of colorblind racial attitudes (CoBRA), they posited, is the ignorance, denial, and distortion of the reality that race plays a role in people's lived experiences. Thus CoBRA are an ultramodern form of racism that is distinguished from the overt bigotry of Jim Crow (Neville et al., 2001). This more modern form of racism is characterized by persistent negative stereotyping, blaming the victims of oppression, and resistance to meaningful efforts to remedy problematic social situations and institutions. Neville et al. (2001) cite the work of Schuman and Krysan, who found that ultramodern racism mirrored changes in White individuals' beliefs about racial disadvantage over a 32-year period. For example, there was a significant increase, from 51% in 1963 to 80% in 1995, in beliefs that Blacks are to blame for their present condition. In addition, CoBRA are posited to be cognitive schema with affective correlates for processing racial material. They are multidimensional and complex in nature, and people of color may also adopt them.

Implications for Prejudice Reduction

We have presented evolutionary theories that view racial prejudice as a mechanism related to self-preservation in humans during prehistoric times. In addition, a review of the historical record provided a context for understanding the ubiquitous nature of contemporary racial prejudice. We demonstrated that racism has long permeated the social and cultural beliefs of those who are today classified as White. As was noted, racism has evolved and mutated into newer, more insidious expressions that are often undetectable by the victims and denied by the perpetrators. As such, we note that the efforts of counselors, educators, parents, and others seeking to reduce racial prejudice will be more difficult.

Given a probable evolutionary link and biological predisposition, a long and odious history in our social and cultural institutions, and a change to more subtle forms of expression, it is likely that racial prejudice will remain a fixture in our society for many years to come. Acknowledgment of racism's permanent place in society does not suggest that the problem is insurmountable but provides a realistic frame of reference for formulating intervention strategies. We must begin with the understanding that eliminating racial prejudice is unlikely to occur in the short term, if at all; therefore, it may be more realistic to strive toward reducing its expression.

Eradicating racial prejudice altogether will require strategies that seek to prevent our innate tendency toward tribalism from developing. Interventions that target children are likely to be the most successful, because children lack exposure to the social and cultural reinforcement of racial prejudice that one encounters daily in society (Parks, 1999). Moreover, some attention must be directed toward correcting the institutional and cultural mechanisms that maintain and perpetuate racism. There must be a national consciousness that rejects the tenets of the White racial superiority and "other" racial inferiority. These topics and other strategies for preventing prejudice are covered in depth in subsequent chapters of this book.

Chapter Summary

This chapter examined the historical origins of racial prejudice. To begin with, we presented a theory linking racial prejudice to the survival efforts of prehistoric man. Next, we discussed the prevalence of race prejudice in ancient and pre-Christian Europe. It was observed that attitudes toward Blacks were not necessarily negative to begin with but slowly evolved as more and more Europeans made contact with Black Africans. Following our discussion of the influence of religious doctrine on the ideology of White racial superiority, we provided an overview of science's role in legitimizing racism. A section was devoted to elucidating the changing nature of racism; we noted that old-fashioned racism had been replaced with more modern expressions of racial prejudice. Finally, we discussed the implications of racism's origins and evolution on efforts to reduce its expression in society. We now move to Chapter 3, which explores some of the causes and consequences of racial prejudice.

3

Causes and Consequences
of Racial Prejudice

Deep rooted prejudices entertained by the whites; ten thousand recollections, by the blacks, of the injuries they have sustained; new provocations; the real distinctions which nature has made; and many other circumstances, will divide us into parties, and produce convulsions which will probably never end but in the extermination of the one or the other race.

—Thomas Jefferson, *Notes on Virginia*
(as cited in Jordan, 1968, p. 436)

The deleterious effect of prejudice and racism on African Americans and other ethnic minority groups is well documented. A number of scholars have built long and illustrious careers delineating the exact mechanisms by which racism diminishes the quality of life experienced by African Americans and other racial and ethnic minorities living in the United States and elsewhere (e.g., Gordon Allport, Na'im Akbar, Philomena Essed, Joe Feagin, Franz Fanon, James Jackson, James Jones). In contrast, little evidence, empirical or otherwise, exists regarding the negative consequences of racism for White Americans. The lack of attention given to understanding how racism affects the lives of White Americans is due to the commonly held belief that it is an issue germane only to people of color. This fallacy has been perpetuated by research scientists, educators, politicians, policy makers, and, to some degree, well-intentioned civil rights leaders and organizations. Moreover, and to a greater degree, the privilege of Whiteness allows persons so classified to be oblivious to racism and its deleterious effects (see McIntosh, 1988, 1998; Neville et al., 2001).

There is little doubt as to how insidious racism is and that it permeates every facet of American life. Intuitively, we know that racism is harmful for both the victims and perpetrators and that eliminating it from our society would be in everyone's interest. However, a number of scholars (e.g., D'Andrea & Daniels, 2001; Helms, 1984) have suggested that only when Whites are convinced that racism is detrimental to their own quality of life and accept responsibility for its elimination can we expect to eradicate it from our society. This chapter will make the case that racism is not only a bad thing for African Americans and other minority group members but that it negatively affects the quality of life and psychological well-being of White Americans.

We would like the reader to note that the focus of this chapter is White racism. Some might argue that members of other racial and ethnic groups can be racist and to focus on only Whites is in and of itself a form of racism. Here we would direct the reader back to Chapter 1, where we define racism and distinguish it from prejudice and discrimination. True, anyone can be a bigot and harbor hatred based on race, ethnicity, national origin, sexual orientation, and related demographics. These behaviors, though reprehensible, do not constitute racism. The focus on White racism, however, is not based on these distinctions but is used for historical accuracy and conceptual clarity. White racism is the progenitor of all the other forms of racism that pervade the social and cultural fabric of U.S. society. To begin this discussion anywhere else would be misleading.

The current chapter will address several areas pertinent to the deleterious effects of racism on both Black and White Americans. First, we discuss the psychological mechanisms responsible for the development and maintenance of racial animosity. Particular attention is given to unconscious psychological processes and how they protect the ego from the threat, both real and imagined, ignited by anxiety related to racial fantasies. Second, we examine the deleterious effects of racism on the mental health of Whites; particular attention is given to reviewing recent empirical evidence on the topic. In the next section, we devote space to a discussion of the negative consequences of racism on the quality of life and general well-being of African Americans. We conclude with a summary of the chapter.

Racism and White Americans

Psychological Mechanisms of White Racism

White Privilege

White privilege, according to McIntosh (1988, 1998), is a means whereby Whites achieve societal rewards based on skin color and other socially determined indicators of race rather than on merit. White privilege is based on the assumption that Whiteness confers powers, both real and imagined, on the beholder that are not available to people of color (Neville et al., 2001). McIntosh posits that there are two types of White privilege: (a) *unearned entitlements* and (b) *conferred dominance.* Unearned entitlements refer to things that all people should enjoy (e.g., feeling safe in public spaces, being valued for what one contributes, working in a place where one feels one belongs) but that are restricted to Whites and result in *unearned advantage.* It is this unearned advantage that results in a competitive edge that most Whites are unwilling to admit to, let alone relinquish. The other form of privilege, conferred dominance, goes even further by giving individuals classified as White power over individuals classified as non-White. For example, the second author (S. O. Utsey), an African American male, was once questioned about his presence in a predominantly White community by an ordinary citizen who felt empowered to do so.

Like racism, White privilege is maintained and reinforced via cultural symbols that perpetuate the superiority of Whites and the inferiority of all other racial groups. As a result, White privilege has become institutionalized, permeating virtually all aspects of American life. Neville et al. (2001) suggest that White privilege is a multidimensional phenomena occurring at both macro and micro levels. Macrolevel White privilege is systemic in nature and manifests itself in the benefits, rights, and immunities afforded Whites in institutional settings in the United States. For example, in times of economic hardship, the "first-hired-last-fired" policy practiced by many U.S. corporations tends to benefit Whites because Blacks and other people of color, due to historical discrimination in hiring, tend to be the last hired and therefore the first to be fired. Microlevel White privilege is characterized by the individual and group advantages that Whites enjoy. According to Neville et al., advantages at the microlevel of White privilege are primarily intrapsychic and interpersonal (e.g., sense of entitlement, social validation of Whiteness). What makes White privilege so insidious is that it is invisible, omnipresent, and unacknowledged by its beneficiaries.

Colorblind Racial Attitudes

The concept of colorblind racial attitudes was first introduced in Chapter 2. As was noted, racism is less an individual-level psychological attitude than it is a social, cultural, and institutional phenomenon (Neville et al., 2001). As such, Neville et al. (2001) posited that colorblind racial attitudes (CoBRA) were an attempt to deny and distort the reality of race and racism in the lives of people of color. In this context, CoBRA are viewed as a more modern form of racism, distinguishable from old-fashioned racism and bigotry. Expressions of CoBRA are characterized by negative stereotyping, "blaming the victim" (assuming that people of color are to blame for their own racial victimization), and resistance to any meaningful effort to dismantle institutional barriers to racial equality. Moreover, Neville et al. (2001) noted that CoBRA are multi-dimensional and complex attitudes characterized by positive cognitive schema, with affective correlates for processing racial material, and that it is possible for people of color to adopt them.

White Racial Identity Development

White racial identity theory posits that racial attitudes toward self, for individuals who classify themselves as "White," develop in relation to their attitudes toward Blacks (Helms, 1990). The model posited by Helms (1984) initially consisted of a five-stage cognitive model describing the phases Whites experienced as they moved toward a nonracist identity. She later expanded her model to include six statuses (formerly stages) that delineate the abandonment of racism by Whites (Helms, 1995). The six statuses of White racial identity development are as follows: (a) contact, (b) disintegration, (c) reintegration, (d) pseudoindependence, (e) immersion-emersion, and (f) autonomy. According to Helms (1990), the six statuses comprise the following two themes: (a) the abandonment of racism (contact, disintegration, and reintegration), and (b) developing a positive, nonracist White identity (pseudoindependence, immersion-emersion, and autonomy). (See Chapter 6 for a more detailed discussion of the White racial identity statuses.)

In the updated model, Helms (1995) described each racial identity status and its concomitant style of cognitive-emotional information processing. For example, Whites who operate primarily from the contact status often use obliviousness to alter reality. In the disintegration status, the primary information-processing strategies include disorientation, confusion, and suppression of information. Information processing in the reintegration status is marked by distortion of information in an own-group–enhancing manner. The reshaping of race-related material to fit one's societal framework is the preferred style of information processing for individuals in the pseudoindependence status. The autonomy status is characterized by a more complex approach to integrating race-related stimuli, such as searching for internally defined racial standards and open and flexible interpretation and responses to racial material. Furthermore, Helms suggested that the thematic content of these strategies might vary according to the era in which a given individual was socialized. That is, a person internalizes race-related messages in the context of what society and the developing ego will allow (Kovel, 1970).

Psychodynamic Formulations of White Racism

The psychoanalytic literature posits that anxiety and racial intolerance are interrelated constructs. Accordingly, the more underlying anxiety one has, the greater one's propensity toward racial prejudice (Bettelheim, 1964). An individual whose personal control is weakened by the pressure of his or her anxiety may be inclined to seek relief through prejudice and racial animosity. This facilitates the discharge of hostility, thereby reducing anxiety. An individual's anxiety is reduced because he or she is able to convince the ego of its superiority, and therefore the person need not feel anxious (Bettelheim, 1964; Welsing, 1991; Wright, 1981).

Some psychoanalytic theoreticians have posited that racial prejudice represents the defensive efforts of the ego and superego. Meerloo (1961) observed that prejudice is more common among individuals with fragile egos and a deep fear of loneliness. From this theoretical perspective, racial animosity is viewed as an ego-strengthening experience that permits the prejudiced individual to better function in society. This is particularly true in a society in which racial prejudice is condoned. Moreover, the primary psychological benefit of racial animus is the reestablishment of the threatened ego's control over the individual's instinctual forces (Ryan & Buirski, 2001).

Identity formation theory has also received considerable attention in the early psychoanalytic literature in relation to racial prejudice. Bettelheim (1964) posited that racial prejudice offers individuals protection from the threat of identity diffusion or a complete loss of identity. For the extremely prejudiced person, feeling superior to members of an identifiable racial or ethnic group forms the basis for his or her identity. Any perceived infringement of the rights and privileges of the dominant group is viewed as a threat to the identity of the individuals who rely on their group membership as a source of ego strength (Bettelheim, 1964). In this regard, racial prejudice is viewed as an attempt by a weak ego structure to secure a social, ethnic, or personal identity.

More recently, object relations theory has been used to conceptualize the psychological mechanisms associated with White racism. In this framework, the unconscious source of racism is located deep within a primitive layer of the human psyche (Timimi, 1996). Here racism has its origins in the paranoid-schizoid split that occurs when an individual attempts to control or dominate, through projection and projective identification, those external objects that are different or separate from the self. Just as children less than one year old use fantasy to control objects that are external to themselves but at the same time projectively identify with them, highly prejudiced individuals are prone to the same behavior (Ryan & Buirski, 2001; Timimi, 1996). This is done to manage the anxiety of feeling separate and apart from them. For example, by viewing Blacks as inferior and as representing all that is evil, the highly prejudiced individual is able to project those aspects of self that are despised and disowned onto Blacks, thereby reducing her or his own feelings of anxiety.

The Disease Model of White Racism

Skillings and Dobbins (1991) proposed a disease model that characterizes White racism as a form of psychopathology whose etiology is similar to that of an addictive disorder. According to Skillings and Dobbins (1991), the addiction is to the seductive and distorted worldview that the success of White Americans is exclusively the result of their individual effort. The phenomenon of *cognitive dissonance* is integral to Skillings and Dobbins's conceptualization of racism as a disease. Cognitive dissonance is a psychological state characterized by anxiety and emotional discomfort that results when a person holds beliefs and cognitions that are incongruent with each other. Accordingly, when White Americans begin to realize that many of the privileges they enjoy are at the expense of people of color, feelings of anxiety, guilt, and shame may result. Skillings and Dobbins (1991) posit that White Americans have formed an addiction to a worldview steeped in denial, rationalization, and projection in an effort to avoid the anxiety and emotional pain associated with any cognitive dissonance they may experience.

The disease model of White racism has come under attack by a number of scholars writing in the area. For example, Wellman (2000) takes issue with the disease model of racism because it fails to meet the criteria for a disease. *The American Heritage College Dictionary* (1993) defines a disease as "A pathological condition in an organism resulting from infection or genetic defect" or "A condition or tendency, as of society, regarded as abnormal and harmful" (p. 397). Wellman argues that because racism is socially acceptable in the United States and is sanctioned by social and cultural institutions of society, the model of racism proposed by Skillings and Dobbins (1991) cannot be classified as a disease. Furthermore, he warns that by "medicalizing" racism we run the risk of absolving White America of the responsibility for dismantling the racial hierarchy created to give individuals classified as White advantage over individuals classified as non-White.

Negative Consequences of Racism for White Americans

In spite of a dearth of empirical research, anecdotal evidence suggests that Whites do experience psychological and emotional distress related to White racism. For example, several researchers have reported that Whites experience anxiety, frustration, guilt, and shame when confronted with issues related to their own racism or racism in general (Bowser & Hunt, 1996; Pettigrew, 1996; Utsey & Gernat, 2002). Similarly, Jones and Carter (1996) reported that Whites experience feelings of guilt, shame, anxiety, and helplessness, interwoven with a sense of intense confusion, around issues related to racism. Furthermore, Whites who consider themselves to be egalitarian but simultaneously hold that the second-class status of Black Americans is justified have been found to experience emotional and psychological discomfort (Hass, Katz, Rizzo, Bailey, & Moore, 1992).

Much of the early research that examined the psychological correlates of racial prejudice has produced dissimilar results. For example, in a study using a sample of psychiatric patients, researchers failed to detect any relationship between racial animosity and severity of psychiatric diagnosis (Ackerman & Jahoda, 1950). However, the highly prejudiced patients tended to have little awareness of their feelings and lacked insight into their psychological problems. Moreover, these patients often suffered from generalized anxiety, had physical symptoms of anxiety with somatic complaints, and experienced high levels of nonspecific rage (Ackerman & Jahoda, 1950). Research with psychiatric populations has consistently found racial prejudice to be correlated with symptoms of hypochondriasis, depression, psychopathic deviations, schizophrenia, and hypomania. Studies involving normal samples have not produced significant differences between highly prejudiced and unprejudiced individuals (Ackerman & Jahoda, 1950).

In a study conducted by Claney and Parker (1989), Whites who exhibited little racial consciousness experienced increased amounts of psychological discomfort during interactions with Blacks. A similar study by Hass et al. (1992) found that making Whites aware (i.e., conscious) of their ambivalence toward Blacks aroused emotional tension and psychological discomfort. Furthermore, European Americans who harbor racial animosity are at risk of developing maladaptive coping behaviors (Skillings & Dobbins, 1991). An earlier study by Bettelheim (1964) found that personal insecurity, subjective feelings of deprivation, anxiety, and hostility positively correlated with racial animosity. One study found that Whites who harbor racial prejudice are less likely to benefit from psychotherapy (Dowling, 1955). The empirical evidence suggesting that Whites experience psychological threat of varying levels of intensity during interracial interactions has clear implications for efforts aimed at reducing racial prejudice in society.

Racism and the Black Experience

Mechanisms of Anti-Black Racism

White Supremacy

Several renowned scholars have examined the psychological and cultural mechanisms of White supremacy and domination (Ani, 1994; Fuller, 1969; Kambon, 1998; Welsing, 1991; Wilson, 1998). White supremacy is defined as a system of power and domination, determined consciously or subconsciously, and embedded in the logic, thought, speech, action, perceptions, and affective response of people who classify themselves as White. According to Fuller (1969), White supremacy permeates cultural, economic, ideological, military, political, psychological, religious, and social structures in the service of European global conquest and domination.

The system of White supremacy and domination is perpetuated and maintained through violence, cultural hegemony, and the myth of White superiority (Ani, 1994; Fanon, 1963; Kambon, 1998; Sutherland, 1993). The European worldview, which values rugged individualism, dominance over nature, competition, materialism, and aggression, is congruent with a White supremacy orientation toward relations with others (Ani, 1994; Kambon, 1998; Myers, 1993). According to Welsing (1991), it is the culture and system of White supremacy and its thrust toward the global domination of people of color that produces the phenomenon of racism. Fuller (1969) posits that in spite of any self-professed economic and political independence on the part of individuals of color, all "non-White" people are victims of White supremacy.

Oppression

Freire (1970) views oppression as an act (or acts) of violence that by its very nature interferes with a person's ability to evolve as a complete human being. He defines oppression as any attempt by an individual or group of individuals to exploit, block, or hinder a person's or group of persons' pursuit of self-determination. Not only is oppression achieved and maintained by violence, but the violence gradually permeates all aspects of the social order, through which it affects the everyday lives of the oppressed (Fanon, 1963, 1967). In the course of time, such violence becomes normalized, subtle, and embedded into the institutional structure of society. The violence of oppression, once established in the culture, consumes and dehumanizes both the oppressed and the oppressor (Bulhan, 1985; Fanon, 1963, 1964).

Racism

According to Bulhan (1985), racism is characterized by the generalization, institutionalization, and assignment of values to phenotypic and cultural distinctions between persons from various racial and ethnic groups. These distinctions are typically used to justify the privilege of one group over others, unequal distribution of resources, and acts of aggression and violence directed at individuals from less powerful out-groups. Essed (1990) defined racism as "a complex aggregate of prejudice and discrimination based on an ideology of racial domination and oppression" (p. 11). Jones (1997) described racism as "resulting from the transformation of race prejudice and/or ethnocentrism through the exercise of power against a racial group defined as inferior, by individuals and institutions with the intentional or unintentional support of the entire culture" (p. 280). As far back as four decades ago, Fanon (1964) recognized that traditional racism, grounded in vulgar notions of the biological inferiority of certain racial groups, usually dark-skinned people, had become transformed into a more sophisticated and insidious form of cultural racism.

Negative Consequences of Racism for Blacks

Researchers have elucidated the exact psychological and physiological stress response associated with racism and discrimination (see Clark, Anderson, Clark, & Williams, 1999; Harrell, 2000; Hashfield et al., 1989; Krieger & Sidney, 1996; Outlaw, 1993). Psychologically, racism has been associated with increased levels of depression (Brown et al., 2000; Noh, Beiser, Kaspar, Hou, & Rummens, 1999), increased hostility (Utsey, 1999), lowered life satisfaction and self-esteem (Broman, 1997; Jackson et al., 1992), and feelings of trauma, loss, and helplessness (Fernando, 1984). According to Clark et al. (1999), perceptions of a racially stressful situation may result in the amalgamation of maladaptive feelings of anger, anxiety, paranoia, hopelessness, frustration, resentment, and fear. In some cases, these emotional and psychological responses are exacerbated by maladaptive coping strategies (Dobbins & Skillings, 2000; Lalonde, Majunder, & Parris, 1995; Plummer & Slane, 1996). For example, suppressing anger that results from encounters with racism potentially results in increased blood pressure, hostility, substance use, and other maladaptive coping responses (Clark et al., 1999; Krieger & Sidney, 1996).

The cumulative impact of the psychological stress and strain of racism may, in time, have negative somatic health consequences for African Americans. For example, the stress associated with chronic exposure to racism has been implicated in the onset of a number of stress-related diseases, including hypertension (Krieger & Sidney, 1996), cardiovascular disease (Armstead, Lawler, Gorden, Cross, & Gibbons, 1989), cirrhosis of the liver (McCord & Freeman, 1990), and lung ailments (Karlsen & Nazroo, 2002). Several studies have examined the relationship between noxious racial stimuli and blood pressure reactivity in African Americans. For example, Sutherland and Harrell (1987) found that racist encounters resulted in increased heart rate activity for a sample of African Americans. Armstead et al. (1989) found that racial stressors resulted in increased blood pressure in a sample of African American college students. A study by Clark (2000) found that perceptions of racism resulted in increased blood pressure responses in a sample of college women.

A number of other scholars have reported that African Americans experience a diminished quality of life due to their chronic exposure to invidious racism and general life stress (Essed, 1990; Jones, 1997; Outlaw, 1993; Utsey, Bolden, Brown, & Chae, 2001; Utsey, Chae, Brown, & Kelly, 2002). According to data from the National Study of Black Americans, racism was responsible for lowered life satisfaction among African Americans (Jackson et al., 1992). Another study by Broman (1997) found that the life satisfaction of African Americans was negatively affected by their experiences with racism. Jackson, Williams, and Torres (1995) found an inverse relationship between African Americans' life satisfaction, general happiness, and the stress associated with racism. Harrell (2000) noted that the interaction between race-related stress and general life stress increases the potential for African Americans to experience deleterious health consequences and a decreased quality of life.

Effects of Prolonged Exposure to Racism

In the context of American society, institutionalized racism is so sinister and ubiquitous that its victims are very often unable to fully recognize it in all its forms, even when they personally experience it (Akbar, 1984; Feagin, 1991; Jones, 1997). Firmly held notions of Black inferiority and White superiority have consummated the cultural legacy of racism in American society. Anti-Black sentiments are casually, commonly, and openly expressed daily in American society, both directly and through cultural symbolism (Ani, 1994; Wilson, 1998). To the extent that African Americans have internalized these anti-Black attitudes and accepted their subordinate status in society, as prescribed to them under a social order of White supremacy, a most damning and irreversible effect will occur—self-alienation (Akbar, 1984; Fanon, 1963, 1967; Wilson, 1990, 1998). Table 3.1 delineates this and other negative consequences of racism.

Fanon (1963) believed that adoption of the cultural reality of the oppressor and abandonment of one's own resulted in a profound sense of alienation for the oppressed. He proposed the following five aspects of alienation as a reaction to conditions of oppression: (1) alienation from the self—to be alienated from one's personal identity, (2) alienation from significant others—estrangement from one's family or group, (3) alienation from others in general—characterized by violence between Blacks and Whites, (4) alienation from one's culture and history—estrangement from one's language and history, and (5) alienation from creative social praxis—denial of or abdication from self-determination and from socialized and organized activity, which is at the core of the realization of human potential.

Akbar (1984) proposed an Africentric classificatory system of mental disorders that result from the assimilation of an alien worldview (i.e., European) for people of African descent. The first, *alien-self disorder,* is characterized by a conscious rejection of one's African reality, a denial of the reality of racism, and the active attempt of African Americans to emulate the European worldview and reality. The second, *anti-self disorder,* shares some characteristics with alien-self disorder but has the added element of covert and overt hostility toward all things African. *Self-destructive disorder,* on the other hand, reflects the ineffective and destructive attempts of African Americans to cope with the unnatural conditions of White supremacy and domination. Finally, *organic disorder* refers to those physiological and biochemical diseases that have their etiology in the oppressive conditions typical of the victims of White supremacy (ecological racism, poor nutrition, substandard health care, etc.).

Table 3.1   Classification Systems Characterizing the Negative Consequences
of Racism for Persons of African Descent

Authors	Classificatory System of Racism Reactions	Notes
Fanon (1963)	1. Alienation from self 2. Alienation from significant others 3. Alienation from others in general 4. Alienation from culture and history 5. Alienation from social praxis	According to Fanon, alienation results from the cultural deracination of Blacks via the imposition of European cultural hegemony
Akbar (1984)	1. Alien-self disorder 2. Anti-self disorder 3. Self-destructive disorder 4. Organic disorder	Like Fanon, Akbar's taxonomic model focuses on the cultural identity of Blacks as the etiology of psychological dysfunction

Kambon (1998)	1. Cultural misorientation (CM)
	  a. Minimal
	  b. Moderate
	  c. Severe
		Kambon's model is an extension of both Fanon's and Akbar's but adds degrees of dysfunction (i.e., minimal, moderate, severe)

Utsey, Bolden, & Brown (2001)	1. Racism-related trauma 2. Racism-related fatigue 3. Anticipatory racism reaction 4. Race-related stress and distress 5. Racism-related frustration 6. Racism-related confusion	This model is behaviorally focused in that the symptoms are directly observable and measurable

Kambon (1998) proposed that African Americans who are alienated from their natural African self-consciousness experience *psychological and cultural misorientation*. Hence, those of an individualistic orientation, expressing or exhibiting anti-African or -Black behavior, manifesting self-deprecating or self-destructive tendencies, or who are exploitative of or hostile to other African Americans, suffer from the Africentrically defined mental disorder cultural misorientation (CM). According to Kambon, African Americans can experience cultural misorientation with varying degrees of severity (i.e., minimal CM, moderate CM, or severe CM). For example, persons experiencing minimal cultural misorientation have a weak propensity for a Eurocentric worldview. In individuals experiencing moderate cultural misorientation, there is a tendency to internalize Eurocentric cultural values, beliefs, attitudes, and behaviors and at the same time manifest some pro-Black cultural values, beliefs, attitudes, and behaviors. Severe cultural misorientation is characterized by a predominance of internalized Eurocentric cultural values, beliefs, attitudes, and behaviors. A most insidious feature of psychological and cultural misorientation is that individuals with severe CM appear "normal" when viewed through the lens of a Eurocentric worldview (Kambon, 1992).

Acute Racism Reactions

In addition to the impacts of long-term exposure to racism and oppression, African Americans are at risk of experiencing a number of acute racism reactions. Utsey, Bolden, and Brown (2001) proposed six racism-related reactions that characterize African Americans' response to the psychological and physiological processes associated with the experience of racism and oppression. Although the reactions may occur simultaneously, each response is distinctive in its functionality and interpretation by the respondent. The racism-related reactions are as follows: (a) race-related trauma, (b) racism-related fatigue, (c) anticipatory racism reaction, (d) race-related stress and distress, (e) racism-related frustration, and (f) racism-related confusion. The following sections provide further explanations of the racism-related reactions and examples of their physical and psychological manifestation.

Race-Related Trauma

Race-related trauma is the spiritual, psychological, and physiological devastation African Americans experience following exposure to stressors involving the (a) direct personal experience with, (b) witnessing of, or (c) learning about actual or threatened violent death, serious injury or harm, or other threat to one's physical integrity on the basis of their race or skin color or as a result of the vicious and aggressive encroachment of oppression and White supremacy. Symptoms associated with race-related trauma include recurring thoughts or nightmares regarding the traumatic event, anxiety, fear, sleeplessness, and depression. Race-related trauma is not a pathological reaction per se but a logical and predictable response to racism and oppression.

Events that can trigger the onset of a race-related traumatic episode include being victimized with regard to housing or employment discrimination; race-based exclusion from goods and services; humiliation and degradation in public places; witnessing or experiencing mob violence (i.e., lynching, being attacked by a hate group); and being harassed, detained, arrested, or beaten by the police or other law enforcement personnel. Notable race-related events that have traumatized the collective psyche of African Americans include the dragging death of James Byrd in Jasper, Texas; witnessing the videotaped beating of Rodney King by members of the Los Angeles Police Department; the brutal beating and sodomy of Abner Louima by New York City police; the murder of Eleanor Bumpers by New York City police; and the murder of Amadou Diallo, also by New York City police (note that this list is hardly exhaustive). These horrific events, as soon as they are known by the masses, cause fear, anger, outrage, and shock in the African American community.

Racism-Related Fatigue

Racism-related fatigue is the tremendous psychological and physiological exhaustion that African Americans experience as a result of and in response to the chronic exposure to racism and oppression. Racism-related fatigue is a physiological manifestation of the constant, sweltering, and grinding toll taken on the individual who must combat racism, oppression, and White supremacy daily. The more determined the struggle against racism and oppression, the more taxing to one's ability to maintain focus in daily routine tasks, concentrate, or participate in activities that require physical exertion.

Similar to the physical fatigue one experiences as a result of exhaustive training and the chronic fatigue that women experience during pregnancy, racism-related fatigue is just as exhaustive and debilitating, making daily chores and routine tasks challenging or impossible. The causality of race-related fatigue often goes unrecognized because of its coupling with the daily challenges of life, such as dealing with family, school, intimate relationships, financial obligations, and work environments.

Anticipatory Racism Reaction

An anticipatory racism reaction is a defense mechanism that African Americans develop after being the victim, recipient, or combatant of racial discrimination and racially motivated hostility. The development of the anticipatory racism reaction is necessary and functional, as it forces the individual to remain aware at all times, in all situations involving Whites, based on previous interracial experiences. Although functional for self-protection and environmental awareness, the extreme amount of energy that the individual expends in attempting to maintain this high level of awareness increases his or her anxiety and becomes too taxing and burdensome to sustain.

The fear and threat of being attacked results in a state of hypervigilance for African Americans, who are constantly confronted with personal and shared experiences of racism and oppression (Essed, 1990; Feagin, 1991). Even in an environment that is perceived to be nonthreatening, the mechanisms of anticipatory racism reaction are unable to disengage, consequently making the situation uncomfortable for others. The effort that the individual must exert in anticipation of a race-related incident occurring may be more anxiety producing and stressful than the anticipated encounter itself (Essed, 1990).

Race-Related Stress and Distress

Chronic exposure to racism and oppression has been shown to have a deleterious effect on the psychological and physical well-being of African Americans (Utsey, 1998b). Racism is viewed as a major source of stress in the lives of African Americans and results in increased incidences of stress-related diseases (Outlaw, 1993). Stress is recognized as a person-environment encounter that is appraised as relating to one's well-being and that taxes or exceeds the person's resources to cope with a situation (Lazarus & Folkman, 1984, as cited in Outlaw, 1993). In this regard, encounters with racism and oppression result in an acute source of stress for African Americans.

Some symptoms associated with race-related stress and distress include the onset of tension headaches, muscle tightness, inability to concentrate, intrusive thoughts regarding a specific racism encounter, and a general sense of anxiety and tension. Moreover, race-related stress and distress may result in greater susceptibility to minor (e.g., common cold, flu) and major (e.g., hypertension, cancer) illnesses due to a weakened immune system.

Racism-Related Frustration

Racism-related frustration occurs when African Americans realize that they are powerless over the way in which they are treated because of their race. This experience often results in feelings of anger, irritability, aggravation, disappointment, dissatisfaction, and lack of fulfillment and satisfaction. Encounters with racism and oppression that are neither traumatic nor life threatening are still bothersome and upsetting. The individual involved in the incident recognizes that the encounter is both unnecessary and frivolous but must be entertained and managed until a conclusion is reached. If the situation is not resolved, closure cannot occur, and the individual will remain frustrated until a new racism encounter is experienced and the existing frustration is magnified.

Racism-Related Confusion

Racism-related confusion is a reaction that occurs when an individual in the midst of an onslaught of racist exchanges asks the question, "Who am I?"

This consuming question and the search for identity must be undertaken in an oppressive society, and the oppressed, now psychologically and physically fatigued, are thus left to function in bewilderment. Partially because of this disorientation, other questions now need answering: "What is going on?" "Whose problem is this?" and the unanswerable "Why me?" In this state of racism-related confusion, the oppressed begin to look at events and individuals differently. Things that were once certain are now uncertain; positions known are now unknown. As the oppressed are continuously attacked and placed in compromising positions, they now question their own involvement and skills and internalize the plight of the deserving victim.

Chapter Summary

We began this chapter by examining the mechanisms of White racism and discussing their role in the expression of racial animosity. Specifically, we provided an overview of White racial identity and psychodynamic formulations of White racism. The literature on White racial identity development and psychoanalytic theory highlighted the unconscious processes associated with the development and maintenance of racial animosity in Whites. Next, we presented evidence to demonstrate that racism not only negatively affects African Americans and other people of color but that it has deleterious consequences for White Americans. Most scholars conducting research in this agree that until Whites are convinced of racism's harmful effects, there will be little progress toward its eradication.

At the outset of our discussion, we indicated that the literature examining the negative impact of racism on African Americans and other people of color was extensive. Therefore, in our discussion of this topic our aim was not to duplicate that literature. To this end, we focused our discussion on the structural mechanisms that maintain and perpetuate racism and discrimination. In this section, we discussed White supremacy, oppression, and racism as acts of violence directed at its victims. In our coverage of the deleterious effects of racism, we first discussed the long-term, intrapsychic consequences of racism for African Americans. Here we examined the work of Na'im Akbar, Franz Fanon, and Paulo Freire, all of whom are internationally renowned scholars who have written extensively in the area of racism and oppression. Next, we presented a number of acute reactions commonly experienced by African Americans who are the victims of racism. Utsey, Bolden, and Brown (2001) developed a classificatory system for use by clinicians working with the victims of racism and discrimination. They outlined and named several symptom clusters to describe potential short-term reactions to encounters with racism and discrimination.

This chapter has a number of implications for reducing racial prejudice and racism. In writing this chapter, it was our intention to make real the causes and consequences of racism. It was especially important to make the case for racism's harmful effects on White Americans. Counselors, educators, and parents who want to reduce expressions of racism should be cognizant of the intrapsychic mechanisms that maintain and perpetuate racial animosity. Moreover, it is equally important for counselors, educators, and parents to be familiar with the negative effects of racism on the victims; this awareness is crucial for developing prevention and intervention programs.

Part II

Racial, Biracial, Multiracial, and Lesbian and Gay Identity Development and the Multicultural Personality

Part II of *Preventing Prejudice* includes four substantive chapters that cover the theoretical basis for the applied interventions outlined in Parts III and IV of the book. Knowledge of models of identity development and of multicultural personality dispositions is essential for a thorough understanding of prejudice and racism. Effectively intervening in the area of prejudice reduction, whether as a teacher, counselor, or parent, requires the solid theoretical grounding provided in this section.

Chapter 4, "Person of Color (Minority) Identity Development, Mental Health, and Prejudice," reviews influential models of racial and ethnic minority identity development, including the landmark models of William Cross and Jean Phinney. This chapter summarizes the research linking stages of racial and ethnic identity development to prejudicial attitudes and psychological health.

Chapter 5, "European American (White) Racial Identity Development, Mental Health, and Prejudice," reviews leading models of White racial identity and White racial consciousness development. Although these areas have not been as well researched as minority identity development models, there is clear evidence that higher stages of White identity and consciousness correlate to lower levels of prejudice and higher levels of psychological health. Therefore, as with minority identity models, the study of White identity is critical to the day-to-day work of all mental health professionals and educators.

Biracial, multiracial, and lesbian and gay identity development is the focus of Chapter 6. Research in these areas is relatively limited in comparison to empirical research on White and single racial and ethnic minority identity models. Nonetheless, knowledge of biracial, multiracial, and lesbian and gay models is critical, given the increasing numbers of biracial and multiracial families and the continuing stigma associated with homosexuality. As in the models reviewed in Chapters 4 and 5, in these models it is hypothesized that individuals who reach the highest stages of biracial, multiracial, and lesbian or gay identity will experience greater psychological health and more positive and open attitudes toward diversity in general.

Finally, Chapter 7 focuses on a relatively new construct in psychology, the *multicultural personality*. Integrating research from Europe and the United States, our model of the multicultural personality draws from theory and research in counseling psychology, social psychology, organizational psychology, feminist studies, and African-centered psychology. We expect that multicultural personality dispositions will be predictive of psychological health and intercultural comfort in our increasingly culturally diverse U.S. society. The multicultural personality will be a major area of psychological study in the next decades.

4

Person of Color (Minority) Identity Development, Mental Health, and Prejudice

How we feel about ourselves predicts, in part, how we relate to others. A critical component of our self-esteem, self-concept, and personal identity is our scnsc of racial and ethnic identity. How do we feel about ourselves as racial, ethnic, and cultural beings in an increasingly multicultural society that has a history of oppression and subjugation of non-White racial groups? This is a critical question for all Americans to ask themselves.

This chapter reviews and integrates both general and race- or ethnic-specific models of identity development. Research on the mental health correlates of various identity stages is summarized, and the relationship of prejudice to racial and ethnic identity is discussed. We begin our discussion of identity development by reviewing the landmark theories of Erik Erikson, James Marcia, and Rita Hardiman. With these conceptual models in hand, we move to a discussion of both general and race-specific models of minority identity development. The focus of Chapters 5 and 6 is on biracial or multiracial and gay identity development, and White racial identity development, respectively.

Erikson's and Marcia's Models of Identity Development

Erikson (1950, 1968) introduced an influential theory of ego identity formation in which he proposed that an achieved identity results from a period of exploration and experimentation that usually takes place in adolescence. Working through the exploration, the adolescent comes to solidify decisions and personal commitments in various areas, such as religious ideology, occupational identity, and political orientation. Marcia (1966, 1980) extended Erikson's work in his adapted model of ego identity development. Marcia outlined four distinct ego identity statuses centered on the elements of crisis and commitment. He believed that to form a healthy adult identity, each individual must experience a crisis in ideas derived from childhood identity development. The adolescent must explore possibilities, experiment with different options, and eventually make decisions and commitments about what to believe, how to behave, and what to become.

According to Marcia (1980), an adolescent is in the status of *identity diffusion* if she or he has not experienced an identity crisis, engaged in exploration, or made identity commitments in various areas. Let's use political affiliation as an example to clarify Marcia's statuses. When asked her or his political party affiliation, an adolescent in identity diffusion might respond, "Well, I haven't really thought about it, and I don't really care about politics."

Marcia's second identity status is termed *foreclosed identity* and describes the adolescent who makes an identity commitment based on external influences carried on from childhood, without undergoing her or his own identity crisis and exploration. This unexplored commitment often is based on the values of parents, who were so influential in childhood. Returning to our political ideology example, an adolescent in this status may respond to the question about party affiliation as follows: "My whole family is Republican, so I am a Republican."

The *moratorium* status describes the adolescent in the midst of an identity crisis who is still exploring and experimenting with options but has not yet made a commitment to aspects of identity. This status is characterized by an active identity search. Returning to our political example, the adolescent in moratorium may respond to the party affiliation question something like this: "Well, I have been thinking about that for a few months, and to be honest, I am really torn and confused. I like some Democratic ideas, such as a pro-choice stand and gay rights, but I also like the Republican emphasis on low taxes, the privatization of social security, and high defense spending. I need to think about it further and talk about it some more with a few more trusted friends and mentors. Ask me again in a few weeks."

Finally, an *achieved identity* characterizes the individual who has had an identity crisis, has explored and experimented with options, and has now come to a commitment regarding what to believe and what to become. Returning for the last time to our political example, the adolescent in this status may state, "You know, I've thought about this long and hard for a few months now, and I've decided that issues of a woman's right to choose, affirmative action, and gay rights are so important to me that I have decided to join the Democratic party."

Hardiman's Stages of Social Identity Development

Hardiman (1982) examined the constructs of racial identity and sex-role identity within the broader conception of what she termed "social identity." She defined social identity as "all the various social groups that an individual consciously or unconsciously has membership in and the conscious or unconscious use of that social frame of reference in self-perception, in social perception or in social interaction" (Hardiman, 1982, p. 76). Building from the work of sociologists (e.g., Dashfsky, 1976), anthropologists (e.g., Robbins, 1973), and psychologists (e.g., Erikson, 1968; Tajfel, 1974), Hardiman developed a model of social identity consisting of five stages: *no social consciousness*, *acceptance*, *resistance*, *redefinition*, and *internalization*.

No Social Consciousness

This first stage is characterized by spontaneous, natural behavior with regard to one's social attitudes or behavior. Individuals in this stage are unaware of or confused about their expected social role. Pressures to conform to particular social norms and behaviors have not yet been internalized.

Acceptance

Stage 2 is characterized by identification with role models and imitation or modeling of behavior. At this point, stereotypes are developed and rigidly adhered to. The individual in acceptance conforms to social expectations of appropriate behavior as a member of a particular social group (racial group, gender group, etc.). Stage 2 is also characterized by a rejection and devaluing of behaviors or characteristics that do not fit the social group's expectations.

Resistance

In Stage 3, the individual begins to question previously held beliefs about herself or himself as a member of a particular social group. Feelings of discomfort and anger emerge as one acknowledges his or her conformist attitude with regard to the social group. Individuals in this stage begin to reject the social group's pressures to conform, and a new perspective or consciousness about the group is formed.

Redefinition

Stage 4 is characterized by introspection about the social group and the beginning of a definition of specific needs that are separate from the group as a whole. There is a rediscovery of and a renewed interest in one's heritage and culture as a member of the social group. This stage is characterized by pride and esteem in one's group membership.

Internalization

The final stage of Hardiman's social identity development model involves the integration of aspects of identity achieved in the previous stage into the individual's overall social identity. The individual in internalization is flexible, open minded, and, to some degree, autonomous. There is interest and development in other aspects of one's social identity. The Stage 5 individual also displays empathy for individuals of the same social group who are at earlier stages of development. Perhaps the clearest explication and example of Hardiman's social identity model is reflected in her influential model of White racial identity development, which we cover in depth in Chapter 6.

General Models of Minority Identity Development

This section reviews three general models of minority identity development. The first model reviewed is that of Phinney and her colleagues (Phinney, Lochner, & Murphy, 1990) who extend the identity development work of Erikson and Marcia to the topics of race, ethnicity, and minority status. Phinney's work is anchored in extensive research in developmental psychology, and her model focuses on minority adolescents. The second model we summarize is named the minority identity development (MID) model and was developed by a team of counseling psychologists (Atkinson et al., 1989). The MID model is focused primarily on adults. The third general model summarized is Helms's (1995) people of color racial identity model. Helms is a counseling psychologist who studies both the general and clinical implications of racial identity (Helms, 2001; Helms & Cook, 1999).

Phinney's Model of Ethnic Identity Development

The extensive work of Phinney (1989, 1990; Phinney & Alipuria, 1990; Phinney, Lochner, & Murphy, 1990; Phinney & Rotheram, 1987a; Phinney & Tarver, 1988) and her colleagues has provided a secure bridge linking ethnic identity development to more general models of adolescent identity development. Phinney et al. (1990) note:

> It is our thesis that a commitment to an ethnic identity is an important component of the self-concept of minority youth and a factor that mediates the relationship between minority status and adjustment. That is, adolescents

who do not explore and take a stand on issues regarding their status as minority group members, nor develop a secure ethnic identity with which to obtain meaning and self-direction in an ethnically heterogeneous society, may be at risk for poor self-concept or identity disorders. (p. 54)

Phinney et al. (1990) suggest that minority group members need to resolve two primary issues or conflicts that result from their status as members of a nondominant group in society. The first issue is the existence of dominant-group stereotyping and prejudice toward their group. Phinney et al. (1990) review the work of Tajfel (1978) and Gibbs (1988), who note that individuals belonging to a group that is disparaged and stereotyped by the majority group face a threat to their self-concept. The second issue revolves around contrasting value systems. Minority individuals must choose between (or negotiate) their own cultural value system and that proffered by the dominant society (refer back to Chapter 1 for more on value systems in human behavior). Phinney et al. (1990) maintain that the way in which minority adolescents deal with and come to accept their status as members of society who face prejudice and who must negotiate a bicultural value system affects their sense of ethnic identity. Those adolescents who actively explore and resolve these struggles develop an achieved ethnic identity, whereas those who fail to do so develop a diffused or foreclosed identity.

Integrating the work of Tajfel (1978), Berry and Kim (1988), and others, Phinney et al. (1990) posit four possible coping outcomes that minority-status individuals use to deal with ethnic identity conflicts. *Alienation and marginalization* describe individuals who accept the negative self-image presented by society (what is also termed *internalized racism*), become alienated from their own racial or ethnic cultural group, and do not adapt to the majority culture. *Assimilation* describes those individuals who attempt to become part of the dominant culture and do not maintain ties with their own racial or ethnic cultural group. *Withdrawal* or *separation* describes individuals who emphasize their own culture and withdraw from contact with the majority or dominant group. Finally, *integration and biculturalism* describe those individuals who retain their ethnic culture and also adapt to the dominant culture by learning the skills necessary to succeed in the culture. There is some evidence that this integration is the most psychologically healthy in terms of traditional measures of mental health, such as high self-esteem and lower levels of stress and anxiety. More will be said about this research later in the chapter.

Phinney and her colleagues (Phinney, 1989; Phinney & Alipuria, 1990; Phinney et al., 1990; Phinney & Tarver, 1988) have presented an ethnic identity development model consistent with Marcia's (1966) ego identity model. Phinney's model has three distinct stages—*diffusion and foreclosure, moratorium,* and *achievement*—that elucidate the process by which minority adolescents explore ethnic issues and achieve a positive sense of themselves as minority group members.

Ethnic Identity Diffusion and Foreclosure

In the initial stage of ethnic identity development, adolescents have not yet explored their feelings or attitudes about their ethnicity. Adolescents may lack interest in the topic or see it as a nonissue (*diffusion*), or they may have attitudes about ethnicity derived from significant others carried over from childhood (*foreclosure*). Phinney et al. (1990) note that some minority adolescents in this stage may accept the values and attitudes of the dominant culture toward their group. These youth are at risk of internalizing negative stereotypes about their own group and expressing preferences for the dominant group. The majority of individuals at this stage, however, does not express preferences for the dominant group. Instead, individuals simply appear to be unconcerned about ethnicity or may not have given the topic of their ethnicity much thought.

Table 4.1 outlines the link and crossover between Phinney's stage conceptualization and that of Marcia and other ethnic identity theorists. The last two rows of Table 4.1 summarize the researched mental health correlates to the stages, as well as our hypothesized prejudicial dispositions associated with each stage.

Ethnic Identity Search or Moratorium

The second stage is characterized by an increasing awareness and exploration of ethnic identity issues. This newfound awareness is sometimes precipitated by a sudden experience or encounter that causes the adolescent to pause and consider the meaning of her or his ethnic background. The encounter may be blunt, such as an experience with overt racism, or it may be more subtle, involving a number of less dramatic experiences that cause the adolescent to acknowledge that she or he is perceived (by the dominant group) as unequal by virtue of racial or ethnic affiliation. This awareness leads to an ethnic identity search (moratorium), through which the adolescent attempts both to clarify the personal implications of race and ethnicity and learn more about her or his racial or ethnic group. This stage, like parallel stages in other identity models (see Table 4.1), is often characterized by emotional intensity. Individuals may experience anger and outrage toward the dominant White society. Guilt, embarrassment, and self-directed anger may result from an acknowledgment of past naiveté with regard to racial and ethnic issues.

Ethnic Identity Achievement

In the final stage of adolescent ethnic identity development, the individual has come to terms with racial and ethnic issues and has accepted her- or himself as a member of a minority group. The intense emotions characteristic of the previous stage have moderated. The individual has a

Table 4.1 Models of Racial and Ethnic Identity Development

General Identity Model

Marcia (1980)	Identity diffusion	Foreclosed identity	Moratorium		Achieved identity	

Racial- and Ethnic-Minority Transcendent

Phinney, Lochner, & Murphy (1990)	Diffusion and foreclosure		Search or moratorium		Achievement	
Atkinson, Morten, & Sue (1998)	Conformity	Dissonance	Resistance and denial		Introspection	Synergetic articulation
Helms (1995; Helms & Cook, 1999)	Conformity	Dissonance	Immersion	Emersion	Internalization	Integrative awareness

Racial- or Ethnic-Minority Specific

African American

Cross (1995)	Pre-encounter	Encounter	Immersion and emersion		Internalization	Internalization and commitment
Cross & Vandiver (2001); Vandiver et al. (2002)	Pre-encounter: assimilation, miseducation, or racial self-hatred	Encounter	Immersion-emersion: anti-White or Black involvement		Internalization: nationalist, biculturalist, or multiculturalist	

Japanese American

Kim (1981)	Ethnic awareness	White identification	Awakening	Redirection	Incorporation	

(Continued)

Table 4.1 (Continued)

Mexican American or Latino

Arce (1981)	Forced identification	Internal quest	Acceptance	Internalized
Ruiz (1990)	Causal Cognitive	Consequence	Working through	Successful resolution

Integrative Model

Ponterotto, Utsey, & Pedersen (2006)	Identification with the White majority	Awareness, encounter, and search	Identification and immersion	Integration and internalization
Psychological adjustment	Lower self-esteem and lower levels of psychological health	Lower self-esteem and lower levels of psychological health	Lower levels of psychological health	Higher levels of self-esteem and general psychological health
Multicultural interests and prejudicial inclinations	Less interest in diverse multicultural contacts	Some negative bias toward other racial and ethnic groups but higher interest in multicultural activities (perhaps with own cultural group)	Negative views of other racial and ethnic groups; higher levels of involvement in own-group cultural activities	More interest in diverse multicultural activities; more accepting of culturally diverse others

calm, secure demeanor with regard to her or his cultural group and is, at the same time, open to experiences outside the culture. In essence, a healthy bicultural identity is developed.

Atkinson, Morten, and Sue's Minority Identity Development Model

Atkinson et al.'s (1989, 1998) minority identity development model is anchored in the belief that all minority groups experience the common force of oppression, and, as a result, all will generate attitudes and behaviors consistent with a natural internal struggle to develop a strong sense of self- and group identity in spite of oppressive conditions. The MID model is presented as a stage theory; however, the authors caution that the model is best conceptualized as a continuous process in which the stages blend into one another without clear or abrupt demarcations.

Each stage in the MID model is defined with respect to four attitudinal groupings: (a) attitudes toward oneself, (b) attitudes toward others in the same reference group, (c) attitudes toward members of other minority groups, and (d) attitudes toward the White majority group. The five stages are briefly described here.

Conformity

Minority individuals in Stage 1, conformity, have an unequivocal preference for the values and norms of the dominant culture. They have a strong desire to assimilate and acculturate into the dominant culture. Individuals in this stage have negative, self-deprecating attitudes toward themselves as racial beings, as well as toward their racial group in general. Their view of other minority groups is dependent on how the dominant culture evaluates the groups. Conformity-stage attitudes toward the dominant group are positive.

Dissonance

The dissonance stage marks that point when minority individuals begin to question their conformity-stage pro-White attitudes. Movement into the dissonance stage is a gradual process, often stimulated by a personal race-related experience. For example, an individual who has been denying her or his racial or ethnic heritage (i.e., displaying conformity attitudes) may meet and be strongly influenced by another member of her or his cultural group who displays ethnic pride and a cultural connection. Other conformity individuals reach the dissonance stage after a personal experience with racism. The dissonance stage is one of transition: The individual is straddling both self- and group-appreciating and depreciating attitudes. Similarly, attitudes toward other minority groups and the majority group represent a mixture of both positive and negative attitudes. The dissonance individual is in a state of flux and confusion.

Resistance and Immersion

At Stage 3, resistance and immersion, the minority individual comes to embrace his or her own racial or ethnic group completely. This stage is characterized by a blanket endorsement of one's group and all the values and attitudes attributed to the group. At the same time, there is a rejection of the values and norms associated with the dominant group. The individual has now completely broken through the denial characteristic of the conformity stage and questioned in the dissonance stage and now acknowledges racism and oppression as a reality. Resistance attitudes are associated with guilt over previously held (and now believed to be naïve) conformity attitudes. Anger, even rage, is experienced now as the individual contemplates his or her role as an oppressed member of society. Attitudes toward the dominant group in resistance and immersion are very negative, and attitudes toward self and members of the same racial or ethnic group are unequivocally positive. Resistance-stage attitudes toward members of other minority groups are conflictual, characterized simultaneously by an empathic understanding and an overpowering ethnocentric bias.

Introspection

During introspection, the rigid ethnocentric views of the previous stage begin to attenuate. There is a comfort and security in one's racial identity that allows the questioning of rigid resistance-stage attitudes. There is a feeling that much of the anger and negativity previously directed toward the "White system" could be better used in the positive exploration of identity issues. During this stage, the minority individual feels concern with regard to the basis of self- and group-appreciating attitudes. There is some conflict between one's allegiance to his or her ethnic group and issues of personal autonomy. Views toward one's racial or ethnic group are now not blindly positive, and individual differentiation is considered. Attitudes toward the dominant group are also conflictual. Although there is still distrust of the "system" to some degree, individual variation is acknowledged, and Whites are not stereotyped as a monolithic group.

Synergetic Articulation and Awareness

This final stage of the MID model is characterized by a sense of self-fulfillment with regard to cultural identity. The individual has a confident and secure racial identity, and there is a desire to eliminate all forms of oppression, not just oppression aimed at one's own group. Synergetic attitudes reflect a generally high level of positive regard toward self and toward one's group. Unlike the resistance and immersion stage, however, the synergetic stage is not characterized by a blanket acceptance of all group values and norms. Racial group membership constitutes just one important facet of the person's life, and there is a high level of personal autonomy. Synergetic attitudes toward other minority groups are positive. There is respect and appreciation of other cultural groups, as well as acknowledgment that other minority groups in America have their own unique history of oppression. Finally, synergetic attitudes toward the dominant group are characterized by selective appreciation. The individual is receptive to dominant culture persons who themselves seek a halt to minority group oppression, and there is an openness to constructive elements of the dominant culture.

Helms's People of Color Racial Identity Model

Like other identity models reviewed in this chapter, Helms's (1995; Helms & Cook, 1999) model is anchored in the belief that various minority groups in the United States "have been subjected to similar (but not necessarily identical) deplorable political and economic conditions because they were not perceived to be 'pure' White" (Helms, 1995, p. 189). A result of this societal racism is that persons of color absorb the dominant White society's negative perceptions of the group and develop an internalized racism. Therefore, overcoming this internalized racism—internalized racial stereotypes and negative self- and own-group conceptions—is a defining characteristic of developing a healthy racial identity.

In her writing, Helms (1995; Helms & Cook, 1999) prefers the use of the terms *people of color, ALANA* (an acronym referring to African Americans, Asian Americans, Latinos, and Native Americans [indigenous peoples]) or *visible racial or ethnic group* (VREG) to the term *minority,* given the semantic meanings attached to the latter term. "Minority" implies less than or a subordinate status and is, furthermore, an inaccurate term, as persons of color are not always the numerical minority in certain circumstances, and Whites are not always the numerical majority in certain circumstances. The model considers race or color the defining characteristic in how people in the United States are perceived and treated. Helms and Cook (1999) provide a helpful explanation:

> Thus, for example, if a person's ancestry is English, Jewish, or German and the person's perceived race is White, then the United States society's rules, privileges, and sanctions for White people usually pertain to the individual. However, if one's ancestry is English, Jewish, or German and one is perceived as Black, then the person's Blackness rather than ethnicity more strongly determines the social conditions to which the person will be exposed. (p. 17)

Helms's (1995; Helms & Cook, 1999) people of color model was influenced by the landmark Black racial identity work of Cross (1971; to be reviewed later in this chapter), the integrative identity work of Atkinson et al. (1989), and the more general collective identity model of Erikson (1968) and the self-psychology work of Kohut (1971). The Helms model consists of six ego statuses, described briefly here.

Conformity

This status represents the least sophisticated ego identity and centers on the person's internalization of White society's perspectives of one's group. This internalized racism is demonstrated either by conformity to White society's stereotypes of the group or by attempts to become White and assimilated into White culture. Persons in this status are usually unaware of the racial dynamics in their environment and may demonstrate little knowledge of the group's sociopolitical history.

Dissonance

In this status, the person of color begins to acknowledge her or his lack of fit with the White world. The status is characterized by confusion, disorientation, and unpredictable responses to racial events. Individuals in this status experience ambivalence and anxiety over their lack of own-group knowledge; they lack positive own-group information to replace their attenuating idealization of the White group.

Immersion

The anxiety characteristic of the previous stage is now addressed by the quest for positive group information to replace the negative group perceptions held in the conformity status. Cognitively, persons in immersion exhibit rather simplistic thinking, with a focus on idealizing everything associated with their own racial or ethnic group and denigrating anything associated with the White world.

Emersion

The person in the emersion status feels grounded and anchored when in the presence of same-group members. There is a strong sense of commitment to and communalism with one's own socioracial group. This status is characterized by joy and pride in response to the accomplishments of one's group. The defining focus of this status is the need for development of a positive group definition.

Internalization

This status represents a cognitively sophisticated state. Individuals have a strong positive commitment to and identity with members of their own group and are able to assess and respond objectively to members of their own group as well as the dominant White group.

Integrated Awareness

This status is the most sophisticated cognitively and is characterized on the one hand by a continuing identification with and commitment to one's own group, coupled with the capacity to identify in some ways with members of other visible racial and ethnic groups. In a sense, the biculturalism characteristic of the previous status is extended to multiculturalism. Integrated persons are cognitively flexible and manifest healthy intrapsychic and interpersonal functioning. There is a component of global humanistic expression in life decisions.

Race- and Ethnicity-Specific Models
of Minority Identity Development

The adolescent model of Phinney et al. (1990) and the adult models of Atkinson et al. (1989, 1998) and Helms (1995; Helms & Cook, 1999) are relatively recent developments. These models, to a large degree, have been extensions and integrations of longer standing race- and ethnicity-based identity models. This section of Chapter 4 reviews four such models that cover the following groups: African Americans (Cross, 1991), Asian Americans (more specifically, Japanese Americans; Kim, 1981), and Mexican Americans and Latinos (Arce, 1981; Ruiz, 1990). Of all the racial and ethnic identity models, Cross's model has received the most conceptual attention and empirical scrutiny. It is also the longest standing model of those we have chosen to review, and therefore we begin our discussion with this ground-breaking theory.

Cross's Psychology of Nigrescence

Perhaps the most well-known and most often cited model of racial identity is the psychological nigrescence model developed by William E. Cross, Jr. (1991, 1995, 2001). This model was first introduced in 1971 in a classic article on the "Negro-to-Black" conversion experience (Cross, 1971). In the more than three decades since this article appeared, Cross has continued to develop and revise the model based on research findings and further conceptual thinking (see Cross, 1991, 1995; Cross & Fhagen-Smith, 1996; Cross, Smith, & Payne, 2002; Cross & Vandiver, 2001; Vandiver, Cross, Worrell, & Fhagen-Smith, 2002). Recently, Cross (2001) presented his "life story," detailing his personal and professional journey in 30+ years of work on the nigrescence model.

In reviewing Cross and colleagues' nigrescence model, we first summarize some of his earlier conceptual positions (Cross, 1991, 1995) and then move to his most recent theoretical explication (Cross & Vandiver, 2001; Vandiver, 2001; Vandiver, Fhagen-Smith, Cokley, Cross, & Worrell, 2001; Worrell, Cross, & Vandiver, 2001). Initially, Cross posited a five-stage model that explains how assimilated Black Americans are transformed by a series of circumstances and events into persons who are more Afrocentrically aligned. The first stage, pre-encounter, describes the pre-existing, non-Afrocentric identity. Individuals with pre-encounter attitudes vary along a continuum from low salience to anti-Black. Individuals with low salience do not place much significance on being Black and see this physical characteristic as being unrelated to their happiness and sense of well-being. Cross (1991) notes that "some low-salience types simply have not given much thought to race issues; they seem to be dumbfounded and naïve during racial discussions" (p. 191). Other low-salience individuals have given some thought to being Black but focus on race as a stigma, as a hassle that has to be dealt with. On the other end of the continuum are those Blacks with high salience in that they ascribe much importance to their race but process this identity in a negative light. These individuals have anti-Black sentiments and feel alienated from other Blacks.

Stage 2 in Cross's (1995) revised nigrescence model, encounter, pinpoints those circumstances and events facilitating identity reconsideration in the individual. Cross (1991) noted that the pre-encounter attitude is resistant to change because of the power of early Eurocentric socialization, and therefore the shift to encounter attitudes is stimulated by a critical event, or series of events, that catches the individual off guard. Specifically, Cross (1991) noted that "the encounter must work around, slip through, or even shatter the relevance of the person's current identity and worldview, and at the same time provide some hint of the direction in which to point the person to be resocialized or transformed" (p. 199).

The critical encounter can be a single event, such as a personal encounter with racism, or it can be a dramatic event in the community that launches identity reconsideration. For example, Cross (1991) points out that the assassination of Dr. Martin Luther King, Jr., sent many pre-encounter Blacks searching for a deeper understanding of Afrocentricity. Cross (1991, 1995) felt that it was important to understand that the encounter stage is a two-stage process: The person must experience the encounter and then personalize it. Referring again to the King assassination, Cross (1991) stated, "In April 1968, not every Black person who heard about the death of Dr. Martin Luther King, Jr. was transformed into a Black Power advocate. Some people experienced the event, but it did not lead to change" (p. 200). For other Blacks, however, the trauma of the King assassination led to a questioning of previously held integrationist views.

Cross (1991) also points out that the encounter experience can be a positive one. For instance, individuals might be exposed to historical information about the Black culture or Afrocentric philosophy of which they were previously unaware, thus leading to identity reconsideration. However, regardless of whether the initial encounter penetrating the pre-encounter identity is abrupt and traumatic or more subtle and sequential, the encounter individual "becomes enraged at that thought of having been previously miseducated by White racist institutions" (Cross, 1991, p. 200). Thus, in all cases, the encounter stage engenders a wide range of emotions: alarm, confusion, guilt, depression, anxiety, and anger.

The third stage in the Cross (1991, 1995) model is called immersion-emersion and centers on abandoning the old perspectives and constructing what will become the person's new frame of reference. Cross notes that this stage represents the vortex of psychological nigrescence, given the intense emotions and attitude shifts engendered. In this two-component stage, Black individuals first immerse themselves into their newfound Afrocentric world and begin to embrace all things Black; simultaneously there is a forceful rejection of that White or Eurocentric worldview held during the pre-encounter stage. The intensity of the immersion phase of this stage is best captured in Cross's (1991) words:

> This immersion is a strong, powerful, dominating sensation that is constantly energized by rage (at White people and culture), guilt (at having once been tricked into thinking Negro ideas), and a developing sense of pride (in one's Black self, in Black people, and in Black culture). (p. 203)

After a period of intense immersion, individuals in this stage begin to develop a more balanced perspective of racial attitudes; they acknowledge that their pro-Black immersion attitudes were at times romanticized and exaggerated. Cross (1991) describes the emersion phase of the immersion-emersion stage as

> an emergence from the emotionality and dead-end, either-or, racist and oversimplified ideologies of the immersion experience. The person regains control of his of her emotions and intellect. In fact, he or she probably cannot continue to handle the intense emotional phase [of immersion] and is predisposed to find a way to level off. (p. 207)

The fourth stage in the Cross (1991, 1995) model is called internalization, which defines the new identity. The internalized person is secure in her or his Blackness and has a deep sense of connection to the Black community, at the same time nourishing relationships with healthy models of all racial groups. The internalized individual has a broadened multicultural perspective, seeks and embraces new cultural experiences, and demonstrates a commitment to social justice and human rights issues for all oppressed groups. Thus the internalization stage is linked to the current authors' conception of the multicultural personality. How long a sustained and active commitment to Black and other-group social issues is maintained will vary among internalized individuals.

Cross (1995) has hypothesized a fifth stage in his nigrescence model that he calls internalization-commitment. This stage describes internalized individuals who maintain a lifelong commitment to Black affairs and social justice issues. However, no instrument has been developed that can measure this final stage, and thus it has not been investigated empirically or elaborated upon conceptually.

In more recent years, Cross and colleagues have emphasized the complexity of nigrescence theory and have expanded impressively their theoretical vision and empirical research program. With an understanding of Cross's (1991, 1995) earlier models, we move to a review of his latest revised model (Cross & Vandiver, 2001; Vandiver et al., 2002), which posits three levels of the pre-encounter stage (assimilation, miseducation, and self-hatred), two levels of the immersion-emersion stage (anti-White and intense Black), and three levels of the internalization stage (nationalist, biculturalist, and multiculturalist). Cross and Vandiver (2001) refer to these stages as *identity profiles, identity types,* or *nigrescence exemplars.* Identity types that reflect nonengagement are the pre-encounter exemplars, those that reflect engagement are the internalization exemplars, and those that reflect immersion-emersion represent exemplars characterized by "a curious mixture of extreme or militant pro-Blackness and livid anti-Whiteness" (Cross & Vandiver, 2001, p. 375). The immersion-emersion exemplars represent markers of the transition from a nonengaged identity in pre-encounter to one of the engaged identities of internalization. Here we summarize the current identity exemplars, all of which are paraphrased directly from Cross and Vandiver (2001).

Pre-encounter Assimilation

This exemplar describes Black persons whose social identity is organized around being American and being an individual. There is little emphasis placed on one's racial group identity, and therefore Black culture is not engaged. In the more passive version of this type, the Black person simply fails to engage Blackness. In the more active type, the person may actually work with the dominant White group to speak or act against "race-based" programs (e.g., affirmative action). This identity type exhibits disdain for multiculturalism generally and for Black culture and all-Black groups specifically.

Pre-encounter Miseducation

Black persons of this exemplar accept inaccurate and stereotypical information about their group. These individuals can compartmentalize their own self-group stereotypes to maintain their own personal, individual self-image. Generally, such persons are hesitant to engage Black culture and issues because they see so little strength in the Black community.

Pre-encounter (Racial) Self-Hatred

As the exemplar name implies, Black people in this type have deep negative feelings and self-loathing in regard to being Black. The personal dysfunction and group hatred characteristic of this identity type clearly limit positive engagement in Black culture.

Immersion-Emersion Anti-White

Black persons representing this exemplar hate White people, White society, and all that this society may represent. Such persons do engage Black problems and Black culture but are frequently unpredictable and emotionally volatile.

Immersion-Emersion Intense Black Involvement

Persons in this identity type or exemplar romanticize Blackness and are obsessively dedicated to all things Black. These individuals tend to engage Blackness in a cult-like fashion and are subject to Blacker-than-thou social interactions with other Blacks. Blacks in this type exhibit more simplistic and either-or thinking vis-à-vis complex issues.

Internalization Nationalist

This exemplar is characterized by individuals who stress an Africentric perspective about themselves, Black people in general, and the surrounding world. These individuals are highly engaged in Black culture and Black problems.

Internalization Biculturalist

This identity type is represented by Black people who are bicultural in the sense that they give equal weight and importance to being Black and to being American. They are very engaged in and proud of their African identity and are also engaged in and value mainstream culture. These individuals are comfortable in both predominantly Black settings and chiefly White environments.

Internalization Multiculturalist

Whereas biculturalists possess a dual identity commitment of sorts, the multiculturalist fuses three or more social categories or identities. These individuals do indeed engage Black culture and Black problems, but they also engage issues representing other identities. An example might be a Black person who is Jewish and female and who engages nearly equally all three identities.

Kim's Model of Asian American Identity Development

Kim (1981) conducted an exploratory study to "examine the process by which Asian Americans resolve their identity conflict around being Americans of Asian ancestry, living in a predominantly White society" (p. vi). Kim's sample consisted of ten Sansei (third-generation) Japanese American women. Kim's retrospective results indicate that identity conflict is resolved through a developmental, progressive, and sequential process. This process involves five stages; progressing through them moves the individual from a state of negative self-concept and identity conflict to one of positive self-concept and a positive identification with Asian Americans. The five stages identified and described by Kim are *ethnic awareness*, *White identification, awakening to social-political consciousness, redirection to Asian American consciousness*, and *incorporation*.

Ethnic Awareness

This first stage occurs prior to entering elementary school, at around 3 or 4 years of age, when the individual first comes to know his or her ethnic origins. This awareness comes primarily through interactions with family members and relatives.

During these early childhood years, the attitudes of Kim's research participants toward being Japanese were either positive or neutral, depending on the extent of family involvement in ethnic activities. The children with greater exposure to Japanese culture and ethnic activities had a more positive self-concept and a clearer ego identity. The children with less exposure recalled having a more neutral self-concept and a confused ego identity as Japanese Americans.

Stage 1 lasts until the children begin school. This developmental change—beginning school—brings the children into more frequent and often less-hospitable contact with White society. For Kim's (1981) adult participants who were reflecting back to this time, this movement into the formal educational structure was invariably a negative one with regard to the effects of others' prejudice on their self-perception.

White Identification

Through increased contact with the White society, Asian American children begin to develop a sense that they are different from their peers. Feeling different was primarily the result of negative encounters with other children's racial prejudices. The Asian American children were not prepared for this and responded by personalizing their situation, leading them to believe it was their fault. Invariably, the participants in Kim's study remembered this period as a painful experience, a time when their self-concept became negative.

Being treated as different and inferior led Kim's participants to identity with White people. They began to internalize White society's values and become alienated from self and from other Asian Americans. Kim (1981) notes that "during this stage all subjects have subconsciously internalized overt, positive, White images, especially regarding standards of physical beauty and attractiveness. Hence, alienation from oneself is experienced primarily as a negative self-image focused around physical attributes" (p. 129).

Buying into White society's view that Asian Americans are less attractive, Kim's (1981) participants were not very involved in dating during adolescence and instead focused their energy toward involvement in formal organizational and leadership roles (e.g., class president, club leaders, yearbook editor) and in academic pursuits.

The extent of "White identification" during this stage varied among the study participants. Some identified *actively,* considering themselves as very similar to White peers and not consciously acknowledging cultural differences. These participants saw themselves as White and acted accordingly. They did not want to be seen as Asian in any way. In contrast, during *passive* White identification, participants did not consider themselves as White, although they did accept, as a reference point, White standards, values, and beliefs.

Kim points out that those participants who experienced the ethnic awareness stage as neutral (those whose families were not very involved in Japanese ethnic culture and activities) were more likely to identify actively with Whites, whereas those participants who were more culturally involved during the ethnic awareness stage were more likely to identify only passively with Whites and White cultural norms.

Awakening to Social-Political Consciousness

During this stage, individuals develop a new perspective of who they are in society. This perspective involves seeing oneself as a minority in society. Often a significant life event (e.g., moving to the West Coast and having increased contact with politically conscious Asian Americans) initiates the awakening to political consciousness. Kim's participants' awakening was stimulated and activated by the social environment—for example, the civil rights and women's movements of the 1960s and 1970s, or by politically active family members, partners, or friends.

At this stage, participants shed their previously held White-identified values and critically reassess the merits of White standards. This reassessment sometimes leads to political alienation from White society. Now the participants' reference group centers on political and social philosophy. Their ego identity is now "centered around being a minority, being oppressed, not being inferior, and feeling connected to experiences of other minorities" (Kim, 1981, pp. 144–145). It is during this stage that self-concept becomes more positive.

Redirection to Asian American Consciousness

In the preceding stage, Kim's participants changed their identification from White oriented to minority oriented. In the redirection stage, individuals begin to embrace their Asian American identity. Their political-social involvement in the previous stage bolstered their self-concept, and now they desire to embrace their own racial and ethnic identity and immerse themselves in Asian American heritage.

During this immersion period, subjects can feel very angry and outraged at White society. They realize that White racism was the foundation for their negative experiences and for their previous identification with White standards and values. In time, individuals in this stage are able to work through this emotionally laden reactionary phase and come to a realistic reappraisal of both themselves and other Asian Americans. In this redirection stage, self-concept is positive, and individuals feel good about themselves and proud to be Asian American.

Incorporation

In the final stage of the Asian American identity development model put forth by Kim (1981), individuals come to a healthy and secure balance, feeling comfortable with their own identity and appreciative of other racial groups. Individuals at this stage do not feel the driving need to identify either with or against White people. They develop a realistic appraisal of all people. In the incorporation stage, Asian American identity is very important but constitutes only one aspect of an overall identity. There is a healthy blending of racial and ethnic identity with other identities central to the individual's overall view of self and self-concept (e.g., religious identity, political ideology, sexual and sex-role orientation, and career or professional identity).

Arce's Model of Chicano Identity

Arce (1981) reviews the literature on group consciousness processes for Chicanos and describes a transition during which people stop thinking of themselves as Mexican American and begin to see themselves as Chicano. Reaching *Chicanismo* involves two forms of self-awareness: (a) political awareness, which is the knowledge of the Mexican people's history in the United States and an awareness of the effects of discrimination on the group, and (b) cultural awareness, which is manifested in pride in one's language and cultural values.

Arce (1981) does not name specific stages in the ethnic identity process, as do other theorists, yet his transitional descriptions in many ways closely parallel other identity stages reviewed throughout this chapter. For ease of cross-reference to other stage models, we have given names to Arce's stage process. Arce's model can be organized along four stages: *forced identification, internal quest, acceptance,* and *internalized ethnic identity.* The context for this identity model stems from the experiences of Mexican American students studying in a health sciences program.

During *forced identification,* students are identified as Hispanics or Mexican American by others, often by school officials who need to document affirmative action data. According to Arce (1981), some individuals "disavow the identification by muting ethnic characteristics or by reconstructing their personal histories" (p. 185). Some individuals may acquiesce to this forced identification and then find that it stimulates an internal quest for their cultural roots. This leads to an acceptance of their group, which is characterized by group loyalty and pride. Finally, the acceptance of and pride in the group lead to an internalized ethnic identity. This final stage is characterized by a deep sense of belonging to one's cultural group, by a desire to be accepted by the group, and by a desire to do something for the group. Arce (1981) states that in this final stage,

> Associated preferences shift inward, particularly toward people who will reciprocate the new identity. A strong, new kinship develops with all Chicanos, and individual personal commitments include action in behalf of the group. When the person finally comes to feel at one with the group, the internalization process has been completed, and ethnic identity [is] established. (p. 186)

Arce further notes that the identity process is generally directional, but it is not fully linear, as students may go back and forth between points on the stage continuum.

Ruiz's Model of Ethnic Identity
for Chicano and Latino Populations

Unlike the other identity models reviewed in this chapter, the Ruiz model of ethnic identity was formulated through the analysis of case studies of individuals representative of Mexican American and other Latino populations. In explicating his model, Ruiz was guided by the following assumptions generated from his clinical experience: (a) that the marginal status of Latinos, along with their forced assimilation, are destructive to the individual, and (b) pride in one's cultural heritage and ethnic identity leads to greater mental health and greater freedom in life choices. Here we summarize briefly Ruiz's (1990) five-stage model.

Causal

Due to internalizing messages and injunctions from a racist environment, individuals lack an affirmation of their ethnic identity, and they may experience traumatic experiences related to their ethnicity. Individuals in the causal stage do not identity with their ethnic culture.

Cognitive

As a result of negative and distorted messages that Latino people receive starting in the previous stage, three outcomes become apparent in the cognitive stage. Individuals in this stage may associate ethnic group membership with prejudice and poverty, they may consider strict assimilation into the dominant White society as an escape from this poverty and prejudice, and they may associate successful assimilation with possible life success.

Consequences

Consequences refers to the outcomes of attempted assimilation into and association with White culture. Shame and embarrassment result, given possible ethnic markers such as skin color, cultural customs and traditions, name, or language accent. The individual becomes estranged from and rejects her or his ethnic heritage.

Working Through

This stage is marked by extreme stress over ethnic identity conflict: The individual can no longer tolerate the pretense of Anglo assimilation. This intrapsychic stress leads individuals to search out and reclaim their culture of origin, and ethnic-specific consciousness increases.

Successful Resolution

In this final stage, individuals come to have high acceptance of their culture and ethnicity. There is a positive psychological disposition with increased self-esteem and a worldview that ethnic identity represents a highly positive and success-promoting life experience.

Integration of Identity Models and Relationship to Mental Health and Prejudice

As you read through the different racial and ethnic identity models, you probably noticed that there are many commonalities that transcend the various models. As there are similarities, there are also some unique aspects to individual models. For example, Kim's (1981) first stage, ethnic awareness, has no direct parallel in the other models. This stage begins in early childhood, whereas the first stage in the other models takes place in adolescence or young adulthood. Another unique stage is the internalization-commitment stage of the Cross (1991) model. This stage represents an advanced commitment to social causes and is characterized by a life's devotion to work on racial justice. Only the Cross model extends racial identity development to this level.

Of all the models reviewed in this chapter, it is the Cross model that is most theoretically and empirically robust. There has been extensive research supporting the construct validity of the model, as well as criterion-related validity linking attitudes reflective of different stages to psychological and behavioral correlates.

This concluding section of Chapter 4 discusses the mental health correlates of diverse stages. Furthermore, we review the available (though limited) research on the relationship between racial identity stages and attitudes toward other racial and ethnic groups and toward multicultural interaction and involvement generally.

Although the models reviewed in this chapter differ with respect to the number of stages or phases represented in the process of racial and ethnic identity development, common themes can be extracted. Collapsing stages across the seven different identity models reveals the four transcendent themes (or stages) discussed here (see Table 4.1).

Identification With the White Majority

Many of the models posit a point at which minority individuals identify primarily with White majority culture. The degree or intensity of this identification can vary. In Phinney et al.'s (1990) diffusion and foreclosure stage, the adolescent may simply lack interest in the concept of race or ethnicity and not see it as relevant to her or his life. In other models, there is a more active identification with Whites and even a disavowal of one's own racial or ethnic group. In Cross's (1991) pre-encounter stage and Atkinson et al.'s (1989, 1998) conformity stage, there is an unequivocal preference for dominant cultural values. Kim's (1981) White-identified stage, Helms's (1995) conformity status, Ruiz's (1990) cognitive stage, and Arce's (1981) forced identification stage also posit a preference for the standards, norms, and values of the dominant White culture. In Cross's revised model, the Black person in the pre-encounter (racial) self-hatred status holds "profound negative feelings and deep-structure self-loathing because of the fact she or he is Black" (Cross & Vandiver, 2001, p. 376).

Awareness, Encounter, and Search

The second stage of our four-stage model is characterized by an examination and questioning of previously held White-preference attitudes. Minority adolescents and adults begin to question their status as minorities in a racist society (see Sue, 2003), and they begin a search for their own racial or ethnic identity. This search can be stimulated by a single blunt encounter with an oppressive or racist experience or by an accumulation of more subtle experiences. All seven identity models have stages that fit into this integrative stage: Phinney et al.'s (1990) search and moratorium, Atkinson et al.'s (1989) dissonance, Helms's (1995) dissonance status, Cross's (1991) encounter, Kim's (1981) awakening to social-political consciousness, Arce's (1981) internal quest, and Ruiz's (1990) consequences and working through stages.

It is interesting that although the revised Cross model (Cross & Vandiver, 2001) no longer includes a formal encounter-type stage, the encounter process is critical to the transition from the nonengaged (pre-encounter) identity types to the engaged (immersion-emersion and internalization) identity types. Cross and Vandiver (2001) state this clearly when they note that

> the label Pre-Encounter is derived from the fact that there is always the possibility that a person who currently holds an identity that signals nonengagement will have an experience, a racial-cultural epiphany, an "encounter" that causes the person to go through a conversion experience, which results in the displacement of the nonengaged identity by a new identity that does engage Blackness. (p. 375)

Identification and Immersion

Stage 3 of our integrative model depicts individuals who have searched for their own identity (a process begun in Stage 2) and are now committing to and immersing themselves in their own racial or ethnic cultural roots. Stage 3 individuals are likely to completely endorse the norms, values, and customs of their own racial or ethnic group and at the same time completely reject values or norms associated with the White establishment. Phinney et al.'s (1990) search and moratorium level has aspects of this stage, as does Helms's (1995) immersion status, Atkinson et al.'s (1989) resistance and denial stage, the immersion portion of Cross's (1991) and Cross and Vandiver's (2001) immersion-emersion stages, Kim's (1981) redirection to

Asian American consciousness stage, and, to some degree, Arce's (1981) acceptance stage and Ruiz's (1990) working through stage.

An important component of Stage 3 as reflected in a number of the identity models is intense emotionality. For example, in Ruiz's (1990) working through stage, Chicanos and Latinos are no longer able to cope with the psychological distress of ethnic identity conflict and are propelled to reclaim their previously disowned ethnic identity. In other models, anger and even rage are directed at the White majority, concurrent with an almost idealized and romanticized view of one's own racial or ethnic group. This is best exemplified in the immersion-emersion intense Black involvement and the immersion-emersion anti-White exemplars in the Cross and Vandiver (2001) model. Cross and Vandiver speak quite directly when they note that Black persons in the immersion-emersion, anti-White identity stage "are nearly consumed by a hatred of White people and White society" (p. 376).

Integration and Internalization

One commonality across all seven models reviewed in this chapter is that after a period of intense identification or immersion in one's own culture, there is a reassessment and reappraisal, out of which emerges a more balanced bicultural or even multicultural identity. Atkinson et al.'s (1989) introspection stage and the emersion portion of Cross's (1991) and Cross and Vandiver's (2001) immersion-emersion stages specifically describe this reappraisal. Also, the intense emotion characterizing the previous stage—highly negative toward Whites and highly positive toward one's own group—becomes attenuated in this final stage. A major characteristic of this stage is the development of a healthy and secure racial or ethnic identity, coupled with an appreciation of other cultures. In essence, a bicultural or multicultural identity development is established. Phinney et al.'s (1990) achievement stage, Atkinson et al.'s (1989) synergetic articulation and awareness stage, Helms's (1995) internalization and integrated awareness statuses, Cross (1991) and Cross and Vandiver's (2001) internalization stages, Kim's (1981) incorporation stage, Arce's (1981) internalized stage, and Ruiz's (1990) successful resolution stage all fall under our fourth and final integrative stage.

Summary of Research
Correlates of Identity Stages

The last two rows of Table 4.1 summarize research on the psychological and behavioral correlates of the various stages represented in our four-stage transcendent model. Table 4.2 then presents specific research findings (column 2) and associated references (column 3). Most of the research

summarized in Table 4.2 used correlational survey methods and incorporated the racial identity scales developed by Janet Helms (1990, 1995) and
colleagues. A few of the studies used William Cross and Beverly Vandiver's
(2001) new racial identity scale or instruments based on the work of Jean
Phinney (1992).

The findings represented in Tables 4.1 and 4.2 represent trends in the
research studies. The findings are not absolute or always consistent, as some
studies have not found some of the associations reported in the tables.
Findings can differ based on the researchers' sample, procedures, and score
reliability variance due to sampling or testing conditions. There are also
natural limitations to studying racial identity, a very complex construct
(Ponterotto, Casas, Suzuki, & Alexander, 1995, 2001), using mainly paper-
and-pencil survey instruments. Clearly there is a need for additional research,
particularly that which we would label qualitative or mixed-method research
(see Haverkamp, Morrow, & Ponterotto, 2005). Despite the limitations of the
research on racial identity, the findings reported in Table 4.2 are fairly convincing, particularly with regard to the psychological benefits for those in the
stages and statuses falling under the integration and internalization stage of
our transcendent model.

Table 4.2 Research Findings on Minority Identity Development

Integrative Identity Stage	Research Findings	Research Studies
Identification with the White majority	Lower self-esteem; higher anxiety and global psychological distress, increased memory impairment, paranoid thoughts, auditory hallucinations, and alcohol concerns; lower levels of academic and general autonomy; less mature interpersonal relationships; lower multicultural involvement on college campuses; a belief that counseling or psychotherapy can be a helpful process; problems identifying and expressing feelings; lower psychological well-being and increased depression	Carter (1991), Cokley (2002), Delphin & Rollock (1995), Dinsmore & Mallinckrodt (1996), Goodstein & Ponterotto (1997), Mitchell & Dell (1992), Poindexter-Cameron & Robinson (1997), Pyant & Yanico (1991), Taub & McEwen (1992), Vandiver et al. (2002)
Awareness, encounter, and search	Lower self-esteem and psychological well-being, higher depression, problems identifying and expressing feelings, higher perceived culture-specific stress, lower levels of academic autonomy, less mature levels of interpersonal relationships and intimacy, bias toward other racial and ethnic groups, higher satisfaction in counseling from White therapists rather than own-group therapists, and higher levels of multicultural campus activities	Bradby & Helms (1990); Dinsmore & Mallinckrodt (1996); Goodstein & Ponterotto (1997); Martin & Hall (1992); Mitchell & Dell (1992); Neville, Heppner, & Wang (1997); Pyant & Yanico (1991); Taub & McEwen (1992)

(Continued)

85

Table 4.2 (Continued)

Integrative Identity Stage	Research Findings	Research Studies
Identification and immersion	Greater perceived general stress, lower problem-solving appraisal ability, greater avoidance of problem-solving activities, lower levels of academic autonomy, less mature levels of intimacy and interpersonal relationships, lack of self-examination of feelings, fewer memory difficulties, more negative views of other racial and ethnic groups and more traditional attitudes toward women, lower awareness of available campus mental health services, less confidence in the value of college counseling services, preference for an ethnically similar counselor, high levels of campus involvement in cultural organizations and greater involvement with college fraternity or sorority, more antisocial attitudes	Carter (1991); Delphin & Rollock (1995); Dinsmore & Mallinckrodt (1996); Goodstein & Ponterotto (1997); Martin & Hall (1992); Mitchell & Dell (1992); Neville et al. (1997); Taub & McEwen (1992); Taylor & Howard-Hamilton (1995); Whatley, Allen, & Dana (2003)
Integration and internalization	Higher self-esteem; stronger internal locus of control; higher levels of trusting others; deeper levels of psychological closeness; more goal-oriented behavior and hope in achieving goals; tendency to rely on a rational (versus dependent or intuitive) decision-making style; lower levels of culture-specific stress; fewer somatic complaints; more comfort in examining internal emotional states and fewer problems	Bradby & Helms (1990); Brookins, Anyabwile, & Nacoste (1996); Carter (1991); Delphin & Rollock (1995); Dinsmore & Mallinckrodt (1996); Goodstein & Ponterotto (1997); Helms & Parham (1990); Jackson & Neville (1998); Johnson, Buboltz, & Seemann (2003); Martin & Hall (1992); Mitchell & Dell (1992); Miville et al. (2000); Neville & Lilly (2000); Neville et al.

Integrative Identity Stage	Research Findings	Research Studies
	identifying and expressing feelings; strong sense of ethnic identity and, for women, strong sense of womanist identity; strong sense of self and commitment to convictions; preferences for both Black and White counselors as well as for counselors of a similar economic background; for counselors, greater self-rated multicultural competence; greater awareness of campus mental health services; higher involvement in campus multicultural and general activities; for women, higher vocational identity; more accepting of both similarities and differences in others (Note that Carter [1991] and O'Dougherty & Littleford [2002] found higher levels of paranoid ideation, but Carter [1991] notes that for persons of color, higher paranoid ideation may have some healthy and adaptive functions in a racist society)	(1997); O'Dougherty & Littleford (2002); Parks, Carter, & Gushue (1996); Poindexter-Cameron & Robinson (1997); Taylor & Howard-Hamilton (1995); Vinson & Neimeyer (2000, 2003); Whatley, Allen, & Dana (2003); Wilson & Constantine (1999)

5

European American (White) Racial Identity Development, Mental Health, and Prejudice

Historically, in the progression of the psychology and education professions, White racial identity development models were developed after minority identity development models. Whereas the psychology literature in the early 1970s introduced models of Black racial identity development (e.g., Cross, 1971; Dizard, 1970), the late 1970s and 1980s witnessed the introduction of racial identity models focused on White persons (e.g., Hardiman, 1982; Helms, 1984; Ponterotto, 1988; Terry, 1977). The Black identity theories focused on the "oppressed"—individuals who were in a numerical minority; who had less power, fewer resources, and diminished life-quality access; and who had been the subject of violent physical and psychological torture for centuries. White racial identity models focused on the "oppressors"—individuals who were in the numerical majority; who had power, resources, and countless unearned life privileges; and who were responsible for racism in the United States (see D'Andrea & Daniels, 2001; Sue, 2003).

There was a sense among White identity theorists, who, interestingly, were both scholars of color (Janet Helms) and scholars of White European ancestry (Rita Hardiman and Joseph Ponterotto), that if American society were to improve with regard to racial equality and respectful and appreciative interracial interaction, White Americans would have to take stock in, and responsibility for, their legacy of oppression and their ongoing participation in an oppressive society either directly or through passive acceptance of the racist status quo (Sue, 2003). This perception was relevant to society in general and to the counseling and education professions, particularly as the overwhelming majority of mental health professionals and educators at the time were of White racial heritage. As a result of the influence of the White identity theorists, a good amount of empirical research has been conducted on the study of White identity development and its psychological correlates. We will review and integrate this research later in the chapter. First, it is important to review some of the theoretical assumptions inherent in all theories of White racial identity development.

Whites, because of their privileged status in society (Helms, 1995; Neville et al., 2001) have not been led, or forced, to examine their own roles in race relations in the United States (Sue, 2003; Sue et al., 1998). The White racial identity development process involves coming to terms with one's own unearned privilege in society, followed by an honest self-examination of one's role in maintaining the status quo and ending with a balanced identity perspective characterized by self-awareness and commitments to social justice for all groups.

Sue et al. (1998) provide more specific and detailed assumptions of White racial identity models, as follows:

- Racism is integral to U.S. life and permeates all aspects of our institutions and culture.
- Whites are socialized into society and therefore inherit the biases, stereotypes, and racist attitudes, beliefs, and behaviors of the larger society.
- How Whites perceive themselves and process their reactions as racial beings follows an identifiable sequence that can occur in progressive (linear) or nonprogressive (nonlinear) fashion.
- White racial identity status will affect an individual's interracial interactions and relationships.
- The desirable outcome of the White racial identity development process is that individuals accept their status as White persons in a racist society and define their identity in a nonracist manner (p. 56).

As the theoretical assumptions of White racial identity theory have now been elaborated, it is appropriate to review popular and often-referenced models of White identity development. In subsequent pages of this chapter we review the models of Rita Hardiman, Janet E. Helms, Joseph G. Ponterotto, and Wayne Rowe and his colleagues. We then review two integrative models of White racial identity development presented by Haresh B. Sabnani and colleagues and Derald Wing Sue and colleagues.

Hardiman's White Identity Development Model

To examine White racial identity development in the context of social identity theory, Hardiman (1982) studied six autobiographies written by White authors describing their experiences and lives as White Americans. Each author discussed her or his growth and development regarding racial issues and racism. Represented among the six authors were four women and two men, and various regions of the country were represented in the stories. The autobiographies examined by Hardiman were *Killers of the Dream* (Smith, 1963), *The Wall Between* (Braden, 1958), *Confessions of a White Racist* (King, 1971), *The Education of a WASP* (Stalvey, 1970), *Hey, White Girl* (Gregory, 1970), and *White on White: An Anti-Racism Manual for White Educators in the Process of Becoming* (Edler, 1974).

One strength of the Hardiman (1982) study is its creative and descriptive methodology. Hardiman used qualitative methods to read, study, and integrate major themes, insights, and experiences from the six autobiographies. The result is a stage model that is highly descriptive and poignant. In the next section, you will read exact quotes from the six authors that help capture the emotion and thinking of the time. Hardiman's qualitative study (like Kim's 1981 study, described in the previous chapter) is refreshing in that the overwhelming majority of identity research in psychology has relied on quantitative methods and the use of survey instruments.

Hardiman's (1982) model consists of five stages, the names of which correspond to the social identity stage names listed previously.

Lack of Social Consciousness

Stage 1 individuals are unaware of the complex codes of appropriate behavior for White people. Individuals in this first stage naïvely operate from their own needs, interests, and curiosity. As a result, they break many social rules and are chastised for their thoughts and actions. It is at this point that White people begin to learn what it means to be White and what other Whites consider appropriate attitudes and behaviors with regard to racial issues. Hardiman (1982, p. 159) cites the autobiography of Anne Braden (1958), in which the author recalls a childhood conversation with her mother. During the course of this conversation, Anne happened to use the term "colored lady," at which point her mother quickly retorted, "'You never call colored people ladies, Anne Gambrell [maiden name].' I can hear her voice now. 'You say colored woman and white lady—never a colored lady'" (p. 21).

Hardiman's Stage 1 covers birth to about 4 or 5 years of age. The White authors recall this period as the time that awareness of racial differences began. Given the early-life period of this stage, the authors recalled the time as confusing. During this early stage, White children do not feel hostile, fearful, or superior to Blacks, but they may experience some discomfort in interracial situations. The authors also described this period as one in which they were curious about racially diverse persons.

Acceptance

The transition to Stage 2, *Acceptance,* occurs as a result of socialization by parents, educators, peers, the church, the media, and the larger surrounding community (Hardiman, 1982). In the transition period, White children quickly learn the systematic ideology of race. They learn what shared opinions and behaviors (with regard to racial issues and interactions) are acceptable and unacceptable—which will be met with punishment and derision and which will be met with glowing approval. This powerful socialization results in the staunch acceptance of behavior and beliefs that support the social codes. The dominant belief system becomes internalized, and no conscious effort is needed to remind the individual what thoughts or actions are socially appropriate. The prevailing unspoken attitude with regard to Black and White racial beliefs was captured in Braden's autobiography (1958).

> It was most regrettable that the Negroes had ever been brought to this country in the first place and slavery had certainly been wrong. The presence of the Negroes in the South today was probably our punishment for the sins of our forefathers in bringing them here as slaves. . . . Negroes were really not bad creatures and certainly they had their uses, as they were available as domestic servants so white women could be freed from the burden of housework. . . . The point was to treat then kindly, not only because this was of course right according to Biblical teaching but also because if you treat a Negro with kindness he is also good to you—somewhat in the way a pet dog is good to the master who is good to him. And of course, the Negro people are happy in this relationship, there is not a reason to feel sorry for them—goodness, they are more carefree and there's nothing they like better than having some white folks who will take care of them. (pp. 19–21, cited in Hardiman, 1982, pp. 170–171)

Hardiman (1982) notes that unlike Stage 1, which is relatively brief in duration, Stage 2 can last many years, even a lifetime. Most of the autobiographies describe this stage in great detail, and many of the authors were in their adult years before encountering circumstances that would facilitate the transition to Stage 3.

Resistance

The transition from Stage 2 to Stage 3 is often a confusing and painful one. It is at this point that the White authors acknowledge the reality of the Black experience in America. The transition to Stage 3 is frequently stimulated by interaction with people, social events, or information presented in the media or in books. For example, King (1971) found his acceptance-stage belief system challenged by reading a library book:

I was a grown man before discovering that George Washington and Thomas Jefferson (those wise, saintly men whose pronouncements on liberty and justice leaped from my textbooks and echoed from the mouths of our Independence Day orators . . .) had owned slaves. It was shocking to learn that demigods who had influenced documents affirming the thrilling, limitless doctrine that *all men are created equal* had been otherwise capable of holding men in bondage for the profit from their sweat. I well remember discovering these new lessons in the Midland County Library, in my twenty-first year, and then standing outside, looking up at the windswept streets, and thinking, "Hell, if they lied to me about *that*, they've lied to me about everything." (p. 17, cited in Hardiman, 1982, p. 180)

Hardiman notes that Whites experience painful emotions during the transition to Stage 3. These feelings range from guilt and embarrassment at having been foolish enough to believe the racist messages they received to anger and disgust at the system and the people who lied to them. Stage 3 individuals acknowledge their Whiteness, and they understand that they have been socialized by a racism woven into the fabric of American society. Individuals come to understand minority group anger at White society, and they see all minority groups as victimized in some way by White racism.

White people in Stage 3 are not sure what their role should be in addressing racism. Feelings of guilt emerge as they contemplate their previously held Stage 2 identity. They harbor negative feelings about Whiteness, and they are angry at themselves and at other Whites. Resistance individuals are likely to attempt to reeducate themselves and other Whites about racism. They will devote time to learning accurate information about other cultures. They may challenge and confront racist institutions through letter writing, boycotts, and demonstrations. At times, the Stage 3 individual feels ostracized from other Whites and uncertain about being accepted by minority peers. Stage 3 can be both emotionally draining and stimulating.

Redefinition

Having experienced conflict in Stage 3 between their own values and values deemed appropriate by their racial group, Whites at Stage 4 now begin to search for a new White identity. Whites at the redefinition stage acknowledge the reality and pervasiveness of racism and act to change undesirable situations. This involvement facilitates the development of a more positive White identity. Whites in redefinition begin to search out aspects of White identity not linked to racism, they learn more about their culture (e.g., Western philosophy, art, and music), and they develop a sense of pride in their group. It is important to note that there is a recognition that cultures may vary in values, but no culture or race is superior to another and they all contribute to the enrichment of human life. The redefinition person is aware of the strengths and limitations of White history and culture. She or he has a desire to help other Whites redefine themselves, has empathy for the difficulties Whites have at earlier stages, and sees that it is in Whites' self-interest to eradicate racism.

Internalization

Having established a sense of pride in their identity during the previous stage, White people in internalization integrate and incorporate this new racial identity into their overall social identity. A positive White identity is now a healthy part of the individual; it is natural and spontaneous; it requires no conscious thought or effort.

The internalized individual has balanced his or her racial identity with other aspects of identity. Energy is directed toward liberating other Whites from racism and educating oneself about other forms of oppression (e.g., sexism, homophobia, ageism) and their relationship to race (e.g., the interaction of racism and sexism). Internalized Whites voluntarily alienate themselves from some aspects of the social environment and actively engage with other aspects. The placement of Hardiman's stages in relation to Marcia's (1980, see Chapter 4) general stages and other race-based models is shown in Table 5.1.

Helms's White Racial Identity Model

Helms (1984) was working independently of Hardiman (1982) when she developed and presented her initial model of White racial identity development. Over two decades, Helms has continued to elaborate and refine her model (e.g., Helms, 1990, 1995, 2005; Helms & Cook, 1999), and her theoretical model is by far the most discussed and researched in the psychological literature. The process of White racial identity development involves abandoning one's racism and developing a realistic and self-affirming racial identity. Because Whites are socialized in an environment in which they are privileged relative to other groups, they internalize a sense of entitlement and learn to maintain their privilege by distorting race-related reality and, at times, by aggressive actions against perceived threats to the racial status quo. Helms's latest formulation of her White identity model (see Helms & Cook, 1999) consists of seven ego statuses. Helms notes as important that individuals may simultaneously exhibit characteristics of multiple statuses but that one status may be more dominant.

Contact

Contact is a primitive status characterized by denial of or obliviousness to White privilege. Thus when this status is dominant in a White person, she or he will react to racial stimuli (e.g., discussion about racism) with avoidance,

Table 5.1   Models of White Identity Development

Source					
General Identity Model					
Marcia (1980)	Identity diffusion		Foreclosed identity		Moratorium	Achieved identity
White Racial Identity Development Models					
Hardiman (1982)	No social consciousness		Acceptance	Resistance	Redefinition	Internalization
Helms & Cook (1999)	Contact	Disintegration	Reintegration	Pseudo-independence	Immersion-emersion	Autonomy
Ponterotto (1988)	Pre-exposure		Exposure	Zealot-defensive		Integration
Sabnani et al. (1991)	Pre-exposure or precontact		Conflict	Prominority and antiracism	Retreat into White culture	Redefinition and integration
Sue et al. (1998)	Conformity		Dissonance	Resistance and immersion	Introspection	Integrative awareness
White Racial Typology Model					
Rowe et al. (1994, 1995)	Conflictive		Dominative		Reactive	Integrative
LaFleur et al. (2002)	Racial justice (conflictive and reactive types)		Dominative		Racial acceptance (dominative and integrative types)	

denial, or obliviousness. Understandably, as these individuals do not acknowledge the reality of racism in society, they take no action to understand their own privilege or work toward creating a more just society.

Disintegration

This status is characterized by disorientation, guilt, and anxiety as the realities of racism seem to break through the obliviousness of the contact stage. The individual is caught between wanting to be accepted by the normative (White) group and at the same time experiencing a moral dilemma over treating (or considering) Blacks as inferior to Whites. One solution to mitigating the anxiety of this stage is to reembrace the ideology of the normative White group and its racist social pressure. If a person in disintegration adopts this solution to dealing with her or his ambivalence and anxiety, the reintegration status has been entered.

Reintegration

Reintegration is characterized by denigration of and intolerance toward non-White groups and by the forceful protection of one's privilege and the racial status quo. Reintegration represents the purest racist status in the Helms model. Negative conditions associated with minority individuals are thought to reflect their own failings or lack of effort. The residual feelings of anxiety and guilt from the previous status are now transformed into anger and fear of minority group individuals.

Pseudoindependence

In pseudoindependence, the individual acknowledges the responsibilities of Whites for past and ongoing racism. These individuals are not comfortable with a racist stance and begin the search for a new White identity. However, in this status Whites operate more from an intellectual understanding of racism rather than from a sense of personal responsibility based on their own racism. Attention is directed more toward dissatisfaction with other Whites rather than a deep level of personal self-analysis with regard to their own socialized racism.

Immersion

During immersion, individuals immerse themselves in the search for accurate information about race and in a deeper understanding of their own racist socializations as White people in America. An individual in immersion might be involved in social activism to fight racism.

Emersion

In Helms's latest model (Helms & Cook, 1999), emersion involves a withdrawal from the previous frantic search for a new identity that is characteristic of immersion and the embracing of a community of reeducated Whites where one can be rejuvenated and empowered in continuing one's identity development.

Autonomy

Autonomy is the most advanced status of racial identity development for White Americans. The autonomous person is cognitively complex and flexible and may avoid life options that involve participation in racial oppression. Such individuals have the capacity to relinquish White privilege. The autonomous person is humanistic and involved in activism regarding many forms of oppression (e.g., fighting sexism, ageism, homophobia). It is the autonomy status of Helms's model (1995; Helms & Cook, 1999) that closely resembles aspects of the multicultural personality discussed in Chapter 7.

Ponterotto's White Racial Consciousness Development Model

Ponterotto (1988) presented a four-stage model of racial consciousness development for White counselor trainees. Unlike the majority of models reviewed in this chapter, which focused on White identity in the general public, Ponterotto was specifically interested in the racial consciousness development of counselor trainees. At the time he began work on his model, Ponterotto was a professor at the University of Nebraska in Lincoln, working primarily with White graduate students. Building on the landmark White identity work of Janet Helms and Rita Hardiman (reviewed earlier in this chapter) and contextualized within his experiences as a White man teaching multicultural counseling to numerous White students, Ponterotto sketched a progressive model with the following four stages: pre-exposure, exposure, zealot-defensive, and integration.

Pre-exposure

In the pre-exposure stage, White graduate students have given little thought to multicultural issues. They are generally naïve about both racial issues and their inherited, unearned privileges (see Neville et al., 2001; Vasquez, 2001) as White people in America. Students in this stage often believe that racism no longer exists or that if it does exist, it does so only to a limited degree with the few remaining Americans who are "old-fashioned bigots" (refer back to Chapter 2). White students in this stage are unaware of the concepts of subtle racism or modern racism (Dovidio, Kawakami, & Gaertner, 2000; Gaertner & Dovidio, 1986) or of institutional and cultural racism (Jones, 1997).

Exposure

Students enter the exposure stage when they are first confronted with multicultural issues. In the Ponterotto (1988) model, this occurred when they began their Multicultural Counseling course. At this point, students were exposed to the realities of continuing racism in the United States. They began to understand the nature of modern racism, as well as the individual, institutional, and cultural manifestations of racism. Students then acknowledged that Whites and minority group members were treated differently (regardless of the person's economic status) and that minorities faced barriers with which White people never had to deal. This newfound insight was enlightening to the students, and they initially felt a sense of empowerment over their new and accurate knowledge.

Quickly, however, White students in exposure began to realize that they had been lied to throughout their education. They learned that even the counseling profession, which professed to be objective and fair to all, was a tool of institutional and cultural racism because of the profession's centering on White middle class values (refer back to Chapter 1). Whites in this stage begin to experience anger and guilt over their naïveté in accepting without question myths and stereotypes of minorities fostered by the education and counseling profession. The students began to see how they themselves were subtly racist. During exposure, the students also felt some ambivalence as they contemplated whether to share their newfound insights with family and friends and to confront them with their prejudicial beliefs. Doing so risked alienation from other White people they had been close to for years. They risked inciting family or friendship conflict, as they might be seen as "going native" or turning too liberal (or simply being insulting). White students' processing of and responses to the multitude of strong feelings emerging during exposure signaled their entrance into Stage 3.

Zealot-Defensive

Ponterotto (1988) observed that White graduate students in the counseling field often responded to their array of newfound mixed feelings in one of two ways. Some became very zealous about the multicultural topic. These students dove head first into minority issues, studied the topic extensively, and became very prominority in philosophy. Ponterotto (1988) states that "this pro-minority directed energy enables the student to deal with his or her personal, or White society's collective, guilt in regard to being a White member of society" (p. 152).

Other students responded to their anger and guilt in a very defensive manner. Some students took the criticisms of the "White system" very personally and begin to withdraw from the multicultural topic. Ponterotto (1988) observed that students in this stage stopped participating in class discussions, moved to sit in the back of the classroom, and seldom made eye contact with the professor. These students were quite angry at the professor and saw him (in this case) as anti-White.

Integration

Ponterotto (1988) noted that as students were led to process and express their feelings (guilt, anger, defensiveness), they began to demonstrate a renewed interest and openness to multicultural issues. The intense feelings of Stage 3 were attenuated to a large degree, and students achieved a more balanced perspective on the topic. At this point the integration stage was achieved. Students then accepted the realities of modern racism (refer back to Chapter 2), acknowledged their own subtle racism, and felt a sense of empowerment about eliminating racism in themselves and in society. Students at this point felt good about themselves as individuals and as members of the White cultural group. They often developed a renewed interest in their racial group (White) and in their ethnic roots (e.g., Italian, Polish, Irish). There was an appreciation of other cultures and a desire to learn more about various groups. Students also begin to devote energy to other identity commitments, such as gender and lesbian or gay identity, where effort was directed toward understanding and combating sexism, heterosexism, and homophobia (see Croteau, Lark, Lidderdale, & Chung, 2005; Moradi, Subich, & Phillips, 2002). It is the integration stage in this model that is reflected in the multicultural personality discussed in Chapter 7.

Rowe, Bennett, and Atkinson's White Racial Consciousness Model

The most recent comprehensive model of White racial consciousness was introduced by Wayne Rowe, Mark Leach, and colleagues (LaFleur, Rowe, & Leach, 2002; Leach, Behrens, & LaFleur, 2002; Rowe, Behrens, & Leach, 1995; Rowe, Bennett, & Atkinson, 1994). Part of the stimulus for their model came from a dissatisfaction with the identity theory aspects of existing White race-based conceptualizations (e.g., Helms, 1990, 1995; Sabnani, Ponterotto, & Borodovsky, 1991). Rowe and his colleagues were of the opinion that how Whites felt about their own racial group and other racial groups did not follow a linear or progressive developmental process.

They believed that anchoring Whites' racial attitudes in developmental psychology (e.g., variations of social identity theory; refer back to Chapter 4) was not justified empirically. These authors believed that identity theory was too abstract and intangible (LaFleur et al., 2002) to serve as a conceptual anchor for understanding racial beliefs and that a more parsimonious understanding of Whites' racial attitudes could be studied through social-cognitive psychological research on attitude development and expressions (see Ponterotto, Potere, & Johansen, 2002, on measuring the cognitive, affective, and behavioral components of racial attitudes).

Therefore, Rowe and colleagues set out to develop a concise and parsimonious model that accurately classified commonly held racial attitudes that White people have toward persons of color. They defined attitudes as the "affective orientation regarding the favorableness of a thing" (LaFleur et al., 2002, p. 148), and they assumed that "attitudes are most frequently acquired through observational learning, are rather impervious to verbal persuasion, and, subject to situational influences, tend to result in intentions that guide observable behaviors" (p. 149). Furthermore, the model specifies that attitudes can change in the face of direct or vicarious experience that is dissonant or inconsistent with previously held attitudes. The focus of the Rowe et al. (1994) model is to label empirically identified constellations of racial attitudes held by White people in the United States. In essence, the model is an attitude typology model rather than a sequenced developmental model.

The initial explication of the Rowe et al. (1994, 1995) model specified seven *types* or constellations of racial attitudes. The types were organized into two groupings, *achieved* and *unachieved*. These terms were borrowed from the identity literature (see discussions of Erikson, Marcia, and Phinney in the previous chapter), which is surprising, because the authors seem to want to stay away from identity conceptualizations. In identity studies, achieved types have both explored and committed to their racial attitudes and unachieved types lack personal exploration, commitment, or both. We now briefly summarize achieved and unachieved types.

Achieved Types

Dominative persons hold White ethnocentric attitudes, believe in the superiority of Whites, and may act out racist attitudes passively or directly.

Conflictive individuals do not support obvious racism or inequality yet still value a Eurocentric worldview (e.g., individualism) over alternate worldviews (e.g., collectivism).

Integrative persons hold positive racial attitudes, relate to a variety of racial and ethnic issues, and are rational and pragmatic in orientation.

Reactive individuals hold strong prominority attitudes yet may be unaware of their personal responsibility in maintaining a racist status quo.

Unachieved Types

Avoidant persons have not explored racial issues and appear to ignore, deny, or minimize racial issues.

Dependent types hold a narrow and limited understanding of racial issues that are heavily influenced by others.

Dissonant individuals are conflicted between their racial beliefs and some contradictory experiences that call into question their belief system; they are wavering in their racial attitudes.

A Revised White Racial Consciousness Conceptualization

One great strength of the Rowe et al. (1994, 1995) White racial consciousness model is that it has been closely linked to empirical research at the outset. We will talk more about instruments used to operationalize White racial identity and consciousness theory later in this chapter and in Chapter 15. Suffice it to say that as a result of systematic research on their model, Rowe and colleagues have recently revised it (see LaFleur et al., 2002). The revised model now centers on two broad constructs: *racial acceptance* and *racial justice*, each the result of an integration of typologies discussed earlier.

Racial Acceptance

The racial acceptance construct results from the bipolar placement of the dominative and integrative typologies. The main theme here appears to be acceptance of racial minorities, characterized by strong positive views at one pole (integrative attitudes) and highly negative views at the opposite pole (dominative attitudes).

Racial Justice

The theme of racial justice stems from the perception that conflictive and reactive typologies both possess an underlying focus on justice. In the conflictive typology, Whites condemn racism and racial oppression but feel that efforts to assist minorities (such as affirmative action) constitute reverse discrimination and therefore serve as an injustice to White people. On the other hand, in the reactive typology, Whites believe there are unearned advantages to being White in America (see discussions of White privilege in Neville et al., 2001; Sue, 2003; and Vasquez, 2001) and that therefore ameliorative efforts to help minorities achieve equality (e.g., affirmative action) are more justified.

In Rowe et al.'s revised model (LaFleur et al., 2002), the distinction between achieved and unachieved types has been discontinued. Instead, racial acceptance and racial justice are regarded as one's orientation regarding racial attitudes, and statuses formerly labeled as unachieved measure simply the degree to which one admits to being unconcerned about racial issues (avoidant), being uncertain about such issues (dissonant), or basing racial attitudes on the influence of others (dependent).

Integrative Models of White Racial Identity

Two teams of authors have integrated the various models of White racial identity and consciousness in an attempt to explicate a more general and inclusive model. Sabnani et al. (1991) examined the models of Hardiman (1982), Helms (1984, 1990), and Ponterotto (1988) and extracted a five-stage developmental model: pre-exposure or precontact, conflict, prominority and antiracism, retreat into White culture, and redefinition and integration. Sue et al. (1998) examined the models of Hardiman (1982), Helms (1990, 1995), and Rowe et al. (1994) to arrive at a five-stage descriptive model: conformity, dissonance, resistance and immersion, introspective, and integrative awareness. As these models are integrations and extensions of preexisting models, we will review them only briefly here.

Sabnani et al.'s White Racial Identity Model

Pre-exposure or Precontact

The chief characteristic of this stage is a lack of awareness of oneself as a racial being. The White person in pre-exposure or precontact is unaware of social expectations and roles with regard to race and is generally oblivious to cultural or racial issues. Persons in this stage have not yet begun to explore their own racial identity, nor have they given thought to their roles as White people in a society with a history and ongoing legacy of White oppression and racism (see D'Andrea & Daniels, 2001; Sue, 2003). At this point there is also an unconscious identification with Whiteness and an unquestioned acceptance of stereotypes about minority groups.

Conflict

Stage 2 of this integrative model centers on the experience of emotional conflict over developing race relations knowledge and an evolving perspective on race relations. At this point there is an expansion of knowledge about racial matters that is facilitated by interaction with members of minority groups or by information gathered elsewhere (e.g., independent reading, a multicultural counseling or education course). New information challenges individuals to reconsider the status of race relations in the United States (and elsewhere) and to reflect on what it means to be a White person in a country with a legacy of oppression of non-White groups. The central feature of this stage is conflict between wanting to conform to majority norms (i.e., peer pressure from some White friends, colleagues, and family members) and a desire to uphold humanistic, nonracist values. Key affective components of the conflict stage are confusion, guilt, anger, and depression.

Prominority and Antiracism

Sabnani et al. (1991) posit that White people often have one of two reactions to emotional outcomes central to Stage 2. The first response (characterizing this stage) is a strong prominority stance, during which Whites begin to resist racism and identify with minority group members. This behavior serves to alleviate the strong feelings of guilt and confusion arising in the previous stage. White people in this stage experience self-focused anger and continuing guilt over their previous conformity to White, Eurocentric socialization, as well as anger directed outward toward the White culture in general.

Retreat Into White Culture

Stage 4 is marked by the second of two extremes that are a response to the conflict stage. Whereas some Whites deal with Stage 2 conflict by identifying with minorities, others deal with it by retreating from situations that would stimulate such conflict. This latter response is characterized by a behavioral and attitudinal retreat from interracial contact back into the comfort, security, and familiarity of same-race contacts. White people in Stage 3 are often challenged on their prominority views by White peers who sense a racial disloyalty or betrayal. Moreover, these Whites may be confronted by minority peers who question their newfound supportive attitudes. As a result of peer pressure and minority group rejection, some White people feel life will just be easier and less complicated if they retreat into the "White world." Stage 4, therefore, is characterized by an overidentification with Whiteness and a defensiveness about White culture.

Redefinition and Integration

In this final stage, White individuals come to redefine what it means to be White in today's society. There is a transition to a more balanced and healthy racial identity. Whites acknowledge their responsibility for maintaining racism and at the same time identify with a White identity that is nonracist and healthy. They see good and bad in their own group as they do in other groups. Large-scale ethnic and racial categorization and stereotyping is consciously avoided. Energy is now devoted to nonracial issues, and there is an interest in fighting all forms of oppression (e.g., sexism, homophobia, anti-Semitism, anti-Muslim sentiments, ageism, and so on). White people in redefinition and integration are flexible and open with regard to culture-learning activities, both from their own racial group and other groups. This stage represents components of the multicultural personality presented in Chapter 7.

Sue et al.'s Descriptive Model of White Racial Identity

The goal of the Sue et al. (1998) model was to integrate the strengths of the more developmental models (Hardiman, 1982; Helms, 1995) with those of the consciousness typology model (Rowe et al., 1994, 1995). According to Sue et al. (1998), the strength of the developmental identity models is that they provide a historical framework for the process of developing a healthy White identity. On the other hand, the strength of the typology model is that it allows for greater conceptual latitude, as it is independent of developmental sequencing. In fact, even developmental theorists (e.g., Parham, 1989) acknowledge that identity attitudes recycle and that identity development is not a linear process moving from one stage to another. Furthermore, the typology model is less bound by time frames and social movements (see Rogler, 2002) that may affect developmental models.

Conformity

In conformity, the White person is ethnocentric and possesses minimal awareness of him- or herself as a racial or cultural being. Individuals at this stage have limited knowledge of other racial or ethnic groups, and whatever impressions they have of culturally different persons is often stereotypical, inaccurate, and overgeneralized. They espouse a "colorblind" approach, valuing individualism and denying (or being unaware of) the existence of White privilege. They tend to believe that racism is a thing of the past and that everyone in the United States has an equal chance of success if they just worked hard enough and stopped complaining about civil rights.

Dissonance

During dissonance, the White person experiences internal conflict between a previously held belief and contradictory evidence regarding the existence of racism. For instance, a person who thought that racism was a practice of the past may witness an act of racism. This individual may be confronted with her or his own racism; for example, if anxiety is raised at the knowledge that a new neighbor may be African American or Puerto Rican. Whereas this person had denied having racist attitudes, she or he now realizes and acknowledges personal discomfort about a culturally different person moving next door. Such a realization may result in feelings of guilt, shame, depression, or anger. What does the White person now do with these unwelcome strong emotions? Sue et al. (1998) say that the person will either retreat back to the conformity stage or will process these emerging emotions and move toward Stage 3, resistance and immersion. Whether a White person retreats back into the denial of conformity or forward to the insight and personal responsibility of resistance and immersion will depend on individual personality traits (e.g., cognitive flexibility, self-esteem; see discussion of the multicultural personality in Chapter 7) interacting with social forces (e.g., family and peer group attitudes).

For example, if an emotionally insecure person's immediate environment is characterized by conformity attitudes and the person risks ostracism, criticism, and isolation for acknowledging racism, she or he may re-embrace the denial and racial obliviousness of the previous conformity stage. On the other hand, if the person has enough internal strength of character or has allies in acknowledging and discussing the ongoing realities of racism, she or he may enter Stage 3—resistance and immersion.

Resistance and Immersion

In this third stage, the individual considers and acknowledges the realities of ongoing White racism (see D'Andrea & Daniels, 2001; Sue, 2003) in the United States (and elsewhere). This person begins to contemplate and understand how she or he has perpetuated racism, either overtly or covertly. It is important to note that the resistance and immersion person comes to understand and acknowledge his or her own unearned White privilege (see Neville et al., 2001). According to Sue et al. (1998), White persons in this stage feel both anger at having been misled about the notion of equality and justice for all and guilt for not being aware of their own White privilege and their socialized participation in oppression.

Some individuals in this stage operate out of guilt and become overzealous in their non-White identifications. They may become the paternalistic or maternalistic "protector" who consistently champions minority causes and sees racism readily in many venues. Alternatively, such individuals may overidentify with minority groups, to the point of rejecting their own Whiteness.

Introspection

The introspective White person strikes a balance or compromise between the naïve unconditional acceptance of Whiteness characteristic of the conformity stage and the rejection of Whiteness that characterizes the resistance and immersion stage. Stage 4, as its name implies, involves introspection and relative quiescence as individuals reformulate what it means to be a White person who has participated in the oppression of others and has benefited from White privilege. These individuals acknowledge that racism continues to be an integral part of U.S. society. However, introspective individuals are less motivated by guilt and defensiveness about their Whiteness and are actively engaged in a personal search for deeper understanding and meaning as a White person in this society. Individuals in this stage may experience some existential angst characterized by feelings of isolation, confusion, and loss. This angst is due to the realization that they will never fully understand the "minority experience" and due also to the feeling that they are disconnected from their own European American group.

Integrative Awareness

This final stage reflects the formation of a nonracist White European American identity. According to Sue et al. (1998), individuals with integrative awareness have a deep understanding of themselves as racial and cultural beings, are aware of racism socialization in society, value racial diversity in their personal lives, and fight multiple forms of oppression in society. These individuals have a strong inner sense of security even though they are a minority among their White peers. This stage is reflective of the multicultural personality discussed in Chapter 7.

Why Is White Racial Identity Development Important? What Does the Research Say?

It has long been hypothesized that one's racial identity attitudes relate to sense of self, comfort with one's own racial group, and comfort with persons of diverse racial groups. Furthermore, level of racial identity has been hypothesized to correlate to a broader array of psychological variables. In this section, we briefly review the results of research on White racial identity development. Most of the extant research on White racial identity development has used Helms's model and her White Racial Identity Attitude Scale (Helms & Carter, 1990). Table 5.2 summarizes the results of this research. Column 1 lists Helms's (1990) White racial identity status, column 2 lists the variables that the statuses correlate with, and column 3 cites the source of the research findings.

As shown in Table 5.2, research has identified statistically significant correlations between statuses of White racial identity development and various measures of psychological health and prejudice. The trend in the findings is that White people in the higher statuses, particularly autonomy, tend to self-report higher levels of psychological health and quality of life, and they appear to be more comfortable in multicultural environments and exhibit less prejudice toward those who are culturally different. It is this autonomy status that is related to the multicultural personality discussed in Chapter 7.

If one reads the research studies listed in Table 5.2 in their entirety, one will notice that in addition to robust findings with the autonomy status, there are also consistent findings with the reintegration status. Reintegration attitudes consistently correlate with prejudiced and racist views and with lower levels of psychological health. The accumulated findings relative to the other statuses are less consistent but tend in the direction of lower statuses (i.e., contact and disintegration), relating to lower levels of mental health and mixed attitudes about cross-cultural interaction. On the contrary, higher statuses (e.g., pseudoindependence) tend toward higher mental health indexes and positive views toward other racial groups.

As we will review in Chapter 7, racial identity is not without limitations; nonetheless, the study of White identity theory is critical to our understanding of prejudice and racism in White persons. As noted in Chapter 1, we believe that White racism constitutes a significant and widespread phenomenon in the United States. The study of White identity models, particularly those of Helms (1995) and Rowe et al. (1995), are critical to all parents, teachers, administrators, and mental health professionals.

Table 5.2   Research Findings on White Racial Identity Development

Helms's (1990) Stages of White Racial Identity	Research Findings	Research Studies
Contact	Lower levels of inner directness and reduced capacity for intimate contact, more dualistic and rigid thinking, reduced capacity to consider past events and future goals when contemplating present state of affairs, lower levels of racism in women, more positive views of other racial and ethnic groups, lower levels of multicultural counseling competence (in counselors), higher working alliance perceptions in cross-cultural counseling, higher general identity achievement	Burkard et al. (2003); Carter (1990); Goodstein & Ponterotto (1997); Miville, Darlington, et al. (2005); Neville et al. (1996); Steward et al. (1998); Tokar & Swanson (1991); Vinson & Neimeyer (2000, 2003)
Disintegration	Lower levels of mature interpersonal relationships, lower ability to consider present circumstances in light of past events and future goals, more negative views of other racial and ethnic groups, lower multicultural counseling knowledge and negative perceptions of the working alliance in an analog counseling study, preferences for White counselors, and lower levels of general identity achievement levels	Burkard, Ponterotto, Reynolds, & Alfonso (1999); Helms & Carter (1991); Goodstein & Ponterotto (1997); Miville, Darlington, et al. (2005); Tokar & Swanson (1991)
Reintegration	Lower capacity for intimate contact, lower levels of mature interpersonal relationships, more dualistic thinking, higher levels of racism and more negative attitudes toward other racial and ethnic groups, lower ratings of the therapeutic alliance regardless of client's race, and lower levels of multicultural counseling competence in counselors	Burkard et al. (1999, 2003); Carter (1990); Goodstein & Ponterotto (1997); Miville, Gelso, et al. (1999); Miville, Darlington, et al. (2005); Pope-Davis & Ottavi (1992, 1994); Steward et al. (1998); Taub & McEwen (1992); Tokar & Swanson (1991); Vinson & Neimeyer (2000, 2003)

(Continued)

Table 5.2 (Continued)

Helms's Stages of White Racial Identity	Research Findings	Research Studies
Pseudoindependence	Higher levels of autonomy and mature interpersonal relationships; lower levels of racism in women; more positive views of other racial and ethnic groups; higher levels of self-reported multicultural counseling competence among counselors, as well as more positive expectations for the therapeutic alliance with potential clients across race; some preference for White counselors; higher general levels of identity achievement	Burkard et al. (1999); Goodstein & Ponterotto (1997); Helms & Carter (1991); Ladany et al. (1997); Miville, Darlington, et al. (2005); Neville et al. (1996); Pope-Davis & Ottavi (1994); Taub & McEwen (1992); Vinson & Neimeyer (2000, 2003)
Autonomy	Higher inner directedness and autonomy, positive opinions of other racial and ethnic groups, higher self-reported multicultural counseling competence among counselors and stronger perceived therapeutic alliance with racially diverse clients among counselors, higher general levels of identity achievement	Burkard et al. (1999, 2003); Goodstein & Ponterotto (1997); Miville, Darlington, et al. (2005); Neville et al. (1996); Ottavi et al. (1994); Taub & McEwen (1992); Tokar & Swanson (1991); Vinson & Neimeyer (2000, 2003)

6

Biracial, Multiracial, and Gay or Lesbian Identity Development

After identifying totally with Whites for a while, I went through a period of rejecting the White race and trying to compensate for what I felt was lacking by totally immersing myself in Black culture (or what I thought was Black culture). This was no resolution either. Eventually I came to accept myself as a product of both races and realized the futility of trying to fit anyone's expectations of me.

—Helen Brody (1984, p. 15, as cited in
Kerwin & Ponterotto, 1995, p. 213)

Biracial and Multiracial Identity Development

Theory and research on racial identity development presented in Chapters 4 and 5 focused on the process of identity development within a single individual racial or ethnic group. However, increasing numbers of Americans are born into biracial or multiracial families. In fact, Root (1992b) used the phrase "biracial baby boom" to characterize the rapid growth rate of biracial populations in the United States (see discussions in Choi-Misailidis, 2003; Wehrly, Kenney, & Kenney, 1999). The 2000 U.S. Census, which was the first census to allow people to identify with more than one race, estimates that there are roughly 7 million multiracial individuals in the United States (Miville, 2005). This figure is likely a gross underestimate for multiple reasons: (a) multiracial individuals may have chosen to just check off (on the census form) one race rather than all those that the person may represent, and (b) the individual may be raised in a foster or single-parent home and may not be sure of the racial origins of one or both parents. Although we do not have an exact count of the number of multiracial people in the United States, we do know that with continuing demographic shifts and immigration trends, coupled with more accepting societal attitudes and decreasing stigma of interracial relationships, the numbers of children born to parents representing two or more racial groups will continue to grow rapidly.

It is clear that single-race models of racial identity development cannot account for the complexity of identity development in biracial and multiracial individuals (see Kerwin & Ponterotto, 1995; Poston, 1990). This section of Chapter 6 reviews popular models of biracial or multiracial identity development. These models are relatively recent compared to the longer standing, single-group identity models focusing on Blacks (Cross, 1971), Whites (Hardiman, 1982; Helms, 1984), Chicanos (Arce, 1981), and Japanese Americans (Kim, 1981) reviewed in the last two chapters. However, before reviewing identity models for mixed race people, it is first important to provide a little historical context for the study of multiracial identity.

Antimiscegenation Laws and the Supreme Court

In June 1958, Mildred Jeters, an African American and Native American woman, and Richard Loving, a European American man, fell in love and were married in Washington, DC. Shortly after returning to their home in Caroline County, Virginia, they were arrested and convicted because their marriage was in violation of Virginia's antimiscegenation laws. A condition of the conviction was that they were forced to leave Caroline County and the state of Virginia, thus leaving family and friends behind. (Wehrly et al., 1999, p. 7)

This quotation, taken from Wehrly et al.'s (1999) outstanding book *Counseling Multiracial Families,* provides a snapshot of life for interracial couples in the late 1950s. At the time the Lovings were arrested, 16 states still prohibited interracial marital unions. The Lovings decided to fight the State of Virginia's conviction, and the case worked its way up to the Supreme Court of the United States, where in 1976, in *Loving v. Virginia,* our highest court struck down the remaining antimiscegenation laws on grounds of equal protection and individual rights (see Wehrly et al., 1999).

Models of Biracial and Multiracial Identity Development

The terms *biracial* and *multiracial* are often used interchangeably in the literature. Biracial is most often used to describe first-generation children of two parents differing in racial background. Multiracial more accurately reflects the person who has two or more racial heritages. The term *multiracial* has a broader scope than *biracial* and has become the preferred term among a number of multicultural research scholars (e.g., Choi-Misailidis, 2003; Wehrly et al., 1999). In this chapter, we use the terms preferred by the authors whose work we are reviewing.

Poston's Biracial Identity Development Model

Poston (1990) presented a tentative five-stage model that is progressive and moves from an initial self-focus exclusive of racial group affiliation through a period of identity turmoil and ends with a balanced and integrated multiracial identity. In Stage 1, personal identity, a young's person's sense of her- or himself is independent of an identification with a racial reference group. The individual's sense of personal identity (e.g., self-esteem) emanates from early childhood family experiences and contexts.

In the second stage, choice of group categorization, the young person feels compelled to select an identity, usually of just one racial group. Which racial group affiliation is selected is dependent on the social-cultural context and may be influenced by factors such as primary peer group, one's physical features, family preferences, and so forth. Poston (1990) hypothesized that the young person may not have the cognitive sophistication to form multiple racial identities at this early state.

Enmeshment and denial represents the third stage in Poston's model and involves the person identifying with one racial group at the expense of the other. This is an emotionally intense and difficult stage, and the individual feels some guilt and self-hatred whatever the choice. One positive avenue to take in dealing with these negative emotions is to broaden one racial identity affiliation to include that of both parents, thus moving the person into the next stage.

In Stage 4, appreciation, the person now begins to acknowledge, accept, and discover the previously denied aspect of his or her racial heritage. The primary racial group affiliation may still lie with the racial identification embraced in the previous stage, but the person is open to and interested in exploring the component of her or his racial identity that had previously been neglected.

Finally, in the integration stage, the individual comes to fully appreciate and explore both racial identities. A balanced biracial or multiracial identity emerges and the individual feels secure, proud, and anchored in the newly integrated multiracial identity.

Jacobs's Model of Biracial Identity Development

Jacobs (1977, 1992) generated his model of identity development based on interviews and doll-play studies with children from Black and White interracial couples. He proposed three stages, the first of which is labeled pre-color constancy: play and experimentation. During this stage, biracial children under the age of 4½ years come to understand that one's skin color is permanent. For young children, skin color is usually nonevaluative; however, if children have had negative experiences or have low levels of self-esteem, they may develop negative feelings regarding skin color.

In Stage 2, post-color constancy: biracial label and racial ambivalence, which begins roughly at 4½ years of age, children develop somewhat ambivalent feelings regarding their own skin color. Jacobs found that the ambivalence is sequential, usually starting with a preference for Blackness and a rejection of Whiteness, followed by a preference for Whiteness and a rejection of the child's own Blackness. Jacobs (1992) sees this ambivalence as both a normal and necessary process, as it allows children to reconcile discordant elements into a unified biracial identity. During this stage, the ambivalent feelings gradually diminish as children come to understand that their skin color will remain constant and as they come to understand and integrate a biracial or multiracial label with which they can identity. Jacobs notes that parents play a pivotal role in helping children acquire, understand, and embrace a multiracial label with which they can be comfortable. A final important component of Stage 2 is that children begin to develop an awareness of racial discrimination in society.

From the time they are about 8 to 12 years old, biracial Black-White children are in Jacobs's biracial identity stage, during which a more complex understanding of multiracial identity emerges. Children come to understand that racial group membership is determined by parentage, in that one parent represents the Black social group and one the White social group. Skin color is still important here and may correlate with parents' diverse heritages, but the focus is more on parental lineage per se rather than on skin color. During this final stage of childhood biracial identity development, the children continue to work through any ambivalent feelings remaining from the last stage, but mixed feelings about self can resurface as the children enter adolescence and the developmental challenges associated with that stage of life.

Kich's Three-Stage Model of Japanese-White Biracial Identity Development

Kich's (1992) model is based on his 1982 qualitative dissertation, in which he interviewed 15 adults between the ages of 17 and 60. In interpreting his research findings, Kich also relied on his clinical and anecdotal experience as a basis for helping to frame and support his empirical findings from the interviews. All the participants interviewed by Kich appeared to progress though three stages, moving over time from a sense of questioning and sometimes devaluing their interracial self concept to a level of comfort and security in their biracial identity. Kich emphasizes that biracial identity development for his research participants was and is a lifelong process.

Awareness of differentness and dissonance (3–10 years old) constitutes the first stage and involves biracial children feeling different in various ways as they leave the security of family and home and begin to interact with other social networks outside the home such as classmates, neighborhood peers, and community residents. Kich emphasizes that this sense of feeling different can be positive if ensconced in a secure family context. It can, however, also become a source of rejection by peers and others outside the home who may be confused or have difficulty with understanding the biracial experience. Parents and other family members play a pivotal role in helping the children develop a secure self-concept and a positive interracial label for self-identification. Healthy biracial identity development is facilitated by parents and family members demonstrating cultural pride, being open to discussion with the children, and participating in cultural and other events that demonstrate a pride in the multiple heritages of the parents.

Stage 2 is called struggle for acceptance and occurs from the time the child is about 8 years old through late adolescence or early adulthood. During this time period, Kich's interviewees became more involved with a wider network of friends, peers, and the community at large. These experiences reinforced the notion of being different discussed in the previous stage. Individuals feel some shame about their multiracial heritage and some anger over being persistently judged or identified by their "differentness." In an attempt to resolve this internal conflict, some individuals try to maintain a separation between family and social life, but Kich notes that this denial strategy can only be used temporarily as a defense against perceptions and feelings of rejection. Also common to this stage is an effort to identify racially or culturally with one parent over the other for a time. Often, during high school or college, the subjects in Kich's study began to experiment with interracial labels and make an effort to integrate positive aspects of each parent's racial or cultural heritage. This is important identity development groundwork that lays the foundation for the final stage.

Self-acceptance and assertion of an interracial identity is Kich's (1992) third stage. Typically it occurs after high school, often during transitions to or from work or college. In this final stage, Kich's subjects developed a secure identity that was independent of others' definitions or stereotypes. Persons in this stage seek out and embrace information relative to their multiple racial identities and also acknowledge an American identification. The person feels integrated as a biracial person and as an American. In this stage, rather than being annoyed at questions from others about their racial background, individuals demonstrate patience toward others and understand that these questions may not represent prejudice but a genuine confusion on the part of others.

The Kerwin-Ponterotto Model of
Biracial Identity Development

This model of identity development was primarily based on qualitative interviews conducted by Christine Kerwin with biracial (Black and White) children and their parents, the results of which were reported in Kerwin (1991) and Kerwin, Ponterotto, Jackson, and Harris (1993). The model also integrates the findings of other theoretical models reviewed earlier, as well as a number of empirical studies reviewed in Kerwin and Ponterotto (1995). The model is developmentally based and acknowledges that biracial identity development is influenced by many variables, including personal, societal, and environmental factors. The resolution and integration of identity is also individual, and there are many variations in the complex process of establishing racial identity. The Kerwin and Ponterotto (1995) model includes the following stages: preschool, entry to school, preadolescence, adolescence, college and young adulthood, and adulthood.

During the preschool stage, children (up to 5 years old) develop a racial awareness that includes understanding the differences between their White and Black parents through physical features such as skin color and hair texture. The developing recognition of differences and similarities in one's parents and others can vary depending on parents' attitudes toward and discussions of racial issues, exposure of children to racially diverse people inside and outside the home, and other factors.

In Stage 2, entry to school, children are asked by peers, "What are you?" and they begin to develop labels or descriptive terms to define themselves. For example, Kerwin (1991) found that some children used descriptive terms of skin color, such as "coffee and cream" to label themselves, whereas others used terms taught to them by their parents, such as "interracial." As in the previous stage, there is variety in how children negotiate this stage, and their development through this stage is affected by attitudes in the school environment, availability of Black and White role models, and parental perceptions and discussion on the topic.

In preadolescence, children's sense of self as a racial being becomes more complex as they become aware that physical appearance and perhaps language spoken, in addition to skin color, helps to define one's social group affiliation. Increased awareness of one's own group membership as well as of one's parents' varied racial group memberships is stimulated by interaction with the larger environment, such as experiencing racism firsthand or entering a more integrated (or more segregated) environment for the first time.

The adolescence stage is considered to be perhaps the most challenging for biracial youth due to the combination of general developmental factors and societal pressure faced by biracial youth and teens. Kerwin's (1991) interviews uncovered that her sample felt a strong pressure from peers to identify with or choose one racial group over another, usually the group represented by the parent of color. Because the will to belong to an "in-group" is so strong during adolescence, biracial youth may not be able to resist peer pressure to identify with the parent of color's racial background (see also Miville, Constantine, Baysden, & So-Lloyd, 2005). Another stressor for biracial adolescents at this stage is dating, as for the first time individuals may be confronted with the prejudices of a date's parents, who may not approve of their son or daughter being romantically involved with a biracial person. It is interesting that Kerwin's interviews found that other group affiliations, such as sports teams and school clubs, attenuated some of the peer pressure to identity and socialize with only one racial group.

During the next stage, college and young adulthood, there may be continuing efforts to identity with only one parental racial group. However, as a more secure identity develops within this stage, biracial youth have a greater ability to reject others' expectations and pressures, and the individuals develop a more balanced biracial and bicultural identity. Individuals begin to see advantages as well as disadvantages to having a biracial heritage. One of these advantages or strengths is the ability to have "bicultural vision" ("Bicultural Vision," 1994; Kerwin & Ponterotto, 1995), which speaks to the ability to understand situations and people in a more in-depth and multifaceted fashion.

The final stage of the Kerwin-Ponterotto (1995) model is termed adulthood and focuses on biracial identity development as a lifelong process that is fluid and involves continuing efforts to integrate the many facets that make up one's racial identity. If resolution of earlier developmental stages has been reached, this final lifelong stage will be characterized by ongoing interest in and exploration of one's own cultures, as well as diverse cultures in society. Individuals at the adulthood stage are integrated and balanced. They further develop their bicultural vision and resultant flexibility and competence in a wide variety of interpersonal situations.

Root's Evolving Model of Multiracial Identity

I never wanted to be White growing up. It is a good thing because I was not. But now, I am almost White in some people's eyes. How this happened tells not only a piece of some of my lifestory but, in hindsight, has allowed some of my critical thinking around racial and ethnic identity formation.

When I came to the United States with my mother as a small child, we were not White. My mother is Filipina, not Filipina American, as she always reminds me even after 40-plus years. Whereas my father is a White American, he sustained some subtle and not so subtle demotions in status as a result of marrying a non-White person. Certain neighborhoods, while not closed to him as an individual, became closed to him as part of our family. (Root, 2001, p. 13)

This quotation is taken from the life story of Maria P. P. Root (2001), who is a pioneer in the study of biracial and multiracial identity development. Her work has been extremely influential to psychologists and researchers around the world, and her edited books, *Racially Mixed People in America* (Root, 1992a) and *The Multiracial Experience: Racial Borders on the New Frontier* (Root, 1996), have had a profound impact on the profession.

Root's (1990, 1998, 1999) "schematic metamodel" focused on biracial identity as a resolution process rather than as a developmental stage process. She hypothesized that there are four ways by which biracial people can resolve the challenges of having two racial identities. Root's model is particularly valuable because it points out that there is not one true or best resolution to identity formation for biracial persons and that the process of integrating an identity is complex, with multiple successful alternatives.

One resolution is to accept the identity assigned by society. This resolution can be a positive choice if the individual is happy with the assigned identity and has support for the resolution choice from family, both nuclear and extended. A challenge for this resolution choice is that if the individual relocates to another geographic locale, a different identity may be assigned by the new community, and thus the individual's original sense of self may be called into question, causing internal identity conflict.

A second resolution option is to identify with both racial groups. Biracial individuals may identify with the racial groups of both parents. This resolution is positive in that one draws on the strengths of two cultures, and the person is well anchored in and proud of her or his dual heritage. This resolution choice can be challenging if individuals cannot maintain their basic personality in different racial group contexts.

A third choice is to identify with a single racial group. Unlike the first resolution choice, in which the person passively accepts the single identity ascribed by society, in this resolution option the biracial person actively chooses his or her racial group identification. This resolution strategy can be positive if the person feels accepted by the group with whom she or he identifies and if the person does not deny aspects of the racial group identity not selected. When successful, biracial people using this resolution option do not feel marginalized and are not in denial. A challenge may arise in this resolution choice when an individual's single identity choice is at odds with how he or she is perceived by others in the community.

The fourth resolution strategy is to identify with a new racial group, a mixed race group. In this strategy, biracial persons do not identify particularly with either of their individual racial group heritages but instead identify with a new group, a multiracial group. This resolution is successful if the new identity incorporates all parts of the person's racial heritage. An advantage of this resolution option is that individuals are able to negotiate interactions with multiple groups.

Since her 1990 resolution model, Root has continued to explore the complexity of multiracial identity. She emphasizes (Root, 1998) the limits of applying singular racial identity models to the experiences of multiracial people, and she advocates for an ecological identity model that considers racial identity in the context of gender, class, sexual orientation, and regional history of race relations.

Choi-Misailidis's Multiracial-Heritage Awareness and Personal Affiliation Theory

Among the most recent theoretical and empirical work on multiracial identity is the work of SooJean Choi-Misailidis, a professor in the Department of Psychiatry at the University of Hawai'i's John A. Burns School of Medicine. After a careful review, integration, and critique of existing theory and research on biracial identity development, Choi-Misailidis (2003) summarized some of the limitations of our knowledge base in the area. First, there are few empirical studies that study people of mixed race descent. Choi-Misailidis attributes this dearth of empirical work to the inability of researchers to identify multiracial people and to the absence of reliable and valid research measures to be used with multiracial people. Second, much of the available theory and research focuses on particular combinations of biracial identity, such as Black-White (e.g., Jacobs, 1992) and Japanese-White (e.g., Kich, 1992), and the models and findings may not be applicable across biracial or multiracial combinations. Third, a majority of the studies that have been conducted on biracial and multiracial persons have relied on qualitative methods (usually interview studies) incorporating small samples whose life experiences may not be generalizable to the larger population of multiracial people.

Although the theory reviewed earlier in this chapter based on qualitative research is indeed valuable, there is clearly a need to incorporate larger-sample quantitative research, as well. We believe strongly that theory development and best practice strategies (of parents, educators, and counselors) should be based on a combination of quantitative and qualitative methods (see Haverkamp et al., 2005; Miville, 2005). Choi-Misailidis set out to address the limitations she noted by first presenting an integrated theory that would be applicable to all people of mixed race backgrounds and then developing a quantitative measure of identity statuses that could be used for large-sample testing.

Choi-Misailidis (2003) introduced the multiracial-heritage awareness and personal affiliation (M-HAPA) theory, which includes three identity statuses: marginal status, singular status, and integrated status. M-HAPA theory is conceptualized as fluid and dynamic; mixed race people will primarily identify with one of the three statuses but may broach other statuses and use alternate strategies dependent on social and environmental contexts.

In marginal status, multiracial individuals are disconnected from their multiple heritages and lack a sense of belonging to any racial group. They feel alienated from other people because they feel different from them, particularly from those representing single racial groups. Choi-Misailidis notes that such individuals may not appreciate, understand, or participate in the cultural practices and beliefs of their multiple racial heritages.

Singular identity describes those mixed race people who internalize the racial group identification that society might ascribe to them based on physical characteristics. This status is similar to Root's (1990) first resolution strategy, accept the identity assigned by society. Wehrly (1996) cites a biracial participant from Funderburg's (1994) interview study who comments:

> But I feel like when I walk down the streets or anything that I do in this world, people look at me as a Black person or an African-American woman, and so I felt like I had to at some point accept that. (p. 204, cited in Wehrly, 1996, p. 121)

According to Choi-Misailidis's M-HAPA theory, this status is characterized by an immersion in the cultural practices of only one racial group and the exclusion of others to which the person may belong. The singular status individual will perceive that his or her position in society matches that of the singular reference group selected. Behaviorally, persons in this status will relate to friends, romantic partners, and family members who represent the singular status.

Choi-Misailidis hypothesized also an integrated status, in which individuals blend and integrate all aspects and components of their racial heritage. Such individuals maintain meaningful connections with multiple racial groups and use multiracial labels that highlight their connection and commitment to multiple heritages. Integrated status people will relate well to family members representing all of their racial heritages and will have a culturally diverse set of friends. Such individuals demonstrate increased tolerance toward cultural differences generally, are culturally flexible, and can adapt to many social contexts. M-HAPA theory notes that the integrated person does not necessarily value or integrate her or his multiple heritages equally but instead may tap various components of the multiple identity as the context requires.

To test and validate her M-HAPA theory, Choi-Misailidis (2003) developed a revised 45-item Likert-type survey instrument that assesses where multiracial people fall or to what degree they identify with the different statuses. In a carefully planned and well-executed study, Choi-Misailidis sampled 364 mixed race individuals from three Hawai'i university campuses. These mixed race participants represented a wide variety of mixed race heritages. The majority of the sample reported being biracial; however, there was good representation as well of students who reported representing three or four races. For example, Choi-Misailidis's sample included 61 students who reported being Asian-White, 5 were Black-White, and 33 represented Asian-Black-Hispanic-Native American heritage.

It is interesting to note that in empirically testing her M-HAPA theory with her new instrument, Choi-Misailidis discovered that the integrated status was best conceptualized as including two dimensions: integrated identity status–combinatory factor, which is characterized by the integration of the different racial groups making up one's heritage, and integrated identity status–universality factor, which focuses on the person's appreciation of commonalities among all racial groups and on an appreciation for diversity at large. The breaking up of the integrated status into two dimensions reminds us of the latest developments in Cross's nigrescence model (Cross & Vandiver, 2001), covered in Chapter 4. Both Cross and Vandiver (2001) and Choi-Misailidis (2003) demonstrate impressively how good instruments developed from theoretical constructs can lead to findings and insights that can inform and modify the initial theoretical propositions. Choi-Misailidis's research findings supported or partially supported the majority of her initial hypotheses, which included the following: (a) both integrated statuses (combinatory and universality) were positively correlated with self-esteem, with a healthy sense of ethnic identity and pride, and with positive attitudes toward people from other racial and ethnic groups; (b) marginal status correlated negatively to a measure of positive ethnic identity and to a measure of attitudes toward other groups (people in this status were more prejudiced) and correlated with lower levels of self-esteem; and (c) singular identity correlated positively with a measure of ethnic identity, negatively with a measure of attitudes toward other racial and ethnic groups, and negatively with a measure of self-esteem (this last finding was not expected).

Lesbian, Gay, and Bisexual Identity Development

Among the most oppressed people in the United States are those who label themselves lesbian, gay, or bisexual (LGB). In Chapter 1, we pointed out the extent of ongoing hate crimes directed at LGB persons. Prejudice toward LGB people is pervasive in society and starts early in homes, neighborhoods, and schools (Lattarulo, 2005). For example, the 2001 National School Climate Survey of close to 1000 LGB students from 48 states found that 94% of the respondents reported hearing derogatory language toward LGB students frequently or often, and 24% even reported hearing such negative comments coming from school faculty and staff at least occasionally. As such derogatory comments were rarely confronted or challenged by other students or faculty, it is not surprising that 69% of LGB students reported feeling unsafe in their school (Kosciw, 2001, as reviewed in Lattarulo, 2005).

In this section, we briefly review some landmark and more recent models of gay and lesbian identity development. Knowledge of these models will be helpful to counselors, educators, administrators, and parents as we all strive to better understand the processes of identity development in their many forms.

Models of Gay and Lesbian Identity Development

In this section, we review select models of lesbian and gay identity development. We begin our overview with the landmark work of Cass (1979) and then cover more briefly the influential models of Coleman (1982) and Fassinger (1998). This section closes with a brief summary of the most recent research in the area (Lattarulo, 2005).

Cass's Theoretical Model of
Homosexuality Identity Formation

One of the first and most influential models of gay and lesbian identity development was that proposed by Vivienne C. Cass (1979) almost 30 years ago. Cass developed her six-stage model based on clinical experience with gay and lesbian clients. Theoretically speaking, Cass's model was anchored in interpersonal congruency theory, which assumes "that stability and change in human behavior are dependent on congruency or incongruency that exists in [the person's] environment" (p. 220). Thus the individual's effort to deal with incongruity between perceptions of self and others leads to self-examination and reflection and, ultimately, movement through the stages. Cass (1979) notes that the incongruence that stimulates identity processes at each stage can be addressed with multiple options, some that lead more directly to advanced stages and others that serve to block or foreclose (at least temporarily) movement to subsequent stages.

Cass's model, like others reviewed in this and the previous chapter, can be perceived as a developmental person-environment interaction model in that (a) identity, or the acquisition of "an identity of 'homosexual' fully integrated within the individual's overall concept of self" (p. 220) is a developmental process, and (b) that the identity formation process begins and continues as a result of the gay or lesbian person's interaction with a heterosexual-dominated environment.

An important aspect of this model is Cass's (1979) distinction between private and public aspects of identity. Thus, Cass is proposing a bilinear or dual-process model. For example, it is possible for a gay man to maintain a private identity as a gay person and a public image or persona as a heterosexual man. Given U.S. society's generally negative view toward homosexuality, and given the threat of violence that gay people face every day (see Chapter 1), it is understandable how one could operate in the dual-process model.

Stage 1 is identity confusion, and it focuses on questioning assumptions regarding one's sexual orientation. The gay or lesbian person develops a growing awareness of thoughts and sexual feelings toward same-sex persons, yet because of societal values against homosexuality, these feelings and thoughts are not shared with others, and the person feels an inner turmoil and confusion. This incongruity between personal thoughts and feelings toward same-sex persons and the previous stable situation before such thoughts and feelings became active leads the individual to deal with the incongruence in one of three ways. In the first option, the individual may perceive these gay feelings as both correct and acceptable, in which case she or he expends energy in learning more about gay persons and gay life. A second option is that the individual accepts the emergent feelings and thoughts but sees them as undesirable, in which case he or she may expend considerable energy inhibiting, restricting, or denying such thoughts, feelings, and behaviors. The third option is that the Stage 1 person sees the emergent feelings toward same-sex persons as both incorrect and undesirable and attempts to redefine what may be considered homosexual behavior. Cass (1979) gives the example of the prison environment, in which some inmates may engage in homosexual behavior without defining it as such or seeing themselves as gay or lesbian.

Dealing with the inconguence through the first option leads to Stage 2 of the model. Options 2 and 3 can lead to foreclosure, in which the individual does not advance along the stage model. However, if attempts at denial or redefining "homosexual behavior" are not successful, persons using options 2 and 3 may also then move into Stage 2.

Stage 2, identity comparison, marks the "first tentative commitment to a homosexual self" (Cass, 1979, p. 225). As the individual acknowledges that she or he may be homosexual, the implications of this identification become clearer, and the person experiences deep feelings of social alienation. These strong feelings of alienation may lead a student or young person to the counselor's office, where, Cass notes, they may exclaim, "I do not want to be different" (p. 226). Individuals in Stage 2 use one of four options to deal with these painful feelings of isolation. First, individuals may work through feelings of alienation by acknowledging that they always felt different, and now by accepting their homosexuality they understand this differentness and work to identify with other gay and lesbian people. For a while, these persons may continue to present a public image of heterosexuality although they have accepted a private image of homosexuality. This is done because they may not want to be confronted with other persons' negative views of the gay lifestyle, and maintaining a public heterosexual persona (what Cass calls "passing") allows them time to absorb and manage a growing commitment to a gay or lesbian self-image.

The second option for reducing feelings of incongruence in Stage 2 is characterized by those who accept the homosexual label of their behavior but see a homosexual self-image as undesirable. To reduce the self-image of homosexuality, this option might entail seeing homosexuality in relation to one person only (a special circumstance); considering oneself bisexual (e.g., "I could act heterosexual if and when I wanted to"; Cass, 1979, p. 227); noting a temporary state of homosexuality, implying that the future may hold a heterosexual lifestyle; or accepting a passive innocence strategy that emphasizes that the person was born this way and cannot help the way he or she is (Cass notes that this last strategy can lead to a self-hate perception).

In Stage 3, identity tolerance, individuals acknowledge that they are probably gay or lesbian. They tolerate rather than accept their homosexuality and make efforts to contact other gay and lesbian people as a means of dealing with the alienation they may feel. Cass emphasizes that positive contacts with others (affirmation of gay people and gay identity) at this point serve to help individuals integrate their gay identity further. On the other hand, negative contacts with others, particularly for those who had a negative self-image as a gay person at the start of this stage, may lead to further devaluation and a more negative identity. Such negative contacts can lead the person to an attempt to inhibit gay or lesbian sexual behaviors and may prevent further identity development.

Individuals who reach Stage 4, identity acceptance, have acknowledged that "I am homosexual" (Cass, 1979, p. 231). This stage is characterized by increasing contacts and identification with other gay and lesbian persons. Individuals' developing gay identity is normalized and validated through this expanded social network. As in the previous stages, individuals will vary in how they negotiate this stage. Some fully legitimize their identity both privately and publicly; others will legitimize the identity privately but may be selective in their public selves. These latter individuals will continue to use the strategy of passing or may choose to have limited contact with certain heterosexuals who may not be accepting and will only selectively disclose their private selves to those viewed as accepting.

Identity pride constitutes Stage 5 and involves a deep immersion into gay and lesbian culture, coupled with a rejection of heterosexual values. The Stage 5 person has both pride in his or her gay identity and anger resulting from previous feelings of frustration and alienation. This individual is likely to become more activist, and if he or she was still holding onto a gay private self and heterosexual public self, the public self becomes open and aligned with the gay-identity private self. Thus both selves come into congruence.

Finally, in Stage 6, identity synthesis, the gay or lesbian identity is integrated into the overall personal identity and self-concept and is no longer seen as a separate or independent aspect of self. The negative view toward heterosexual society characteristic of the previous stage is brought into balance, and now the individual has increasing contact with accepting heterosexuals.

Cass (1984) developed a questionnaire to test her theoretical model (Cass, 1979). She found that individuals could indeed be distinguished by varying characteristics tied to discrete stages and that the predicted sequence of stages generally held up as hypothesized. She did find, however, that some stages were blurred together and that the overall model might better be represented as a four-stage model rather than the hypothesized six-stage model.

Contemporary gay identity theorists and researchers have noted some limitations in Cass's (1979) landmark model. Among these are the limited empirical testing of the model, the association of identity self-disclosure (coming out) as a prerequisite to reaching the highest stage of identity (thus downplaying the dangers or consequences of coming out in certain social-cultural contexts), and questioning the possible generalizability of Cass's results from an Australian sample to U.S. gays and lesbians (see Lattarulo, 2005; McCarn & Fassinger, 1996).

It is understandable that Cass's (1979) model, presented over a quarter of a century ago, would hold some limitations by today's theoretical and empirical standards. Nonetheless, we consider Cass's model to be a major breakthrough in psychology and education, and her model is still frequently cited in the literature.

Coleman's Stages of the Coming Out Process

Coleman (1982) presented a five-stage model that expanded on Cass's model by extending the coming out process over the entire lifespan. Furthermore, Cass's model was more sequential and invariant in that her model posited that individuals would have to resolve the identity challenges at each stage before moving to a higher stage. Coleman's model was less sequential, and he acknowledged that individuals may be fixated at certain stages or may tackle tasks associated with higher stages before moving back to the identity tasks of earlier stages.

Coleman's (1982) Stage 1 is pre–coming out: At an early age, both the child and his or her parents understand on some level that the child's sexual orientation differs in some way from the expected norm. This knowledge creates tension in children, for as they grow they can sense society's heterosexual emphasis, and they develop feelings of alienation and isolation. These individuals use defense mechanisms, such as denial or repression, to avoid acknowledging same-sex feelings. Coleman notes that denying one's sexuality takes its toll and there is risk in acting out the internal conflicts through psychological symptoms such as lowered self-esteem, depression, and anxiety and behavior problems such as somatization, substance abuse, and even suicide attempts. For Coleman, a healthy resolution to this stage is to face up to and process the existential crisis of being different.

Stage 2 is called coming out and is initiated as individuals acknowledge their same-sex feelings. There is variability at which age this acknowledgment occurs; younger persons may be aware of homosexual feelings but may not have formally labeled them as such yet. A critical aspect of this stage is to externally validate one's sexual orientation identity by self-disclosing feelings to another person. This self-disclosure is risky in that if the gay person is rejected for his or her disclosure, the gay stigmatization is confirmed and personal self-esteem is damaged. However, if the disclosure is met with understanding and acceptance, it provides a positive push toward further healthy identity development and integration. Coleman (1982) states that "once an individual gains acceptance from a number of persons, it is much easier to withstand rejection, or even indirect rejection by society" (pp. 34–35).

In the third stage, exploration, individuals experiment with their new sexual identity and develop a sense of sexual competence and personal attractiveness. Persons in this stage actively socialize with other gay and lesbian individuals, which serves to further develop their identity and enhance self-esteem. The next stage is first relationships and refers to a period during which individuals desire to move beyond sexual experimentation and increase the general social interaction of the previous stage in search of a committed, stable relationship. The challenge is functioning in a same-sex relationship in a society in which opposite-sex relationships are considered the norm. At times, the first committed relationships are rocky, with one or both partners feeling possessive or lacking trust in the other. Finally, in the last stage, integration, individuals develop an integrated gay identity that continues through the adult lifespan. Some of the challenges inherent in the early committed relationships established in the previous stage are worked through, and relationships when both partners are in this final stage are more successful and are characterized by mutual trust, respect, and freedom.

Fassinger and Colleagues' Inclusive Model of Lesbian and Gay Identity Formation

Ruth Fassinger (1998) and her colleagues (Fassinger & Miller, 1997; McCarn & Fassinger, 1996) have proposed a four-phase model that espouses two separate but reciprocal processes of identity formation: an internal, individual process of awareness and identification and a group membership or group affiliation process of awareness and identity. The individual identity process asks the question "Am I lesbian or gay?" whereas the group identity process asks "What does it mean, to me and to other LGB people, to be lesbian or gay in this society at this time?" (Fassinger, 1998, p. 16). The Fassinger and colleague model was first described in relation to lesbian women (McCarn, 1991; McCarn & Fassinger, 1996). One interesting outcome was that the lesbian-based model also appeared to be valid for gay men after the model was modified to reflect greater sexual exploration and activity (Fassinger & Miller, 1997).

The work of Fassinger and her colleagues is a major breakthrough for the psychology profession in that the model successfully integrates and extends the work of gay identity pioneers (e.g., Cass, 1979; Coleman, 1982), racial identity scholars (e.g., Atkinson, Morten, & Sue, 1989; Cross, 1971), and feminist theorists (e.g., Downing & Roush, 1985; Ossana, Helms, & Leonard, 1992). This model is also noteworthy because it emphasizes the dual nature of lesbian or gay identity "as an *individual sexual identity* that results in *membership in an oppressed minority group*" (McCarn & Fassinger, 1996, p. 509). Another defining feature of the model is that it does not equate higher levels of lesbian or gay identity development with coming out or self-disclosing one's sexual orientation to the public. More specifically, McCarn and Fassinger (1996) state that "disclosure is so profoundly affected by environmental oppression that to use it as an index of identity development directly forces an individual to take responsibility for her own victimization" (p. 522).

In presenting the Fassinger and colleague model, we review the individual sexual identity development process and the group membership identity development process for each of the proposed four phases. Note that McCarn and Fassinger (1996) prefer the term *phases* to *stages* to highlight the flexibility implied in a model that represents a continuous and circular process. As individual identity is affected, it has an effect on one's group membership identity, and vice versa.

Awareness marks the first phase of the model. In the individual identity development branch of this phase, the person acknowledges having thoughts and feelings regarding sexuality that are different from both society's norms and socialized self-expectations for heterosexual preference. The person now can no longer assume that everyone is heterosexual. In the group identity branch of the model, awareness is characterized by the perception that heterosexuality is not a universal norm and that there are persons who are heterosexual and persons who are lesbian or gay. The individual comes to understand that there is a community of lesbian and gay persons in society. This realization leads to the conscious acknowledgment that there is a heterosexist bias in U.S. society.

Phase 2 is called exploration, and in the individual identity branch of this phase, individuals more deeply explore their sexual feelings and may or may not act on these feelings in terms of sexual behavior. Women in this phase experience strong feelings or relationships with other women or with a particular woman. In the group identity branch of this phase, individuals actively pursue increased knowledge about lesbian or gay people to learn more about their newly identified group and to explore their sense of belonging to the group. Persons in this phase may feel some guilt and anger for having bought into society's heterosexist and homophobic socialization. Equally salient, however, are feelings of excitement, joy, and energized curiosity as a result of exploring affiliation with and belonging to a community of lesbians or gays.

Deepening or commitment is the name of Phase 3, and in the individual identity branch, the individual develops greater self-knowledge with regard to sexual identity. In reference to lesbians, McCarn and Fassinger (1996) note that

> Some may see relationships with women as only one possibility and iden-
> tify as bisexual, and others may decide in favor of men as sexual partners.
> It is here that the emerging lesbian is likely to recognize her desire for
> other women as within herself and, with deepening self-awareness, will
> develop sexual clarity and commitment to her self-fulfillment as a sexual
> being. (pp. 522–523)

Sexual intimacy and sense of identity become more interconnected as individuals acknowledge that their chosen forms of intimacy imply something about their personal identity, and as a result, individuals now embrace their developing identity as a lesbian or gay person. The group identity branch of the deepening or commitment phase centers on considering the unique aspects and values of the lesbian and gay community as well as under-standing and acknowledging the historic and ongoing oppression experi-enced by this community. Individuals at this phase may strongly and passionately identify with their lesbian or gay culture and simultaneously reject heterosexual society. This phase is often accompanied with strong mixed emotions, such as rage and a deep feeling of pride.

The final phase of the model is called internalization and synthesis, at which point the individual identity component is characterized by deeper self-acceptance of emotional and physical attraction for same-sex persons and the integration of this acceptance into one's overall personal identity. Individuals at this phase have typically spent many years processing thoughts and feelings with regard to their sexual identity. They have achieved an inte-grated sexual orientation and personal identity, and they are comfortable and confident in their newly achieved identity. Persons in this phase may or may not be "out," depending on the environmental context. For example, a woman may decide not to self-disclose her identity as a lesbian at work for fear of heterosexist repercussions. However, as long as the decision about where and to whom to come out is made by the individual, the level of iden-tity achieved is not attenuated.

In the group identity branch of this final phase, individuals have iden-tified themselves as a member of a minority group, have probably redefined the meaning of the group, and have synthesized their personal identity com-fortably with their group identity. Individuals in Phase 4 interact with and make evaluative judgments of both gays and nongays on an individual basis rather than on a group membership basis. Individuals in this phase experi-ence a sense of inner peace and fulfillment, and they are able to maintain their integrated identity across different contexts.

Empirical testing of the Fassinger (1998) model is in its infancy, but early findings are promising with regard to the construct validity of the model as applied to both lesbian women and gay men. A recent qualitative study by Lattarulo (2005) found strong support for major propositions in the Fassinger model as applied to a diverse group of gay men.

Lattarulo introduced an emergent grounded theory of coming out experiences of gay men anchored in the concept of "self-monitoring." Specifically, gay males interviewed by Lattarulo became hypervigilant and hyperaware of their surroundings as a coping strategy for the barrage of antigay messages, hate language, and violence they were exposed to from their earliest recollections. Always concerned for their safety, these men became adept at keeping feelings and thoughts secret, and they continuously self-monitored their behaviors and presentation to the outside world. Lattarulo's (2005) findings support the conflation of two separate but interdependent processes proposed by Fassinger (1998; McCarn & Fassinger, 1996) and also extend Fassinger's work by identifying the specific sources of oppression faced by the men as well as the self-monitoring processes developed to maintain a perception of safety in a hostile world.

Chapter Summary

This chapter has briefly reviewed landmark as well as emerging theories of biracial, multiracial, and lesbian or gay identity development. Compared to the status of research on single-group racial identity models, parallel research on multiracial and lesbian or gay identity is in its infancy. However, these are crucial areas for more model building and empirical testing using quantitative, qualitative, and mixed-method approaches.

7

Multicultural Personality Development

We believe, and research generally supports the position, that a healthy level of racial and ethnic identity development is a prerequisite to being an accepting, tolerant person. Furthermore, there is mounting evidence that advanced stages of racial and ethnic identity development correlate to healthier psychological functioning. Clearly, part of our role as counselors, educators, administrators, and parents is to model healthy levels of ethnic identity and to promote racial and ethnic identity development among those we influence.

Despite the critical role of racial and ethnic identity development in mental health and in race relations, the construct itself is not without limitations. For example, most of the theory and research in racial and ethnic identity development stems primarily from counseling and developmental psychology and does not tap the resources of other specialties within the profession. This narrow focus naturally confines the scope and application of racial identity theory. Also, research on racial identity is relatively recent in comparison to other constructs in psychology (e.g., Allport's [1954] "tolerant personality"), and the research has relied mainly on paper-and-pencil instruments that are limited with regard to external validity (real-world applications). Another limitation is that most racial and ethnic identity models are culture or group specific (emic) and cannot be applied to people in general. Having a broader, more universally inclusive (etic) model of cultural self-integration and multicultural interpersonal competence would be useful to researchers and teachers.

In this chapter, we expand on the construct of racial and ethnic identity development by examining and integrating related theory and research across many specialties within psychology, including social psychology, organizational psychology, international psychology, feminist psychology, and African-centered or Black psychology. The result of this integration is the introduction of a fairly new construct called the *multicultural personality.* We believe the multicultural personality serves as a useful conceptualization for identifying and promoting traits in people that may relate to lower levels of prejudice as well as higher levels of quality of life for those persons living in an increasingly heterogeneous society.

What Is the Multicultural Personality?

The term *multicultural personality* was first coined by Ramirez (1991) to describe individuals who could successfully negotiate and thrive in multiple cultures simultaneously. Ramirez's (1991) work was rooted in clinical psychology and focused on helping culturally diverse clients develop bicultural skills and a multicultural orientation to life. For Ramirez (1999), a multicultural orientation to life is characterized by the individual who (a) strives for maximum personality development, in part achieved by interacting with diversity; (b) adapts well to different environmental situations; (c) enjoys leadership roles in diverse groups and develops innovative solutions for resolving conflict in diverse groups; (d) works for social justice for all citizens; and (e) seeks exposure to as much diversity as possible through friendships, colleagues, readings, travel, and so on. Ramirez (1991) defined the multicultural personality as a "synthesis and amalgamation of the resources learned from different peoples and cultures to create multicultural coping styles, thinking styles, perceptions of the world (world views) and multicultural identities" (p. 26).

Since Ramirez's (1991) early work on the multicultural personality, other researchers anchored in diverse psychology disciplines have further expanded the construct. For example, working from the context of personnel and cross-cultural psychology, Van Der Zee and Van Oudenhoven (2000, 2001) have focused on the multicultural personality within the context of expatriates (people living abroad) adapting to work and life in international contexts. Ponterotto and colleagues (Brummett, Wade, Ponterotto, Thombs, & Lewis, in press; Ponterotto, Costa, & Werner-Lin, 2002; Ponterotto, Mendelsohn, & Belizaire, 2003), writing from a counseling psychology perspective, addressed the multicultural personality as a positive indicator of enhanced quality of life for Americans living in an increasingly culturally diverse society. The multicultural personality construct is consistent with the growing body of literature and research (see Seligman, Steen, Park, & Peterson, 2005) on "positive psychology," with its emphasis on enhancing optimal human functioning (Ponterotto et al., 2005).

In addition to all these authors, who specifically address the "multicultural personality," select theorists in multicultural education have discussed constructs that appear to be related to the multicultural personality. For example, Nieto (2000) believes that for teachers to work effectively in culturally diverse classrooms, they must develop as "multicultural persons."

Becoming a multicultural person involves reeducation in three areas: (a) learning more about cultural pluralism, (b) confronting one's own racism and biases, and (c) learning to see reality from a variety of perspectives.

In related though independent work, Banks (2001) believes that one important yet neglected goal in education, starting in the early grades, is to develop "multicultural citizens." Teachers who model multicultural citizenship are characterized by (a) having a balance of cultural, national, and global identifications and understanding multiple ways in which knowledge is constructed; (b) becoming knowledge producers; (c) being thoughtful, caring, and reflective and being socially active in efforts to create a more humane nation and world.

Perhaps the most comprehensive conception of the multicultural personality is that recently offered by Ponterotto (2004, in press). Integrating and extending this work, we note that the multicultural personality is characterized by an individual who is emotionally stable; is secure in her or his racial, ethnic, and other identities; embraces diversity in her or his personal life and makes active attempts to learn about other cultures and interact with culturally different people (e.g., friends, colleagues); has a spiritual essence with some sense of connectedness to all persons; has wide-reaching empathic ability in multiple contexts; is self-reflective and cognitively flexible; has a sense of humor; effectively negotiates and copes within multiple roles and cultural contexts; possesses the ability to live and work effectively among different groups and types of people; understands the biases inherent in his or her own worldview and actively learns about alternate worldviews; understands the impact of internalized racism (and homophobia) and unearned privilege in her or his personal life; and is a social activist, empowered to speak out against all forms of social injustice (e.g., racism, homophobia, sexism, ageism, domestic violence, religious stereotyping).

This expansive definition represents an integration of related theory and research in different specialties within psychology, including counseling, clinical, developmental, social, and organizational psychology, as well as Black and feminist perspectives in psychology and mental health. We will review these theories and the related research studies later in this chapter; but first it is important to (a) summarize the evolving research on personality traits and (b) highlight the relationship of the multicultural personality to established models of personality.

How Does the Multicultural Personality Relate to Broader Models of Personality?

Landmark work on measuring personality traits and developing personality profiles can be traced back to Allport and Odbert (1936), who conducted a lexical study of terms in an unabridged English dictionary. They identified some 18,000 terms of some relevance to four aspects of personality: traits (e.g., sociable), temporary states (e.g., rejoicing), evaluative judgments (e.g., worthy), and physical characteristics (e.g., strong). Allport and Odbert defined personality traits as "generalized and personalized determining tendencies—consistent and stable modes of an individual's adjustment to his environment" (as cited in John & Srivastava, 1999, p. 103).

Working with some 4500 trait terms identified by Allport and Odbert (1936), Cattell (1943) used factor analyses (a sophisticated empirical procedure for the time) to arrive at just 12 personality factors. Picking up and extending Cattell's (1943) work, Tupes and Christal (1961) further condensed the list of personality traits down to five consistently recurring factors or dimensions. These are collectively labeled the "five-factor model": extraversion, agreeableness, conscientiousness, neuroticism, and openness. These broad traits have subsequently been validated in hundreds of studies by researchers around the world. In fact, McRae and Costa (1999, p. 139) note that the five-factor model "is the Christmas tree on which findings of stability, heritability, consensual validation, cross-cultural invariance, and predictive utility are hung like ornaments" (we acknowledge that this example will be more meaningful to our Christian readers than readers of other religions). Table 7.1 summarizes McCrae and Costa's (1999, 2003; Costa & McCrae, 1992) five-factor model.

Table 7.1   Summary of the Five-Factor Model

FFM Dimensions	*Opposing Factors*
Extraversion: warm, enthusiastic, affectionate, talkative, fun loving	Introversion: reserved, quiet, sober
Agreeableness: good natured, trusting, altruistic, modest, generous	Antagonism: critical, irritable, suspicious, stingy, unforgiving
Conscientiousness: organized, hard working, efficient, ambitious, punctual	Lack of direction: disorganized, tardy, aimless, unfocused
Neuroticism: anxious, depressed, perfectionistic, vulnerable, moody	Emotional stability: stable, calm, even tempered, self-satisfied, hardy
Openness (to experience): original, creative, curious, imaginative, diverse interests	Closed (to experience): conventional, routine oriented, down to earth

SOURCES: Adapted from John and Srivastava (1999) and McCrae and Costa (2003).

Note: FFM indicates the five-factor model.

The multicultural personality is conceived as a narrow matrix of personality traits that are subsumed within broader personality conceptions, such as the big five model of Costa and McCrae (1992). It is important to note that Paunonen (1998) and colleagues (Ashton, Jackson, Paunonen, Helmes, &

Rothstein, 1995; Paunonen & Ashton, 2001; Paunonen & Gardner, 2001; Paunonen & Jackson, 2000; Paunonen, Rothstein, & Jackson, 1999), in their systematic research program, have demonstrated the significant incremental value of narrow personality traits over broader aggregate traits in predicting human behavior in a variety of contexts. Adapting to, and thriving in, an increasingly multicultural society is one such context.

We believe that individuals who possess a "multicultural personality" will be more successful in our evolving multicultural society, and they will experience higher levels of life satisfaction and quality of life. Although the comprehensive definition of the multicultural personality presented earlier is a relatively recent development, components of this personality disposition have been presented in related constructs across diverse psychology specialties. Here we review theory and research in related psychological specialties that formed the basis of our definition of the multicultural personality. Specifically, the following topical areas formed the foundation for our model of the multicultural personality: racial and ethnic identity development, coping with cultural diversity, the tolerant personality, the universal-diverse orientation, an expansionist theory of gender roles, Afrocentric perspectives on mental health, and the expatriate adjustment literature. Within each topical section, select research is reviewed that demonstrates the link between the specific construct, the multicultural personality, and various psychological correlates.

Racial and Ethnic Identity Development

As evident in Chapters 4 through 6 of this book, one of the most vibrant areas of research in mental health over the last two decades has centered on the psychological correlates of racial and ethnic identity development for both minority groups and the White majority in the United States (Ponterotto, Casas, et al., 1995, 2001). Racial and ethnic identity represents one of seven anchors forming the foundation for our definition of the multicultural personality presented earlier. Because we covered the theory and research on racial and ethnic identity development in depth in previous chapters, here we will only summarize briefly the general focus of identity models.

An interpretive context for understanding racial and ethnic minority development models rests on the following assumptions. First, the United States has a racist history and both overt and more covert prejudice continues to thrive in society (Burkard, Medler, & Boticki, 2001; Gaertner & Dovidio, 2000; Sue, 2003; Sue et al., 1998). Second, non-White individuals in the United States may undergo a developmental process, with identifiable stages, during which internalized negative images of themselves engendered from cultural racism (Jones, 1997; Utsey & Ponterotto, 1996) are challenged, a racial or ethnic self-exploration ensues, a strong identification with their own racial or ethnic group develops, and finally, a balanced positive racial or ethnic or multiculturalist identity emerges.

For White Americans in the United States, a modified identity development process is hypothesized. Assumptions of White identity theory are as follows. First, Whites, because of their privileged status in society (Helms, 1995; McIntosh, 1998; Neville et al., 2001) have not been led, or forced, to examine their own roles in race relations in the United States (Sue, 2003). Second, the White racial identity development process involves coming to terms with one's own unearned privilege in society, followed by an honest self-examination of one's role in maintaining the status quo, and ending with a balanced identity perspective characterized by self-awareness, a relinquishing of unearned privileges, and commitments to social justice for all groups.

The last two decades have witnessed the generation of numerous racial, ethnic, and other-group identity development models, which we reviewed in earlier chapters. What is most relevant to our discussion of the multicultural personality is the advanced stages of these models. In all cases, it is the final stages of each model that are the critical components and anchors of the multicultural personality. Table 7.2 lists the identity models and associated stages that we relate to multicultural personality development.

Coping With Cultural Diversity Within the United States

An important line of research related to the present authors' conception of the multicultural personality has been initiated by Coleman (1995; Coleman, Casali, & Wampold, 2001; LaFromboise, Coleman, & Gerton, 1993), who conceptualized and tested diverse strategies for effectively coping with diversity in a culturally heterogeneous society. Coleman (1995; Coleman et al., 2001) argues that the strategies that individuals incorporate when adapting to a second culture are dependent on the goals they have in the new cultural context. For example, the second-culture acquisition goals of an IBM executive traveling to Japan for 2 weeks of meetings are probably different from the goals of a college student studying abroad for a year and different still from an American who marries someone from another country and moves permanently to the spouse's home country. Coleman (1995; Coleman et al., 2001) borrows the construct of "behavioral episode schemata" (Ford, 1992) to explain that the goals one has in a new culture and the strategies used to adjust to the new environment are varied and context dependent.

The six strategies for coping with cultural diversity presented by Coleman et al. (2001) are separation, assimilation, acculturation, alternation, integration, and fusion. Three of these strategies, separation, assimilation, and acculturation, reflect second-culture acquisition strategies that are unilinear: "Individuals either let go of their culture of origin and join the second culture or they remove themselves from contact with the second culture" (Coleman et al., 2001, p. 356). An individual who uses the separation strategy attempts to avoid contact and interaction with host culture persons

Table 7.2   Models of Racial, Ethnic, and Gender Identity Development,
With Advanced Stage Component Subsumed Within the
Multicultural Personality

Author of Identity Models	Advanced Stage
Racial- or Ethnic-Minority Specific	
African American	
Cross (1995)	Internalization and internalization commitment
Cross & Vandiver (2001) and Vandiver et al. (2002)	Internalization (multiculturalist inclusive)
Japanese American	
Kim (1981)	Incorporation
Mexican American/Latino	
Arce (1981)	Internalized
Ruiz (1990)	Successful resolution
Racial- or Ethnic-Minority Transcendent	
Atkinson, Morten, & Sue (1998)	Synergetic articulation
Helms (1995)	Integrative awareness
Phinney et al. (1990)	Achievement
Ponterotto & Pedersen (1993)	Integration and internalization
European American (White) Racial Identity	
Helms (1995)	Autonomy
Ponterotto (1988)	Integration
Sabnani et al. (1991)	Redefinition and integration
Sue et al. (1998)	Integrative awareness
Biracial and Multiracial Identity Development	
Choi-Misailidis (2003)	Integrated identity
Jacobs (1992)	Biracial identity
Kerwin & Ponterotto (1995)	Adulthood
Kich (1992)	Self-acceptance and assertion
Poston (1990)	Integration
Feminist Identity Models	
Downing & Roush (1985)	Active commitment
Lesbian and Gay Identity Models	
Cass (1979)	Identity synthesis
Coleman (1982)	Integration
Fassinger (1998)	Internalization and synthesis

(and values and traditions) and remain ensconced within home country personal interactions (as in an ethnic enclave within the community). An individual who assimilates or acculturates,[1] according to Coleman et al. (2001),
is one who lets go of her or his culture of origin and joins the host culture.

The remaining second-culture acquisition strategies are conceived as bilinear, maintaining involvement and competence with one's home culture and simultaneously developing interactive comfort and competence in the host culture. The alternation strategy assumes that it is possible to alternate between the home and host cultures, much in the same way a fully bilingual individual can easily adapt to the context-necessary language. In the integration strategy, the two cultures are more deeply integrated into the personality structure, and the person becomes bicultural, maintaining her or his culture of origin and incorporating language, customs, and values from the host culture.

Finally, in the fusion strategy, culturally diverse individuals in regular contact with one another fuse to create a new culture that subsumes the value systems, behaviors, and traditions of the individually represented cultures. An example of fusion is the White Anglo-Saxon Protestant value system that predominated in the colonists arriving in America. Colonists from different European countries arrived, interacted, and, over time, developed new, integrated political and value systems that were somewhat distinct from their European origins and very distinct from the Native American indigenous cultures, the Afrocentric cultures, and the Eastern hemisphere value systems (see Katz, 1985; Sue, 2003; and Sue et al., 1998, for extensive discussion of cultural value systems in the United States). Of the six culture-acquisition strategies presented by Coleman (1995), it is the integration strategy that most closely parallels characteristics of the multicultural personality.

Coleman et al. (2001) hypothesized and empirically validated, to some degree, that the six second-culture acquisition coping strategies are sequential. That is, when the individual comes into contact with a second culture, she or he makes a series of decisions over time that will lead to commitment to one of the six strategies. Specifically, Coleman et al. (2001) pose a series of questions, the answers to which lead to a sequential path of second-culture acquisition. An example is as follows: "Do you associate with more than one cultural group?" If the answer is "yes," then the question is asked, "Do you attempt to associate with your culture of origin and a second culture at the same time?" If the answer is "no," the person has selected the alternation strategy; if "yes," then "Do you seek to combine two or more cultures?" is asked. If the answer is "yes," the fusion strategy has been selected; if "no," the integration strategy has been selected. A similar sequential path leads to the selection of one of the other strategies if the response to the first question was "no" (Coleman et al., 2001, p. 358). At present, there is no extant research testing the correlation between the integration strategy and quality-of-life indicators. However, the integration strategy appears to closely parallel bicultural affiliations in bilinear acculturation models (see Kim & Abreu, 2001) and is reminiscent of Oetting and Beauvais' (1991) orthogonal theory of identity, which posits that individuals may embrace multiple cultural identities simultaneously and without confusion. There is some limited research to support the relationship between bicultural and multicultural identity and psychological health and life satisfaction (e.g., Lieber, Chin, Nihira, & Mink, 2001; Roysircar-Sodowsky & Maestas, 2000).

The Tolerant Personality

Allport (1954, 1979) coined the term "the tolerant personality" in his classic text *The Nature of Prejudice*. The tolerant personality is reflected in the individual who is on friendly terms with a wide variety of people. Important components of the tolerant personality, according to Allport (1979), are empathic ability, self-insight, intropunitiveness, and tolerance for ambiguity.

In discussing empathy, Allport is referring to the ability to size up people, a social sensitivity, and "a flexible capacity to know another's state of mind and adapt to it" (Allport, 1979, p. 436). Allport laments the limits of the English word "empathy" in fully capturing the intricacies of the construct and prefers instead the German terms *Menschenkenntnis* and *Menschenkenner* (a deep understanding of people) as more accurate depictions of the empathic person.

The tolerant person is also characterized by a high degree of self-insight. According to Allport (1979), individuals with self-insight are self-aware, know and accept their capabilities and shortcomings, and are self-critical. These individuals are also likely to possess a sense of humor and can laugh at their own misgivings: "One who can laugh at oneself is unlikely to feel greatly superior to others" (Allport, 1979, p. 437).

A third characteristic of the tolerant personality is what Allport labels *intropunitiveness*, referring to a tendency to look inward for responsibility and blame rather than projecting blame outwardly. An intropunitive person feels genuine sympathy for the "underdog" and empathizes keenly with the suffering of others. This type of person also finds great reward in helping others. Finally, the tolerant personality, according to Allport (1979), has a tolerance for ambiguity and is flexible and cognitively complex rather than cognitively rigid or bifurcated. Clearly, the tolerant personality parallels components of the multicultural personality discussed earlier.

There are countless measures of tolerance, multicultural sensitivity, and racial prejudice (see Chapter 15, as well as critical reviews in Biernat & Crandall, 1999, and Burkard et al., 2001). Many of these are fraught with psychometric limitations and vulnerability to social desirability contamination (Krosnick, 1999). One measure, the Quick Discrimination Index (QDI; Ponterotto, Burkard, et al., 1995; Utsey & Ponterotto, 1999; Ponterotto, Potere, & Johansen, 2002), has received positive psychometric critiques by independent scholars in social psychology (Biernat & Crandall, 1999) and counseling psychology (Burkard et al., 2001). The QDI is a broader, less overt measure of multicultural tolerance and was designed to apply across racial groups; it provides a measure of openness to multicultural interaction both personally and professionally and a belief in equity across races and genders. High scores on the QDI would therefore represent components of the multicultural personality. For the sake of delimiting the review and providing some focus, we briefly summarize research incorporating the QDI.

High scores on the QDI, which represent an openness to interracial interaction and a commitment to racial and gender equity, have been correlated to positive attitudes toward gay men and higher stages of racial identity development (Driscoll & Hoffman, 1997), awareness of White privilege and institutional racism (Neville, Lilly, Duran, Lee, & Browne, 2000), lower levels of self-reported racism (Ponterotto, Burkard, et al., 1995), and higher levels of multicultural competence among counseling professionals (Ponterotto, Burkard, et al., 1995; Pope & Mueller, 2000).

Universal-Diverse Orientation

The universal-diverse orientation (UDO) is a construct introduced by Miville and colleagues (Miville et al., 1999; Miville, Rohrbacker, & Kim, 2004). Anchored in the influential existential writings of Vontress (1988, 1996), the construct of UDO reflects a level of multicultural awareness and an attitude of acceptance toward both differences and similarities among people. Higher UDO scores represent components of the multicultural personality. Specifically, Miville et al. (1999) define UDO as

> an attitude toward all other persons that is inclusive yet differentiating in that similarities and differences are both recognized and accepted; the shared experience of being human results in a sense of connectedness with people and is associated with a plurality or diversity of interactions with others. (p. 292)

Miville et al.'s (1999) UDO construct appears to extend earlier work on universal orientation (see Phillips & Ziller, 1997) that addressed the tendency toward multicultural tolerance vis-à-vis perceived similarities between the self and diverse others.

The UDO construct has been successfully operationalized through the Miville-Guzman Universality-Diversity Scale (Miville et al., 1999) and through a short-form version (Fuertes, Miville, Mohr, Sedlacek, & Gretchen, 2000). Collectively, findings indicate that individuals high in UDO have corresponding high levels of positive racial identity, healthy narcissism, empathy, feminist views, androgyny, multicultural-focused education, academic self-concept, interdependent self-construal (the person is connected, attentive, and responsive to others), self-efficacy, openness, positive thinking, and coping skills, and correspondingly low levels of dogmatism and homophobia (Fuertes, Sedlacek, Roger, & Mohr, 2000; Miville, Romans, Johnson, & Lone, 2004; Miville et al., 1999; Thompson, Brossart, Carlozzi, & Miville, 2002; Yeh & Arora, 2003).

An Expansionist Theory of Gender Roles

Writing in the *American Psychologist,* Barnett and Hyde (2001) introduced "an expansionist theory" of gender, work, and family. The rationale for the new model rests on their perception that extant theories of gender role identity are obsolete and unsupported by recent empirical literature. Barnett and Hyde's theory rests on four primary principles. First, multiple roles are, in general, beneficial to women and men as manifested in the quality-of-life indicators of mental health, physical heath, and relationship health. Second, the beneficial effects of multiple roles are both moderated or mediated by a number of factors, including the following, which are directly relevant to the present discussion: buffering, social support, success experiences, an expanded frame of reference, and similarity of experiences.

Buffering is a moderating variable through which success in one role (e.g., a man's rewarding family and child-care role) may offset negative stress in another (e.g., disempowerment at work). Barnett and Hyde (2001) integrate recent empirical findings supporting this buffering effect for both women and men. The multiple roles of men and women also increase their opportunities for social support, thus enhancing quality-of-life indicators. Furthermore, multiple roles widen the array of contexts in which success can be experienced, therefore enhancing levels of self-confidence and self-efficacy (see Bussey & Bandura, 1999). Barnett and Hyde (2001) emphasize that negative experiences in multiple contexts will have the opposite effect and contribute to a decreased quality of life.

According to Barnett and Hyde (2001), multiple roles facilitate the development of expanded frames of reference and increased self-complexity. Specifically, an individual in multiple roles interacting with role partners who have different viewpoints can lead "to an amplification of one's successes" (p. 788). Furthermore, higher self-complexity attenuates the impact of stressful life events. Finally, multiple roles promote a "similarity of experiences," which results in improved spousal communication and marital quality (Barnett & Hyde, 2001, p. 788).

Barnett and Hyde's (2001) third primary principle is that the benefits of multiple roles for men and women are moderated by the number of roles and the quality of roles. Specifically, these authors note that there is an upper limit to the number of roles one can play given the time demands of each. Too many roles will lead to overload and emotional and physical distress. Similarly, the quality of the roles is a greater predictor of life quality than the number of roles. Meaningful and esteem-enhancing experiences in two roles are more beneficial than four life roles that are only partially satisfying.

The fourth and final primary principle introduced by Barnett and Hyde (2001) is that gender differences in personality, workplace behavior, and family behavior are smaller than hypothesized in earlier gender role research. The authors review a number of recent studies supporting their hypothesis that gender differences are neither large nor immutable and that, therefore, the magnitude of male-female differences does not support highly differentiated life roles. One can see how Barnett and Hyde's (2001) expansionist gender role theory overlaps with the universal-diverse orientation described earlier. Furthermore, the UDO and multiple role benefits overlap with the multicultural personality, as presented earlier.

African-Centered Values and Mental Health

Our construct of the multicultural personality also draws on the rich tradition of African psychology. The origins of the patterned study of psychology and health can be traced back to the land in Africa known as Kemet, "Land of the Blacks." The Greeks would later call Kemet "Aegyptos" (Egypt). Perhaps the first psychologist (and philosopher and physician) in recorded human history is Imhotep, who lived around 2700 BCE (long before the Greek philosophers who influenced European and American psychology and medicine: Thales, 600 BCE, Plato, 430 BCE, and Aristotle, 390 BCE). We believe it accurate to designate Imhotep as the father of psychology (see Asante, 2000, for a thorough overview of Egyptian philosophy).

Modern-day American psychologists who are very influential in the study of African (or Black) psychology include Thomas Parham, Linda James Myers, Shawn Utsey, and James Jones, among others (see Jones, 1997, 2003; Myers, 1988, 1993; Parham, 2002; Utsey et al., 2001). It is the writing of these scholars that we rely on in providing this brief summary of African-centered perspectives on mental health.

Myers (1993) has outlined an Afrocentric optimal conceptual system anchored in a traditional African worldview. Central to Myers's work is "spirit," which

> refers to that permeating essence we come to know in an extrasensory fashion (i.e., via energy/consciousness/God). Within this spiritual/material ontology we lose the sense of individualized ego/mind, and experience the harmony of the collective identity of being one with the source of all good. (Myers, 1993, p. 12)

There is a communal emphasis in the African American perspective that proffers that one's sense of self and survival is derived from meaningful connections with others (physical and spiritual). In fact, all humans are interconnected in meaningful ways (Grills & Ajei, 2002).

The African-centered mental health perspective calls for African American students and clients to reclaim and realign with their spirit force, a force that had been stolen and misaligned as a result of pervasive and destructive racism. Through deep self-knowledge, a sense of spirit, and connections to self, family, community, and ancestors, one's spirit is liberated and realigned, and deep existential meaning and strong mental heath result (see Parham, 2002; Utsey et al., 2001).

Jones (2003) has presented an influential psychological theory of the African legacy in America. The centerpiece of this theory is the TRIOS model, which refers to time, rhythm, improvisation, "orality," and spirituality. TRIOS is conceptualized as a self-protective and self-enhancing model for African Americans who live in the context of racism. Similar to the work of Parham (2002) and Myers (1988, 1993), the TRIOS model is one of psychological liberation. Specifically, Jones (2003) notes that "TRIOS can be used instrumentally as a means of recovering certain forms of physical and psychological freedom, and that can frame the foundation of a humanized existence in a hostile environment" (p. 11). Now let's look more closely at the five components of the TRIOS model.

Time refers to personal perspectives on the past, present, and future. Jones (2003) notes that for early Africans, time was slow moving and practical, associated with specific tasks and behaviors. Jones believes that a present-past time orientation was central to early Africans (see also Grills & Ajei, 2002; Parham, 2002). *Rhythm* refers to patterns of behavior in time, movement, and flow. It serves as an internal response linking a person to her or his environment. Music and dance are examples of rhythm and a way of being in synch and connected to the environment (see Parham, 2002). *Improvisation* refers to a distinctive style of goal-directed creative problem solving (see also Nobles, 1986; Parham, 2002). *Orality* emphasizes the importance of language and spoken words, a preference for oral face-to-face communication, a personally expressive style, and a deep valuing of oral tradition and history (see also Grills & Ajei, 2002). Finally, *spirituality,* as emphasized earlier, refers to a connectedness to all things, a communal sharing of life forces, and the belief in a higher power and unknown forces that influence all living things (see also Cervantes & Parham, 2005; Myers, 1988, 1993; Parham, 2002).

At present there is not extensive research linking the African-centered worldview to correlates of psychological and physical health, but this is a growing and promising area for research. Jones (2003) has introduced a TRIOS scale to measure attitudes relative to the five TRIOS factors, and research on the instrument is in progress.

Expatriate Adjustment Literature

A good amount of research on the multicultural personality has emanated from the fields of personnel psychology and organizational psychology, in which the focus has been on assessing the adjustment of expatriates working in an international context. This research has looked at the topic of "multicultural effectiveness," defined as "success in the fields of professional effectiveness, personal adjustment and intercultural interactions" (Van Der Zee & Van Oudenhoven, 2000, p. 293).

After an extensive review of the expatriate literature, Van Der Zee and Van Oudenhoven (2000) identified seven factors that appeared consistently across studies relevant to the success of international assignees: cultural empathy, open-mindedness, emotional stability, orientation to action, adventurousness and curiosity, flexibility, and extraversion. Cultural empathy refers to the ability to project an interest in others and gather an accurate sense of the thoughts, feelings, and experiences of culturally different persons. Open-mindedness is reflected in unprejudiced attitudes toward members of another culture and toward that culture's possibly variant values and norms.

Emotional stability refers to the tendency to stay calm in stressful situations. More specifically, an emotionally stable person can effectively deal with stress, frustration, divergent political systems, social alienation, and interpersonal conflict. The fourth factor, orientation to action, points up that working effectively in a multicultural environment requires an action-oriented perspective. Individuals who are oriented toward action have clear goals and a tendency to seek results, and they take initiative to solve problems.

The fifth factor identified by Van Der Zee and Van Oudenhoven (2000) is adventurousness and curiosity, which they define as "a tendency to actively search and explore new situations and to regard them as a challenge" (p. 294). An international employee who displays this characteristic also has a high ability to tolerate ambiguity. Flexibility is the sixth component of the multiculturally effective person, and it is characterized by the ability to adjust and alternate behavior to adapt to the host culture, as well as the ability to learn quickly from work-related and interpersonal mistakes or miscues common in adopting to a new cultural environment. The final critical factor correlated to multicultural effectiveness across numerous studies is labeled extraversion by Van Der Zee and Van Oudenhoven (2000). Extraverted expatriates develop culture-relevant social skills, establish and maintain contacts, and actively participate in the host culture.

Van Der Zee and Van Oudenhoven (2000, 2001) developed the Multicultural Personality Questionnaire (MPQ) to capture empirically the seven factors deemed critical to intercultural effectiveness. After a series of factor analyses and an examination of the pattern of correlations among subscales, the authors settled on a factor solution that included five reliable and robust factors: cultural empathy, open-mindedness, emotional stability, flexibility (which combines the original flexibility and adventurousness items), and social initiative (which combines the original extraversion and orientation to action items).

Scores on the MPQ have correlated significantly with multicultural activities (e.g., travel, cross-cultural friendships); furthermore, in a hierarchical regression model, MPQ factor scores demonstrated significant incremental value over and above the big five personality factors (in the NEO Personality Inventory; Costa & McCrae, 1992) in predicting international orientation and international career aspirations. Additionally, higher scores on one or more of the five multicultural personality dispositions have been correlated to higher scores on measures of life satisfaction, quality of life, and physical and psychological health (see Ponterotto et al., 2005; Van der Zee & Van Oudenhoven, 2000, 2001; Van der Zee, Zaal, & Piekstra, 2003; Van Oudenhoven, Mol, & Van der Zee, 2003).

Chapter Summary

Table 7.3 summarizes the seven models reviewed in this article, and Figure 7.1 displays the interplay between the multicultural personality and broader conceptions of personality. Column 1 of Table 7.3 lists the model of focus, column 2 extracts key defining characteristics of the model as they relate to the "multicultural personality," and column 3 shows sample instruments that have been developed to test the constructs.

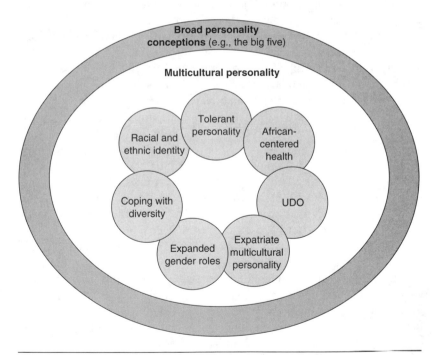

Figure 7.1   Interaction Between Broad Concepts of Personality and
                    Multicultural Personality

Note: UDO indicates universal-diverse orientation.

Table 7.3   Components of the Multicultural Personality

Model	Descriptors	Sample Research Instruments
Racial and ethnic identity theory (higher stages)	Connectedness to one's own racial or ethnic heritage, openness to people of other cultural groups, cognitively flexible, seeks opportunities to interact across cultures, aware of possible internalized racism and unearned privilege, commitment to social justice for all oppressed groups	Cross Racial Identity Scale (Cross & Vandiver, 2001), Helms's (1990) Black and White Racial Identity Attitude Scales
Coping with cultural diversity (integration strategy, balanced biculturalism)	Balances multiple roles, has bicultural and multicultural interaction and coping skills	Coping with Cultural Diversity Scale (Coleman et al., 2001)
Tolerant personality	Empathy skills with a broad spectrum of people; self-aware, introspective, and self-analytic; cognitively sophisticated; sense of humor	Quick Discrimination Index (Ponterotto, Potere, & Johansen, 2002)
Universal-diverse orientation	Appreciative of similarities and differences between self and others, sense of connectedness and shared experience with all people	Miville-Guzman Universality Diversity Scale (Miville et al., 1999) and Short Form version (Fuertes, Miville, et al., 2000)
Expansionist theory of gender roles	Transcends multiple roles, thus enhancing social support and interpersonal anchoring. Increased self-complexity, multiple roles promote similarity of experiences and enhanced empathy skills	Feminist Identity Composite (Fischer et al., 2000)
African-centered values and mental health	Collectivist and spiritual essence to human interaction and self-growth	Africentrism Scale (Grills & Longshore, 1996), TRIOS Scale (Jones, 2003)
Expatriate multicultural personality construct	Empathic, open-minded, emotionally stable, action oriented, adventurous, and curious	Multicultural Personality Questionnaire (Van der Zee & Van Oudenhoven, 2000)

The reader will note that there is overlap among the defining characteristics of each model as presented in column 2 of Table 7.3. This is to be expected, given their relationship to the broader multicultural personality construct as conceptualized by the present authors. The models in Table 7.3 vary along a continuum of complexity and breadth of coverage. The UDO model (Miville et al., 1999) is perhaps the most focused, with the expatriate model of the multicultural personality (Van der Zee & Van Oudenhoven, 2000) presenting the broadest and most complex coverage. The remainder of the models seem to fall somewhere between these two complexity anchors.

This chapter has integrated theory and research in multiple specialties within psychology in an effort to explore and define the construct of "multicultural personality." As a relatively new construct for psychology, this construct is in need of systematic validity testing. First, to further clarify the construct validity of the multicultural personality, the relationship among the seven components undergirding the construct (refer back to Table 7.3, column 1) must be tested. Second, when and if the construct is clarified and optimally operationalized, it needs to be correlated to both mediating and criterion variables. For example, Figure 7.2 presents a simple path diagram hypothesizing the relationship between the multicultural personality and select mediating and criterion variables (see alternate model presented in Ponterotto, Costa, & Werner-Lin, 2002). It is hoped that the path model, and this chapter in general, will stimulate increased research into effective adaptation and adjustment to an evolving, multicultural, multilingual society.

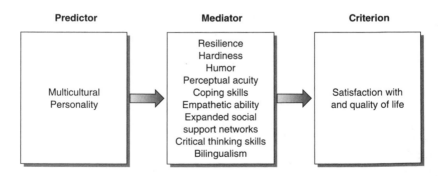

Predictor	Mediator	Criterion
Multicultural Personality	Resilience Hardiness Humor Perceptual acuity Coping skills Empathetic ability Expanded social support networks Critical thinking skills Bilingualism	Satisfaction with and quality of life

Figure 7.2   Relationship Between Multicultural Personality and Selected Variables

Note

1. Coleman et al. (2001), in presenting the construct of acculturation, rely on an old formulation of the construct (i.e., Stonequist, 1935), in which individuals who become acculturated to the host culture abandon their culture of origin. More recent formulations of acculturation show the process as bilinear: Immigrants or expatriates simultaneously negotiate a balance of both cultures along continuums (e.g., Cuellar, Arnold, & Maldonado, 1995). Therefore persons can be simultaneously low or high (or mixed) in commitment to both cultures (see a recent integrative review by Kim & Abreu, 2001).

Part III

Proactive Roles in Reducing Prejudice

With a firm understanding of the nature, prevalence, and manifestations of prejudice (Part I) and the theoretical anchors for prejudice prevention work (Part II), the reader may move to Part III of *Preventing Prejudice,* which examines critical parental and professional roles for reducing prejudice in children, adolescents, and adult peers. Here we focus on interventions and programs that can be implemented by counselors (Chapter 8), teachers (Chapter 9), and parents (Chapter 10). These individuals are the first adults to work with children in the area of cultural empathy, intellectual flexibility, and respect for those who differ in race, religion, ethnicity, gender, and sexual orientation. We all serve as critical role models for our youth, either directly or indirectly, and Part III highlights our responsibilities in this regard.

8

Counselor Roles in Prejudice Reduction and Race Relations

In Germany, they came first for the Communists, and I didn't speak up because I wasn't a Communist. Then they came for the Jews, and I didn't speak up because I wasn't a Jew. Then they came for the trade unionists, and I didn't speak up because I wasn't a trade unionist. Then they came for the Catholics, and I didn't speak up because I was a Protestant. Then they came for me, and by that time no one was left to speak up.

—Widely disseminated quote by Pastor Martin Niemoller (cited in Sue, 2003, p. 278)

Counselors and psychologists working in all settings—schools, universities, clinics, corporations, hospitals—have a social responsibility to help individuals understand themselves and appreciate others. Because of their intensive training in understanding people, communicating with them, and helping them change for the better, mental health professionals have a particular responsibility to work in the area of prejudice prevention and race relations (Grieger & Ponterotto, 1998). In this chapter, we review traditional roles of the counselor, as well as important roles for prejudice prevention work. The need for counselors to be proactive and work in prejudice prevention as well as remediation is stressed.

Traditional Roles of the Counselor

Three important roles have characterized the counseling psychology profession: the remedial, the preventive, and the educative and developmental (Gelso & Fretz, 2001). In remedial work, counselors assist individuals and groups in solving problems that have developed. Also included within remedial efforts is the critical role of the counselor in crisis intervention. In preventive work, counselors focus on assisting clients and students to anticipate, circumvent, and possibly forestall problems that may arise. Finally, in educative and developmental work, counselors guide students and clients to seek out and make the best of experiences that will facilitate personal growth.

Another helpful model for understanding counselors' roles in combating prejudice is the tripartite model of prevention anchored in community psychology, which includes primary, secondary, and tertiary levels. Primary prevention "refers to intentional programs that target groups of currently unaffected people for purposes of helping them to continue functioning in healthy ways, free from disturbance" (Coyne, 1987, p. 6). Therefore, teaching young children to appreciate and welcome cultural diversity would serve as an example of primary prevention. Secondary prevention refers to early detection of problems followed by immediate intervention. Thus, for example, an elementary school teacher might hear prejudicial remarks made by her or his fifth graders and decide that a unit on tolerance and multiculturalism is in order. Finally, tertiary prevention refers to intervention after serious problems have emerged. An example might be counselors called into a community or school where race-based physical violence has erupted. In summary, the goal of primary prevention is to prevent problems from developing, whereas the goal of secondary and tertiary prevention is to prevent the escalation or continuation of problems that have developed.

To a large degree, counselors working in the area of prejudice prevention and race relations have focused on remedial and crisis intervention efforts or on secondary and tertiary levels of prevention. That is, counselors are often called on to deal with racial tensions after they have developed. Schools, colleges, and communities have often relied on counseling professionals to diffuse racial animosities. Although the remedial role is a critical one for counselors, we believe that counselors need to be more involved in preventive, educative, and developmental aspects of prejudice reduction efforts. Here we elaborate on how counseling professionals can be more proactive in dealing with issues of prejudice and racism.

Counselor Skills and Prejudice Prevention Work

As noted at the start of this chapter, counselors are ideally trained to work in the area of race awareness and prejudice prevention. Counseling and other mental health professionals are highly skilled in interpersonal communication, conflict mediation, social influence mechanisms, behavior and attitude change, group process, and human development. Counselors and psychologists are also ethically and professionally mandated to receive cultural competence training (see American Psychological Association, 2003; Pack-Brown & Williams, 2003; Sue et al., 1998). This cadre of theoretical bases, concomitant skills, and ethical mandates equips counselors with important tools for studying, preventing, and combating prejudice in its many forms.

In Chapter 1, we affirmed that the seeds of prejudice are ethnocentrism, lack of meaningful intergroup contact, and the natural tendency to cognitively categorize information. Therefore, counselor prevention and education efforts need to focus, at least to some degree, on these three areas.

Reducing Ethnocentrism Through Racial and Ethnic Identity and Multicultural Personality Development

Part II of this book highlighted the critical role of racial and ethnic identity development and multicultural personality dispositions in enhancing one's quality of life in a multicultural environment. The first step for counselors in their efforts in this area is to work through their own ethnocentrism by examining their own levels of racial or ethnic identity and multicultural personality development. Obviously, counselors who are at lower stages of identity development and who have not developed multicultural personality dispositions will be ineffective in helping others acquire these strengths and attributes. Counselors who feel that they did not receive adequate multicultural training must take it upon themselves to seek continuing education and ongoing supervision in multicultural counseling. Continuing study can easily be acquired at conferences and in workshops that occur throughout the nation. Counselors should also be well grounded in the 34 specific multicultural counseling competencies endorsed by multiple divisions of both the American Counseling Association and the American Psychological Association (see Sue et al., 1998). These competencies are reprinted in Table 8.1.

We want to emphasize that multicultural development, in its various forms, is a lifelong task, and even seasoned multicultural counselors need to stay informed, update their training, and perform thorough self-examination on a regular basis.

There are a myriad of ways that counselors can promote racial and ethnic identity and multicultural personality development in clients and students of all ages. These include everyday role modeling, lectures, discussions, workshops, seminars, film and book discussions, and counseling itself. We discuss this further later in this chapter and provide demonstrations in Part IV of the text.

(Text continues on page 155)

Table 8.1   Multicultural Counseling Competencies

Dimension 1: Counselor Awareness of Own Assumptions, Values, and Biases

Attitudes and Beliefs

1. Have moved from being culturally unaware to being aware and sensitive to their own cultural heritage and to valuing and respecting differences.

2. Are aware of how their own cultural background and experiences, attitudes, values, and biases influence psychological processes.

3. Are able to recognize the limits of their competencies and expertise.

4. Are comfortable with differences that exist between themselves and clients in race, ethnicity, culture, and beliefs.

Knowledge

5. Have specific knowledge about their own racial and cultural heritage and how it personally and professionally affects their definitions and biases or normality-abnormality and the process of counseling.

6. Possess knowledge and understanding about how oppression, racism, discrimination, and stereotyping affect them personally and affect their work. This allows them to acknowledge their own racist attitudes, beliefs, and feelings. Although this standard applies to all groups, for White counselors it may mean that they understand how they may have directly or indirectly benefited from individual, institutional, and cultural racism (White identity development models).

7. Possess knowledge about their social impact on others. They are knowledgeable about communication style differences, how their style may clash with or facilitate the counseling process with minority clients, and how to anticipate the impact it may have on others.

Skills

8. Seek out educational, consultative, and training experiences to enrich their understanding and effectiveness in working with culturally different populations. Being able to recognize the limits of their competencies, they (a) seek consultation, (b) seek further training or education, (c) refer out to more qualified individuals or resources, or (d) engage in a combination of these.

9. Constantly seek to understand themselves as racial and cultural beings and actively seek a nonracist identity.

Dimension 2: Understanding the Worldview of the Culturally Different Client

Attitudes and Beliefs

10. Are aware of their negative emotional reactions toward other racial and ethnic groups and that these reactions may prove detrimental to their

---

clients in counseling. They are willing to contrast their own beliefs and attitudes with those of their culturally different clients in a nonjudgmental fashion.

11. Are aware of the stereotypes and preconceived notions that they may hold toward other racial and ethnic minority groups.

Knowledge

12. Possess specific knowledge and information about the particular group with which they are working. They are aware of the life experiences, cultural heritage, and historical background of their culturally different clients. This particular competency is strongly linked to the minority identity development models available in the literature.

13. Understand how race, culture, ethnicity, and so forth may affect personality formation, vocational choices, manifestation of psychological disorders, help-seeking behavior, and the appropriateness or inappropriateness of counseling approaches.

14. Understand and have knowledge about sociopolitical influences that impinge on the life of racial and ethnic minorities. Immigration issues, poverty, racism, stereotyping, and powerlessness all leave major scars that may influence the counseling process.

Skills

15. Should familiarize themselves with relevant research and the latest findings regarding mental health and mental disorders of various ethnic and racial groups. They should actively seek out educational experiences that enrich their knowledge, understanding, and cross-cultural skills.

16. Become actively involved with minority individuals outside the counseling setting (community events, social and political functions, celebrations, friendships, neighborhood groups, and so forth) so that their perspective of minorities is more than an academic or helping exercise.

Dimension 3: Developing Appropriate Intervention Strategies and Techniques

Attitudes and Beliefs

17. Respect clients' religious beliefs and values, spiritual beliefs and values, or both in regard to physical and mental functioning.

18. Respect indigenous helping practices and respect minority community intrinsic help-giving networks.

19. Value bilingualism and do not view another language as an impediment to counseling (monolingualism may be the culprit).

Knowledge

20. Have a clear and explicit knowledge and understanding of the generic characteristics of counseling and therapy (culture bound, class bound, and

(Continued)

Table 8.1 (Continued)

monolingual) and how they may clash with the cultural values of various minority groups.

21. Are aware of institutional barriers that prevent minorities from using mental health services.

22. Have knowledge of the potential biases in assessment instruments and use procedures and interpret findings keeping in mind the cultural and linguistic characteristics of clients.

23. Have knowledge of minority family structures, hierarchies, values, and beliefs. They are knowledgeable about the community characteristics and the resources in the community, as well as in the family.

24. Should be aware of relevant discriminatory practices at the social and community level that may be affecting the psychological welfare of the population being served.

25. Have knowledge of models of minority and majority identity and understand how these models relate to the counseling relationship and the counseling process.

Skills

26. Are able to engage in a variety of verbal and nonverbal helping responses. They are able to send and receive both verbal and nonverbal messages accurately and appropriately. They are not tied down to a single method or approach to helping but recognize that helping styles and approaches may be culture bound. When they sense that their helping style is limited and potentially inappropriate, they can anticipate and ameliorate its negative impact.

27. Are able to exercise institutional intervention skills on behalf of their clients. They can help clients determine whether a "problem" stems from racism or bias in others (the concept of healthy paranoia) so that clients do not inappropriately blame themselves.

28. Are not averse to seeking consultation with traditional healers or religious and spiritual leaders and practitioners in the treatment of culturally different clients when appropriate.

29. Take responsibility for interacting in the language requested by the client; this may mean appropriate referral to outside resources. A serious problem arises when the linguistic skills of the counselor do not match the language of the client. This being the case, counselors should (a) seek a translator with cultural knowledge and appropriate professional background or (b) refer to a knowledgeable and competent bilingual counselor.

30. Have training and expertise in the use of traditional assessment and testing instruments. They not only understand the technical aspects of the instruments but are also aware of the cultural limitations. This allows them to use test instruments for the welfare of diverse clients.

31. Should attend to as well as work to eliminate biases, prejudices, and discriminatory practices. They should be cognizant of sociopolitical contexts in conducting evaluations and providing interventions and should develop sensitivity to issues of oppression, sexism, and racism.

32. Take responsibility for educating their clients about the processes of psychological intervention such as goals, expectations, legal rights, and the counselor's orientation.

33. Can tailor their relationship-building strategies, intervention plans, and referral considerations to the particular stage of identity development of the client and take into account their own level of racial identity development.

34. Are able to engage in psychoeducational or systems intervention roles in addition to clinical roles. Although conventional counseling and clinical roles are valuable, other roles, such as the consultant, advocate, adviser, teacher, facilitator of indigenous healing, and so on, may prove more culturally appropriate.

SOURCE: Adapted from Sue, Arredondo, and McDavis (1992, pp. 482–483) and Sue et al. (1998, pp. 38–42); reprinted with the permission of the American Counseling Association and Sage Publications.

NOTE: This list represents the 34 specific multicultural counseling competencies necessary for counselors to be considered culturally skilled.

Promoting Meaningful Intergroup Contact

An important component of racial identity development and the multicultural personality is having interpersonal contact with people of diverse cultures. However, it is important to emphasize what kinds of contacts are most helpful. Integrated schools, corporations, and communities do not in and of themselves promote harmonious relationships. According to the well-researched *Contact Hypothesis* (Allport, 1979), a number of conditions must be satisfied if interethnic contact is to promote positive relationships. First, there must be equal status between individuals in the given context. In contrast, contact in a hierarchical system or between individuals who perceive one another as a threat or between people who equally lack status (poor Whites and poor Blacks) leads to increased prejudice (Allport, 1979).

Second, the contact must be substantial enough (not casual or superficial) to allow the interethnic dyad to disconfirm stereotypes about the respective groups. For example, interracial friendships may meet this second condition, whereas interracial work colleagues or neighbors may not if there is not meaningful contact and deep shared discussion. Third, the contact should revolve around necessary interdependence to achieve group goals, thus promoting cooperation. Fourth, the situation or context must include social norms that favor the respective groups equally, and those in authority positions must sanction (approve) the contact.

An example of a context where all of the conditions of the contact hypothesis are met might include an integrated athletic team in which the athletes have equal power; share a common goal (winning games); and have intimate contact in that they travel, study, train, hang out together, and share personal stories through mutual trust and respect, and in which team member contact and cooperation is encouraged by the coaches and administration. A similar example of facilitative contact hypothesis conditions can be found in some military units (see Pettigrew & Tropp, 2000).

There is a significant amount of research supporting the tenets of the contact hypothesis as well as related models. Social psychologists Thomas Pettigrew and Linda Tropp (2000), of the University of California at Santa Cruz, conducted a meta-analysis (a quantitative-based integrative review of research findings) of 203 separate intergroup contact studies that operationalized one or more components of the contact hypothesis. Findings of the meta-analysis overwhelmingly supported the tenets of the contact hypothesis and, furthermore, there appeared to be a generalization of findings beyond the small contact group to the larger groups being represented and even to other groups not represented in the contact simulation.

A strong line of related research conducted in both laboratory and field settings focuses on the "common ingroup identity model" (CIIM; Gaertner & Dovidio, 2000), which is an extension of the contact hypothesis that aims to demonstrate how intergroup contact reduces prejudice. In a nutshell, the CIIM model identifies situational, structural, and social factors that reduce bias "by changing *cognitive representations* of the memberships from two groups to one involving common ingroup membership, that is, by changing conceptions from 'us' and 'them' to a more inclusive 'we'" (Gaertner & Dovidio, 2000, p. 156). These authors emphasize that developing a shared common identity in no way detracts from individuals' own sense of positive racial identity and that when a "dual identity is compatible with the goals of the superordinate organization (e.g., a multicultural high school), it too can be an important mediator of lower levels of intergroup bias" (p. 158). Thus the findings from social psychology on dual identity are consistent with findings from counseling psychology on racial and ethnic identity development (refer back to Part II of this book): Higher stages of identity and biculturalism relate to lower prejudice.

Counselors, educators, administrators, corporate supervisors, and others can promote the conditions of the contact hypothesis or CIIM by incorporating cooperative learning and task activities to foster interethnic collaboration. When individuals share common problems, goals, and rewards with culturally diverse peers, positive interethnic feelings emerge. Furthermore, when individuals can hold on to a healthy sense of their own racial or ethnic identity and simultaneously develop a shared identity with fellow group or team members, intergroup harmony and goal progress ensues.

Cognitive Categorizations and
Transforming Negative Racial Attitudes

As we noted in Chapter 1, individuals in the 21st century are bombarded with stimuli from multiple sources—radio, television, the Internet, iPods, newsprint—and so forth. To absorb this incoming tidal wave of data, people naturally tend to chunk and categorize data into a reduced and more manageable number of categories. Unfortunately, data, perceptions, and attitudes about difference—race, ethnicity, gender, sexual orientation, and so forth—often get categorized in uninformed and stereotypical ways.

Counselors are highly skilled in helping clients and students transform misinformed or negative cognitions, beliefs, and attitudes into more accurate perceptions. In fact, whole schools of counseling and psychotherapy are based on changing maladaptive thinking patterns. Such therapeutic orientations include cognitive therapy, rational emotive therapy, and their many variants (for a review, see Corsini & Wedding, 2004). By changing maladaptive thinking patterns and distorted cognitions, counselors can also modify negative behavior and painful affect. Counselors have the ability to help people restructure their cognitions, which is known as cognitive restructuring. This skill is a powerful tool in the fight again prejudice and racism.

To combat the roots of prejudice effectively, prejudice prevention programs must address individuals' attitudes. It is critical to foster cognitive complexity and critical thinking in our children and students, starting at developmentally appropriate times. In our earlier definition of prejudice (refer back to Chapter 1), we noted both a belief and attitude component. Allport (1979) stresses that individual beliefs (e.g., "All Asian Americans are good at math and science") can be altered in the face of factual evidence but that the underlying attitude at the root of the erroneous belief is more resistant to change. An individual with prejudicial attitudes can quickly present another erroneous belief for each one that is refuted by factual evidence. Let's provide a couple of examples to make our point.

First we present a poignant example taken directly from Allport (1979) that focuses on anti-Jewish prejudice:

Mr. X: The trouble with the Jews is that they only take care of their own group.

Mr. Y: But the record of the Community Chest campaign shows that they give more generously, in proportion to their numbers, to the general charities of the community than do non-Jews.

Mr. X: That shows they are always trying to buy favor and intrude into Christian affairs. They think of nothing but money; that is why there are so many Jewish bankers.

Mr. Y: But a recent study shows that the percentage of Jews in the banking business is negligible, far smaller than the percentage of non-Jews.

Mr. X: That's just it; they don't go in for respectable business; they are only in the movie business or run nightclubs.

This example in the dialogue between Mr. X and Mr. Y highlights how resistant Mr. X's negative Jewish prejudice is to change. In the face of factual evidence, a refuted stereotyped belief is just replaced by another stereotype because the underlying attitude about Jews has not been altered. Let's now turn to another example. This dialogue involves two university students, Michelle and Gregory, who are discussing the men's basketball team at University X. The team is composed of roughly 85% African American players.

Gregory: I bet most University X athletes are failing out, particularly the guys on the basketball team.

Michelle: Actually, Gregory, I recently read an NCAA report that shows University X has an exceptionally good 4-year graduation rate among its athletes. And with regard to the men's basketball team, the *Chronicle of Higher Education* recently ranked the team 13th in the nation with regard to graduation success in Division I schools.

Gregory: Well maybe, but I bet they get assigned the easiest courses and take classes from professors who are "basketball junkies."

Michelle: It is interesting, Gregory; last night I ran into Dr. L., the academic dean, and I asked her about this topic. She said that University X athletes, regardless of their sport, are given no slack whatsoever in required academic work.

Gregory: Ah, perhaps! But I bet they have instant access to great tutors, and they probably get free computers.

Here again, we see how if there is an underlying negative attitude about male basketball players, even factual evidence that disputes stereotypes does little to alter the underlying prejudice. In designing prejudice prevention programs, counselors must work on modifying these stubborn, ingrained attitudes. Attitudes and prejudices develop early in a person's life, and they are thus quite immutable to change. To effectively reduce prejudice, counselors need to penetrate the attitudinal wall underlying the stereotypical belief. To do so necessitates cognitive restructuring, more experiential and affective interventions, and, most important, the facilitation of the contact hypothesis conditions discussed earlier.

Counselor Roles in Working With Prejudice

We believe that counselors and mental health professionals should be more involved in prejudice reduction training at all developmental levels. The specific roles they can play involve parent training, faculty and administrative consultation, group counseling and support, individual and family counseling, crisis intervention, and the counselor as activist. Although some of these roles are more relevant to a professional counselor's training (e.g., individual, family, and group counseling), other roles fall clearly within the training and work environments of educators (see Chapter 9) and administrators as well. Ideally, professionals from these diverse disciplines would work in an interdisciplinary fashion.

Parent Training

Katz (1987) stated that "although parents generally have been blamed for negative intergroup attitudes in their children, there has been remarkably little attempt to provide parents with methods of raising children with positive attitudes toward themselves and others" (p. 99). How much influence do parents have over their children's development of attitudes toward diverse groups? This is a critical question that we address more fully in Chapter 10. Suffice it to say at this point that young children, particularly, seek and desire the approval of their parents, and if parents feel a sense of "White superiority" or distrust of others, then on some level, this attitude base will influence young children.

There are hundreds of parent training programs throughout the Untied States, but very few of them focus on raising prejudice-free children. Counselors need to be more involved in working with parents on the topic of multicultural personality development. They might consider speaking to parent groups, as most schools already have formal mechanisms for school-parent dialogue. Again, counselors must instill in parents the attitude that cultural diversity in and of itself is rewarding and that students are academically and socially enriched by diversity.

Specifically, counselors can collaborate with teachers and administrators in the development of multicultural education programs. They can consult on the development of multilingual pamphlets focusing on cultural pluralism. In this regard, the innovative work of Casas, Furlong, and de Esparza (2003) with *fotonovelas* (bilingual storybooks) for children and their parents provides a model with great impact. It is important to note that parent training in multicultural appreciation should not be limited to preschool through high school. Most colleges and universities have parent orientation weekends, and cultural similarity and diversity issues should be a component of such programs. We strongly suggest that counselors, particularly White counselors, consult with minority elders in the community when designing parent education programs.

Faculty and Administration Consultants

All three of the authors of this book are active multicultural consultants to faculty and administrators at all levels of education. One lasting impression we have formed is that faculty and administrators, as well as schools themselves, are a microcosm of the larger society, and as such, school leaders and teachers representing the dominant White culture develop unconscious racial prejudices similar to those of the society at large. Gilbert Wrenn (1985) used the now famous term "culturally encapsulated" to describe White individuals, usually well intentioned, who harbor unconscious racial prejudices through normal societal socialization processes (refer back to Chapter 5 on White racial identity development).

Culturally competent counselors can serve as valuable consultants to faculty and administrators through multiple venues. First, they can be involved in continuing education programs for faculty and staff that deal with diverse prejudice prevention and multicultural personality development topics. Second, they can serve as consultants to individual faculty looking to infuse multicultural topics into their lesson plans and course syllabi. They can also advise faculty and administrators on culturally influenced aspects of the education process, such as cognitive and learning styles across and within cultures, the critical role of oral history for many subgroups, expected teacher-parent and teacher-student interpersonal interaction and communication styles, and so forth. It is important that counselors consult with multicultural and minority leaders in the schools, on campus, and in the local community before designing consultation programs.

Group Counseling and Support

Counselors are highly trained group facilitators, and, in some cases, group formats may be an ideal way to discuss and process issues of prejudice, tolerance, and race relations. Mixed racial groups provide an ideal route to cultural sharing, to hearing firsthand the effects of prejudice and discrimination on individual group members, and to establishing deep empathic understanding.

In terms of conflict resolution and crisis intervention, counselors may first work with same-race groups to allow for free and uninhibited cathartic expression. Allport (1979) noted that "in part, catharsis may be effective because one's irrational outburst shocks one's own conscious [mind]" (p. 498). At that point, interracial groups can be run. The decision of whether to facilitate same-race or interracial support groups will vary by the specific situation, the age of the clients, and the emotional intensity present in the school or institution. For example, we have often been called into high schools or college campuses to diffuse already established racial tensions (remediation rather than prevention), and at times the feelings of anger are so strong in some students or faculty that we first run same-race groups to listen carefully and validate people's anger or frustration, moving only eventually to running interracial groups to promote dialogue. Counselors should consult with campus and community minority leaders and one another before deciding on the specific group approach taken at a particular point in time.

Counselors can also serve as consultants and supervisors of peer counseling, support, and mediation programs focusing on cultural tolerance. School-age children are heavily influenced by peers, and a number of outstanding peer-helper programs have been established in schools throughout the country. Pedersen (2003) recently provided an excellent overview of successful peer group models.

Individual and Family Counseling

If prejudice is deeply embedded in one's personality, counseling and therapy may be required to modify attitudes. Two researchers who have done innovative work in this area are James Dobbins and Judith Skillings (Dobbins & Skillings, 2000, 2005; Skillings & Dobbins, 1991). These authors conceptualize the racism of White Americans as a mental health disorder that "manifests on the individual level based on institutional and cultural foundations" (Dobbins & Skillings, 2005, p. 443), and they see White racism

> as an addiction to power and privilege, whereby members of the dominant culture suffer from problems of denial in regard to the irrelevance they ascribe to others and the false entitlements that come to them by virtue of conferred dominance. Thus they lose touch with an accurate sense of themselves in context, possibly leading to manifestations of depression, anxiety, aggression, and distortions of information processing as well as the more obvious and salient acting-out that is stereotypically associated with the behavior of bigots. (Dobbins & Skillings, 2005, pp. 443–444)

Students involved in more active expressions of prejudice, for example discrimination and physical attacks (refer back to Chapter 1), may be required to see a counselor (in addition to undergoing established school and community or criminal policy sanctions) for a specified period of time as part of their remediation. Naturally, the counselor can expect either resistance or faked acquiescence in the initial stages of counseling;

nonetheless, a skilled counselor may assist such a client in understanding the consequences of his or her action and in developing empathy skills. Again, group counseling may be an option for students violating school policy and civil rights mandates. Given the growing body of conceptual and empirical knowledge on racial and ethnic identity development and multicultural personality development (refer back to Part II of this book), it appears that focusing on these areas would be beneficial to counseling generally and to multicultural education.

An option that we seldom find discussed in the literature is family counseling that focuses on prejudice awareness and prevention. If we can assume that the family, particularly parents and older siblings, plays a pivotal role in "teaching" prejudice to children, then family counseling may provide effective avenues for family attitude change and cognitive restructuring.

Crisis Intervention

Schools, colleges, and communities will always be faced with crises at various points in time, and counselors have the requisite cadre of skills to work in the critical area. Crisis intervention would fall in the remedial role of the counseling psychology model (Gelso & Fretz, 2001) and in the tertiary prevention role in the community psychology model (Coyne, 1987). A comprehensive and effective model of crisis intervention is the "integrated problem-solving model" (IPSM) developed by counseling psychologists John Westefeld and Carolyn Heckman-Stone (2003) from the University of Iowa. The IPSM model is different from most existing models of crisis intervention in that it was developed by counseling psychologists and has an emphasis on (a) exploring in detail various options and plans, (b) focusing on quickly establishing and maintaining rapport, (c) considering cultural context and empowerment, (d) focusing on client assets and strengths rather than weaknesses, and (e) carefully evaluating intervention outcome.

The 10 specific stages of the Westefeld and Heckman-Stone (2003) IPSM model are (1) establish and maintain rapport, (2) ensure safety, (3) assess client or student and begin processing trauma, (4) set goals, (5) generate options, (6) evaluate options, (7) select plan, (8) implement plan, (9) evaluate outcome, and (10) follow up. In their detailed presentation of the IPSM model, Westefeld and Heckman-Stone demonstrate its application with the trauma of sexual assault. We feel the model works well with a wide variety of crises involving prejudice and racism, such as hate crimes, whether they involve property damage, intimidation, assault, or other manifestations.

Activism and Social Justice

In addition to working with individuals, families, and small groups, counselors can affect society on a larger scale. Through their own professional activism and social justice activities, counselors and psychologists, along with their parent organizations, the American Counseling Association and the American Psychological Association and related professional organizations, can influence institutions on all levels, as well as both state and federal legislation. D'Andrea et al. (2001) stress the work of Dr. Martin Luther King, Jr., who discussed the intimate "links that exist between a nation's mental health, spiritual well-being, and genuine commitment to promote justice and democracy among all of its citizens" (p. 227). The goal of social justice is

> full and equal participation of all groups in a society that is mutually shaped to meet their needs. Social justice includes a vision of society in which the distribution of resources is equitable and all members are physically and psychologically safe and secure. (Bell, 1997, p. 3, cited in Vera & Speight, 2003, p. 259)

From this definition we can see that there can be no social justice in a racist society, as racism implies unequal distribution of resources and the lack of psychological and physical safety. Although counselors can promote social justice in their traditional one-on-one or small group activities, they need to take on a greater role in the fight for social justice. Such roles include advocate, consultant, facilitator of indigenous support systems, community organizer, and others (see Atkinson, Thompson, & Grant, 1993; Grieger, 1996; Lewis, Lewis, Daniels, & D'Andrea, 1998; Vera & Speight, 2003).

Two critical avenues for social justice intervention are with the media and government agencies. A powerful socializing factor confronting all children and parents is television and the Internet. With all the technical, scholarly, and pragmatic resources available to the American Counseling Association and the American Psychological Association, these organizations might consider television programs that facilitate cultural harmony for both children and adults. Naturally, such a far-reaching media strategy could be used to promote other social issues as well. Most children and adults do not work with counselors and psychologists in any significant capacity, and if we are to reach a majority of the population, we must access common communication channels.

Individual counselors and their umbrella organizations can be more involved in lobbying government for support of civil rights and affirmative action for racial and ethnic minorities, women, sexual orientation minorities, and other oppressed groups (see an excellent review in Atkinson & Hackett, 2004). Allport (1979) provides convincing evidence that presidential executive orders and Supreme Court decisions, if enforced, can serve as sharp tools in the battle against discrimination. It appears that although legislation is intended to control outward expressions of intolerance, such laws, over time, affect inner attitudes and feelings. Thus, for example, high schools with safe zones where antigay, sexist, or racist language will not be tolerated and in fact will be punished can, over time, influence once-biased students to come to believe in the equity of all groups and refrain from such prejudicial behavior outside the safe zones and outside the school. As we know, attitudes can affect behavior; Allport (1979) has shown that facilitated behavior can also affect underlying attitudes.

Chapter Summary

This chapter reviewed both traditional roles of the counselor and critical roles in the fight against prejudice and racism. We stressed that counselors should facilitate in their students and clients healthy racial and ethnic identities and multicultural personality development, increased intergroup communication under the conditions of Allport's (1979) contact hypothesis, and the transforming of negative racial attitudes. Important venues for counselors' work in the area of prejudice include parent training, faculty and administrator consultation, group counseling and support, individual and family counseling, crisis intervention, and social activism.

9

Teacher Roles in Prejudice Reduction

Given the increasing regularity with which acts of racism, including violent hate crimes, are being committed by persons under 20, the opportunity for early intervention is clearly best made available in our schools and classrooms. Teachers are uniquely positioned to facilitate the prosocial development of their students and thereby reduce the likelihood that they will become adults who are prejudiced and intolerant of others who are different. This chapter will outline and discuss several techniques that teachers can use in their efforts to prevent or reduce prejudice in students. In the first section, we discuss the *invitational method* proposed by Haberman (1994) that is intended to facilitate teachers' self-awareness with regard to their own prejudice. As part of this discussion, we introduce *Purkey's rule of five C's,* a conflict management model couched in invitational theory and incorporated by Haberman as the action component for reducing prejudice in students. Next, we present a number of critical thinking skills in which students may be trained. Teachers should encourage students to use these skills in examining their attitudes and behaviors. In addition, we suggest several curriculum-based interventions and instructional techniques that provide teachers with opportunities to incorporate prejudice prevention into their overall pedagogical thrust. Finally, we make recommendations for creating an environment free from prejudice and racism.

Teacher- and Student-Centered
Strategies for Reducing Prejudice

An Invitational Approach to Reducing Prejudice

Haberman (1994) proposed a model for reducing prejudice that calls on educators to face their own prejudice as a necessary precursor to assisting others in reducing prejudice and racism. He proposed a five-step model to assist teachers with this process. Here we outline and discuss Haberman's model, anticipating that teachers will find his techniques useful for reducing prejudice in their own schools and classrooms.

Analyzing Prejudices

Teachers are encouraged to examine the content of their own prejudices, specifically as it relates to their beliefs about the inferiority or superiority of others who are different (see Table 9.1, "Teacher Awareness"). By analyzing the exact nature of these prejudices, it is possible to discover how these beliefs hinder efforts to provide a quality education to all students. Haberman recommends a number of critical questions teachers may ask themselves to promote the thorough analysis of their own prejudice. For example, teachers are encouraged to ask themselves if they believe that one language is superior to another; if so, which one, and why? This same question is to be posed for gender, race, and religion. Most important, teachers should ask themselves if they hold lower expectations for those students they deem inferior or different. Most people will have difficulty admitting that they view a particular group as inferior, for to do so is socially unacceptable. However, even for those teachers who are unable to acknowledge their prejudice, there will be some benefit from an examination of the attitudes they hold toward others.

Seeking the Sources of Beliefs

Teachers and educators are advised to uncover the source of their attitudes and beliefs about the world (see Table 9.1, "Teacher Awareness"). This process entails examining the experiences, people, environments, and events that shaped their current thinking. Each individual has a worldview or lens from which he or she views the world and others in the world. Our worldview determines what we believe, what we value, our preferences, our dislikes, and how we interpret information from others in our environment. Consequently, when we hold faulty beliefs about others, we can usually trace them back to our earliest memories and the messages we received from our sources of socialization. Haberman (1994) recommends several questions that get at the sources of our beliefs. These questions are as follows:

Table 9.1   Teacher Multicultural Competencies

Teacher Awareness

1. I understand that becoming a multicultural teacher is a continuous process that all teachers must address. I personally have progressed in my development by moving from being less culturally aware to becoming more aware of and sensitive to my own cultural heritage and to valuing and respecting differences. I am aware of how my own cultural background and experiences, attitudes, values, and biases influence my views of education and social processes.

2. I am comfortable with differences that exist between students and myself in race, ethnicity, culture, gender, sexual orientation, beliefs, and other areas. Part of this process includes recognizing my preconceived notions, stereotypes, and negative emotional reactions toward historically oppressed groups (as well as other groups) and understanding how these reactions may prove detrimental to my students in their education and social development. I am willing to contrast my beliefs and attitudes with those of my culturally different students in a nonjudgmental fashion.

3. I possess knowledge and understanding about how oppression, racism, discrimination, and stereotyping affect me personally and in my work. In addition to recognizing how I am discriminated against based on my group memberships, I must acknowledge my own discriminatory attitudes, beliefs, and feelings about race, sexual orientation, class, gender, and so on. I understand how I may have experienced privilege in my own life and how I may have directly or indirectly benefited from individual, institutional, and cultural racism or sexism.

4. As a teacher, I am aware that I have the potential for tremendous social influence on my students, as well as their families. As an employee of the board of education, I recognize the education system and the school as being extremely powerful socializing agents. I also understand how this socializing process may act to oppress minorities.

5. I view diversity in my classroom as an asset to my students' educations, as well as my own. I understand that diversity benefits the learning of all the students in my classroom. I am aware of the need, and have the ability, to incorporate the multitude of human experiences into my lesson plans and course materials.

6. I am committed to becoming more socially active to fight oppression in my classroom, my school, my community, and my personal life.

Teacher Knowledge

1. I possess specific knowledge and information about the particular groups with which I am working. I am aware of the cultural heritages and historical backgrounds of my culturally different students. I understand that a superficial knowledge of other cultures may further my stereotyping, and therefore I seek an in-depth knowledge of other cultures, beliefs, values, and lifestyles.

(Continued)

Table 9.1 (Continued)

2. I understand how variables such as culture, race and ethnicity, sexual orientation, gender, and so forth may affect the educational processes (learning styles; educational choices; the identification of learning disorders; relationships with teachers, elders, and authority figures; help-seeking behavior; etc.). Furthermore, I am able to apply information from various racial, ethnic, gender, and sexual orientation identity development models to assist in my understanding of my relationships and communications with individual students. Educators can take such variables into account when determining a variety of teaching approaches.

3. I understand and have knowledge of sociopolitical influences that impinge on the life of minorities. Immigration issues, poverty, racism, stereotyping, institutional barriers, and powerlessness all leave major scars that may influence the education and social development process.

4. I value differences in communication styles, including bilingualism, and view them as assets to education. I recognize the challenges that students may face within our education system when English is not the native language. I encourage all my students to develop bilingual skills, and I work to improve my own bilingual competence.

5. I am aware that various forms of testing and assessment may be culture and class bound and therefore may place certain students at a disadvantage. I attempt to ameliorate the negative impact of standardized testing by creating varied forms of testing and evaluation within my classroom. Furthermore, I recognize the large-scale effects of biased assessment, such as overrepresentation of minorities in special education and lower level tracks.

6. I have knowledge and respect for minority family structures, hierarchies, values, and beliefs. I am knowledgeable about the community characteristics and the resources in the community as well as the family. I understand how this may affect my students and how I communicate with them and their families. I understand the great heterogeneity existing within cultural groups.

7. I understand that being a multicultural teacher must be pervasive through all facets of my professional work. It extends to all of my students, the faculty with whom I work, my lesson plans, my classroom environment, and so forth, with the goal of creating a more open place in which students from various backgrounds can thrive. On a personal level, I strive to develop a multicultural personality.

Teacher Skills

1. I am able to incorporate various teaching styles, course materials, and lesson plans that benefit all of my students. I understand the limitations of using only one instructional method and that teaching styles and approaches may be culture bound. When I am unable to provide appropriate instruction,

I take the appropriate steps, which may include consultation, supervision, and coteaching. Furthermore, I continuously seek to further my skills by seeking consultation, supervision, and continuing education.

2. I am able to implement various forms of assessment within my classroom, in ways that will allow students from various backgrounds to thrive in their education. I use both individualistic and collectivistic evaluation tools.

3. I attend to and work to eliminate biases, prejudices, and discriminatory practices within the education system. I am cognizant of sociopolitical contexts in conducting evaluations and providing education and am developing sensitivity to issues of oppression, sexism, elitism, and racism. I am a social activist on behalf of my students and their families.

4. I am able to engage in advocacy or systems intervention roles, in addition to my teaching role. Although the conventional teaching roles are valuable, other roles, such as consultant, advocate, adviser, facilitator (of indigenous education models), and so on, may prove more culturally appropriate.

5. I am able to create a multicultural environment in my classroom, both physically and emotionally. My students, their caregivers, and other faculty can see in my classroom setup, as well as my teaching methods, that various cultural, racial, ethnic, religious, gender, and other backgrounds are valued in my space.

6. I am a skilled communicator and respect the differences in communication styles between culturally different faculty members and myself. I take responsibility for communicating to my students who do not speak English (or speak limited English); this may mean appropriate use of outside resources.

7. I am able to communicate multiculturalism to my students. I understand the negative impact of discriminatory peer interactions, and I continuously promote appreciation of diversity in students' relations with each another.

SOURCE: Adapted from Ponterotto, Mendelsohn, and Belizaire (2003), with the permission of Sage Publications.

(a) Who are the sources of my ideas? (b) When did I learn these ideas? (c) How much of what I believe is based on myth or stereotypes? (d) Have any of my beliefs been substantiated by actual experience? (e) How much of what I believe is influenced by my race, culture, gender, religion, or social background? Seeking the source of one's own beliefs is seen as a valuable exercise in that it reduces the likelihood of teachers interacting with students from diverse racial, cultural, and social backgrounds through a lens tainted with unintentional (or intentional) prejudice.

Examining Benefits of Prejudice

Teachers should take inventory of the ways in which they benefit from their prejudices and the unearned privileges granted them by virtue of their group membership (e.g., race, gender, social class, sexual orientation). In addition, it is helpful to examine ways in which one is negatively affected by one's prejudices. For example, are opportunities for new social and cultural experiences lost due to an aversion to others who are different or considered inferior? Questions that facilitate the process of critically examining the benefits and liabilities of personal prejudice include the following: (a) What privileges do I or members of my group derive from prejudice? (b) Are these privileges earned or granted? (c) What are the liabilities related to my prejudices? A critical examination of the benefits one receives for one's membership in a privileged group (race, class, gender, etc.) is essential for preventing prejudice in others who share in the benefits of prejudice.

Considering the Effects of Prejudice

It is important for teachers to consider how their prejudice influences their beliefs about their role as educators, the ability of all students to learn, and the meaning of racial and cultural differences in relation to the classroom environment (again, see Table 9.1, "Teacher Awareness"). If, for instance, a teacher believes that some students are less able to learn because of their racial, cultural, or linguistic background, that teacher is likely to behave in ways that will perpetuate the failure of those students. Keep in mind that these messages of low expectations regarding the academic achievement of racially, culturally, and linguistically different students are subtle and often unintentional. To facilitate an examination of how one's prejudices may affect the academic experiences of students from diverse racial, cultural, and linguistic backgrounds, Haberman recommends the following questions: (a) What is my role as an educator? (b) Do I believe all students can learn? (c) Do my teaching style, curriculum, and student evaluations reflect the interest and diversity of the students in my class? Keep in mind that this list of questions is not exhaustive, and teachers are encouraged to include other pertinent self-evaluative questions for the purpose of considering the effects of their prejudice on others.

Planning to Eliminate Prejudices

According to Haberman (1994), it is essential that teachers go beyond examining and understanding prejudice to formulating an action plan for its elimination. He lists several possibilities for eliminating prejudices, including acknowledging them, unlearning them, counteracting them, and getting beyond them. Taking action against prejudice requires personal awareness, commitment, skill, and planning (see Table 9.1, "Teacher Skills"). In planning for the elimination of prejudice, teachers are advised to partner with parents, colleagues, supervisors, persons from the community, and civic organizations. Plans for eliminating prejudice should include long- and short-term goals, specific steps for reaching goals, and timeframes for achieving each step. Goals should be realistic and achievable within the allotted timeframe.

Rule of Five C's

The invitational model continues with the application of Purkey's (1992) rule of five C's. Purkey's rule of five C's provides the praxis by which the invitational model is effectively implemented toward reducing prejudice. Purkey's model is intended to build on the work begun in the application of Haberman's model for overcoming personal prejudice.

Perceiving Concern

This step requires teachers to establish personal concern about the impact of prejudice on the lives of their students. Teachers are invited to reflect on past behaviors that might have revealed prejudiced attitudes or beliefs regarding students from diverse backgrounds. As noted, examining one's prejudices involves some level of risk and may result in feelings of anxiety, guilt, and shame. These are all necessary emotions in overcoming personal prejudice and are usually short lived. Finally, having engaged in honest self-reflection regarding their own prejudice, teachers must commit to changing the undesirable behaviors.

Conferring With Oneself

Here teachers engage in a nonthreatening internal dialogue with themselves. During this process, the teacher is free to select positive or negative self-statements for the purpose of modifying his or her behavior. Note that although it is important to have an open and honest dialogue with oneself, and negative self-statements are permissible, the process should not result in devaluation or ridicule. According to Stanley (1991), self-talk should be rational, accurate, functional, task focused, and positive.

Consulting With Colleagues

When teachers encounter difficult situations related to their efforts to reduce personal prejudice, they are advised to seek peer consultation and support. In some instances, it may be necessary for the school administration to mandate a peer consultation. Mandated interventions are warranted when a teacher expresses racist beliefs or engages in discriminatory behavior toward students or colleagues and is unwilling to acknowledge his or her prejudice or accept responsibility for his or her actions (Reed, 1996). The peer consultant should confront the attitudes and behaviors of the offending teacher without being judgmental or insulting. The teacher should be allowed to express his or her feelings without interruption or rebuttal. During this process, the peer consultant facilitates a deeper exploration of the offending teacher's beliefs, values, and behaviors. More important, the teacher is given concrete strategies for changing his or her offensive attitudes and behaviors. The peer consultant should be a fellow teacher who is seen as fair and impartial. Only as a last resort should the school's administration be involved in the intervention process.

Confronting the Crisis

When all intervention efforts have failed and a teacher remains unable or unwilling to acknowledge his or her problematic behavior, the situation has become a crisis. Many times a crisis surfaces as a result of some outside source, such as a formal complaint by a student, parent, or colleague. Given the potential legal ramifications of a crisis, care should be taken to document the incidents leading up to the crisis, steps taken to resolve it, and recommendations made for corrective action on the part of the teacher. Moreover, at the crisis stage, the teacher is made aware of the potential consequences of his or her behavior and how his or her actions negatively affect his or her performance as an educator. Teachers who are committed to change but lack the knowledge, awareness, and skill necessary to increase their multicultural sensitivity should receive additional training by attending professional conferences and seminars on relevant topics.

Combating Prejudices

This fifth and final step requires a more drastic approach toward combating the personal prejudice of teachers. However, it is important to keep in mind that we are combating the *attitudes and behaviors* of the individual, not the individual. Reed (1996) reminds us that it is important to remember that people can change, given the proper opportunity, support, and resources. However, if a teacher, after having spent time and effort working the earlier steps of Purkey's five C's model (i.e., concern, conferring, consulting, and confronting), continues to resist attitudinal and behavioral change, more extreme measures may be required. Once the teacher is cognizant of the negative impact his or her attitudes and behaviors are having on his or her students and, in spite of this awareness, continues with the offensive behaviors, there is no other choice than to remove the teacher from all contact with students. Given the severity of this course of action, it is advisable to carefully document the process and consider termination only as a last resort.

Fostering Critical Thinking Skills in Reducing Prejudice in Students

Cognitively sophisticated children are less likely to become prejudiced adolescents and adults than are children who "think" simply and unquestioningly (Gabelko, 1988). Walsh (1988) has provided a valuable contribution to our topic through her integration of work on critical thinking (D'Angelo, 1971) in prejudice prevention. She presents 10 factors related to the best climate for and development of critical thinking (or cognitive sophistication; Gabelko, 1988) in children. Here we paraphrase and expand on Walsh's (1988) 10 points.

Climate of Respect and Trust

For students to challenge their own thinking and that of others, teachers must create an atmosphere of trust and support in the classroom and school setting. Children (and adults) are not likely to share personal thoughts and feelings if they fear being ridiculed. We suggest that teachers set ground rules (much the way counselors do in group counseling situations) for the discussion of prejudice and racism. Such ground rules would include requiring students to respect others' opinions, allowing students to finish their statements before being challenged, and so forth.

Community of Inquiry

Teachers and educators can help students learn to ask the right questions instead of focusing on getting the "right" answers. Furthermore, not all questions have one right answer; some may have multiple correct responses.

Allow Students to Be Heard

Students need to feel that their thoughts, opinions, and feelings matter. They need to be heard and listened to, just as the teacher or educator expects to be listened to. Students should be led to discuss and grapple with ideas and problems.

Self-Esteem and Success

Evidence points to a strong correlation between high self-esteem and lower levels of prejudice (Byrnes, 1988; Pate, 1988; Walsh, 1988). Teachers and educators should be encouraged to foster self-esteem development in children, adolescents, and adults. Building a healthy sense of racial identity contributes to this process, as does ensuring that students achieve success in the classroom.

Analyze Thinking

Walsh (1988) notes that "getting students to think about their thinking is extremely important" (p. 18). Students can be led to analyze their thought process in arriving at decisions that influence their beliefs about others and the world.

Intellectual Curiosity and Being Systematic

It is important that students be methodological when considering the complexity of human diversity. Walsh (1988) suggests that after identifying a topic, students should brainstorm and then plan carefully the questions of greatest importance to the topic.

Objectivity and Respect for Diverse Viewpoints

It is human nature to believe that your position or point of view is the "best" or only "correct" way of seeing the world. It is easy to see how this rigidity could facilitate prejudice and lower levels of racial and ethnic identity development. Using debates in which students take both sides of an issue could facilitate cognitive flexibility. As mentioned earlier, setting ground rules for discussion (e.g., allowing assertive expression but not aggression or name calling) serves as an important strategy for promoting the development of critical thinking skills.

Flexibility and Open-Mindedness

A challenge for teachers is to teach our students to be open-minded and flexible. Do our students make judgments without bias and prejudice? Can they consider a variety of beliefs and views equally legitimate, although different? Are they willing to change their beliefs or methods of inquiry to expand their view of the world and reality? These questions pose important challenges to professionals, given that it is human nature to cherish one's beliefs and opinions. Individuals with lower self-esteem may be particularly rigid, as the thought of being "wrong" can be ego threatening. Once again, we see the need to promote the development of healthy self-esteem in children and adolescents.

Decisiveness

Although it is important to consider alternate positions on an issue, it is equally important to reach and defend a conclusion when the evidence warrants. For example, we, the authors of *Preventing Prejudice* (2nd ed.), have reached the conclusion that prejudice and racism continue to be pervasive in U.S. society and abroad. Yes, we were flexible and did consider competing interpretations of recent events. For example, we explored the theory that prejudice is not a major problem but that it is perceived so simply because the media have been more persistent in its coverage. We reviewed research, we interviewed many people, and we ran countless focus and discussion groups. For us, the evidence is conclusive that racism is a major, worldwide problem. An important component of critical thinking is to be able to take a stand and present a position that is supported by the evidence.

Intellectual Honesty

It is easy to be swayed by emotional appeals for support of a given topic. Students can be taught to distinguish between appeals to reason and appeals to emotion. By analyzing reports (e.g., newspaper accounts, biographies, history) in terms of the language used (e.g., quality of reasoning, extent of rhetoric and emotionally laden language), adolescents and adults can become effective at assessing the credibility of sources.

Using Curricula and Instructional Techniques to Reduce Prejudice

Teachers have exceptional opportunities to reduce the degree to which students develop attitudes and behaviors that express prejudice and racism. Through the use of culturally appropriate curriculum and instructional materials, teachers can teach tolerance and appreciation for differences. A number of educators suggests that exposure to multicultural and ethnically diverse curricula reduces the likelihood that students will develop attitudes associated with prejudice and racism (Bigler, 1999; Pohan, 2000). Other educators have used intensive 6- to 8-week intervention programs aimed at countering the stereotypical information about racial and cultural groups that emanate from the media. What we advocate for is an experiential approach that, in addition to the previously mentioned culturally inclusive instructional materials and methods, requires students to conduct multicultural field assignments.

School-Based Prejudice Reduction Program

Curriculum of Inclusion

Educators have recommended a number of approaches to the development and implementation of a curriculum that promotes multicultural awareness and sensitivity. If prejudice results from our ignorance about persons who are different from us, a "curriculum of inclusion" can be used to expose students to multicultural material that reflects the diversity of our society (Bigler, 1999; Pohan, 2000). A curriculum of inclusion with the aim of facilitating prejudice reduction can be used to present counterstereotypic information about various racial and cultural groups (Bishop, 1992; Pohan, 2000). For example, given the negative stereotypes of African Americans found in the media, teachers might introduce some of the many historical or contemporary African American figures who have made substantial scientific, cultural, or artistic contributions to our society. Teachers should exercise caution with regard to selecting Black athletes and entertainers as celebratory figures so that they do not perpetuate the stereotype that the contributions of African Americans is limited to sports and entertainment. Others (Pedersen, 2004; Short & Carrington, 1991) have recommended the use of explicit curriculum-based lessons regarding prejudice, racism, and discrimination that include role-playing exercises intended to teach students how to recognize and confront prejudice and discrimination.

Culturally Appropriate Instruction

Teachers should seek out opportunities to infuse prejudice prevention and reduction strategies into their daily instructional activities (Hansman, Spencer, Grant, & Jackson, 1999). We recommend that teachers encourage increased intercultural contact by implementing cooperative learning methods that require students to work cooperatively across racial, cultural, ethnic, and gender boundaries. More important, the effectiveness of the cooperative learning method is predicated on the assumption of equal status among the participants (Singh, 1991). Therefore, teachers should construct learning tasks that encourage an atmosphere of interdependence whereby each student's contribution, regardless of race, ethnicity, or gender, is equally important to the successful outcome of the group's effort. The cooperative learning method can be used in a variety of educational settings and learning situations (see Slavin & Cooper, 1999). Teachers are encouraged to be creative in developing and implementing cooperative learning strategies.

Experiential Field Assignments

Multicultural scholars agree that the most effective learning tool when it comes to increasing multicultural awareness and sensitivity is experiential learning (Utsey, Gernat, & Bolden, 2002). Like the cooperative learning method, the experiential approach to prejudice prevention and reduction is grounded in the conceptual framework of the contact hypothesis (Cook, 1978). The contact hypothesis holds that prejudice toward members of an out-group is reduced through frequent and intimate contact with members from that out-group. Hence, experiential field assignments are intended to facilitate students' exposure to persons from diverse racial, ethnic, and cultural groups. We recommend that teachers structure assignments to demand increasing levels of intimacy between students and persons from the target cultural group. For example, the initial assignment might require students to visit a religious or cultural celebration of the target group. Next, students might be required to spend a day interacting with individuals from the target cultural group. Finally, students might be instructed to conduct an in-depth interview of a person from the target cultural group for the purpose of gathering information about similarities and differences between the student's own worldview and the worldview of the individual from the target cultural group. Again, teachers are encouraged to be creative in developing experiential learning opportunities and not to be limited by their own prejudices and fears.

Postprogram Evaluation

An important part of any intervention program is the evaluative component. How do we know when our efforts to reduce prejudice and discrimination are working? Postprogram evaluation is an effective method to use to determine which prejudice reduction strategies are having the greatest impact. Based on this feedback, we are able to adjust our focus, redirect resources, or eliminate ineffective components of the program. There are several means by which to conduct a postprogram evaluation. Formal methods include pre-post self-report paper-and-pencil measures, behavior checklists, and observer ratings. Informal methods for conducting postprogram evaluation include student feedback, parent interviews, and teacher journals.

Creating a Prejudice-Free Classroom and School Environment

Eliminate Unnecessary Distinctions

Classrooms are natural environments for the development and perpetuation of prejudice and discrimination. In most instances these forms of prejudice are not intentional but are based on pedagogical practices aimed at grouping students according to ability. Tracking and grouping by ability often result in de facto segregation in schools and classrooms. Teachers should understand that at times it may be in the interests of all students to create situations in which students can be challenged to their fullest potential. However, in many instances, grouping is unnecessary and avoidable. Even in cases wherein grouping by ability does not result in a disparate racial distribution, it creates a hierarchy grounded in inequality. Teachers are encouraged to seek alternatives to unnecessary grouping and to avoid labeling students in ways that assign value judgments (e.g., gifted, talented, challenged).

Uncover and Confront Unintentional Racism

The most insidious form of racism and prejudice is that which is subtle and unintentional (Ridley, 1995). Teachers are human, and like others who have been socialized in a race-conscious society in which prejudice and racism are rampant, they normally harbor prejudice and may exhibit unintentional racism. Moreover, having been socialized in a society in which some forms of prejudice have been normalized, it can be difficult to recognize when others are displaying attitudes and behaviors that marginalize some individuals because of their group membership. Teachers should actively seek to uncover subtle and unintentional forms of prejudice and racism as they exist in the school and classroom environment (Hansman et al., 1999). This task will become easier as teachers increase their multicultural awareness and engage the invitational approach to prejudice reduction as outlined earlier in this chapter.

Promote Equity and Justice

At every opportunity, teachers should promote equity and justice in an effort to create a safe learning environment in which their students can thrive (Hansman et al., 1999). By using some of the strategies outlined in the "Fostering Critical Thinking Skills" (e.g., trust and respect, community of inquiry, analyze thinking) section, teachers can promote a climate of fairness and equality in the classroom. Students should be encouraged to take these principles out into the community and practice them when away from school.

Work to Eliminate Institutional Racism

Institutional racism is prejudice and discrimination manifested in the policies and practices of institutions that operate (intentionally or unintentionally) to restrict the rights, mobility, access, or privileges of persons belonging to a subordinate social group (Jones, 1997). Eliminating this kind of intolerance is perhaps the most daunting task of all, as it relates to reducing prejudice and working to eliminate racism. However, the first step in this process requires teachers to examine how power and privilege operate in their schools and classrooms. Given that institutional racism is so insidious and omnipresent, efforts aimed at dismantling the barriers erected by this type of racism will require long-term, sustained activism (Reed, 1996). Teachers must be willing to commit to agitating, provoking, and facilitating institutional change, be able to develop strategies for change, and be active in supporting those who advocate change. Paulo Freire's (1970) *The Pedagogy of the Oppressed* is an excellent text for those interested in liberating their schools and classrooms from the insane asylum that is institutional racism.

Chapter Summary

This chapter discussed teacher roles in reducing and preventing prejudice in students. We outlined a number of techniques and strategies that have been developed by educators for the purpose of reducing prejudice among students. Our focus was on those techniques and strategies aimed at teacher self-awareness and action, developing critical thinking skills in students, infusing multicultural material into the curricula, use of innovative instructional strategies that provide opportunities for cooperative learning, and creating an environment free of prejudice and inequality. We recognize the important role that teachers play in the emotional, psychological, and social development of students and hope that this chapter will assist them with the very valuable contribution they make to our society.

10

Parent Roles in Prejudice Reduction

A day on the school bus. . . .
One day, a large White boy, about two or three years older, who often bullied us all, came and roughly pushed my sister and me into a corner of our seat because he wanted to sit in that space, across from his friends. I remember the fear and humiliation I felt for myself and for my sister. Yet, we did nothing but sit silently, squashed by his large size. An African American young girl, about his size, saw what happened, and came up, pushed his shoulder and said in a very loud and assertive voice, "What are you doing? You can't do that to them. They're sitting there, can't you see, and you're crowding. Move. Now!" He looked at her defiantly, and said, "This ain't your business." She glared back, and said, "It is now." The whole bus got quiet. She repeated in a low voice, "Move. Now." He got up and moved. The young Black girl went to her seat, came back, gave us each a piece of candy, and watched over us and others like us for the rest of the year.

—From the life story of Dr. Melba J. T. Vasquez (2001, p. 69),
pioneer in multicultural counseling and social justice

One of the most important thing parents can do for their children is to model empathy and ally behavior toward others. The opening quote, by Melba Vasquez (2001), captures well the impact that having an ally had on her and her sister as Mexican American children growing up in the

Southwest of the United States. In this chapter, we talk directly to parents about the critical role they play in fostering healthy racial and ethnic identity development and multicultural personality dispositions in their children. We begin the chapter by discussing the importance of addressing issues of prejudice with children. Then we move to a brief review of how and when children develop preferences for "in" or "out" groups. The chapter ends with specific steps and actions parents can take to promote tolerance, empathy, and multicultural personality development in their children.

Children and Prejudice

In Chapter 1 we discussed Allport's (1979) view that prejudice can develop rather easily. Negative racial prejudice does not, however, develop in a vacuum. For children and adolescents to develop racial prejudice, there must be either an implicit or explicit societal message of superiority or inferiority based on race. People have a need to be accepted by significant others, whether it is a child attempting to please his or her parents, a teenager wishing to be accepted by a peer group, or an adult looking for approval from a boss on the job. Given the pervasive nature of negative racial prejudice and modern racism (Sue, 2003), one must conclude that society is condoning racial inequality either directly, through continuing discrimination, or indirectly, through its refusal to alter the status quo.

When people ponder issues of prejudice, they do not usually think about children. After all, most acts of ethnoviolence are committed by young adults and late adolescents. However, as Aboud and Levy (2000) emphasized,

> While it is probably the case that the prejudice of children is not as hostile and intentionally hurtful as that of adolescents and adults, it is nonetheless harmful to the children who possess it, and even more so to those who are its targets. . . . prejudice and discrimination isolate children from others in a society that is becoming increasingly diverse. (p. 269)

Of further alarm is that in recent years, hate activity among children has increased and has become more violent. This trend was documented in a recent Southern Poverty Law Center intelligence report (Willoughby, 2003), which also noted that a number of racist organizations—such as Aryan Nations, the National Socialist Movement, Connecticut White Wolves, and the Agnostic Neo-Nazis—were increasing their recruitment of younger and younger members.

Although the average reader of this book is not likely to have contact with these racist organizations, one of the points we are making is that children are vulnerable to racist messages, and the seeds of tolerance and empathy are planted in the home, by parents. Clearly, parents have a great influence on children's attitude development. Children learn quickly what behaviors, attitudes, and values are likely to be met with either approval or disapproval from parents (refer back to the Hardiman model in Chapter 5). If dominant-group parents believe that the White race is superior or "better" than other races, then children are very likely to acquire (in a very short amount of time) a similar racial attitude.

As we pointed out in Chapter 8 when we discussed the critical roles of professional counselors in working with prejudice programming, parent training programs have not focused much attention on teaching tolerance in children (Sandhu & Aspy, 1997). However, childhood is a critical time for the development of a healthy racial or ethnic identity and for developing realistic and positive attitudes toward others who come from different racial, ethnic, and religious groups. Aboud and Levy (2000) assert that children and adolescents can undergo significant developmental change in emotional, social, and cognitive skills and that racial attitudes are malleable. Thus it is critical that parents talk with their children and adolescents about issues of race, prejudice, and racism.

Early Formation of Racial
Attitudes and Preferences

Children first come to recognize their racial or ethnic background when they are about 3 or 4 years old (Aboud, 1987; Katz, 1987). From this time until they are about 7 or 8, children demonstrate increasing competence in perceiving their similarity to their own group. Children at this point can accurately categorize different groups based on perceptual cues (e.g., language, race), they can label groups consistent with adult labels, and they understand the notion that race and ethnicity are unchangeable (Ponterotto, 1991).

The expressed racial and ethnic attitudes and preferences of children across age levels have been a topic of research interest for some time. White children 4 to 7 years old consistently express a same-group ethnic preference and hold negative or moderately negative attitudes toward other racial groups. This is the case regardless of the research methodology employed to access the children's preferences (Aboud, 1987). When they are around 8 years old, White children's same-group preference either levels off or declines until they are about 12. Furthermore, there is evidence that in adolescence and young adulthood, White females are less prejudiced than their male counterparts (Fishbein, 2002).

Speaking to White children's decline of same-group preferences around the age of 8, Aboud (1987) notes that this decline in expressed prejudice may be due to perceived social desirability pressure experienced by the children. By this age, children are fairly perceptive in picking up cues from the researcher, family, or society generally that prejudice is not a desirable trait (see also Baker & Fishbein, 1998).

In reviewing research on the racial attitudes and preferences of Black children 3 to 8 years old, Aboud (1987) found that 27% of samples expressed same-group preference and negative attitudes toward Whites. These negative attitudes often remained high until the children were about 12 years old. Sixteen percent of the respondents expressed White identity preference; however, these preferences were neutralized or became anti-White with increasing age. Finally, 57% of the Black children displayed no ethnic preference. In a more recent integrative review on the research regarding Black children's racial preferences, Fishbein (2002) found that Black children tended to express a White racial preference from the time they were about 4 to 6 years old, and then between the ages of 7 and 10, they exhibit Black preferences. However, when they are about 8 to 10, Black children's same-group preferences decline somewhat and their attitudes toward Whites become more neutral.

Although childhood research on racial and ethnic preferences provides some information on when and how children begin to express racial attitudes, it is important not to overinterpret the meaningfulness of such research. First, the results of later childhood (rather than early childhood) studies can vary depending on the methodology used, the amount of exposure children have to other racial and ethnic groups, and the prevalent socioeconomic conditions in the household and community (Phinney & Rotheram, 1987b). Second, racial attitude statements made by children may have different meanings than the same statements made by adults. Children's expressed attitudes are likely to be in part an artifact of the method used to elicit the attitudes, as well as of the developmental stage of the child (Ponterotto, 1991). Katz (1987) stated that "the expression of prejudice in young children may reflect the child's perceptual and cognitive limitations more than any stable, organized predisposition to act in a certain way" (p. 93).

Other limitations of early research on Black children's preferences for the same or the White racial group are eloquently discussed by William Cross (1991), whose work we featured in Chapter 4. For example, previous research that found some Black children preferring to play with White dolls tended to be interpreted from a "Black self-hate" framework. A more appropriate explanation for such findings is that Black children may be socialized to be bicultural or culturally flexible (see Chapter 7 on the multicultural personality), whereas White children (who consistently expressed a preference to play with White dolls) are socialized to be monocultural or culturally inflexible. Therefore, one must be careful not to overinterpret or misinterpret the meaning of research results on racial preferences in children (Cross, 1991; Phinney & Rotheram, 1987a).

How Do Parents, Peers, and Personality Influence Prejudice Levels in Children?

Although it makes intuitive sense that parents and peers can influence children's prejudice levels, what does the research say? In an excellent integrative review of such research, Fishbein (2002) provides some beginning answers to this question. Here we review Fishbein's findings in three areas: parental influences, peer influences, and personality dispositions.

Parental Influence

In a review of eight studies on parental influences on their children's prejudices, Fishbein concluded that parents only have a modest influence on the development of prejudice in their children. In the most recent study Fishbein (2002) reviewed, one he conducted with colleagues (O'Bryan, Fishbein, & Ritchey, 1999), the subjects were 15- and 17-year-old White Catholic school students. Overall, the authors found that there was a small but consistent effect where parents' level of prejudice matched their children's. Of interest, however, was that there were gender differences across parental influence based on the targets of the prejudice. Mothers, but not fathers, influenced their adolescent children's prejudice toward Black people, those infected with HIV/AIDS, and those considered fat. Fathers, on the other hand, but not mothers, influenced their adolescent children's gender sex-role stereotypes and prejudice toward gays and lesbians. It appears that fathers in the O'Bryan et al. (1999) study had a stronger commitment to and thus greater influence on children's sex-role identity and gay attitudes. Mothers, Fishbein hypothesizes, are more socialized in North American culture to be concerned about health and weight issues in their children and therefore were more influential in transmitting these attitude clusters to their children.

Fishbein (2002) concluded in his review of eight studies that White parents generally exert a consistent but small effect on their adolescent children's prejudice; however, for Black and White parents of 6- to 10-year-olds, the findings were mixed and inconsistent, and therefore no conclusions could be drawn. The collective findings of these eight studies may be somewhat surprising to the reader, given the general perception of parental influence on children's attitudes. It is important to keep in mind, however, that the number of studies was limited, they used different methodologies, and two of the eight studies were conducted outside of the United States (one in Canada and one in England). Specific and coordinated replication studies were not conducted, and as a result, we need to be cautious in drawing definitive conclusions from the results of these few studies.

Peer Influence

Fishbein (2002) reviewed three studies, two conducted in the United States and one in Canada, that examined the correlations (relationships) between friends' racial prejudice and sex-role stereotypes. The results may surprise you. Fishbein's (2002) rigorous integrative review found that "friends have essentially no influence on each others' prejudices" (p. 286). Fishbein provides four possible explanations for these findings. First, the youth in the studies were already low in prejudice levels, and there was not enough variance in or salience of prejudice scores to transmit to peers or to capture in quantitative analyses. Second, adolescents may not actively discuss issues of prejudice with one another, and thus there would be little opportunity to influence each other in this way. Third, it may be that adolescents assume peers have similar race and gender-role attitudes and simply do not challenge their assumptions. Fourth, adolescents may not be influenced by the race attitudes of peers, even if they feign attitude similarity to appear loyal to the peer group. Clearly more coordinated research with replication is needed to more fully understand how friends' prejudices influence one another. Furthermore, most of the research in this area has been quantitative in nature, and more in-depth qualitative studies (e.g., in-depth personal interviews, focus group analyses, participant observation) are in order.

Personality Differences

Personality can be defined as "a hierarchically organized pattern of relatively enduring internal dispositions and behavioral characteristics of the self that partially determine how an individual interacts in the environment" (Fishbein, 2002, p. 273). Personality can affect how and whether individuals accept or reject prejudices endemic to a particular society.

Fishbein (2002) reviews and integrates research in four areas of personality development: religiosity (see Altemeyer & Hunsberger, 1992; Batson & Burris, 1994), right-wing authoritarianism (see Altemeyer, 1996), social dominance orientation (see Sidanius & Pratto, 1999), and humanitarianism-egalitarianism (see Katz & Hass, 1988).

With regard to the relationship between religiosity and prejudice, Fishbein (2002) concludes that those adults who perceive religion as an internal *quest* for personal truths and truths about human nature and God have distinctly lower levels of prejudice. Those adults whom we define as *religious fundamentalists* are consistently higher in levels of prejudice. Altemeyer and Hunsberger (1992) define religious fundamentalism as

> the belief that there is one set of religious teachings that clearly contains the fundamental, basic, intrinsic, essential, inerrant truth about humanity and deity; that this essential truth is fundamentally opposed by forces of

evil which must be vigorously fought; that this truth must be followed today according to fundamental, unchangeable practices of the past; and that those who believe and follow these fundamental teachings have a special relationship with the deity. (p. 118)

Right-wing authoritarianism is manifested in three ways: *authoritarian submission,* characterized by those who believe people should submit to the perceived authority; *authoritarian aggression,* characterized by those willing to harm others if they sense the perceived authorities would condone such violence; and *conventionalism,* characterized by those persons who adhere strongly to social convention and norms of the culture. One can see that all three of these authoritarian versions are guided by extrinsic (outside the self) forces, somewhat like religious fundamentalism, rather than internal and personal values, which is more like the quest religious orientation just noted. In his review of the research, Fishbein (2002) concludes that persons scoring high in any of the three right-wing authoritarian versions "are prejudiced against almost any conceivable minority group in a culture" (p. 286). Although most of the personality research reviewed by Fishbein focused solely on adults and not on parent-children pairs, there was some indication of a moderate correlation between parents' levels of authoritarianism and those of their college-aged children.

Social dominance orientation refers to the belief that one's in-group (e.g., racial, religious, or gender group) should be superior to and dominant over out-groups (Fishbein, 2002). Research on social dominance is quite consistent and indicates that those scoring higher on scales measuring this construct also score higher on prejudice scales toward virtually all perceived out-groups. Those high in social dominance orientation are also against laws or programs aimed to empower the perceived out-groups (e.g., civil rights laws, affirmative action programs). Furthermore, males score higher than females in social dominance, and Whites score higher than Blacks.

Finally, studies examining the relationship between a humanitarian-egalitarian (the view that all persons are equal and deserve similar kindness and respect) personality trait and levels of prejudice have consistently found that those with high levels of this trait are correspondingly low in their levels of prejudice.

The results of the research on these four personality traits are more extensive and consistent than were found for the topics of peer and parental influence. One reason is that the personality research used adults (who are easier to sample than children, in terms of research procedures such as informed consent) and simply correlated diverse paper-and-pencil measures. Conducting research that matches parents with their children or peers with one another is more time consuming and costly; thus there are relatively few studies in this area.

What conclusions can be drawn, then, for parents? We believe that the empirical research on the relationship between personality traits and prejudice should lead parents to promote in their children (a) a quest type of spirituality that is guided by individual exploration of life's meaning and of God rather than an unquestioned digestion of an extrinsically defined, fundamentalist religious doctrine; (b) the development of a nonauthoritarian attitude and behavioral profile; (c) the development of a nondominant perspective on interpersonal and intergroup relationships; and (d) values of humanitarianism and egalitarianism. Note that these traits and values, emanating from research in social psychology, parallel closely the counseling psychology research reviewed in Part II of this book that promoted the development of higher levels of racial, ethnic, and "other" identities, as well as multicultural personality development.

What Parents Can Do to Promote Tolerance in Their Children

Although the specific correlational research on parental influence on children's prejudice is limited and identifies only a modest effect at best, we believe parents influence children in ways that may not have been captured in this limited pool of studies. Furthermore, Fishbein's (2002) review of the relationship between personality traits and prejudice indicated a strong and consistent relationship between variables in predicted directions. Also, we know that personality traits in children and adolescents are in part inherited (nature) and in part a function of the home and community environment (nurture) (Plomin & Caspi, 1999). Thus, considering the research reviewed in this chapter, along with the extensive corpus of research reviewed in Part II of this book on racial and ethnic identity and multicultural personality development, it makes sense to us that the sooner we can promote humanistic-egalitarian values and the multicultural personality in our children, the more likely they will be to develop as "multicultural citizens" (Banks, 2001).

Here we list seven steps parents can take to promote multicultural personality development in their children. The list is generated from an interpretation of the findings in Part II of this text (Chapters 4 through 7) and the present chapter.

1. Examine your own biases and prejudices. Bias development and subtle prejudices transcend education level, so whether you are a high school graduate or a Ph.D.-level scholar, you need to explore some of your own personal prejudices. Methods for self-examination include reading this book and others (see Chapter 16 for resources), viewing multicultural films, joining multicultural discussion groups, and talking about the topic with

friends of different races and religions. Also, personal and group counseling helps improve quality of life generally, and this avenue is also a safe place to discuss your values, attitudes, and biases with a highly trained professional. Keep in mind that counseling has a preventive and educational emphasis as well as a more traditionally therapeutic emphasis. We feel all people can benefit from professional counseling, even when they perceive that life is going very well.

2. Model multicultural reflection for your children. When our children see us pondering and reflecting on multicultural issues such as racism, homophobia, sexism, ageism, and so forth, it signals to them that such self-reflection is healthy. When children are old enough and when teachable moments arise (e.g., in response to a newscast, school incident, or newspaper article), it may be appropriate to share some of our own prejudices. You may want to talk about what prejudices you held at various points, how you think they developed, and how you came to understand them and break through the prejudicial beliefs.

3. Be proactive in initiating talks with your kids about racism and other topics. Calmly yet assertively confront prejudicial remarks when heard in the company of children—for example, remarks heard on television or remarks made by neighbors or other children.

4. Model multicultural friendships. In Chapter 1, we discussed the "illusion of integration" in the United States and noted that many of us live somewhat segregated lives. Most of our closest friends often come from the same racial or religious groups. Reflect on your closest circle of intimate friends. How many represent racial, ethnic, gender, or religious groups different from your own? If you primarily associate with people within your own race, make efforts to befriend culturally diverse persons. Let your children know how much you value, learn, and grow from talking with and being with others with different backgrounds and cultural worldviews.

5. To take number 4 further, encourage your children to associate with people from different cultures. Traveling, particularly abroad to countries where English is not the primary language, is a great culture-learning, empathy-enhancing tool. One of our own authors, Paul B. Pedersen, who in 2001 was identified as a "pioneer" in multicultural counseling, has spoken about the important effect travel had on him in the summer after his sophomore year in college. He stated,

> My journal from that summer typed out to 120 pages single spaced. We slept in German haystacks, Venetian gondolas, Swiss police stations, and on Italian beaches, but usually in Youth Hostels with other "sophomores" hitching around on the cheap. That summer was the least expensive tuition and the most powerful multicultural education I ever experienced. (Pedersen, 2001, p. 97)

If family, political, and economic conditions allow, encourage your children to study abroad in a supervised environment. If it is not too embarrassing for your son or daughter, visit them while they are living abroad, and have them teach you about the culture they are learning about. Demonstrate your enthusiasm for this new culture and language.

6. Create a physical home environment that honors various cultures. For example, display artwork and artifacts that represent the parents' cultures as well as others. For young children, read aloud books that teach about cultural pluralism and racial and ethnic pride; for adolescents, give them such books to read on their own. On family movie days, whether watching at home or in theaters, view films from different cultures and those with themes of diversity (see Chapter 16).

7. Try to model for your children the positive personality traits we reviewed in this chapter. These include a quest religious orientation, non-authoritarian and nondominant attitudes and behavior, and humanistic-egalitarian attitudes and behavior. Our children do observe the superficially small things we do and say on a daily basis, such as expressions of empathy, concern, and care for others. Examples include letting an automobile driver into your lane ahead of you during a traffic jam or letting someone with only a few items to purchase go ahead of you at the supermarket checkout counter.

Chapter Summary

This chapter has highlighted the important role parents can play in helping their children develop positive attitudes about themselves and about others who differ from them on some demographic such as race, ethnicity, or religion. We reviewed the developmental stages of race-based preferences in young children, and we examined some research studies investigating the relationship between children's prejudice levels and those of their parents and peers. We also reviewed the important relationship found between select personality traits and prejudice levels. The chapter ended with seven action steps parents can take to promote multicultural personality dispositions and higher levels of racial and ethnic identity development in their children.

Part IV

Practical Exercises for Multicultural Awareness and Prejudice Reduction

Part IV of *Preventing Prejudice* presents 16 time-tested exercises and activities that counselors, educators, supervisors, and managers can use with people to help promote intellectual maturity and flexibility, cultural empathy, multicultural understanding, and the highest levels of self-awareness. This section includes four chapters that focus, respectively, on exercises or interventions in elementary and middle schools (Chapter 11), high schools (Chapter 12), colleges and universities (Chapter 13), and the community at large. Facilitating, supervising, and processing these exercises takes high levels of skill and insight, and the solid foundation necessary to achieve these may be laid by background study of Parts I through III of this book.

An Orientation to Practical Exercises for Multicultural Awareness and Prejudice Reduction

In previous chapters, we have discussed the process of ethnic, racial, and cultural identity formation and the role of that identity in prejudice prevention. We know (Sherif & Sherif, 1953) that social influence is particularly strong when the facts are ambiguous and that this social influence is seen through both the formation of in-groups and intergroup friction or conflict.

Tajfel (1970) speaks of social identity and social differentiation growing out of a "we" versus a "they" orientation as a necessary but not sufficient condition for reducing intergroup conflict. We also know from Festinger (1954) that we develop our self-concept through social comparison with others. Prejudice, war, aggression, and discrimination persist as natural phenomena in society. Only when we come to understand this process more adequately can we hope to escape the potential destructive force that prejudice presents.

Multicultural training no longer assumes that every individual belongs to a single culture. Globalization has demonstrated that every individual belongs to many different cultures at the same time. Multicultural training has evolved from preparing people for exotic experiences to a recognition that every group and organization is multicultural. Training is no longer a one-time event but an ongoing process that recognizes the complex and dynamic interaction of cultures. Gudykunst, Guzley, and Hammer (1996) classify multicultural training approaches into "experiential approaches" and "didactic lectures" in one dimension and "culture-general" or "culture-specific" in another dimension. Cushner and Brislin (1997) review examples of all four combinations of multicultural training. The exercises in this book will be primarily experiential and culture-general.

Research on the contact hypothesis and social exchange theory has demonstrated the importance of creating favorable conditions for training or even intergroup contact, if these are to have a positive effect. Favorable conditions for the use of structured cultural contact do not happen spontaneously and require preparation. Some of the arguments favoring structured exercises are as follows:

1. There is research evidence that multicultural exercises and experiential learning will result in favorable outcomes through training.

2. Structured experiences provide learning opportunities for group leaders to use in developing their skills.

3. Structured experiences get a new group warmed up rapidly.

4. Structured experiences often require little preparation time.

5. Structured experiences provide unambiguous and nonthreatening roles to play in rehearsing contact.

6. Structured experiences can now be better matched to desired outcomes.

7. Defining or focusing objectives is easier in structured experiences than in the real world.

8. Structured experiences can contribute to research.

9. Structured experiences force leaders to clarify their objectives.

10. There are now many structured experiences from which to choose.

Not everyone favors the use of structured experiences for multicultural training. There are numerous arguments against structured experiences, such as the following:

1. Structured experiences are culture bound.

2. Some participants may be offended or embarrassed.

3. Some cultures do not value the confrontational style of some structured exercises.

4. Some participants may judge structured experiences as trivial game playing.

5. Some cultures do not value the high level of openness required for many structured exercises.

6. Some participants resent having to reveal their feelings.

7. Structured exercises presume direct rather than indirect communication.

8. Many cultures value silence and passive rather than active learning.

9. Participants from hierarchical cultures might be embarrassed by loss of status.

10. Structured exercises sometimes seem simplistic.

There is a considerable literature supporting the use of structured exercises for multicultural training when those experiences are managed carefully (Arthur & Achenbach, 2002; Merta, Wolfgang, & McNeil, 1993). Pedersen (2000a, 2000b) provides a series of exercises for developing multicultural awareness. Singelis (1998) provides a book of 28 exercises designed for use by teachers working outside the traditional classroom. Goldstein (2000) provides another excellent resource book for including the cultural perspective in a psychology curriculum. Hofstede, Pedersen, and Hofstede (2002) provide a book describing "synthetic cultures" and their usefulness in training. Brislin and Yoshida (1994) and Cushner and Brislin (1997) provide two helpful volumes of multicultural training modules. Critical incidents are widely used in multicultural training. Brislin, Cushner, Cherrie, and Young (1986) and Cushner and Brislin (1997) provide guidelines for the use of critical incidents in multicultural training. Tyson and Pedersen (2000) provide critical incidents in school counseling, and Pedersen (1995) compiled 350 critical incidents from students on the "Semester at Sea" voyage around the world.

These resources share an emphasis on the importance of creating a safe context for multicultural training exercises and providing adequate debriefing after the experience is concluded. The following guidelines suggest how the training might proceed.

1. Know the participants ahead of time with regard to motivation, attitudes, and special needs. A needs assessment might optimally be completed.

2. Prepare participants ahead of time so that they are not blindsided by the unexpected. Materials describing longer exercises might be handed out ahead of time.

3. Protect the confidentiality of participants.

4. Do not impose leaders' values on the participants.

5. Monitor the group carefully during the exercise to make sure the experience is constructive.

6. Help participants go beyond the superficial understanding of a training experience.

7. Be ready to terminate the experience prematurely if necessary.

8. Provide debriefing for all participants after the exercise to find out if the objectives were met.

9. Evaluate the training experience in a formal or informal way.

10. Follow up the training experience with individual members later.

Ivey, Pedersen, and Ivey (2001) describe group microskills that delineate the complex art of training and group leadership as a hierarchy of defined skills. These skills begin with attending and observation microskills, used to assess the training experience. Focusing, pacing, leading, and linking microskills provide a second stage of analysis. Questioning, encouraging paraphrasing, and summarizing describe a third level of expert facilitation. Influencing microskills focus on the constructive outcome of these training exercises. Reflection of meaning microskills help the leader guide participants toward identifying the meaning of what occurs in training. Conflict management microskills are useful in preventing a negative outcome and creating favorable conditions. Finally, each teacher, trainer, or leader will develop her or his own style from training in the ability to teach others.

As you use the following exercises, keep these guidelines in mind so the exercises will have a positive and constructive influence. Preventing prejudice is not a simple process. These exercises do not provide easy answers, and they may result in more questions if completed properly. The exercises do, however, provide a meaningful opportunity for both participants and leaders.

11

Race Relations in Elementary
and Middle Schools

Prejudice prevention in the schools is especially important because it is at this stage of life that youth and adolescents first learn to depend on their cognitive capabilities and are more comfortable with abstract reasoning. It is also at this stage that psychosocial tasks, such as peer affiliation, become more important.

Pedersen (2003) combines the intervention agenda with a training and education model. School students may be more attracted to the educational approach of "learning" about prejudice and prejudice prevention than to the medical model of "treatment." It is also important to focus on training for prejudice prevention that includes the faculty and staff, administrators, family, and community so that the whole context can be changed. Attempts to change the student in isolation from the rest of the school-community culture are apt to meet with limited success.

Although the terms *prejudice* and *discrimination* are often used interchangeably, they are in fact quite different (refer back to Chapter 1). Prejudice means having negative attitudes regarding particular groups. Discrimination means that negative actions have resulted from prejudiced attitudes, and those actions are directed against the victims of prejudice through stereotyping. Stereotyping occurs when all the people in a group are seen as the same, typically negative, fixed and unchanging image. The perception about other group members is most important here, not the actual strengths or weaknesses of those group members (Denmark, 1994). Prejudiced attitudes are thus linked to what people do, what people feel, and what people think. Prejudiced attitudes are learned, and therefore they can be unlearned.

When children enter elementary school, they take an important first step toward becoming responsible adults. Elementary school counselors help the students gain self-confidence as well as communication and social skills needed to demonstrate meaningful relationships with teachers and peers. Likewise, during the middle school period, students explore their academic and personal boundaries and learn the consequences of their choices. The pressures of social status, peer pressure, and adolescent impulsiveness make this a difficult task.

Hayes and Lewis (2002) describe the duties of a school counselor managing these problems as counseling, group and classroom guidance, consultation, and coordination. One might add "training" as a fifth professional duty of the school counselor. Tyson and Pedersen (2000) provide a book of critical incidents in school counseling that explore the problems faced by students in multicultural schools.

Elementary and middle school children are especially vulnerable to society's teachings about prejudice, but they are also highly receptive to a skilled approach to teaching the prevention of prejudice. The success of preventing prejudice will depend on a working relationship between the school, the family, and the community acting together to create the favorable conditions in which cultural contact is likely to have positive constructive outcomes. "For some, the schools are a last hope for societal integration; for others, they are a facile solution to the complex problem of reducing racism and increasing sociability among Whites and minority group members in America" (Khmelkov & Hallinan, 1999, p. 636).

The recent census data documents a rapid growth of Black, Hispanic, Asian, and American Indian populations, especially among school-aged youth, making all schools and organizations multicultural. In addition, there are large numbers of immigrant students in the schools whose rich cultural heritage is often trivialized and overlooked as an educational resource (Bemak & Chung, 2003). It is highly likely that each student will be in frequent contact with persons from other cultures and, if that contact occurs under favorable conditions, positive consequences will result. "Students who have consistent contact over their school careers with members of other racial groups, in a climate supportive of diversity, and who learn through these contacts to respect and like individuals from different backgrounds are likely to carry these attitudes into adult life" (Khmelkov & Hallinan, 1999, p. 641). For students who may still be educated in racially or culturally homogenous schools (e.g., all-White or -Black schools), exposure to cultural diversity and prejudice prevention programming is equally important, as students are likely to continue their education and move on to work and careers in different communities.

Carey and Boscardin (2003) review the measures of academic and interpersonal effectiveness for elementary schools. The more effective schools had high academic expectations of students, an orderly and nonoppressive atmosphere, clear instructional priorities, and frequent monitoring of all students' progress. The key to success is the energetic cooperation of school personnel with students and with the students' families in a combined effort. McKenna, Roberts, and Woodfin (2003) focus on the importance of family-school partnerships in children's and community development. The school counselor is in a unique position to provide a link between the school-based formal and informal curriculum and the students' home and family context.

Cooperative learning programs with a purposive emphasis on preventing prejudice provide one example of a successful intervention (Slavin & Cooper, 1999). Bilingual and dual-language learning programs provide another example of success (Genesee & Gandara, 1999). Successful intervention is not quick or easy, and "previous attempts to reduce children's racial and ethnic stereotyping using multicultural curriculum programs have been relatively ineffective" (Bigler, 1999, p. 701). Television and the public media demonstrate the pervasive influence of prejudice around us that subverts our attempts to prevent prejudice. Teacher-led discussions about prejudice, explicit parental nurturance against prejudice, and purposive peer-group activities must be coordinated to provide a force for prejudice prevention.

Elementary and middle school students are at a developmental stage during which they are constructing their own identities. Helms (2003) discusses the importance of racial identity in the school environment. When we teach prejudice prevention, we are really teaching people about their own identity in a context of many others whose identities are different. Students need to be aware of their own developing identity, both as they see it and as others around them see it. One way to teach the importance of real and perceived identity is with a *label* exercise.

Exercise 1: The Label Game

Objective

Everyone who sees us, from those who pass us on the street to our best friends, probably has his or her own label for us, based on his or her personal perception of our identity. In this exercise, students use feedback from others to discover how they have been labeled and gain some appreciation of the great diversity of both labels and perceptions.

Procedure

1. Prepare a variety of *positive* labels, using adjectives such as Friendly, Helpful, Kind, Smart, Generous, Loving, and others on sticky address labels, with enough labels for all students.

2. Attach one label to the forehead of each student as the student comes into the room. If it would be a cultural taboo to attach the label to the student's forehead, then attach it to the student's back so that the student cannot read it.

3. Allow the students to mingle and interact on a topic of interest to them, or set up a "cocktail party" scene with no structure.

4. Students will be instructed to treat every other individual as though the label that individual is wearing were actually true, thereby saying and doing the things they would say or do to or with that kind of person. It might be useful to divide larger groups into smaller clusters of six or eight students for more thorough interaction.

5. No student is allowed to ask another student to tell what the label says, and students are discouraged from looking at their own reflections to read their label.

6. After 10 minutes of interacting, students are instructed to *first* guess what the label says and *then* remove the label to see if their guess was accurate.

Debriefing

In the discussion following this exercise, students are encouraged to disclose how they decoded feedback from others to discover what was on their labels.

Students are also encouraged to discuss how they felt about being labeled and treated as though the label were accurate. The concepts of stereotyping, prejudice, and communication barriers can be introduced, using examples from the exercise.

Learning Principle

We all wear labels that are perceived by others around us who treat us as though the labels were true. By increasing awareness, we can become more aware of the labels that others perceive on each of us.

If it is not possible to get everyone to agree with one another and work together as a group, the next best outcome is to help students to see the great diversity around them. If you cannot get the students to see how we are all the same—at least on some things—the next best thing is to show them how we are all different. The *least favorable* and *most destructive* outcome is when the group divides itself into a two-sided polarity of "us" and "them" in which each side is against the other. This polarization is like a "war" setting and is to be avoided. The notion of diversity must be taught in such a way that the students can see that there are real differences, that being different is not always bad, and that differences are always important to a person's identity. It is particularly hard to teach diversity to younger children. Exercise 2 suggests one way in which this construct can be taught.

Exercise 2: Patterns of Difference

Objective

We belong to many different groups that function in ways similar to cultures and define our multicultural identity. This exercise was used to teach primary school children the many groups to which they belong, including nationality and ethnicity, which define them as individuals.

Procedure

1. Assemble a group of elementary school students in a large room in which all furniture, tables, chairs, and so on, have been moved to the side or the corner of the room. (The exercise may create noise, so it should be scheduled at a time not disruptive to other classes.)

2. The exercise may begin with a story or talk about prejudice, discrimination, or problems that persons who are "different" may have experienced.

3. Assemble the students into a cluster in the center of the room to await instructions.

4. The teacher or leader will have drawn up a list ahead of time of contrasting characteristics that are likely to divide the group. These may include, for example, such neutral characteristics as black shoes and brown shoes, those wearing red and those not wearing red, those with a penny in their pocket and those without a penny in their pocket.

5. The teacher reads out the instructions, saying, "All those with [name the characteristic] go to this side of the room, and all those without [name the characteristic] go to the other side of the room." In this way, two "teams" will be formed, one team with the named characteristic and one team with a contrasting characteristic. The team whose members identify their similarity first and get all the team members together on their side of the room first "wins" that set.

6. Then the total group reassembles in the middle of the room, and a second set begins, with the teacher reading off a new set of contrasting characteristics that will divide the group differently.

7. After the students have become more familiar with the exercise, the teacher might want to move toward more personal characteristics, such as hair color, height, gender, nationality, and ethnicity.

Debriefing

After about 20 minutes, the teacher could begin a group discussion on how racial differences are just one of the very significant components of our individuality that define us but should not be seen in isolation. The discussion might include the role of competition—winning and losing—in the exercise where the students were on different teams in each set and not rigidly locked into the same group all the time. The students might be encouraged to talk about how they felt about being different from some students and similar to others.

Learning Principle

You will always be similar to some people and different from others, but, depending on the situation, the group to which you belong might change.

Sometimes it is hard for younger students to talk about their culture because that type of discussion is too abstract for their age group. Although differences do matter—in the sense that each set has a winner and a loser— they do not always have to set the same groups against one another. No matter how different the person or group is, there will be similarities. No matter how similar the person or group is, there will be differences. Exercise 3 is an attempt to look at the symbols of our culture.

Exercise 3: Symbols of Our Culture

Objective

Sometimes we become so dependent on abstract verbal jargon about prejudice and racial identity that we lose touch with the less cognitive and more emotional symbols of our cultures. By asking persons to draw the symbols of their culture in a picture that may include anything *but* words, participants are encouraged to explore the less articulate parts of their racial identity.

Procedure

1. Students are assembled in a room with sufficient table space so that each one can spread out a large sheet of paper. Large sheets of poster paper work well, if there is sufficient space in which to spread them out.

2. Students are provided with different-colored crayons or felt marking pens with which to draw.

3. Students are instructed to draw symbols, a picture story, lines, designs, or scribbles on the paper that symbolize their own personal ethnic, racial, or cultural identity.

4. Students are instructed *not* to draw or write words on the paper.

5. Students are allowed to draw whatever they want to (except words) for about 10 to 20 minutes.

6. After drawing the symbols of their culture, students are assembled into small groups of about five persons.

7. Each student is asked to explain his or her drawing and how that drawing symbolizes significant parts of the student's ethnic, racial, or cultural identity.

8. After each group of five students has had about half an hour for members to present and explain the symbols of their culture, the total group of participants is assembled for a discussion.

Debriefing

The teacher may want the students to discuss which symbols appeared most often and least often in the drawings, which symbols were the strongest and most powerful, which symbols indicated a positive experience, and which symbols indicated a negative experience. The teacher might want to ask whether any of the symbols were hard to explain in words and point out how words are not always adequate to express what we feel about our ethnic, racial, or cultural identity. Allowing the drawings to hang in the room might be useful in promoting the continuance of discussion about these symbols among the students.

Learning Principle

Symbols of our ethnic, racial, and cultural identity may be difficult to discuss in words, but they may nonetheless be very important to the individual.

Exercise 4: One Situation But Many Interpretations

Objective

Different students will have different interpretations of the same picture. We do not all see the same situation in the same way. Our cultures and experiences have taught us to see things differently. What seems very clear to one child will be very unclear to another. However, we can learn to see the picture through the eyes of others and accept that our interpretation of that same event may not be the only possible interpretation.

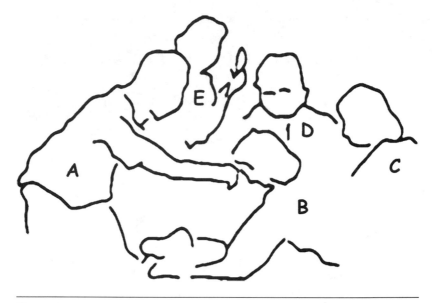

Figure 11.1   Picture for Exercise 4

Procedure

The teacher shows the picture (Figure 11.1) to the group and asks the group members to shout out what they see happening in this ambiguous drawing in as much detail as possible. Teachers should also ask the following:

Who are these people?

What is each person doing?

What objects are shown in the drawing?

What are the clues that helped you identify what is happening?

The teacher can then discuss the meaning of similarities and differences in students' descriptions.

Debriefing

Students should be encouraged to come up with as many different interpretations as possible. Individual students can be asked to explain those cues in the picture that led them to make one interpretation rather than another. Individual students might want to tell a "story" about what is happening in the picture as they see it. How easy is it for the students to change their interpretation after they have heard from others?

Learning Principle

Perception is more important than reality in our decision-making processes because we behave toward others based on how we see them and not necessarily how those people really are.

Chapter Summary

We have examined four different exercises designed to increase awareness of ethnic, racial, and cultural identity in elementary and middle school students. These exercises are designed to help students become more aware of how prejudice happens. Prejudice happens when the normal process of comparing yourself to others gets out of control.

Although elementary and middle school students are especially at risk for learning prejudiced behaviors, they are also receptive to learning how to prevent prejudice, if favorable conditions can be created for those positive outcomes. There is considerable research regarding how those favorable conditions can be constructed, both within the curriculum and in extracurricular activities. The exercises given here provide opportunities for students to examine their own prejudices and make the appropriate changes.

Long-term change, however, will require the continued efforts of teachers, administrators, parents, and the community context in which the student lives. Given that teachers typically carry more than a full load of classes and each school counselor typically serves 400 or more students, the importance of sharing responsibility with parents and others is essential. By consulting with colleagues and culturally informed community helpers who understand diverse students' sociocultural backgrounds, counselors and educators can enrich the curriculum and identify role models for culturally diverse students (Myrick, 1997).

12

Race Relations in High School

Schools can contribute to prejudice prevention by implementing policies and practices that create a climate in which racial stereotyping and prejudiced behavior does not occur and interracial cooperation and friendship are encouraged. Careful attention to the curriculum and to students' extracurricular activities is necessary if the favorable conditions required for racial harmony are to be established.

The vast majority of research on intergroup relations in schools is now 15 to 20 years old and focuses mostly on improving relations between Whites and Blacks (Schofield, 1995). This research gap is particularly true with regard to identifying successful interventions (Bigler, 1999). We do know that racial intolerance exists in schools and that much racial intolerance is a carryover of racist attitudes in the family and community. The combination of prejudice with violence in the media and particularly on television has also had a strong influence on the attitudes of secondary school students (Graves, 1999).

With the increase of violence in secondary schools we are seeing an increase in prejudice and discrimination in schools (Fontes, 2003). It is essential for the school to address this trend directly and explicitly. It is essential for parents to not be afraid of addressing this trend directly and explicitly as well. Parents need to know what their children are learning. Students learn more from one another in the school than they learn from the teachers in constructing a shared cultural model or group culture. This school culture shapes social relationships, establishes rules for what can and cannot be done, provides rewards, and distributes punishments.

The literature is clear about a need to address issues of prejudice explicitly and directly, both in the home and in the school. Some parents and teachers avoid addressing issues of prejudice out of fear that they might contribute to an increase in prejudiced behavior. It can easily become a taboo topic. It is important, therefore, to recognize the generic importance of including issues of racism and prejudice in the curriculum, as it contributes to the student's growth generally.

> The breadth of these variables suggests two key things. First, interventions aimed at attacking the processing strategies and ideologies that contribute to greater levels of prejudice may have an added benefit of helping people become more open-minded about themselves and individual others. Second, targeting broad ideologies and information processing strategies may represent a particularly compelling approach to reducing stereotyping given that interventions aimed at persuading individuals that stereotypes are inaccurate on a trait-by-trait, group-by-group basis have met with limited success with both children and adults. (Levy, 1999, p. 762)

"The American School Counselor Association has targeted the need to provide appropriate multicultural services in schools to promote maximum development since 1988 (ASCA, 1993). In 1992, the association declared a competency in multicultural counseling to be an ethical obligation of school counselors" (Pedersen, 2003, pp. 190–191). This mandate targets the conventional school counselor functions, such as pedagogical services, referral services, accountability services, family consultation, career development and placement, and assessment services, and it applies equally well to the use of training in schools.

Violence in schools has been in the headlines, especially since the late 1990s.

> Some believe that the seemingly random nature of these shootings and the fact that they largely occurred in rural and suburban schools with majority White student bodies indicates that school violence has reached new heights. Others resent the increased national attention paid to these middle-class White victims, claiming that school shootings had already cost the lives of hundreds of children in poor and minority school districts, with scant media or political attention. (Fontes, 2003, p. 212)

Prejudice and conflict tend to go together in school violence, and there is evidence that training helps students manage conflict more effectively. Strategies used by untrained students include withdrawal, suppression, force and coercion, intimidation, and win-lose negotiations. Strategies used by trained students include facing the conflict, learning a set of procedures, applying those procedures, transferring those conflict resolution procedures to nonschool conflicts, problem solving, and integrative negotiations for win-win outcomes (D. W. Johnson & R. T. Johnson, 1996).

We know that students with problems are more likely to go first to peers for help than to counselors or parents. Peer pressure is powerful among school-aged youth, and it makes sense to involve students in preventing prejudice and violence in schools. The Peer Helpers Association (Pedersen, 2003) is a national network focused on mediation. Their guidelines for establishing a program apply equally well to the problem of prejudice prevention.

1. There needs to be a clear and compelling rationale for the development of the program through a formal or informal needs assessment.

2. The purpose of the program needs to be formalized in a mission statement.

3. Program goals and objectives need to fit with the rationale and purpose, be realistic, and be clearly stated.

4. The procedures and activities of the program need to be organized in a clear and systematic format.

5. The program needs to fit with the local, state, and national guidelines for professional and ethical training. (pp. 203–204)

Multicultural schools are complex but not chaotic. Multicultural training needs to be guided by explicit objectives and complement other parts of the curriculum. Training designs need to be comprehensive enough to include both culture-general and culture-specific perspectives and both didactic and experiential methods of presentation. The problem incidents encountered by school counselors can be reframed as learning opportunities. Each problem or crisis that school counselors encounter has something to teach them in preparation for the next crisis. If counselors teach themselves to learn from these incidents, they may better learn from future problems they encounter. The incidents blur boundaries between the classroom and the community in which school counselors work, thus focusing on the community-school connection.

Students in secondary schools regularly report instances of "bullying" in which one student is isolated from the group and punished for being different. The difference may be in how the student looks or dresses, in level of achievement, or some other distinguishing feature. Being bullied is very painful emotionally and can be traumatic; in some cases, it can lead to the abused student acting aggressively toward him- or herself (e.g., suicide) or others (e.g., homicide). It is important for students to accept themselves, even if they are not "typical" for their reference group. Exercise 5 looks at the ways in which the student is different, as well as the positive and negative consequences of that difference.

Exercise 5: Being Normal and Being Abnormal

Objective

We are used to thinking of the construct "normal" both as the way most people *are* and as the way most people *should become*. We therefore help persons "adapt" to this notion of normal so that they can become "well adjusted." This exercise looks at both the positive and the negative consequences of a student being "different" from the different reference groups to which he or she belongs.

Procedure

1. Copies of a worksheet are distributed among secondary school students, indicating 12 or more reference groups.

2. For each reference group, the worksheet indicates that there are positive and negative consequences.

3. Students are instructed to complete the worksheet, indicating how they are different from other typical members of each group, as the student defines *typical*.

4. Students are then instructed to indicate both the positive and the negative consequences of being different.

5. The worksheet will include the categories shown in Table 12.1.

Table 12.1   Worksheet Categories for Exercise 5

Ethnicity	**Place of residence**
positive	positive
negative	negative
Nationality	**Social status**
positive	positive
negative	negative
Religion	**Economic status**
positive	positive
negative	negative
Language	**Educational status**
positive	positive
negative	negative
Age	**Formal affiliation**
positive	positive
negative	negative
Gender	**Informal affiliation**
positive	positive
negative	negative

Debriefing

Some of the students will find some reference group categories easier to discuss than others. In other cases, students may be able to discover only positive or only negative consequences to being different. By sharing both the positive and the negative side of being different, the complex within-group differences of ethnic, racial, and cultural identity groups becomes more clearly defined, both in terms of positive and negative consequences.

Learning Principle

Being different will have both positive and negative consequences for a person's ethnic, racial, or cultural identity.

A first step in prejudice prevention is becoming aware of one's own cultural biases. We often presume that although others may have cultural bias, we are relatively free of bias in our own lives. This self-reference criterion leads us toward what Wrenn (1985) called "cultural encapsulation." In Exercise 6, students are asked to identify specific adjectives describing stereotypes that might be held regarding a particular ethnic, racial, or cultural group.

Exercise 6: Stereotypes

Objective

Sometimes, by focusing on stereotypes directly and explicitly, it is possible to increase our control over the ways in which stereotypes shape our lives. This exercise provides the opportunity for persons to describe "typical" or "frequently expressed" stereotypes about different groups, even though the participant does not believe that stereotype. Students from different ethnic, racial, and cultural groups will probably identify different patterns of stereotypes. By testing these stereotypes against persons who are actually from the different groups, it should be possible to demonstrate the dangers of stereotyping.

Procedure

1. Assemble a group of students willing to look at stereotypes regarding different ethnic, racial, and cultural groups. Because the topic is sensitive, it would be useful to keep the groups small, from 5 to 10 persons, for instance. It would also be useful to include different ethnic, racial, and cultural group members among the participants.

2. Each participant will be asked to complete a checklist indicating different ethnic, racial, and cultural groups at the top of the page and a list of adjectives along one side of the page (see Table 12.2).

Table 12.2   Checklist for Exercise 6

			Groups		
Adjectives	*A*	*B*	*C*	*D*	*E*
Not at all aggressive					
Conceited about appearance					
Very ambitious					
Almost always acts as a leader					
Very independent					
Does not hide emotions					
Very active					
Very logical					
Not at all competitive					
Feelings easily hurt					
Not at all emotional					
Very strong need for security					
Easily influenced					
Very objective					
Very self-confident					
Easygoing					
Has difficulty making decisions					
Dependent					
Likes math and science					
Very passive					
Very direct					
Knows the ways of the world					
Excitable in a minor crisis					
Very adventurous					
Very submissive					
Hardworking and industrious					
Not comfortable with aggression					

Debriefing

Students may work in small groups to compare patterns of similarity and difference as they identify stereotypes typically held regarding one or another ethnic, racial, or cultural group. Because stereotypes tend to be volatile and emotion laden, it is not necessary for individual participants to indicate whether they themselves agree with the stereotypes—although their acceptance or rejection of the stereotype may well come out in the discussion. It would be useful to test these stereotypes against actual persons who are members of the ethnic, racial, cultural groups being mentioned. It might also be useful to search through magazines or publications to find pictures or word descriptions that do or do not support the stereotypes.

Learning Principle

Stereotypes are most powerful when they are unexamined and untested against the reality of the ethnic, racial, or cultural groups being represented. Individual differences are what you were born with. Ethnic, racial, and cultural differences are the result of everything that has happened to you since then.

It is especially crucial to prevent prejudice in the adolescent years, when identity is being shaped and when ethnic, racial, and cultural differences have such a profound impact. In Exercise 7, we look at the unfolding process by which a person's ethnic, racial, or cultural identity is developed.

Exercise 7: Personal Culture History

Objective

History is often underemphasized, both as it relates to individuals and to groups of individuals in the U.S. national culture. Many cultures believe that the extent to which a person knows his or her own history determines the person's level of civilization. This exercise focuses on significant and influential events in a person's own historical development that will help that person see the patterns of ethnic, racial, and cultural identity development as it occurred. By being more aware of our own personal cultural history and by comparing our histories with others, we can become more aware of both our similarities and our differences.

Procedure

1. Assemble a small group of about five students willing to discuss their own personal cultural history.

2. Ideally, this group will be multicultural; that is, from different ethnic, racial, and cultural groups.

3. Each student is given a list of seven questions and is asked to answer each question briefly on paper.

4. When all the students have examined each question, the facilitator will ask each person in turn to respond to the first question and discuss her or his answer.

5. Each of the seven questions will be discussed in turn. The group will go on to the next question after every student has had an opportunity to present his or her answer to the previous question. The questions are as follows:

   a. Describe the earliest memory you have of an experience with a person (people) of a cultural or ethnic group different from your own.

   b. Who or what has had the most influence in the formation of your attitudes and opinions about people of different cultural groups? In what ways?

   c. What influences in your experiences have led to the development of positive feelings about your own cultural heritage and background?

   d. What influences in your experiences have led to the development of negative feelings, if any, about your own cultural heritage or background?

   e. What changes, if any, would you like to make in your own attitudes or experiences in relation to people of other ethnic or cultural groups?

   f. Describe an experience in your own life in which you feel you were discriminated against for any reason, not necessarily because of your culture.

   g. How do you feel _____ [fill in the blank with the name of an ethnic, racial, or cultural group] should deal with issues of cultural diversity in American life?

Debriefing

The debriefing of students will take place during the exercise, as each of the seven questions is discussed in turn by each of the participants. The facilitator will want to point out the process by which ethnic, racial, and cultural identity is developed and how prejudice prevention can be implemented.

Learning Principle

Ethnic, racial, and cultural identity develops as a result of good and bad experiences in one's life that, frequently, involve prejudice.

Exercise 8: Predicting the Decision of a Resource Person From the Community

Objective

To learn how persons from other cultures make decisions.

Procedure

Bring a resource person into the class from a culture or population with which the group members are not likely to have had previous contact. It is important to find a resource person who is both articulate and authentic. It is easy to find people who are authentic to a population but not articulate or who are articulate but not authentic.

Ask the resource person to describe difficult decisions he or she has had to make. Have that person describe the situation up to *but not including* the actual decision that was made. Stop the resource person at that point and have each group member predict what decision the resource person made and why. After all group members have made their predictions, have the resource person explain what decision was made and why it was made that way.

Debriefing

In debriefing this exercise, it is a good idea to have worked with the resource person ahead of time and coached that person to help you teach the concepts of logical consequences or reflection of meaning, as it is different in each cultural context.

Allow the group members to ask their questions directly of the resource person and back off as a leader as much as you can. Be open to the possibility that the resource person's style might be quite different from your own.

There are many ways in which authentic and articulate resource persons from the community can contribute to effective learning in the classroom. Typically, the resource from a particular population has more credibility than teachers or school personnel who do not actually belong to the cultural group being discussed.

Learning Principle

The self-reference criterion that reflects our own view may not apply to others, who may see the world quite differently. It is important for students to recognize the unlimited educational resources in the community that are available to them. It is also important to recognize the educational expertise that many resource persons have and the value of that resource for the curriculum.

Chapter Summary

We have examined four different exercises designed to increase awareness of ethnic, racial, and cultural identity among high school students. Each exercise provides an opportunity to examine prejudice in the context of the school-community culture, as well as among the cultural backgrounds of the students. Without explicit attention to prejudice and carefully planned training, both in the formal curriculum and in extracurricular activities, prejudice may evolve into violence.

The importance of understanding the cultural context of each school culture is evident in all the research. The resistance to confronting prejudice is also evident. The normal developmental process in secondary school continues the identity formation process begun at the elementary and middle school levels. A school training program focused on preventing prejudice therefore becomes a primary prevention strategy to avoid the consequences of escalating prejudice and the resulting violence that has too often occurred in secondary schools.

Prejudice happens when the expectation you have in your own mind of someone else becomes more important than the real, live individual standing in front of you. Prejudice happens when you force other people to fit your own expectations for them. Prejudice happens when you have lost control of your own life and let others make your decisions for you.

13

Race Relations on
the College Campus

The previous chapters focused on students working with identity issues, affiliation needs, and other developmental psychosocial tasks. These chapters focused on building a systematic awareness of racial identity and the basic underlying assumptions that have been taught to school-age youth by their culture teachers. Following from the previous chapters' emphasis on awareness, this chapter will focus on what to do with this awareness and the move toward knowledge and comprehension as a higher stage of development.

There are indications of progress in preventing prejudice at college campuses in the increased representation of minorities among students and faculty, explicit mission statements against prejudice, and courses focused on social problems of racism and prejudice. There are, however, also indications of racial bias in grading, placement, behavioral management, and increased incidents of violence between ethnocultural gender and racial groups on campus (Kiselica, 1999).

In the early 1990s, the California Postsecondary Education Commission (1992) charged colleges and universities with a responsibility to provide a campus climate favorable to racial harmony and further charged that the quality and excellence of an institution will be measured by the extent to which it provides that harmony. Grieger and Toliver (2001) review the research on the inclusion of minorities among students and faculty of colleges and universities and conclude that "clearly on both the undergraduate and graduate levels, predominantly White institutions are not meeting the challenge of recruiting and retaining minority students" (pp. 826–827). The extensive research documents examples of social isolation, alienation and marginalization, stereotyping,

214

invisibility, discriminatory treatment by faculty, language barriers, acculturation problems, a lack of support services, absence of positive role models on
campus, segregation, and hostility toward affirmative action.

Along more positive lines, Smith et al. (1997) review programs to
increase diversity and conclude that

> taken together, this body of research underscores the conclusion that
> attending to issues of diversity is positively related to student success, and
> thus, is directly related to educational excellence. Moreover, the studies
> reveal that higher education is on the right path by addressing diversity in
> multiple ways at all levels of institutions. (p. 5)

In a landmark, state-of-the-art review of research on multiculturalism
at predominantly White campuses in the United States, Grieger and Toliver
(2001) identified 12 research-supported variables that are particularly salient
to promoting campus diversity. Table 13.1 lists these specific variables.

Increased visibility of minorities on the college and university campus
and increased awareness of institutional racism on campus has led to an
increase in multicultural curricula, training, and the development of new
courses focused directly on minority concerns and affirmative action
(Pratkanis & Turner, 1999). Dovidio, Gaertner, Niemann, and Snider (2001)
demonstrate how this new emphasis on multiculturalism can result in a better
understanding of common ground and salience in group membership.
Research documents how "the development of a common group identity
can diffuse the effects of stigmatization, improve intergroup attitudes, and
enhance institutional satisfaction and commitment among college students and
faculty" (Dovidio et al., 2001, p. 167).

Altbach (1991) points out that race relations are not only a "minority
problem" but a concern for everyone in the campus community. Altbach
writes that racial issues are apparent in the campus disruptions that have
increased nationwide. Specifically, this author asserts that

> More important, racial issues pervade the entire university—from debates
> about the curriculum to relations in dormitories, from intercollegiate
> sports to key decisions on admissions. Affirmative action regulations are
> directly linked to concerns about the representation of racial minorities
> (as well as women) on the faculties of colleges and universities. Indeed,
> over the past two decades, racial questions have come to play an unprece-
> dented role in American higher education. (p. 4)

It seems inconsistent for a university to neglect the tools it teaches
for solving community problems through mediation, consultation, and the
search for a balanced harmony. If we teach students how to manage conflict,
should we not be in a good position to teach ourselves? Should not conflict,
such as racial conflict, be handled differently within the university from the

Table 13.1   Twelve Variables Necessary to Enhance Multiculturalism on the
                College Campus

1. A clearly articulated commitment to multiculturalism by the leadership of the institution and an emphasis on the centrality of diversity to the mission of the institution.

2. Multiculturalism and the commitment to the success of all students is a shared value across campus populations, including students, faculty, staff and administrators.

3. A diverse faculty and staff who serve as role models, mentors, and potential experts on diversity-related issues enjoy a visible presence on the campus.

4. Diversity initiatives are not of a "one-shot" haphazard nature, rather, they take place within a coherent framework of multicultural organizational development for institutional transformation. This includes assessment, simultaneous interventions on multiple levels (e.g., mission, policies, climate, curriculum reform and representation), and outcome research.

5. Multiculturally sensitive student services exist that competently address the needs of racial ethnic minority, gay and lesbian, female and other diverse student populations.

6. There is financial aid and other monetary support for the recruitment and retention of a diverse population of students, faculty and staff.

7. Multiple and frequent opportunities exist for interaction, dialogue, contact and collaboration among diverse student populations in the classroom, in co-curricular activities and at social events.

8. There are incentives and rewards for the implementation of faculty, staff and curriculum multicultural development.

9. Faculty actively engage issues of diversity in classroom discussions and across the curriculum.

10. Transition to college and first year experiences that emphasize positive expectations for academic success are implemented for the retention of underrepresented student populations.

11. Mentoring programs are available on both undergraduate and graduate levels, which include student peers, faculty (including White faculty) and staff as mentors.

12. Issues relevant to (a) diversity such as campus climate and minority student representation, (b) retention, and (c) success are assessed regularly; similarly, there is ongoing outcome research to empirically evaluate the impact of diversity initiatives.

SOURCE: Grieger and Toliver (2001), pp. 829–830. Reprinted with the permission of Sage Publications.

way it might be handled in a labor union, in other organizations, or on the street? One traditional method of dealing with problems in the university is debate. Exercise 9 describes how a debate on racial issues might become a useful tool for articulating the issues in a university classroom.

Exercise 9: A Classroom Debate

Objective

The process of debating several sides of an issue goes back to the Socratic method and beyond. The basic premise is that if both sides debate the issue vigorously, carefully, and with meticulous regard for the truth, then the right answer to the question under debate will emerge. This exercise is an attempt to apply the methodology of debate to the articulation of racial issues in a classroom setting.

Procedure

1. A two-sided topic or question is identified regarding ethnic, racial, or cultural issues as they apply to the curriculum in the course for which students are enrolled. For example, one side might emphasize the importance of cultural "similarities" and the other side cultural "differences."

2. Students are divided into two groups and given a week or more to prepare their arguments to debate their side of the ethnic, racial, or cultural issue.

3. It is not necessary for the students to actually believe in the point of view they are presenting, although believing in the issue will no doubt enhance their motivation.

4. It is important, however, for students to spend time preparing their arguments and collecting supporting data to present during the debate.

5. The debate between two groups of students will be organized into a sequence of activities to structure the interaction.

Format of the Debate

- Side one gives opening arguments, allowing 3 minutes per member.
- Side two gives opening arguments, allowing 3 minutes per member.
- Side one has 3 minutes for rebuttal and presentation.
- Side two has 3 minutes for rebuttal and presentation.
- Side one has 3 minutes for a second rebuttal and presentation.
- Side two has 3 minutes for a second rebuttal and presentation.
- Side one has 5 minutes to present concluding arguments.
- Side two has 5 minutes to present concluding arguments.

Debriefing

Following the debate, the other students in the class will score both
debating teams to judge the respective merits of each side as presented in
the debate. The other class members will use the following scoring criteria
for judging the debate, with a low score being 1 and a high score being 10.

1. Analytical skill

2. Clarity of argument and position

3. Sophistication of argument

4. Integration of theory and practice

5. Relation of argument to reported research

6. Relation of argument to current events

7. Effective presentation skills

8. General effort expended by the team

9. Innovative and creative ideas

10. Ability to work within the stated time limits

When both teams in the debate have been scored, the facilitator will
announce the respective scores of each team as judged by the other
students. At that point, the class as a whole may want to discuss alternative
points of view that were not presented but would have strengthened the
argument for one side or the other. The teacher also will want to share notes
indicating factual insights and indications of comprehension of the issue
demonstrated by both teams during the debate.

Learning Principle

The classroom provides a safe place to debate risky topics such as
racial conflict based on data and empirical evidence and to separate truth
from untruth in the process.

Another way to help students in university classrooms apply their skills
to racial problems within the university is through analysis, another traditional method associated with university teaching and learning. Analysis is
the process of turning problems into resources; the problems themselves
become the textbook. The problems under discussion might be from the
examination of elements in a complex situation, to identify patterns and
relationships that make the problem powerful and, ultimately, manageable.
Exercise 10 describes how even a brief newspaper article can become a
valuable resource for the study of racial conflict.

Exercise 10: Analysis of a Newspaper Article Through Role-Playing

Objective

Newspapers and media report large numbers of complex situations every day that are both the cause and the effect of racial conflict. These newspaper articles often seem complex in their description of a problem and—if they are well written—suggest no clear or simple solution. A professor may use selected newspaper stories in the classroom for the application of systematic analysis to the management of even very complex problems. The objective of this exercise is to help students analyze newspaper articles about racial conflict from multiple viewpoints.

Procedure

1. The teacher or facilitator will select an article from a current newspaper that involves racial conflict as either the cause or the effect of a complicated relationship.

2. Key roles in the newspaper article will be identified, and the facilitator should make sure that these roles represent different and contrasting perspectives on the situation being described.

3. Students will be assigned to the various roles identified, either as volunteers or by selection.

4. Students will be given some days to prepare themselves for their roles by becoming more informed about the actual situation or by becoming better informed about the population or viewpoint they represent.

5. If necessary, outside resource persons more closely connected with the situation may be brought into the classroom.

6. At an appointed time, the students will take on their roles and interact *in character* within the classroom for about 10 or 15 minutes. This role-playing can go on for more or less time, depending on the judgment of the facilitator or teacher.

7. Other students in the class will be free to ask questions of the role players, who will respond in their roles.

8. The focus of discussion should be on providing a better understanding of the complex situation described in the article from multiple points of view.

Debriefing

When sufficient data has been gathered describing the same situation from multiple viewpoints, the students will be asked to leave their roles. Each role player will be asked to identify the essential features of this situation of racial conflict from his or her viewpoint. What were the "causes" of the conflict, and what would have to be done to "solve" the problem? Note causes and solutions on the blackboard. When each role player has had an opportunity to report back to the group regarding what she or he learned, the whole class will be asked to discuss (a) how the different viewpoints are different and (b) how the different viewpoints are similar. As they analyze the situation in terms of similarities and differences, class members will be asked to identify the most probable *real* cause and the most likely actual solution to the situation.

Learning Principle

Performing racial conflict as reported in a newspaper as role-play makes it easier to include both the subjective and the objective elements in analysis to determine outcome goals in managing the problem.

Planning is another tool taught in university-based classrooms that can be applied to problems of racial conflict. Planning requires accurate information and careful analysis of complex situations. Planning in a multicultural setting also requires the accommodation of contrasting and sometimes contradictory viewpoints or agendas by the different ethnic, racial, or cultural groups. While teaching a course on education and society at the University of Malaya some years ago, Pedersen (1991) was told it would be illegal to discuss actual ethnic, racial, and cultural issues in the classroom, but it would not be illegal to discuss those issues in a simulation of a society much like Malaysia. As a result, Exercise 11 emerged, in which complex situations involving racial conflict were adapted to a board game designed by groups of students in different ethnic, racial, or cultural roles.

Exercise 11: Designing a Multiethnic Simulation

Objective

Designing a simulation of multiethnic groups interacting together will increase the student's knowledge about the contrasting viewpoints of each ethnic and racial group and the unique advantages or disadvantages of membership in each group. The simulation will provide a safe setting in which to discuss risky topics concerning how different ethnic, racial, or cultural groups interact and manage conflict with one another.

Procedure

1. Students will be organized into planning groups of six, who will work together in contrasting roles to design the simulation.

2. A game board will be provided to each group resembling the game board for *Monopoly,* although the spaces around the perimeter of the board will be blank, and no game rules or instructions will be provided.

3. Each of the six members will take on the role of a different ethnic, racial, or cultural group. Three of the roles must represent low-income members of that group and three must represent high-income members. Each group will determine the appropriate ethnic, racial, or cultural group identity with the teacher or facilitator.

4. Each group will establish a problem situation in which members of their different cultures would be likely to interact, such as a week in a school or university, a 3-day jury session in a trial setting, a month-long series of committee meetings on a community development project, or some other complex multicultural situation.

5. The 30 or 40 empty cells surrounding the game board will each be identified as an event that would be likely to occur within the larger complex situation.

6. Each participating student will then identify the specific advantages or disadvantages of each event for persons from their ethnic, racial, or cultural group and income level. There will essentially be six sets of rules, with different rules for each participant.

7. Students will be encouraged to research the viewpoint of their group to make the consequences of each event as realistic as possible.

8. Currency will be distributed to participants, with twice as much currency being distributed to the high-income as to the low-income players. Each event will have consequences resulting in the increase or decrease of resources for the player.

9. The game is then played, with each player given a marker and the movement of markers being determined by dice.

Debriefing

The game must be playable. The game should also result in players becoming more familiar with the advantages and disadvantages of persons from different ethnic, racial, and cultural groups who compete and cooperate with one another in the same situation. By establishing specific events, the players will have analyzed the components within a complex situation and the consequences of each event for each group. Discussion following the design of this simulation might include questions such as

- Does each group have the same ultimate goal, such as money, influence, popularity, or power?
- Does each group interact with the same amount of resources in terms of money, power, or opportunity?
- What are the policy objectives for each group, and how are those objectives similar or different?
- What would be the appropriate criteria for "winning" this game?
- How large a role is played by chance and how much is determined by skill?
- What did the players learn about the culture they represented that they did not know before?
- What can be learned from this simulation that would apply to racial conflict in society between and among ethnic, racial, and cultural groups?

Learning Principle

There are specific advantages and disadvantages for members of each ethnic, racial, or cultural group as they interact in complex social situations.

Most racial conflict involves competition for limited resources. If you want to see the *real* priorities in an organization, you will find a much clearer ranking of priorities in that organization's budget and allocation of resources than in the rhetoric about what they presume to represent. Consequently, it is important to look at negotiation as still another approach to problem solving that is taught at the university level and can usefully be applied to the study of conflict between ethnic, racial, and cultural groups. In examining the process of negotiation in a simulated budget dispute, it becomes possible to study both the *process* of how these different groups negotiate with one another and the *content* of their various arguments for or against budget allocations. Exercise 12 was developed by Drs. Marshal Singer and Paul Pedersen to look at the processes of competition and cooperation in a multicultural society.

Exercise 12: Lump Sum

Objective

In this exercise, students simulate a gathering of different ethnic, racial, and cultural groups with contrasting or competing agendas as they seek consensus, with the object of gaining a better understanding of the negotiation process in a multicultural setting. The need to reach consensus competes with the need to remain faithful to the best interests of one's ethnic, racial, or cultural group. The fragility of consensus in a multicultural group becomes apparent.

Procedure

1. A group of students ranging in size from 16 to 60 or so is assembled for a simulation on multicultural issues.

2. Once assembled, the larger group is divided, either arbitrarily or by assignment, into four to six constituencies, so that each constituency has a minimum of four members. For example, the constituent groups may be representatives of ethnic groups in a community, subdivisions of an organization, states in a region, country areas in an international association, or branches of a company. The constituent groups are selected to represent a real-world group of special interest to the students; to demonstrate contrasting ethnic, racial, or cultural group memberships; and because students can learn about them either through personal contact or published materials.

3. Once the students are members of their constituent groups, an announcement is made that they have been assembled to decide on the allocation of a large sum of money (usually $1 million to $10 million is about right) by the United Nations. This money must be allocated within the next 2 hours or it will revert to the General Fund. The only requirement that the United Nations places on the allocation decision is that it must be by consensus and total agreement of all groups.

4. Each constituent group is instructed to elect a negotiator (by majority rule voting), decide on the overall division of funds, prepare an argument in support of its allocation, and design bargaining strategies to secure the cooperation of other groups in achieving consensus within the time limit. The group is given 20 minutes for this first planning session.

5. At the end of the first planning session, each group will send a negotiator to a table in the center of the groups. Each negotiator will be given 3 minutes to present his or her group's plan for how the total amount of money should be allocated, presenting the rationale for this division of funds. There will be no discussion during this first presentation.

6. When all negotiators have made their presentations, the negotiators will return to their special-interest groups for 10 minutes to consult with their own group members and members of other groups about modifying their plans, strategies, and tactics.

7. When the second planning session is completed, each group will send a negotiator to the negotiation table for a second 10-minute negotiation session, during which each negotiator will seek to present a modified plan, strategy, or tactic based on his or her discussions with members of his or her own group or other groups.

8. Following the negotiation session, the negotiators will return to their groups for another 10 minutes to discuss further modifications to their plan for allocating funds.

9. The final negotiation session will allow 20 minutes for the negotiators to assemble and negotiate with one another to achieve consensus. If the negotiators do not reach unanimous agreement before the 20 minutes have expired, the facilitator will announce that they have lost the money, which will now be returned to the United Nations General Fund.

Debriefing

Whether the group reaches consensus or not, the session should be followed by at least 20 minutes of debriefing about insights gained through the simulation. Discussion may include the factual content information that members learned about their own or other ethnic, racial, or cultural groups through the discussion. Discussion may also include what the participants learned regarding the process of negotiating in a multicultural group for limited resources. Some of the factors that might have contributed toward either achieving or not achieving consensus might be

- Stubbornness of one or two individuals
- Group pressure not to give in
- Generalized fear of compromising principles for the sake of money
- Indifference about the simulation experience
- A desire to alienate other individuals in other groups
- Disharmony among participants prior to the simulation exercise
- Misguided and unskilled negotiators
- Perception that role authenticity would prevent compromise
- A tendency in the final bargaining sessions to ignore the money and stick to one's principles
- Failure to consider—or having considered, rejected—the idea of setting up a special fund for allocating the money among interest groups at a later date
- Domination of the simulation by one or two interest groups
- Loyalty to the interest group
- Personal self-interest of one or more groups holding out for too much money
- Stubbornness of one or more groups
- Instructor's guidance and direction
- Negotiators functioning as a subgroup independent of their constituent groups

Learning Principle

The relative importance for successful negotiations of tangible goals such as money and intangible goals such as ideals and principles becomes apparent among different ethnic, racial, and cultural groups.

Chapter Summary

This chapter has emphasized the importance of knowledge or comprehension of culturally relevant information as an intermediate stage of developing multicultural awareness. Meaningful knowledge builds on accurate awareness. The various exercises presented build on the awareness exercises in the previous chapter that describe a beginning stage in developing multicultural awareness. The utility of tools appropriate to college- and university-level educational activities, such as negotiation, analysis, debate, and planning, have been illustrated in the exercises of this chapter. In this way, university students can apply the tools they are learning in the classroom to gain a better understanding of ethnic, racial, and cultural differences in the university itself.

There are many ways in which people deal with racial conflict. Some of them involve violence and the overthrow of one group by another or the forceful domination of a more powerful ethnic, racial, or cultural group over competing groups. Of all the alternatives, education provides the most attractive choice as the least expensive and, potentially, the most effective in bringing about long-term harmony. In spite of this, violent "solutions" to racial conflict continue to be popular and to consume a disproportionately large amount of the world's resources.

In an age in which it is cheaper to send a person to Harvard than to prison, we are past the time of decision. If education is to succeed in dealing with racial conflict and in bringing about harmony in our multicultural world, these issues must be dealt with in our schools and universities. If schools and universities are unable to deal with racial conflict in their own organizations, then how will they be able to prepare students to deal with racial conflict in the outside world?

14

Race Relations in the Community

The previous three chapters have focused on developing an awareness of the cultural context and an understanding of how education facilitates that awareness and knowledge-building process. The culturally learned patterns demonstrated in these previous chapters control your life with or without your permission. This chapter will focus on the skills necessary to take appropriate action in prejudice prevention. Skill learning is the most important of the three levels in multicultural development and requires a solid foundation of accurate awareness plus meaningful knowledge.

It is important, for example, to be both aware of and knowledgeable about a particular group's preferred method of receiving help before intruding. A community group will be much more ready to learn from you if you have allowed them to teach you about themselves first. Because problems may be similar across cultures, it is easy to assume that the solutions to those problems will also be similar. However, the appropriate response to problems is almost always culturally unique, and one's self-reference criterion will almost certainly betray the unsuspecting counselor.

Racism in the community is an ideology or belief system based on several assumptions: "(1) Humans differ on the basis of their genetic inheritance. (2) These biological differences are directly linked to intellectual and psychological characteristics. (3) Because of these biologically based differences, some groups are innately superior to others" (Jones, 2002, p. 30). Although *race* as a scientific or biological term has been generally discredited (refer back to Chapter 1), racism continues to be a powerful force in the community, both intentionally and unintentionally (Mio & Awakuni, 2000).

There has been a notable increase of hate crimes in the community context of prejudice and discrimination, and the legal system has not been able to prevent them. In spite of the increase in incidents, Boeckmann and Turpin-Petrosino (2002) point out that there is no universally shared definition of *hate crime*:

> For example, although gender and disability are included as protected statuses under New Jersey's hate crime laws, Pennsylvania, New Jersey's close neighbor to the west does not include either. Many states specify race, religion and ethnicity as protected statuses, yet New Mexico, South Carolina and Texas, for instance, do not. (p. 208)

Within the category of hate crimes is *hate speech*, which is defined as "speech that (1) has a message of racial inferiority, (2) is directed against a member of a historically oppressed group, and (3) is persecutory, hateful and degrading" (Boeckmann & Turpin-Petrosino, 2002, p. 209).

Boeckmann and Turpin-Petrosino (2002) believe that the combined effort of community leaders is needed to develop working coalitions of law enforcement officials, public school administrators, parent-teacher organizations, and others to implement the following:

1. To become educated about hate groups, their potential threat to community youth, and their recruitment tactics.

2. To disseminate this information to community youth, their families, and other educators and law enforcement personnel, as well as civic and business groups.

3. To provide input to local and state law enforcement prosecutors, judges, and victims of hate crime regarding community attitudes on sentencing recommendations and disposition of cases of adjudicated hate crime offenders.

4. To provide periodic reports to the public describing the activities of hate groups in the area, including evidence of infiltration among local youth and the number and type of local hate crimes and bias incidents committed in the public schools as well as the community (p. 216).

Intervention in another culture is most frequently judged by the relevance of that intervention from the receiving culture's viewpoint. The intervention must be judged practical, otherwise the counselor will be guilty of "scratching where it doesn't itch." Problem situations in the host culture can, therefore, become valuable training resources for both understanding and intervention. Critical incident methodology collects examples of problem situations in the host culture that have no easy answers, project serious consequences, and have occurred in a very short (3- to 5-minute) period of time. Critical incidents are similar to brief case studies but differ in their more limited focus on specific aspects.

There is no substitute for real experience. The critical incident technique is an attempt to bring actual experiences or events into the classroom as a resource. The incident is *critical*, meaning important, essential, or valuable, in the way that a part of a machine might be critical to the smooth operation of the machine. The incident is a short description of an event that did or could take place in a 5- or 10-minute period of time. A case study, by contrast, is much more complicated and might take place over weeks, months, or even years.

Critical incidents are based on real-life situations and typically involve a "dilemma" to which there is no easy or obvious solution. The objective of critical incidents is to stimulate thinking about basic and important issues that occur in real life. By reviewing the incident, participants can imagine themselves in the same situation, develop strategies to deal with that situation, and become more realistic in their expectations. Rehearsing what a participant would do in a critical incident in the relative safety of a training situation requires limited risk-taking and yet provides much of the complexity of real-life situations.

Critical incidents do not necessarily imply a single solution or "right way" of resolving the dilemma in the situation. Instead, they allow participants to explore alternative solutions and their implications. Exercise 13 describes the use of critical incidents for appropriate intervention in ethnic, racial, or culturally different communities.

Exercise 13: Critical Incidents

Objective

By taking a "slice of life" critical incident example and studying it in depth, participants will become better able to identify the culturally accurate causes and culturally appropriate responses to the situation. Examining the alternative responses to each situation and the different consequences of each alternative will make it possible to generalize patterns from the critical incident that apply to other situations in that host culture. The critical incident becomes a "window" into the host culture. Focusing on actual incidents also ensures the practicality of this activity, as it puts participants in touch with situations as they actually exist. Finally, critical incidents are valuable in preserving the inherent complexity of each multicultural situation without oversimplification. Some of the alternative skill-building exercises have the danger of oversimplifying cultures in ways that make generalization to the real world very difficult.

Procedure

1. Collect examples of "critical incident" problem situations in a target host culture that have no easy answers, involve serious consequences, and occur with some frequency. If at all possible, the students themselves should

collect the critical incidents. The critical incident format will typically include the following components:

a. Identify the event or occurrence with as much specificity as possible—the problem to be solved, the issue involved, and so on.

b. Describe the relevant details and circumstances surrounding the event so that readers will understand what happened.

c. List the people involved and describe them and their relationships to you and to one another.

d. Describe your own role in the situation—that is, what you did and how you acted—and identify the particular cross-cultural skill or skills involved. What were your other choices, and how would you do things differently next time?

e. Write a brief analysis of the incident, telling what you learned from the experience. State your estimate of the level of development of your particular cross-cultural skills as you reflect on the incident.

f. Identify the specific psychological construct or concept from the class readings or discussion that is illustrated by the dynamics of this critical incident.

2. Divide participants into small, five-person groups to discuss the alternatives to each critical incident and the consequences of each alternative. All groups may work independently on the same critical incident and compare their findings, or the groups may work on different critical incidents to search for culturally learned patterns across situations. It may be useful to role-play the brief situation as well as discussing it, to better understand the dynamics of relationships.

3. Wherever possible, it would be useful to have resource persons from the culture or cultures involved in the situation assist in presenting the incident to the group or groups.

4. In addition to identifying alternative responses and the consequences of each response to the situation, the group or groups may be given additional tasks, such as separating the cultural from the personal element, identifying the feelings that different persons in the situation might have had as a result of the critical incident.

5. After about 30 minutes of discussion, ask each group to report its findings and conclusions back to the total group. Defer discussion by the total group until all groups have reported back, to avoid repetition and to identify patterns across situations.

6. The small group reports should be judged according to specific objectives and scored by other participants for later discussion.

Debriefing

There are several ways in which the participants can be debriefed on their analysis of critical incidents. Critical incidents can be useful in many ways:

- The ability to use many information sources within a social or cultural environment may be increased. The student should work to develop information-gathering skills, such as observing, questioning, and listening carefully.
- Awareness and understanding of the values, feelings, and attitudes of people in another culture and why they behave as they do should be heightened.
- Listening well and speaking clearly to both verbal and nonverbal messages will be recognized as important skills for interpreting physical movements, facial expressions, and the whole range of meanings conveyed in face-to-face encounters.
- Enhanced ability to become involved with people from other cultures may be developed through collecting and analyzing critical incidents. This process involves giving and inspiring trust and confidence and developing a basis for mutual liking or respect. Students may learn ways in which they can be both truthful about and sensitive to the feelings of others.
- The ability to reach conclusions based on assessment of limited data is also an important skill. This form of problem solving requires a systematic approach that will identify cultural salience even as it changes from moment to moment.

Learning Principle

Problems can become useful resources for learning about the culturally complex patterns of an ethnic, racial, or cultural group. There are many different ways culture is defined. Sometimes culture refers to visible or "point-at-able" (Hines & Pedersen, 1980) artifacts or behaviors that are culturally learned and that can be objectively identified or pointed at by both persons within and outside the group. Another definition refers to *subjective culture,* defined by internalized feelings, attitudes, opinions, and assumptions that members of a group consider to be profoundly important. Because this definition is subjective, it is difficult to verify (Triandis, Vassiliou, Vassiliou, Tanaka, & Shanmugam, 1972).

Another polarity of definitions contrasts a narrow definition of culture with a broad definition of culture. The narrow definition of culture is limited almost totally to anthropological descriptors such as nationality and ethnicity. A broader social-system definition of culture includes demographic variables, such as age, gender, and place of residence; status variables, such as social, educational, and economic level; and affiliation variables to formal and informal groups, in addition to ethnographic variables of nationality ethnicity, religion, and language (Hines & Pedersen, 1980).

Still a third polarity contrasts an emphasis on culture-specific with culture-general perspectives. The culture-specific perspective limits the definition to multiethnic or multinational analysis and is mostly a method for helping people learn about or compare different specific groups defined by nationality or ethnicity. An overemphasis on the specific perspective results in politicized and somewhat stereotyped categories that ignore within-group differences. The culture-general perspective presumes that cultural differences are not important and that the best interests of society require us to emphasize only the ways in which we are all the same. An overemphasis on the culture-general approach results in the "melting pot" myth and exploitation of less powerful groups by more powerful groups. The more accurate perspective emphasizes *both* the culture-specific *and* the culture-general perspective at the same time. "Just as differentiation and integration are complementary processes, so are the emic (culture-specific) and the etic (culture-general) perspectives necessarily interrelated" (Pedersen, 1991, p. 7).

Culture can be defined as within the person rather than within the group. If culture is indeed within the person, then an essential part of personality development includes multicultural identity development. This perspective goes beyond the obvious labels used to describe individual groups and collections of groups. The broad definition of culture emphasizes the process of developing a multicultural identity as complex and contextual rather than simple. The subjective definition of culture emphasizes its dynamic and elusive character as the salience changes from one focus to another. In the development of multicultural awareness, knowledge, and skill, it is important to form a clear and accurate picture of one's multicultural identity as the first step to shaping and influencing one's multicultural environment, bringing about desired changes, and comprehending the meaning of culture.

One means of charting both the *intra*cultural ways that culture functions *within* the person and the *inter*cultural ways that culture functions *between* persons is called the cultural grid. The cultural grid is based on the premise that culture is within the person and not within the group. This model was developed to identify and describe the linkage between behavior, expectations, values, and social system variables for a particular decision at a particular point in time. The cultural grid combines social system variables on one dimension and personal variables on another dimension. Rather than describing a person's culture in the abstract, the cultural grid matches a specific decision or behavior to the specific expectations behind that behavior, the specific values behind the expectation, and finally to the specific social system variables from which those values were learned. Culture is complex (linked to a great many different social systems) but not chaotic.

Each behavior is given meaning through reference to the expectations and values behind that behavior. Behavior by itself is not data but meaningless noise. It is only through reference to cultural, learned expectations and values that specific behaviors take on meaning. Exercise 14 will demonstrate how a specific behavior can be analyzed using the intrapersonal cultural grid.

Exercise 14: The Intrapersonal Cultural Grid

Objective

The visual representation of an individual's personal cultural orientation, with social system variables of ethnographic, demographic, status, and affiliation in one dimension and personal variables of behavior, expectation, and value in another dimension, helps to organize the culture within the person. This cultural grid will help individuals understand how culture influences and shapes each specific behavior. *Behavior* is defined as a specific, identifiable action by an individual. *Expectation* is defined as a cognitive variable that includes behavior-outcome and stimulus-outcome expectancies that guide the individual's choice of behavior. *Values* are the belief systems that explain the importance of expectations. *Social system variables* are the sources of understanding, or the "teachers" in society from which the values were learned.

Procedure

1. Distribute blank copies of an intrapersonal cultural grid to all participants (see Table 14.1).

Table 14.1   Intrapersonal Cultural Grid for Exercise 14

Social System Variables	Behavior	Expectation	Value
Ethnographic			
Nationality			
Ethnicity			
Language			
Religion			
Demographic			
Age			
Gender			
Place of residence			
Status			
Social			
Educational			
Economic			
Affiliation			
Formal groups			
Informal groups			

2. The analysis begins by identifying a specific behavior, such as the decision to read this book. Ask all members of the group to analyze the same behavior, whatever that specific behavior may be.

3. Ask participants to identify as many expectations behind that behavior as they can, focusing on two or three that are most important and listing them under the "Expectation" column on the chart. For example, "If I read this book, then I can expect to learn a new approach to preventing prejudice." The expected consequences are what lead the individual to perform a particular behavior. Each specific behavior is linked to many different expectations.

4. Ask participants to identify as many values behind each expectation as they can, focusing on the two or three that are most important and listing them under the "Values" column on the chart. For example, "Learning new approaches to preventing prejudice is important because I value learning." Each expectation is grounded in many different values.

5. Ask participants to identify the social system variables that taught them the particular values they have already listed. The values were learned from a variety of sources in society, indicated in the categories in the "Social System Variables" column. For example, the value "Learning" may be rooted in one's ethnic heritage, one's age group, specific social-economic-educational peer groups, family, organizations, or support groups. Participants should check which social system variables were most important in teaching them the identified values. Each value will be rooted in many different social system variables.

6. Each person should be given about 15 minutes to complete his or her personal-cultural intrapersonal cultural grid.

7. Discuss the linkages among a particular behavior, the expectations behind that behavior, and the values behind the expectations, as well as the social system variables behind the values.

Debriefing

The intrapersonal cultural grid is frozen in time and gives a glimpse of how culture shapes a particular behavior only for that frozen moment. Culture is dynamic, and the combination of variables will change from time to time and place to place, as well as from person to person. Compare and contrast how different members of the group displayed the same behavior but had different expectations and values. Compare and contrast the different social system variables that taught different persons the same value or values. Discuss how the cultural grid provides an accurate and comprehensive assessment of a specific behavior in relation to that person's cultural background. Discuss how dangerous it would be to interpret behavior without reference to culturally learned expectations and values. Discuss how including culture in the analysis results in a more accurate comprehension of the behavior. Discuss how the same behavior might have different meanings and different behaviors might have the same meaning.

Learning Principle

Behavior is not data until and unless it is linked to culturally learned expectations and values.

The cultural grid is also useful in understanding the interactions between two or more culturally different individuals; in this case, it becomes an interpersonal cultural grid. If two persons interpret each other's behaviors without reference to culturally learned expectations and values, those interpretations are certain to be inaccurate. Similar behaviors may have different meanings and different behaviors might have the same meaning, as indicated on the intrapersonal cultural grid. If we extend that insight to the analysis of differences between persons, it is easy to see the extreme importance of judging each behavior according to the expectations and values behind that behavior. If two persons are accurate in their interpretations of each other's behavior and they know it, they do not always need to display the same behavior. The two people may agree to disagree about what behavior is appropriate and still work together in harmony.

For example, think of your very best friend in the world. It will usually be true that your "best friends" behave in different ways from you and display behaviors very different from those you would accept from strangers. Why do you accept that behavior from your best friend? Perhaps because you interpret the different or unacceptable behavior in the context of shared friendship. Dissimilar behaviors are not problematic (and may actually enhance the quality of the relationship) because of the similar expectation of friendship shared by both persons.

This same principle can be applied to the relationships between any two culturally different people, especially when they share the same expectations and values, even though they may behave quite differently. Exercise 15 shows an interpersonal cultural grid that displays how one might accurately analyze differences and similarities across cultures.

Exercise 15: The Interpersonal Cultural Grid

Objective

The interpersonal cultural grid provides a conceptual road map for the accurate interpretation of a culturally different person's behavior in the context of that person's culturally learned expectations. The exercise shows that it is not necessary for two persons to share the same behaviors as long as they share the same positive expectations. The cultural grid analyzes behavior both within persons and between persons, providing practical assistance in managing the complexity of intercultural conflict. There are several ways that this cultural grid can be used.

- The cultural grid provides a framework for separating the personal from the cultural aspects of an interaction.
- Personal-cultural orientation can be compared across time and across people to show how the same behavior can be explained by different expectations or values in different cultural settings.
- The dynamic and changing salience of social system variables is matched with personal-cultural variables for each time and place and person.
- A comprehensively broad description of culture provides those using the grid with the opportunity to consider all sources of culturally learned patterns.
- The culture-specific variable of behavior differences is combined with the culture-general variable of similarities in expectations and values, showing how both the specific and the general perspectives complement one another.

Procedure

1. Identify an example of conflict between two persons from different cultures for analysis using the interpersonal cultural grid.

2. Divide the participants into small groups of two to five persons, working together to analyze the conflict using the grid.

3. Distribute worksheets in which the four quadrants of the interpersonal cultural grid are drawn as shown in Figure 14.1.

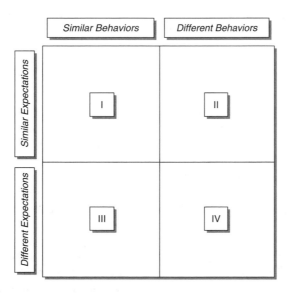

Figure 14.1   Interpersonal Cultural Grid for Exercise 15

4. Each team will identify examples in the first quadrant where the two culturally different individuals have similar behaviors and similar positive expectations. Both persons expect friendliness and both persons smile. There is a high level of accuracy in both persons' interpretation of each other's behavior. This aspect of the relationship indicates intercultural harmony.

5. Each team will identify examples in the second quadrant where the two culturally different individuals have different behaviors but share the same positive expectation. Both persons expect friendliness but only one person is smiling. This part of the relationship is characteristic of intercultural conflict where each person is applying a self-reference criterion to interpret the other person's behavior in terms of the self-reference expectations and values.

6. Each team will identify examples in the third quadrant where the two culturally different individuals have the same behaviors but now have different or negative expectations. For example, both are smiling but only one expects friendship. The two persons may appear friendly to one another but actually be in serious conflict because their expectations are different or negative.

7. Each team will identify examples in the fourth quadrant where the two culturally different individuals have different behaviors and different or negative expectations as well. Not only do they disagree in their behaviors toward one another; now they also openly disagree on their expectations for the future. This relationship is likely to result in hostile disengagement.

8. The teams will now discuss how they can keep the conflict in quadrant two from moving to quadrant three or four by emphasizing the shared and positive expectations between the two culturally different individuals and by not being distracted by culturally different behavior.

Debriefing

Smiling is an ambiguous behavior. It may or may not imply trust and friendliness. The smile may or may not be interpreted accurately. Outside its culturally learned context, the smile has no fixed meaning. Two persons with similar expectations for friendliness may not both be smiling. The salience of intercultural conflict is likely to move from quadrant one to quadrant two to quadrant three and finally to quadrant four unless a skilled facilitator intervenes.

Two persons look forward to working together (quadrant I). Although both persons expect *friendliness*, one person shows that by behaving *formally* and the other person shows that by behaving *informally* (quadrant II). If they are distracted by the behavior, then the less powerful of the two will probably adjust behavior to fit the behavior of the more powerful. Now they have the same behavior, but the less powerful member is expecting an *unfriendly* relationship and the more powerful person might still expect *friendliness* (quadrant III). Finally, the less powerful person becomes fed up with compromising his or her values by pretending to show friendliness, and the two persons separate in anger (quadrant IV).

If, on the other hand, the two people are able to discuss in quadrant II that their behaviors might be very different but their expectations are very similar, the relationship can be salvaged without either person having to change or modify behaviors—as long as there are shared and positive expectations on which they can build a relationship. The debriefing discussion should look at the importance of shared expectations in the critical incident under discussion and discuss how that potentially conflictual relationship can be salvaged by emphasizing similarities of positive expectation and deemphasizing differences of behavior.

Learning Principle

An accurate assessment of interpersonal relationships across cultures must assess both persons' behaviors in the context of their culturally learned expectations and values.

The intrapersonal and interpersonal cultural grids provide tools for understanding how culture is related to behavior and suggest specific procedures for reducing conflict between culturally different persons. There are three steps to applying the cultural grid in practice.

1. Identify one or more specific behaviors of an individual or conflicting behaviors among several individuals from different cultural backgrounds.

2. Identify the positive expectation that each person might potentially attach to the behavior or behaviors. What is expected to happen as a result of that behavior? Each behavior will probably have several positive (at least as perceived by the person him- or herself) expectations.

3. Identify the values that each person attaches to the culturally learned positive expectation. What are the underlying values in which that positive expectation is grounded? What are the meaning and importance of that expectation for the person?

Exercise 16: Outside "Experts"

Objective

The object of this experience is to recognize the importance of cultural patterns in communication. It is particularly insightful for persons who believe they are already sensitive to cultural differences in their daily activities.

Procedure

In this exercise, three or four persons are sent out of the room and the rest of the group is organized into a "culture." When the "outside experts" have left the room, the leader instructs the "cultural group" to follow three rules:

1. Members can only respond yes or no, and this rule will be disclosed to the experts when they return, to help them work.

2. Men may not talk with women experts and women may not talk with men experts because it would be embarrassing and impolite.

3. If the outside expert is smiling, the culture member will respond with a "yes," as that is the response the expert seems to want. If the outside expert is not smiling, the member will respond with a "no," as this answer is appropriate for all serious questions.

When the outside experts return, they are instructed to ask yes or no questions of individual members and try to make contact with each of the group members to gather data on who the group is, what they need and want, how they feel about the outside expert, where they live, and any other relevant information. At the end of 5 or 6 minutes, the experts are asked to report back individually on what they have learned about this group.

Debriefing

In the debriefing the leader will want to point out the importance of nonverbal cues (gender, smiling, etc.), that "yes" may not always mean yes as you understand it, that we tend to evaluate groups quickly as "good" or "bad," that apparent inconsistency may be an artifact of the expert (smiling or not smiling) rather than the group, and that other patterns characteristic of any group are typically even more complicated than in this three-rule cultural group.

Learning Principle

Many cultural misunderstandings are unintentional when we interpret behaviors out of context. The first stage of learning is to ask the right questions, but if we do not know that we are asking wrong questions, we will be led astray.

Chapter Summary

This chapter has discussed skills for preventing prejudice and reducing hate crimes in the community. The emphasis has been on looking at critical incidents or "slices of life" to capture the complexity of culture in a real-life context. The emphasis, furthermore, has been on looking beyond the different behaviors displayed by culturally different persons to search for shared expectations and values. It is only when this area of "common ground" has been identified that two culturally different persons are likely to work together in harmony. If we are to survive in a culturally different and diverse future world, it will be important for us to learn how those cultural differences can become positive rather than negative forces in our lives. That achievement will indicate the highest level of ethnic, racial, and cultural identity development.

Part V

Instruments and Resources
for Prejudice Prevention Work

Part V closes out this second edition of *Preventing Prejudice*. Chapter 15, "Assessments of Prejudice, Multicultural Competence, Stressful Effects of Racism, and the Multicultural Personality," briefly reviews empirical instruments or tools that can be used to study and measure levels of the relevant constructs. The chapter includes specific guidelines for selecting and using instruments for work in prejudice prevention. For the interested reader, we provide a few of these instruments in their entirety, with scoring directions, in the appendixes to the book. Chapter 16 presents "A Race Awareness Resource Guide" for parents, educators, and counselors and reviews important books, organizations, and films useful for work in this area. Guidelines for how best to work with films and books are also provided.

15

Assessments of Prejudice,
Cultural Competence, Stressful Effects
of Racism, Racial and Ethnic Identity,
and the Multicultural Personality

*Terrorists create terror; terror creates fear and anger; fear and
anger create aggression; and aggression against citizens of
different ethnicity or religion creates racism and, in turn, new
forms of terrorism.*

—P. G. Zimbardo, past president of the American
Psychological Association (2001, p. 50)

In Chapter 1, we pointed out how easily prejudice can develop and how
pervasive it is in the United States. This is particularly the case for subtle,
modern racism in White Americans. How can we determine or measure
how racist we are—how racist or prejudiced our children, students, or colleagues may be? In the last half century, researchers, particularly in social
and counseling psychology, have developed countless measures, assessments, and tests to quantify prejudicial thinking and attitudes. In this chapter,
we list some of the more popular and well-researched measures, and we
provide references for readers who may be interested in gathering more
information on a particular assessment.

In this chapter, we also review empirical measures of racial identity development, multicultural personality, and multicultural competence,

because these constructs are correlated with prejudice and multicultural awareness. More specifically, individuals with higher levels of racial identity, multicultural personality, and multicultural competence tend to be less prejudiced and more comfortable and competent when interacting in culturally diverse situations. Furthermore, as noted in Part II of this book, individuals who score higher on the constructs also appear to have higher psychological health and quality of life in general.

Finally, this chapter briefly reviews instruments that measure the stressful effects of racism for select racial and ethnic minority groups.

Measures of Racism, Prejudice, and Homophobia

Table 15.1 summarizes popular and more recently developed measures or assessments of racism, prejudice, and homophobia. The first column of the table specifies the instrument name and the original citations that describe the development and initial validity and reliability of the measure. Column 2 defines the construct that the instrument purports to measure. Column 3 specifies the dimensionality of the instrument. Dimensionality determines, from a psychometric point of view, whether the instrument yields one total score (unidimensional) or multiple, somewhat distinct subscales (or factors), in which case it can be classified as a multidimensional instrument. We also note the number of items per subscale or factor, as well as the total number of items in the instruments.

Columns 4 and 5 note our assessment of the instruments' pattern of score reliability and validity. Instead of getting statistically complex in our assessment here, we use an accessible summative index of the instruments' psychometric strength. Each instrument's score reliability and validity strength is evaluated as *limited, adequate,* or *strong,* based on the following criteria.

Limited

This classification is applied to instruments that may have been used in only a few studies, that have a limited sampling base (in terms of geography, age, and so forth), and that do not have consistently satisfactory indexes of internal score reliability (that we define as coefficient alpha = .70) across diverse samples. These instruments also may not have indexes of stability (test-retest reliability) over time. Furthermore, the measures in this category may not have adequate construct validity as measured by both exploratory and confirmatory factor analyses. Readers should remember that reliability and validity are not stable characteristics of instruments or measures themselves, but are instead characteristics of scores on a measure or assessment administered to a particular sample in a particular place and

Table 15.1   Measures of Racism, Prejudice, and Homophobia

Measure (and Developers)	Construct (and Audience)	Factors (and Item Number)	Reliability	Validity	Psychometric Critiques
Quick Discrimination Index (Ponterotto, Burkard et al., 1995, 2001; Utsey & Ponterotto, 1999)	Subtle racial and gender prejudice (adolescents and adults)	Racial attitudes (9) Racial comfort (7) Gender attitudes (7) Total items = 30	Adequate to strong	Adequate to strong	Burkard et al. (2001), Biernat & Crandall (1999), Ponterotto et al. (2002)
Modern Racism Scale (McConahay, 1986)	Whites' racial attitudes toward Blacks (adolescents and adults)	Unidimensional, 6- and 7-item versions	Adequate	Adequate	Sabnani & Ponterotto (1992)
Institutional Racism Scale (Barbarin & Gilbert, 1981)	Institutional racism (adolescents and adults)	Indices of racism (8) Strategies to reduce racism (11) Extent of strategy use (7) Agency climate (6) Administrative efforts (20) Personal efforts (20) Total items = 72	Adequate	Adequate	
Situational Attitude Scale (Sedlacek & Brooks, 1970)	Initially Whites' attitudes toward Blacks; modified to assess attitudes toward women, male sex roles, persons with disabilities, and children (adolescents and adults)	10 interpersonal scenarios with 10 items each Total items = 100	Adequate	Adequate	

(Continued)

Table 15.1 (Continued)

Measure (and Developers)	Construct (and Audience)	Factors (and Item Number)	Reliability	Validity	Psychometric Critiques
Motivation to Control Prejudice Reactions (Dunton & Fazio, 1997)	Motivation to control expressions of prejudice (adolescents and adults)	Concern with acting prejudiced (11) Restraint to avoid dispute (6) Total items = 17	Adequate	Adequate	Burkard et al. (2001)
Modern Homophobia Scale (Raja & Stokes, 1998)	Heterosexual attitudes toward lesbian women and gay men (adolescents and adults)	Attitudes toward lesbians (24) Attitudes toward gay men (22) Total items = 46	Adequate	Adequate	Burkard et al. (2001)
Lesbian, Gay, and Bisexual Knowledge and Attitudes Scale for Heterosexuals (Worthington et al., 2005)	Heterosexual knowledge and attitudes toward lesbian, gay, and bisexual individuals (heterosexual late adolescents and adults)	Hate (6) Knowledge (5) Civil rights (5) Religious conflict (7) Affirmativeness (5) Total items = 28	Adequate	Adequate	
Racial Bias Preparation Scale (Fisher, Wallace, & Fenton, 2000)	Adolescent perceptions of multicultural preparation messages received from primary caregivers (all adolescents)	Reactive (10) Proactive (10) Total items = 20	Limited	Limited	

at a particular time under certain testing conditions (see Constantine & Ponterotto, 2005; Thompson, 2002). For this reason, it is important that score reliability and validity be calculated for each administration of the measure.

Adequate

We characterize an instrument as generally having adequate score reliability and validity if the measure has been used in multiple studies (usually 5 to 10), has evidenced consistently satisfactory internal consistency score reliability (mean or median coefficient alpha at .70 and higher across studies), and presents some evidence of test-retest reliability (stability) as well. Furthermore, adequate measures also have undergone large-sample exploratory factor analysis (an assessment of construct validity) documenting the proposed factor structure (that is, whether the measure is unidimensional or multidimensional). Finally, adequate measures have also evidenced convergent and criterion-related validity through theoretically predicted significant correlations with related constructs.

Strong

We generally reserve this evaluation for those measures that have been used in many studies (10 or more) across diverse geographic regions and samples and that have evidenced consistently satisfactory levels of score reliability (internal consistency [coefficient alpha] and test-retest stability) across samples. Strong measures most often have construct (factor structure) evidence supported by both large-sample exploratory and confirmatory factor analyses, and they have evidence of score-convergent and criterion-related validity. These measures may also have been used internationally and give evidence of generalizable psychometric support.

Finally, column 6 of Table 15.1 lists references for extensive critical reviews and evaluations of the psychometric strengths and limitations of scores emanating from the specific measures. There are a good number of measures presented that have not yet received such a rigorous evaluation, often by a third party. Some of the measures are too new, with too little use, to warrant an integrative evaluation at this time. For students and professionals or whoever may be interested in using one of the instruments for his or her own research, we highly suggest reading all of the development studies listed in column 1, as well as the critical reviews of the instruments cited in column 6.

Featured Instrument: Quick Discrimination Index

From Table 15.1, we feature the Quick Discrimination Index (QDI; Ponterotto, Burkard, et al., 1995; Utsey & Ponterotto, 1999). The entire instrument, with scoring directions, is presented in Appendix A at the back of this book. The QDI is one of the more frequently used measures of more subtle racial and gender bias. It includes three subscales or factors: Cognitive Racial Attitudes (9 items), Affective Racial Attitudes (7 items), and Cognitive Gender Attitudes (7 items). Critical reviews of the QDI (see column 6 of Table 15.1) have found scores from the QDI across many samples to have consistently satisfactory indexes of internal consistency reliability, with the median coefficient alpha for the Cognitive Racial Attitude factor .85; for the Affective Racial Attitude factor, .77; and for the Cognitive Gender Attitude factor, .71. Indexes of test-retest reliability, construct validity, criterion-related validity, and confirmatory factor structure have also been adequate (see Ponterotto, Potere, et al., 2002, for the latest critical review).

The QDI has also been used internationally, with wording adaptations for samples in the United Kingdom and South Africa and a full translation in Chinese.

Measures of Multicultural Counseling Competence

Table 15.2 summarizes 10 measures of professional counselors' (and other mental health professionals) perceived competence to work with culturally diverse clientele. Seven of the measures focus on competence to work with racially and ethnically diverse clients; two focus on competence in counseling lesbian, gay, and bisexual clients. The 10th measure listed in Table 15.2 tests the multicultural training environment for training programs in counseling. Each measure is evaluated along the same criteria described in detail earlier.

We found all 10 measures to possess generally adequate to strong psychometric properties (score reliability and validity) across samples. The Multicultural Knowledge and Awareness Scale (Ponterotto et al., 1996; Ponterotto, Gretchen, et al., 2002), the Multicultural Counseling Inventory (Sodowsky, Taffe, Gutkin, & Wise, 1994), and the Multicultural Awareness-Knowledge-and-Skills Survey (D'Andrea, Daniels, & Heck, 1991) are the most frequently used self-report measures. The Cross-Cultural Counseling Inventory–Revised (LaFromboise, Coleman, & Hernandez, 1991) is the most frequently used observer or supervisor evaluation form of a trainee's multicultural competence.

Five newer measures that we believe hold strong research promise include Dillon and Worthington's (2003) Lesbian, Gay, and Bisexual Affirmative Counseling Inventory, Bidell's (2005) Sexual Orientation Counselor Competency Scale, Pope and Mueller's (2000) Multicultural Competence in Student Affairs–Preliminary 2 Scale, Holcomb-McCoy and Day-Vines' (2004) Multicultural Counseling Competence and Training

(Text continues on page 252)

Table 15.2 Measures of Multicultural Counseling Competence

Measure (and Developers)	Construct (and Audience)	Factors (and Item Number)	Reliability	Validity	Psychometric Critiques
Multicultural Counseling Knowledge and Awareness Scale (Ponterotto et al., 1996; Ponterotto, Gretchen, et al., 2002)	Self-reported perceptions of multicultural counseling competence (counselors and other mental health professionals)	Knowledge (20) Awareness (12) Total items = 32	Adequate to strong	Adequate to strong	Constantine & Ladany (2001); Ponterotto & Potere (2003); Kocarek et al. (2001); Constantine, Gloria, & Ladany (2002)
Multicultural Counseling Inventory (Sodowsky et al., 1994)	Same as above	Awareness (10) Knowledge (11) Skills (11) Relationship (8) Total items = 40	Adequate to strong	Adequate to strong	Constantine & Ladany (2001), Pope-Davis & Nielsen (1996), Ponterotto & Alexander (1996), Kocarek et al. (2001)
Multicultural Awareness-Knowledge-and-Skills Survey (D'Andrea et al., 1991; Kim et al., 2003)	Same as above	Awareness (20) Knowledge (20) Skills (20) Total items = 60	Adequate to strong	Adequate to strong	Constantine & Ladany (2001), Ponterotto & Alexander (1996), Kocarek et al. (2001)

(Continued)

Table 15.2 (Continued)

Measure (and Developers)	Construct (and Audience)	Factors (and Item Number)	Reliability	Validity	Psychometric Critiques
California Brief Multicultural Competency Scale (Gamst et al., 2004)	Same as above	Nonethnic ability (7) Knowledge (5) Awareness (6) Sensitivity (3) Total items = 21	Adequate to strong	Adequate to strong	
Cross-Cultural Inventory–Revised (LaFromboise et al., 1991)	Observer report assessment of counselor multicultural competency (counseling supervisors)	Unidimensional Total items = 20	Adequate	Adequate	Ponterotto & Alexander (1996)
Multicultural Competence in Student Affairs–Preliminary 2 (Pope & Mueller, 2000)	Self-perceived multicultural competence in student affairs professionals	Unidimensional Total items = 34	Adequate	Adequate	Pope, Reynolds, & Mueller (2004)
Multicultural Counseling Competence and Training Survey–Revised (Holcomb-McCoy & Day-Vines, 2004)	Self-perceived multicultural competence in school counselors	Terminology (4) Knowledge (19) Awareness (9) Total items = 32	Adequate	Adequate	
Lesbian, Gay, and Bisexual Affirmative Counseling Self-Efficacy Inventory (Dillon & Worthington, 2003)	Perceived self-efficacy in working with lesbian, gay, and bisexual clients in an affirmative framework (mental health practitioners and students)	Apply knowledge (13) Advocacy skills (7) Self-awareness (5) Assessment (4) Relationship (3) Total items = 32	Adequate	Adequate	

Measure (and Developers)	Construct (and Audience)	Factors (and Item Number)	Reliability	Validity	Psychometric Critiques
Sexual Orientation Counselor Competency Scale (Bidell, 2005)	Self-perceived competence in counseling gay, lesbian, and bisexual clients	Skills (11) Attitudes (10) Knowledge (8) Total items = 29	Adequate	Adequate	
Multicultural Environmental Inventory–Revised (Pope-Davis et al., 2000; Toporek et al., 2003)	Multicultural integration within counseling graduate programs	Curriculum and supervision (11) Climate and comfort (11) Honesty in recruitment (3) Multicultural research (2) Total items (27)	Adequate	Adequate	

Survey–Revised, and Gamst et al.'s (2004) California Brief Multicultural Competency Scale. These measures are quite new and have not undergone extensive independent use and critique; nonetheless, the development studies introducing these new measures were very strong, and we see the instruments as potential major contributions to the competency research.

Featured Instrument: Multicultural Counseling Knowledge and Awareness Scale

Appendix B presents the Multicultural Counseling Knowledge and Awareness Scale (MCKAS; Ponterotto, Gretchen, et al., 2002) in its entirety, along with scoring directions. The MCKAS is a careful revision of the original Multicultural Counseling Awareness Scale (MCAS; Ponterotto et al., 1996). It includes two factor-analytically derived subscales: Knowledge (20 items) and Awareness (12 items). MCKAS factor scores have witnessed satisfactory internal consistency reliability, with the mean coefficient alpha across 22 geographically dispersed samples falling at .90 (median was .91) for the Knowledge scale, and .78 (median was also .78) for the Awareness scale. The MCKAS subscales also have satisfactory test-retest reliability and criterion-related validity, and the factor structure has been supported using both exploratory and confirmatory factor analyses (see Ponterotto & Potere, 2003, for the latest in-depth critical review).

Measures of Teachers' Multicultural Competence

Table 15.3 summarizes six measures of teachers' multicultural competence. The majority of these measures focus on teachers at the elementary, middle, and high school level. As a group, these measures have undergone less use and less psychometric scrutiny than the measures in the other tables in this chapter. As a result, all of these instruments are rated as only *limited* to *adequate* in regard to psychometric strength. The newest measure in the group is the Multicultural Awareness-Knowledge-and-Skills Survey for Teachers, by D'Andrea et al. (2003). This measure is an adaptation of their popular counselor competency measure of the same name (refer back to Table 15.2). We believe this measure holds good promise, but as of yet there is not enough research on the measure to rate its psychometric strength above the *limited* category.

Featured Instrument: Teacher Multicultural Attitude Scale

The Teacher Multicultural Attitude Scale (TMAS; Ponterotto et al., 1998) is a 20-item unidimensional (yields one total score) measure of K–12

Table 15.3 Measures of Teachers' Multicultural Competence

Measure (and Developers)	Construct (and Audience)	Factors (and Item Number)	Reliability	Validity	Psychometric Critiques
Teacher Multicultural Attitude Survey (Ponterotto et al., 1998)	Multicultural awareness and sensitivity (K–12 teachers)	Unidimensional Total items = 20	Limited to adequate	Limited to adequate	Ponterotto et al. (2003)
Multicultural Awareness-Knowledge-Skills Survey for Teachers (D'Andrea, Daniels, & Noonan, 2003)	Perceived self-reported multicultural competence (K–12 teachers and teacher education students)	Awareness (8) Knowledge (13) Skills (20) Total items = 41	Limited	Limited	
Cultural Diversity Awareness Inventory (Henry, 1986)	Multicultural sensitivity (adult educators)	Unidimensional Total items = 28	Limited	Limited	Ponterotto et al. (2003)
Multiethnic Climate Inventory (P. E. Johnson & R. E. Johnson, 1996)	Cultural attitudes and biases (K–12 teachers)	Cultural encapsulation (5) Cultural hostility (5) Majority dominance (5) Minority suppression (5) Total items = 20	Limited	Limited	Ponterotto et al. (2003)
Multicultural Teaching Concerns Survey (Marshall, 1996)	Concerns regarding working with culturally diverse students (K–12 teachers)	Competence (11) Strategies and techniques (11) Bureaucracy (4) Family and group knowledge (5) Total items = 31	Limited	Limited	Ponterotto et al. (2003)
Racial Ethical Sensitivity Test (Brabeck et al., 2000)	Ethical sensitivity to racial, ethnic, and gender intolerance (K–16 teachers and educators)	Stimulus vignettes of ethical violations, unidimensional, with 37 ethical violations assessed	Limited	Limited	Ponterotto et al. (2003)

teachers' multicultural awareness and sensitivity. More specifically, teachers making high scores on the TMAS are "aware of multicultural issues in education; are open, receptive, and embracing of cultural diversity; and believe cultural diversity and multicultural education enhance the learning environment for all students" (Ponterotto, Mendelsohn, et al., 2003, p. 196). The TMAS has witnessed satisfactory score internal reliability (coefficient alpha = .86) and test-retest stability (.80 at 3-week interval), as well as promising factor-analytic and criterion-related validity support. The TMAS, with scoring directions, is presented in Appendix C.

Measures of the Stressful Effects of Racism

Table 15.4 summarizes six assessments that attempt to measure and quantify, on some level, the impact of racism on the lives of U.S. minority group members. Four of the six measures focus on racism experienced by African Americans, one focuses on the impact of racism on Asian Americans, and one is more general and can apply to the impacts of racism on minority group members in general. As noted in Table 15.4, we perceive a wide variety of psychometric strength in the selected sample of instruments: Some have only limited psychometric support, and others have adequate to strong support. The newest measure in the group is Liang, Li, and Kim's (2004) Asian American Racism-Related Stress Inventory. Although it is relatively new, we already rate this instrument as having *limited* to *adequate* reliability and validity support because of three systematic development studies reported by its authors.

In the study of racism generally, more attention has been paid to measuring racial and prejudicial attitudes rather than on the detrimental impact these attitudes have on both perpetrators and victims. As such, research that measures the impact of racism is critical to researchers' understanding so that prevention and intervention efforts and programs can be better and more holistically informed.

Featured Instrument: Index of
Race-Related Stress–Brief Version

The Index of Race-Related Stress–Brief Version (IRRS-B; Utsey, 1999) is a 22-item factor-analytically reduced version extracted from the longer IRRS (Utsey & Ponterotto, 1996). The IRRS-B includes three factors (or subscales): Cultural Racism, with 10 items; Institutional Racism, with six items; and Individual Racism, also with six items. Coefficient alphas for the three factors were, respectively, .78, .69, and .78. Evidence of score construct and criterion-related validity was demonstrated through confirmatory factor

Table 15.4 Measuring the Stressful Effects of Racism

Measure (and Developers)	Construct (and Audience)	Factors (and Item Number)	Reliability	Validity	Psychometric Critiques
Index of Race-Related Stress (Utsey & Ponterotto, 1996)	Everyday stress experienced by African Americans (late adolescent and adult African Americans)	Cultural racism (16) Institutional racism (11) Individual racism (11) Collective racism (8) Global racism (46) Total items = 46	Adequate to strong	Adequate to strong	Utsey (1998a)
Index of Race-Related Stress–Brief Version (Utsey, 1999)	Same as above	Cultural racism (10) Institutional racism (6) Individual racism (6) Global racism (22) Total items = 22	Adequate to strong	Adequate to strong	Utsey (1998a)
Perceived Racism Scale (McNeilly et al., 1996)	Perceptions of White racism experienced over a lifetime as well as within the past year (late adolescent and adult African Americans)	Employment Academic Public realm Racist statements (Subscale items unclear) Total items = 51	Limited	Limited	Utsey (1998a)
Racism and Life Experience Scale–Brief Version (Harrell, 1994)	Impact of racism (minority group members)	Racism-self (20) Racism-group (12) Total items = 32	Limited	Limited	Utsey (1998a)

(Continued)

Table 15.4 (Continued)

Measure (and Developers)	Construct (and Audience)	Factors (and Item Number)	Reliability	Validity	Psychometric Critiques
Schedule of Racist Events (Landrine & Klonoff, 1996)	Frequency of racial discrimination in past year or over entire lifetime (African American late adolescents and adults)	Recent racist events (6) Lifetime racist events (6) Appraisal of racist events (6) Total items = 18	Limited	Limited	Utsey (1998a)
Adolescent Discrimination Distress Index (Fisher et al., 2000)	Adolescence distress from institutional, educational, and peer contexts (all adolescents)	Institutional (6) Educational (4) Peer (5) Total items = 15	Limited	Limited	
Asian American Racism-Related Stress Inventory (Liang et al., 2004)	Perceptions of race-related stress (Asian American late adolescents and adults)	Sociohistorical (14) General (8) Perpetual foreigner (7) Total items = 29	Limited to adequate	Limited to adequate	

analysis and through theoretically predicted significant correlations with other racism measures. Appendix D presents the complete IRRS-B, along with scoring directions.

Measures of Racial and Ethnic Identity Development

Table 15.5 summarizes basic information on racial and ethnic identity development measures. By far the most extensively used measures in this category are racial identity measures developed by Janet E. Helms and her colleagues, as well as the general ethnic identity measure developed by Jean S. Phinney. Newer measures holding extensive promise in this category are the Cross Racial Identity Scale and the Oklahoma Racial Attitude Scale. Both of these instruments, despite being relatively new, have already received a psychometric rating of *adequate* from us because of careful, systematic development and testing of instrument items (see Table 15.5).

Measures of the Multicultural Personality

The theory of the multicultural personality (refer back to Chapter 7) posits that Americans with more of a multicultural worldview and orientation toward life will not only be more comfortable in an increasingly culturally diverse society but will also evidence higher levels of psychological health and quality of life in general. We believe that the multicultural personality is a promising area for future research.

Table 15.6 lists measures that assess components of the multicultural personality. It is important to remember that instruments reviewed in Tables 15.1 through 15.5 also tap components of the multicultural personality through related constructs (see Chapter 7). The Multicultural Personality Questionnaire (MPQ) profiled in Table 15.6 is the broadest and most comprehensive measure of the multicultural personality currently available. The MPQ consists of five factors (or subscales): Cultural Empathy, Open-Mindedness, Social Initiative, Emotional Stability, and Flexibility. The MPQ was developed in the Netherlands by Professors Karen van der Zee and Pieter van Oudenhoven (2000), and these researchers, along with their colleagues, have conducted a series of studies highlighting the validity and utility of the MPQ in predicting psychological adjustment and quality of life for English-speaking expatriates living in various countries. Ponterotto et al. (2005) have adapted the MPQ slightly for research with North American samples.

The Miville-Guzman Universality-Diversity Scale measures a narrower construct relating to comfort with diversity and the valuing of both similarities and differences among people. This instrument has witnessed

(Text continues on page 261)

Table 15.5 Measuring Racial and Ethnic Identity

Measure (and Developers)	Construct (and Audience)	Factors (and Item Number)	Reliability	Validity	Psychometric Critiques
Black Racial Identity					
Black Racial Identity Attitude Scale (Helms & Parham, 1996)	Cross's (1971) model of psychological nigrescence (African Americans)	Pre-encounter (14) Encounter (4) Immersion-emersion (9) Internalization (12) 11 filler items Total items = 50 (Short form = 30)	Adequate	Adequate	Fischer & Moradi (2001)
Multidimensional Inventory of Black Identity (Sellers et al., 1997; Shelton & Sellers, 2000)	Dimensions of African American Identity (African Americans)	Nationalist (9) Oppressed (9) Assimilationist (9) Humanist (9) Centrality (8) Private regard (7) Total items = 51	Limited	Limited	Fischer & Moradi (2001)
African Self-Consciousness Scale (Baldwin & Bell, 1985)	Baldwin's (1981) Africentric theory (African Americans)	Total items = 42	Adequate	Limited	Fischer & Moradi (2001)
Cross's Racial Identity Scale (Vandiver et al., 2001, 2002)	Cross's (Cross & Vandiver, 2001) revised model of psychological nigrescence (African Americans)	Assimilation (5) Miseducation (5) Self-hatred (5) Anti-White (5) Afrocentricity (5) Multiculturalism (5) Total items = 40	Adequate	Adequate	

Measure (and Developers)	Construct (and Audience)	Factors (and Item Number)	Reliability	Validity	Psychometric Critiques
White Racial Identity White Racial Identity Attitude Scale (Helms & Carter, 1990)	Helms's (1984) theory of White identity (White Americans)	Contact (10) Disintegration (10) Reintegration (10) Pseudoindependence (10) Autonomy (10) Total items = 50	Limited to adequate	Adequate	Helms (2005); Fischer & Moradi (2001)
White Racial Consciousness Development Scale (Claney & Parker, 1989; Parker, Moore, & Neimeyer, 1998)	Helms's (1984) theory of White identity (White Americans)	Contact (3) Autonomy (3) Disintegration (2) Pseudoindependence (2) Reintegration (2) Behavioral autonomy (3) Total items = 15	Limited	Limited	Choney & Rowe (1994)
Oklahoma Racial Attitude Scale (Choney & Behrens, 1996; LaFleur et al., 2002)	Rowe et al.'s (1994) racial consciousness model (White Americans)	Dissonant (4) Avoidant (3) Reactive (8) Dependent (3) Conflictive (8) Integrative or dominant (8) Total items = 34	Adequate	Adequate	Fischer & Moradi (2001)
Multigroup Ethnic Identity Measure (Phinney, 1992)	Social and developmental identity paradigms (all groups)	Ethnic identity (14) Other group orientation (6) Total items = 20	Adequate	Adequate	Fischer & Moradi (2001); Ponterotto, Gretchen, et al. (2003)

Table 15.6 Component Measures of the Multicultural Personality

Measure (and Developers)	Construct (and Audience)	Factors (and Item Number)	Reliability	Validity	Psychometric Critiques
Multicultural Personality Questionnaire (Van der Zee & Van Oudenhoven, 2000, 2001)	Multicultural effectiveness in expatriates (organizational and personnel psychology) (all groups)	Cultural empathy (18) Open-mindedness (18) Social initiative (17) Emotional stability (20) Flexibility (18) Total items = 91	Adequate	Adequate	
Miville-Guzman Universality-Diversity Scale (Miville et al., 1999)	Awareness and acceptance of both similarities and differences among people	Unidimensional Total items = 45	Adequate	Adequate	Burkard et al. (2001)
Miville-Guzman Universality-Diversity Scale-Short Form (Fuertes et al., 2000)	Awareness and acceptance of both similarities and differences among people	Unidimensional Total items = 15	Adequate	Adequate	
Psychosocial Costs of Racism to Whites Scale (Spanierman & Heppner, 2004)	Psychosocial costs of racism for Whites	White empathy (6) White guilt (5) White fear (5) Total items = 16	Adequate	Adequate	
Racial Justice Action Scale (Kingsbury, Schiffner, Qin, & Cheng, 2005)	McClintock's continuum of social action against oppression	Proactive stance (5) Awareness and support (10) Working against equality (5) Total items = 20	Limited	Limited	

adequate score reliability and validity across multiple samples. The Psychological Costs of Racism to Whites Scale and the Racial Justice Action Scale are new measures that we believe have good promise as components of the multicultural personality construct outlined in Chapter 7.

Guidelines for Selecting Multicultural Instruments

This chapter has reviewed a number of multicultural-focused instruments across the areas of prejudice, racism, homophobia, multicultural competence, the stressful effects of racism, racial and ethnic identity development, and the multicultural personality. Paper-and-pencil instruments are one type of tool that counselors, educators, and administrators can use to assist their own professional development and to supplement their work with clients and students. These instruments are not panaceas, and they cannot substitute for meaningful personal and professional experience or seasoned clinical judgment.

Any instrument used by counselors, teachers, administrators, supervisors, or managers should be selected with caution. One general rule is not to administer to clients, students, or parents any instrument that you yourself have not completed. Here are four additional guidelines that we use when selecting instruments for practice, research, program evaluation, and supervision.

1. Does the instrument have face validity to you? Despite the psychometric properties specified for the instrument, are you comfortable with the scale? Are you satisfied with the wording, format, layout, and length of the instrument? Do you believe the instrument items accurately measure the construct of interest? Is the wording (e.g., reading level needed for reliable comprehension) appropriate for your target sample? Are there bilingual or translation issues that need to be addressed? Are you confident that the items will not be offensive to your selected participants?

2. Has the instrument generated scores over multiple samples that could be considered reliable and valid? Have previous research studies using the instrument clearly described the sample, procedures, and indexes of reliability and validity? If the instrument claims to be multidimensional, is there empirical and rational support for scoring and interpreting subscales separately?

3. Remember that when requesting an instrument from an author or publisher it is equally important to request up-to-date research reports assessing score reliability and validity on the instrument. Simply having a copy of the instrument itself with scoring directions will not suffice. You are ethically bound, before using an instrument, to assess its psychometric strengths and limitations.

4. When you use an instrument, it is important to follow the author's or publisher's scoring directions very carefully. For many instruments, certain items need to be reverse-scored before a total score can be tallied; other instruments require complex score transformations. If you have questions about how an instrument is to be used or scored, contact the author or publisher directly. When you write up the results of your study, be sure to include score means, standard deviation, and coefficient alphas for all subscales scored. *Remember, score reliability is a function of instrument scores with a particular sample in a particular place under particular testing conditions; therefore it is essential to report score coefficient alphas for every sample tested.* Furthermore, it is general ethical testing policy to save your actual data for 5 years and make that data available to interested researchers.

16

A Race Awareness Resource Guide

Yet the situation is not without its hopeful features. Chief among these is the simple fact that human nature seems, on the whole, to prefer the sight of kindness and friendliness to the sight of cruelty.

—Gordon W. Allport (1954, pp. xiii–xiv)

For counselors, educators, and parents to work effectively in the area of prejudice prevention, they must have at their disposal a wide array of resources and referrals. This brief chapter discusses select resources covering national organizations, books, and films. These resources can assist readers in promoting multicultural understanding and tolerance in their clients, students, and children.

National Organizations

Major national organizations active in the fight against prejudice and racism in its many virulent forms are listed here. Keep in mind that there are also many local organizations that are probably active in your geographical area. The reader should not neglect to consult these sources when researching these topics and preparing programs. However, the following organizations serve as ideal starting points. We list 12 of them and note the two we relied on most heavily in our work on this book.

Southern Poverty Law Center, 400 Washington Avenue, Montgomery, AL 36104 (334-956-8200), http://www.splcenter.org.

This organization is invaluable, and we referenced it often in this book. The center provides books, magazines, pamphlets, videos, legal support, and more for fighting prejudice and racism. It publishes an award-winning magazine titled *Teaching Tolerance* (http://www.teachingtolerance.org) that is distributed free to educators working in the area. Among the center's helpful and well-prepared publications are *101 Tools for Tolerance, Ten Ways to Fight Hate: A Community Response Guide,* and *Ten Ways to Fight Hate on Campus: A Response Guide for College Activists.*

The Prejudice Institute, 2743 Maryland Avenue, Baltimore, MD 21218 (410-243-6987), http://www.prejudiceinstitute.org.

This institute was an invaluable source to us as we wrote this book. It provides newsletters, publications, research reports, speakers, and more on topics of prejudice, broadly speaking.

American-Arab Anti-Discrimination Committee, 4201 Connecticut Avenue, NW, #300, Washington, DC 20008 (202-244-2990), http://www.adc.org.

American Jewish Committee, 165 East 56th Street, New York, NY 10022 (212-751-4000), http://www.ajc.org.

Anti-Defamation League, 823 United Nations Plaza, New York, NY 10017 (212-490-2525), http://www.adl.org.

Asian American Legal Defense and Education Fund, 99 Hudson Street, 12th Floor, New York, NY 10013 (212-966-5932), http://www.aaldef.org.

National Association for the Advancement of Colored People, 4805 Mt. Hope Drive, Baltimore, MD 21215 (410-358-8900), http://www.naacp.org.

National Council of La Raza, 111 19th NW, Suite 1000, Washington, DC 20036 (202-785-1670), http://www.nclr.org.

National Gay & Lesbian Task Force, 1700 Kalorama Road, NW, Suite 101, Washington, DC 20009 (202-332-6483), http://www.thetaskforce.org/.

Parents and Friends of Lesbians and Gays, 1101 14th Street NW, Suite 1030, Washington, DC (202-638-4200), http://www.pflag.org.

Simon Wiesenthal Center, 9760 West Pico Blvd., Los Angeles, CA (310-553-9036), http://www.wiesenthal.com.

Books

There are probably more than a hundred professional and lay books on prejudice and racism available to readers. Here we list books published since the first edition of *Preventing Prejudice* was released in 1993 (with the exception of Allport's classic work, which was first released half a century ago) that we recommend highly. The first two books mentioned are true classics in the field, and we note an additional nine books for the reader that were instrumental in our learning.

True Classics

Allport, G. W. (1979). *The nature of prejudice*. Reading, MA: Addison-Wesley.

This book, first published in 1954 (the 25th anniversary edition, published in 1979, is the version we worked from), is a classic text and a must read for all counselors, teachers, administrators, managers, and parents. Allport provides an in-depth and comprehensive look at prejudice in all its manifestations and developments. The writing is clear, lucid, and filled with interesting and striking examples and anecdotes. Although it was published more than 50 years ago, the book is still relevant and should be read before more current writing and research.

Jones, J. M. (1997). *Prejudice and racism* (2nd ed.). New York: McGraw-Hill.

The first edition of this book was published in 1972; this second edition is fully updated and significantly expanded. Both the first and present editions are invaluable sources of information and research on prejudice and racism, particularly in the United States. Like Allport, Jones is a social psychologist who has studied racism, and particularly the African American experience in the United States, for roughly 40 years. The book is exceptionally well researched and written, and it should be on the bookshelves of every counselor or psychologist.

Highly Recommended as Well

Bowser, B. P., & Hunt, R. G. (Eds.). (1996). *Impacts of racism on White Americans* (2nd ed.). Thousand Oaks, CA: Sage.

This is the second edition of this book, which was first published in 1981. The editors point out that 15 years after the first edition was published, the problems of White racism continue in society. This is an edited volume that includes contributions from some of the country's leading researchers on the prevalence, manifestations, and consequences of White racism in and for its targets, as well as for White people themselves. The first edition of this book was one of the first to target White racism specifically and to acknowledge the deleterious effects of White racism for Whites and society as well as for the targets of White racism. The chapters are well written, and the book is a valuable resource for educators and practitioners.

Gaertner, S. L., & Dovidio, J. F. (2000). *Reducing intergroup bias: The common ingroup identity model*. Philadelphia: Psychology Press.

Gaertner and Dovidio are highly respected and prolific researchers in the area of intergroup conflict and prejudice. This book guides readers through systematic research, particularly that led by the authors, and it introduces the "common ingroup identity model," which specifies conditions under which prejudice is reduced (see Chapter 8 in this book for more on this model). The book is quite scholarly and user friendly, and the positions taken by the authors are well grounded in solid empirical research.

Kiselica, M. S. (Ed.). (1999). *Prejudice and racism during multicultural training.* Alexandria, VA: American Counseling Association.

This edited book focuses on the challenges inherent in helping counselor trainees understand and overcome their own prejudices and racism. The book is written for counselor educators, practicing counselors, and counseling graduate students. This valuable text includes invited chapters written by experts in multicultural counseling and the study of racism. We found the book to be very well written and organized, and its contents tackle a thorny issue, as counselors are used to studying about "others" and sometimes are unaware of their own socialized prejudices. Counselor trainees can become defensive when asked to examine or admit their own prejudices. This book goes a long way toward helping readers understand the process by which counselors become less prejudiced and more effective in practice across cultures. The chapters all offer excellent strategies for training mental health professionals in this critical area.

Oskamp, S. (Ed.). (2000). *Reducing prejudice and discrimination.* Mahwah, NJ: Erlbaum.

Based on presentations at the prestigious Claremont Symposium on Applied Social Psychology, this edited book includes contributed chapters from renowned social psychologists who work in the area of understanding prejudice. The focus in the book is on how to address racism, and its contents are geared toward educational and mental health professions, as well as allied professionals. Each chapter is well grounded in empirical research, so the strategies and suggestions for combating prejudice presented by each contributor are sound and well formulated.

Ridley, C. R. (2005). *Overcoming unintentional racism in counseling and therapy: A practitioner's guide to intentional intervention* (2nd ed.). Thousand Oaks, CA: Sage.

This is the second edition of Ridley's often-cited work, which was first published in 1995. Like the Sandu and Apsy book reviewed next, this book is aimed at professional counselors, therapists, and psychologists. The contents of the book are invaluable to practitioners, who are led to examine their own unintentional biases, which may be transmitted during counseling and therapy. The book presents concrete and tested strategies for counseling clients from culturally diverse backgrounds. The book is well referenced, up-to-date, and includes helpful case examples.

Sandhu, D. S., & Aspy, C. B. (1997). *Counseling for prejudice prevention and reduction.* Alexandria, VA: American Counseling Association.

This helpful book is written for practicing counselors. It reviews major theories of counseling and how they can be applied to the treatment and prevention of prejudice. Helpful case examples are presented. The authors also introduce their own "multidimensional model of prejudice prevention and reduction," which provides a helpful conceptualization for both understanding and treating symptoms of prejudice.

Sue, D. W. (2003). *Overcoming our racism: The journey to liberation.* San Francisco: Jossey-Bass.

This fairly recent book by Derald Wing Sue was written primarily for lay White audiences. Sue is quite direct and detailed in his coverage of White racism, and he calls on White readers to both acknowledge and work through their racism, which he believes is part of the mind-set of all Whites born in the United States as a result of a racist socialization (similar to Jones's concept of cultural racism). The book is very readable; it is not heavily referenced like the other books in this list, as Sue intended his message for a lay audience. Sue has an engaging and powerful writing style, and we highly recommend this book for both lay and professional audiences. The book also includes many exercises, as well as detailed reading and film lists for interested readers to peruse.

Also Recommended

Adeleman, J., & Enguidanos, G. (1995). *Racism in the lives of women: Testimony, theory, and guides to antiracist practice.* New York: Harrington Park.

Bell, L. A., & Blumenfeld, D. (Eds.). (1995). *Overcoming racism and sexism.* Lanham, MD: Rowman & Littlefield.

Brislin, R. W., & Yoshida, T. (Eds.). (1994). *Improving intercultural interactions: Modules for cross-cultural training programs.* Thousand Oaks, CA: Sage.

Bronstein, P., & Quina, K. (2003). *Teaching gender and multicultural awareness: Resources for the psychology classroom.* Washington, DC: American Psychological Association.

Carter, R. T. (Ed.). (2005). *Handbook of racial-cultural psychology and counseling. Volume 1: Theory and research,* and *Volume 2: Training and practice.* New York: Wiley.

Croteau, J. M., Lark, J. S., Lidderdale, M. A., & Chung, Y. B. (Eds.). (2005). *Deconstructing heterosexism in the counseling professions: A narrative approach.* Thousand Oaks, CA: Sage.

Cushner, K., & Brislin, R. W. (Eds.). (1997). *Improving intercultural interactions: Modules for cross-cultural training programs (Vol. 2).* Thousand Oaks, CA: Sage.

Grevious, S. C. (1993). *Ready-to-use multicultural activities for primary children.* West Nyack, NY: Center for Applied Research in Education.

Kopala, M., & Keitel, M. A. (Eds.). (2003). *Handbook of counseling women.* Thousand Oaks, CA: Sage.

Pedersen, P. B. (2004). *110 experiences for multicultural learning.* Washington, DC: American Psychological Association.

Ponterotto, J. G., Casas, J. M., Suzuki, L. A., & Alexander, C. M. (Eds.). (2001). *Handbook of multicultural counseling* (2nd ed.). Thousand Oaks, CA: Sage.

Salinas, M. F. (2003). *The politics of stereotype: Psychology and affirmative action.* Westport, CT: Praeger.

Sanlo, R. L. (Ed.). (1998). *Working with lesbian, gay, bisexual, and transgender college students: A handbook for faculty and administrators.* Westport, CT: Greenwood Press.

Singelis, T. M. (Ed.). (1998). *Teaching about culture, ethnicity, and diversity: Exercises and planned activities*. Thousand Oaks, CA: Sage.

Sternberg, R. J. (Ed.). (2005). *The psychology of hate*. Washington, DC: American Psychological Association.

Stull, E. C. (1995). *Multicultural discovery activities for the elementary grades*. West Nyack, NY: Center for Applied Research in Education.

Sue, D. W., & Sue, D. (2003). *Counseling the culturally diverse: Theory and practice* (4th ed.). New York: Wiley.

Tatum, B. D. (1997). *"Why are all the Black kids sitting together in the cafeteria?" and other conversations about race*. New York: Basic Books.

For an excellent review of multicultural books for children and adolescents (K–12), the reader is referred to the "Teaching Tools" section of *Teaching Tolerance* magazine (2004, Fall) (http://www.tolerance.org/teach/magazine/teachingtools.jsp?p=0&is=35).

Films and Videos

Research has found that films can reduce prejudice (see Pate, 1988). Recommended films are those that are realistic, have a strong plot, and portray believable characters. It is important that the film audience be able to identify with the emotions, fears, problems, and dreams of the film's characters. There are hundreds of films and videos that can be used in prejudice prevention training. However, there is a select cadre of films that we use repeatedly in our work because of their realism, clarity, and potential to stimulate in-depth discussion and deep feelings on issues of race, prejudice, difference, oppression, hurt, and healing.

Films from Lee Mun Wah (StirFry Seminars & Consulting, 154 Santa Clara Avenue, Oakland, CA 94610, 510-420-8292, http://www.stirfryseminars.com).

Lee Mun Wah is best known for his film *The Color of Fear*, which follows an interracial, interethnic group of nine men attending a retreat (or encounter) to talk about issues of race, prejudice, oppression, and privilege. The film is 90 minutes in length and is one of the most powerful and impactful films on the subject of prejudice and racism that we have ever seen or worked with. More recently, Lee Mun Wah has followed up this first film with *Last Chance for Eden, Part One* (2002, 88 minutes) and *Last Chance for Eden, Part Two* (2003, 70 minutes). This two-part film focuses on the lives of nine men and women of different ethnicities and races who talk openly, honestly, and poignantly about the impact of sexism and racism on their lives.

Films from Jane Elliott (http://www.janeelliott.com).

Jane Elliott is a pioneer in the in-vivo study and experience of racism. As a third-grade teacher in Riceville, Iowa, Jane Elliott was strongly affected by the assassination of Dr. Martin Luther King, Jr., and she decided that she had to do something right away to help her students understand the pain and hurt of prejudice. So in the days following Dr. King's assassination, Jane Elliott divided her third-grade students into two groups—the brown-eyed and the blue-eyed. The groups took turns being the "privileged" and "oppressed" groups over 2 days. This powerful film captures poignantly the pain of the oppressed as well as the feelings of superiority of the privileged. Elliott also emphasizes the impact of the oppression on the students' self-esteem and academic work over the 2-day experimental period. Jane Elliott distributes the following series of videos based on the famous blue eyes–brown eyes experiment: *Eye of the Storm* (ABC News, 1970), *A Class Divided* (1984), *Blue-Eyed* (1996), *The Angry Eye* (2001), and *The Stolen Eye* (2002). We recommend starting with the original film, *Eye of the Storm*, and then moving to the follow-up and expanded versions and discussion.

Films from Microtraining and Multicultural Development (Microtraining Associates, 25 Burdette Avenue, Framingham, MA 01702, 888-505-5576, http://www.emicrotraining.com).

For the last two decades, noted counseling psychologist Dr. Allen E. Ivey has been assembling and producing a wide array of videos for training and educational purposes. His films focus on racism, prejudice, cultural diversity, multicultural counseling, multicultural education, indigenous healing models, and much more. Dr. Ivey has recruited top multicultural psychologists and educators who speak in the videos and who provide counseling and educational demonstrations. These films are highly recommended for counselor and teacher education programs.

Popular Movies

In addition to the specific teaching and training films we have summarized, there are many popular movies, for all age groups, that can be incorporated into prejudice prevention lessons and day-to-day educational goals. Among our favorites for use with late adolescent and adult groups: various Spike Lee Films, such as *Do the Right Thing, Jungle Fever,* and *Malcolm X,* and also

Joy Luck Club

The Wedding Banquet

Monsoon Wedding

Bend It Like Beckham

House of Sand and Fog

Snow Falling on Cedars

Real Women Have Curves

Stand and Deliver

Crash

Working With Films and Books

In their day-to-day lives at home and at work, counselors, educators, and parents come across material (e.g., newspaper and magazine articles, television shows, popular movies, and novels) that could be incorporated into multicultural appreciation talks and discussions with colleagues, students, and children. There are hundreds of films, books (fiction and nonfiction), and Web sites for all age levels that can assist people in developing higher levels of racial identity and multicultural personality. We suggest that readers collect and catalogue such resources that they find helpful and develop their own multicultural awareness and prejudice prevention libraries.

A critical point to consider when selecting and incorporating resources for race appreciation interventions is how the material is to be used and processed. During the last 20 years, the three authors of this book have consulted on multicultural development with K–12 schools, universities, hospitals, various agencies, and corporations. We have found, at times, that staff trainers are not clear on how best to use stimulus materials with their audiences. For example, showing powerful films such as *The Color of Fear* (Lee Mun Wah), *Eye of the Storm* (Jane Elliott), or *Do the Right Thing* (Spike Lee) without adequate processing and debriefing will attenuate the potential for attitudinal and behavioral changes that are desired in such activities. Parents, teachers, counselors, and supervisors who show the films to their children, students, and colleagues must be comfortable and skilled in processing strong emotion. Chief among the necessary skills for work in the prejudice prevention area is group facilitation and counseling skills. We reviewed these skills in greater detail earlier in the book in Chapters 8, 9, and 10. Here are some additional general guidelines for readers to consider when processing emotive and cognitive reactions to video, audio, and print resources.

1. A helpful principle is to attempt to experience the training event first as a participant before serving as group facilitator. For example, we suggest that you participate as an actual member in the blue eyes–brown eyes discrimination experience before facilitating the experiment with students or colleagues. Similarly, be sure to view or read planned stimuli before processing them with others. Also, be sure that the film or reading is appropriate for the age group you are working with. In preparing for your facilitator's role, it is important to attend carefully to the film or reading by considering how it is affecting your thoughts and feelings. Take time to internally process and reflect on the experience before facilitating discussion with others on the stimulus material. Counselors and psychologists know how important such preparation is, as in their own training they spend many hours in a client role before seeing clients; in this way they know what it feels like to be in the client seat—their empathy is enhanced.

2. A second principle or guideline when working with films and other resources is to prepare stimulus questions for group discussion. These

questions are intended to stimulate critical thinking and deep emotive reflection in your participants. Stimulus questions also help to provide some structure and direction for discussion, sometimes making it easier for participants to share their thoughts and feelings. Depending on the age group you are working with and your professional experience, you may want to begin with more general or specific or more or less controversial or thought-provoking questions. As group members begin to develop more feelings of trust and safety with one another and as your competence and confidence as a group leader strengthen, you can move to asking more personal questions for member sharing and group discussion.

Here we provide three example sets of stimulus questions for films cited earlier in this chapter.

Stimulus Questions for *The Color of Fear*

We use this film in adult-level classes and workshops.

1. What one scene was most impactful for you? Why?
2. Which man in the film do you most identify with? Why?
3. At various points in the film, Victor expressed strong emotions of anger. What were you feeling as you listened to him?
4. The film includes two White men, David and Gordon. How were these men similar? How were they different?
5. The men of color were talking about "internalized racism." What does that mean to you?
6. *White privilege* was a topic that came up in the film. What is your understanding of what this term means?
7. What did you think of Lee Mun Wah as the group leader? Talk about some of his interventions.
8. How has the film affected you?

Stimulus Questions for *Eye of the Storm*

This film is excellent for middle school, high school, and college levels, and we use it frequently in our training of educators, counselors, psychologists, and school administrators.

1. What are some of the feelings that emerged for you as you viewed the film?
2. Have there been times in your life when you felt like the blue-eyed or brown-eyed children? Describe these memories.
3. What do you think of Jane Elliott? Could you see yourself using such a simulation with your class (or group)? Why or why not?
4. Does prejudice prevention programming need to incorporate "an experience of discrimination"? Can you understand prejudice without having experienced it directly?

5. What are the ethical concerns you see in subjecting children (or adolescents or adults) to a potentially powerful experience of prejudice? Are the risks worth the benefits? What precautions can be taken to ensure that no lasting psychological damage is done to participants?

6. What does the film say about the effects of the teacher's negative (or positive) expectations on children's academic performance and classroom behavior? Do you think this has been an issue in the education of children in the United States?

Stimulus Questions for *Do the Right Thing*

This movie is rated "R" and is an excellent stimulus for adult audiences.

1. Which character in the movie can you most identify with? Why?
2. What is your personal reaction to the end of the movie?
3. How might the climactic incident of this movie have been avoided?
4. What message is Spike Lee attempting to get across in the movie?
5. Do you believe the riots in Los Angeles, California, in 1992 give some validity to Spike Lee's message? (The movie was produced in 1989.)

Racial Identity Exercises for *The Color of Fear* and *Do the Right Thing*

We have found these two movies to be excellent sources for seeing how different levels of racial identity play out in real-life characters. After reviewing the racial identity models (see Chapters 4 through 6), we show one or both of these films and (in addition to the general processing reflected in the questions provided here) ask participants to try to place different characters in respective stages of racial identity development for their racial group. Participants are asked to provide an evidence-based rationale for their stage placements. The films portray members of several different racial and ethnic groups who are at varying levels of racial identity development, and because of this, the films are excellent models for racial identity development training.

Chapter Summary

This final chapter of *Preventing Prejudice: A Guide for Counselors, Educators, and Parents* provided a very select resource guide for the reader. We recommended that readers build their own multicultural resource library, consisting of books, magazine and newspaper articles, films, and Web sites. Important guidelines for selecting, using, and processing resource aids were presented.

Appendix I

The Quick Discrimination Index (QDI)

The Quick Discrimination Index (QDI)

Dear QDI User:

Below and on the following pages are the QDI, scoring directions, and the "Utilization Request Form," which must be carefully read, endorsed, and returned prior to QDI use. It is important to read the following five articles before using the QDI:

Ponterotto, J. G., Potere, J. C., & Johansen, S. A. (2002). The Quick Discrimination Index: Normative data and user guidelines for counseling researchers. *Journal of Multicultural Counseling and Development, 30,* **192–207. (Should be read first)**

Burkard, A. W., Jones, J. A., & Johll, M. P. (2002). Hierarchical factor analysis of the Quick Discrimination Index. *Educational and Psychological Measurement, 62,* 64–78.

Green, R. G., Hamlin, H. Ogden, & Walters, K. (2004). Some normative data on mental health professionals' attitudes about racial minorities and women. *Psychological Reports, 94,* 485–494.

Ponterotto, J. G., Burkard, A., Rieger, B. P., Grieger, I., D'Onofrio, A., Dubuisson, A., Heenehan, M., Millstein, B., Parisi, M., Rath, J. F., & Sax, G. (1995). Development and initial validation of the Quick Discrimination Index (QDI). *Educational and Psychological Measurement, 55,* 1016–1031.

Utsey, S. O., & Ponterotto, J. G. (1999). Further factorial validity assessment of scores on the Quick Discrimination Index (QDI). *Educational and Psychological Measurement, 59,* 325–335.

Utilization Request Form

In using the Quick Discrimination Index (QDI), I agree to the following terms/conditions:

1. I understand that the QDI is copyrighted by Joseph G. Ponterotto (Ph.D.) at the Division of Psychological and Educational Services, Fordham University at Lincoln Center, 113 West 60th Street, New York, New York 10023-7478 (212-636-6480); Jponterott@aol.com.

2. I am a trained professional in counseling, psychology, or a related field, having completed coursework (or training) in multicultural issues, psychometrics, and research ethics, or I am working under the supervision of such an individual.

3. In using the QDI, all ethical standards of the American Psychological Association, the American Counseling Association, and/or related professional organizations will be adhered to. Furthermore, I will follow the "Research with Human Subjects" guidelines put forth by my university, institution, or professional setting. Ethical considerations include but are not limited to subject informed consent, confidentiality of records, adequate pre- and post-briefing of subjects, and subject opportunity to review a concise written summary of the study's purpose, method, results, and implications.

4. Consistent with accepted professional practice, I will save and protect my raw data for a minimum of five years; and if requested I will make the raw data available to scholars researching the prejudice construct.

5. I will send a copy of my research results (for any study incorporating the QDI) in manuscript form to Dr. Ponterotto, regardless of whether the study is published, presented, or fully completed.

Signature:_____ Date:_____

Name:_____ Phone:_____

Address:_____

_____

_____

If a student, supervisor/mentor's name and phone number, affiliation, and signature:

Name:_____ Phone:_____

Affiliation:_____

Signature:_____ Date:_____

Social Attitude Survey

Please respond to all items in the survey. Remember, there are no right or wrong answers. The survey is completely anonymous; do not put your name on the survey. Please circle the appropriate number to the right.

	Strongly Disagree	*Disagree*	*Not Sure*	*Agree*	*Strongly Agree*
1. I do think it is more appropriate for the mother of a newborn baby, rather than the father, to stay home with the baby during the first year.	1	2	3	4	5
2. It is as easy for women to succeed in business as it is for men.	1	2	3	4	5
3. I really think affirmative action programs on college campuses constitute reverse discrimination.	1	2	3	4	5
4. I feel I could develop an intimate relationship with someone from a different race.	1	2	3	4	5
5. All Americans should learn to speak two languages.	1	2	3	4	5
6. I look forward to the day when a woman is president of the United States.	1	2	3	4	5
7. Generally speaking, men work harder than women.	1	2	3	4	5
8. My friendship network is very racially mixed.	1	2	3	4	5
9. I am against affirmative action programs in business.	1	2	3	4	5
10. Generally, men seem less concerned with building relationships than do women.	1	2	3	4	5
11. I would feel okay about my son or daughter dating someone from a different race.	1	2	3	4	5
12. I look forward to the day when a racial minority person is president of the United States.	1	2	3	4	5
13. In the past few years there has been too much attention directed toward multicultural issues in education.	1	2	3	4	5

14. I think feminist perspectives should be an integral part of the higher education curriculum.	1	2	3	4	5
15. Most of my close friends are from my own racial group.	1	2	3	4	5
16. I feel somewhat more secure that a man, rather than a woman, is currently president of the United States.	1	2	3	4	5
17. I think that it is (or would be) important for my children to attend schools that are racially mixed.	1	2	3	4	5
18. In the past few years there has been too much attention directed toward multicultural issues in business.	1	2	3	4	5
19. Overall, I think racial minorities in America complain too much about racial discrimination.	1	2	3	4	5
20. I feel (or would feel) very comfortable having a woman as my primary physician.	1	2	3	4	5
21. I think the president of the United States should make a concerted effort to appoint more women and racial minorities to the country's Supreme Court.	1	2	3	4	5
22. I think White people's racism toward racial minority groups still constitutes a major problem in America.	1	2	3	4	5
23. I think the school system, from elementary school through college, should encourage minority and immigrant children to learn and fully adopt traditional American values.	1	2	3	4	5
24. If I were to adopt a child, I would be happy to adopt a child of any race.	1	2	3	4	5
25. I think there is as much female physical violence toward men as there is male physical violence toward women.	1	2	3	4	5
26. I think the school system, from elementary school through college, should promote values representative of diverse cultures.	1	2	3	4	5

27.	I believe that reading the autobiography of Malcolm X would be of value.	1 2 3 4 5			
28.	I would enjoy living in a neighborhood consisting of a racially diverse population (e.g., Asians, Blacks, Hispanics, Whites).	1 2 3 4 5			
29.	I think it is better if people marry within their own race.	1 2 3 4 5			
30.	Women make too big a deal out of sexual harassment issues in the workplace.	1 2 3 4 5			

Scoring Directions for the Quick Discrimination Index (QDI)

Introduction

Users of the QDI must have completed the "Utilization Request Form" before incorporating the QDI in their professional work.

The QDI is a 30-item Likert-type self-report measure of racial and gender attitudes. The instrument itself is titled "Social Attitude Survey" to control for some forms of response bias. Users of the QDI should read the development and validity studies on the QDI before use.

Scoring

There are two methods of scoring the QDI. First, you can simply use the total score, which measures overall sensitivity, awareness, and receptivity to cultural diversity and gender equality.

The second scoring procedure involves scoring three separate subscales (factors) of the QDI. This is the preferred method at this time, given that both exploratory and confirmatory factor analysis supports the construct validity of the three-factor model.

Method One: QDI Total Score

Of the 30 items on the QDI, 15 are worded and scored in a positive direction (high scores indicate high sensitivity to multicultural/gender issues), and 15 are worded and scored in a negative direction (where low scores are indicative of high sensitivity). Naturally, when tallying the Total score response, these latter 15 items need to be *reverse-scored*. Reverse scoring simply means that if a respondent circles a "1" they should get five points; if a "2," four points; a "3," three points; a "4," two points; and a "5," one point.

The following QDI items need to be *reverse-scored*:

1, 2, 3, 7, 9, 10, 13, 15, 16, 18, 19, 23, 25, 29, 30.

Score range is 30 to 150, with high scores indicating more awareness, sensitivity, and receptivity to racial diversity and gender equality.

Method Two: Three-Factor Model

If scoring separate subscales (factors), the researcher should not also use the Total score. As expected, the total score is highly correlated with subscale scores, and to use both would be somewhat redundant.

When scoring separate subscales, only 23 of the total 30 items are scored.

Factor 1: General (Cognitive) Attitudes Toward Racial Diversity/ Multiculturalism (Items in parentheses are reverse-scored)

9 items: (3), (9), (13), (18), (19), 22, (23), 26, 27

(Score range = 9 to 45)

Factor 2: Affective Attitudes Toward More Personal Contact (Closeness) With Racial Diversity (Items in parentheses are reverse-scored)

7 items: 4, 8, 11, (15), 17, 24, (29)

(Score range = 7 to 35)

Factor 3: Attitudes Toward Women's Equity (Items in parentheses are reverse-scored)

7 items: (1), 6, (7), 14, (16), 20, (30)

(Score range = 7 to 35)

Appendix II

*Multicultural Counseling Knowledge
and Awareness Scale (MCKAS)*

Multicultural Counseling Knowledge
and Awareness Scale (MCKAS)

Dear MCKAS User:

Below and on the next pages are the MCKAS, scoring directions, and the "Utilization Request Form," which must be carefully read, endorsed, and returned prior to MCKAS use.

Please note that the development and *initial* validity studies on the MCKAS (originally titled the MCAS) were published as a lengthy chapter in the following book:

Ponterotto, J. G., et al. (1996). Development and initial validation of the Multicultural Counseling Awareness Scale. In G. R. Sodowsky & J. C. Impara (Eds.), *Multicultural assessment in counseling and clinical psychology* **(pp. 247–282). Lincoln, NE: Buros Institute of Mental Measurements.**

The revised MCKAS is presented in:

Ponterotto, J. G., Gretchen, D., Utsey, S. O., Riger, B. P., & Austin, R. (2002). A revision of the Multicultural Counseling Awareness Scale. *Journal of Multicultural Counseling and Development, 30,* **153–181.**

The latest presentation, critique, and user guidelines for the MCKAS are presented in:

Ponterotto, J. G., & Potere, J. C. (2003). The Multicultural Counseling Knowledge and Awareness Scale (MCKAS): Validity, reliability, and user guidelines. In D. P. Pope-Davis, H. L. K. Coleman, W. M. Liu, & R. Toporek (Eds.), *Handbook of multicultural competencies in counseling and psychology* **(pp. 137–153). Thousand Oaks, CA: Sage. (Any user of the MCKAS must read this source.)**

Critical reviews of the MCAS/MCKAS and other multicultural competency measures can be found in:

Constantine, M. G., & Ladany, N. (2001). New visions for defining and assessing multicultural counseling competence. In J. G. Ponterotto, J. M. Casas, L. A. Suzuki, & C. M. Alexander (Eds.), *Handbook of multicultural counseling* (2nd ed., pp. 482–498). Thousand Oaks, CA: Sage.

Constantine, M. G., Gloria, A. M., & Ladany, N. (2002). The factor structure underlying three self-report multicultural counseling competency scales. *Cultural Diversity and Ethnic Minority Psychology, 8,* 334–345.

Kocarek, C. E., Talbot, D. M., Batka, J. C., & Anderson, M. Z. (2001). Reliability and validity of three measures of multicultural competency. *Journal of Counseling and Development, 79,* 486–496.

Ponterotto, J. G., & Alexander, C. M. (1996). Assessing the multicultural competence of counselors and clinicians. In L. A. Suzuki, P. J. Meller, & J. G. Ponterotto (Eds.), *Handbook of multicultural assessment: Clinical, psychological, and educational applications* (pp. 651–672). San Francisco: Jossey-Bass.

Ponterotto, J. G., Rieger, B. P., Barrett, A., & Sparks, R. (1994). Assessing multicultural counseling competence: A review of instrumentation. *Journal of Counseling and Development, 72,* 316–322.

Pope-Davis, D. B., & Dings, J. G. (1994). An empirical comparison of two self-report multicultural counseling competency inventories. *Measurement and Evaluation in Counseling and Development, 27,* 93–102.

Pope-Davis, D. B., & Dings, J. G. (1995). The assessment of multicultural counseling competencies. In J. G. Ponterotto, J. M. Casas, L. A. Suzuki, & C. M. Alexander (Eds.), *Handbook of multicultural counseling* (pp. 287–311). Thousand Oaks, CA: Sage.

Utilization Request Form

In using the Multicultural Counseling Knowledge and Awareness Scale (MCKAS), I agree to the following terms/conditions:

1. I understand that the MCKAS is copyrighted by Joseph G. Ponterotto (Ph.D.) at the Division of Psychological and Educational Services, Fordham University at Lincoln Center, 113 West 60th Street, New York, New York 10023-7478 (212-636-6480); Jponterott@aol.com.

2. I am a trained professional in counseling, psychology, or a related field, having completed coursework (or training) in multicultural issues, psychometrics, and research ethics, or I am working under the supervision of such an individual.

3. In using the MCKAS, all ethical standards of the American Psychological Association, the American Counseling Association, and/or related professional organizations will be adhered to. Furthermore, I will follow the "Research with Human Subjects" guidelines put forth by my university, institution, or professional setting. Ethical considerations include but are not limited to subject informed consent, confidentiality of records, adequate pre- and post-briefing of subjects, and subject opportunity to review a concise written summary of the study's purpose, method, results, and implications.

4. Consistent with accepted professional practice, I will save and protect my raw data for a minimum of five years; and if requested I will make the raw data available to scholars researching the multicultural counseling competency construct.

5. I will send a copy of my research results (for any study incorporating the MCKAS) in manuscript form to Dr. Ponterotto, regardless of whether the study is published, presented, or fully completed.

Signature:_____ Date:_____

Name:_____ Phone:_____

Address:_____

_____

_____

If a student, supervisor/mentor's name and phone number, affiliation, and signature:

Name:_____ Phone:_____

Affiliation:_____

Signature:_____ Date:_____

Multicultural Counseling Knowledge and Awareness Scale (MCKAS)

Copyrighted © 1997, 2002 by Joseph G. Ponterotto

A Revision of the Multicultural Counseling Awareness Scale (MCAS)

Copyrighted © 1991 by Joseph Ponterotto

Overview and Scoring Directions

Introduction

The Multicultural Counseling Knowledge and Awareness Scale (MCKAS) is a revision of the earlier Multicultural Counseling Awareness Scale (MCAS). Users of the MCKAS must have completed the "Utilization Request Form" before incorporating the instrument in their professional work. The MCKAS is a 32-item self-report inventory of perceived multicultural counseling knowledge and awareness. Researchers should read the development and validation studies of the MCKAS (Ponterotto, Gretchen, et al., 2002) and its predecessor, the MCAS (Ponterotto et al., 1996), before using the instrument.

The MCKAS is currently undergoing continuing validation research, and its psychometric strengths and limitations are still under study. The instrument should be used only for research at this time. It should not be used as an evaluative tool, and no individual decisions should be based on instrument scores.

The MCKAS is a two-factor instrument that includes 20 Knowledge items and 12 Awareness items extracted from the original 45-item MCAS. The two-factor model has been supported in both exploratory factor analysis and confirmatory factor analysis of the MCAS. Research on the MCAS across multiple samples has shown the two factors to be internally consistent. Coefficient alphas for the Knowledge scale have clustered in the .92 range and for the Awareness scale in the .78 range.

Scoring Directions for the 32-item MCKAS

A number of items (n = 10) in the Awareness Scale are reverse-worded (i.e., low score indicates high awareness) and need to be reverse-scored prior to any data analysis. These items are numbers 1, 4, 7, 10, 11, 18, 20, 24, 25, and 30.

To reverse-score these items, use the following conversion table:

1 = 7, 2 = 6, 3 = 5, 4 = 4, 5 = 3, 6 = 2, 7 = 1

The MCKAS yields two scores that are mildly correlated (r = 0.36), supporting the independent interpretation of separate subscales (see review in Ponterotto & Potere, 2003).

Knowledge Scale (20 items): 2, 3, 5, 6, 8, 9, 12, 13, 14, 15, 16, 17, 19, 21, 22, 23, 27, 28, 31, and 32.

These items are all worded in a positive direction, where high scores indicate higher perceived knowledge of multicultural counseling issues. The score for the Knowledge scale ranges from 20 to 140 using aggregate score, or 1–7 using a mean score (the mean subscale score is derived by dividing the total aggregate score by the number of subscale items, n = 20).

Awareness Scale (12 items): (1), (4), (7), (10), (11), (18), (20), (24), (25), 26, 29, (30).

Ten items in parentheses need to be reverse-scored. After reverse-scoring, the total score for the Awareness Scale ranges from 12 to 84 (or 1 to 7 for mean score; that is, the total score divided by number of subscale items, n = 12), with higher scores indicating higher awareness of multicultural counseling issues.

Note: No cutoff scores establishing "satisfactory" knowledge or awareness of multicultural counseling issues exist.

Multicultural Counseling Knowledge and Awareness Scale (MCKAS)

Copyrighted © 1997 by Joseph G. Ponterotto

A Revision of the Multicultural Counseling Awareness Scale (MCAS)

Copyrighted © 1991 by Joseph G. Ponterotto

Using the following scale, rate the truth of each item as it applies to you.

1	2	3	4	5	6	7
Not at All True			Somewhat True			Totally True

----

1. I believe all clients should maintain direct eye contact during counseling.

1	2	3	4	5	6	7

2. I check up on my minority/cultural counseling skills by monitoring my functioning—via consultation, supervision, and continuing education.

1	2	3	4	5	6	7

3. I am aware some research indicates that minority clients receive "less preferred" forms of counseling treatment than majority clients.

1	2	3	4	5	6	7

4. I think that clients who do not discuss intimate aspects of their lives are being resistant and defensive.

1	2	3	4	5	6	7

5. I am aware of certain counseling skills, techniques, or approaches that are more likely to transcend culture and be effective with any clients.

1	2	3	4	5	6	7

6. I am familiar with the "culturally deficient" and "culturally deprived" depictions of minority mental health and understand how these labels serve to foster and perpetuate discrimination.

1	2	3	4	5	6	7

7. I feel all the recent attention directed toward multicultural issues in counseling is overdone and not really warranted.

1	2	3	4	5	6	7

8. I am aware of individual differences that exist among members within a particular ethnic group based on values, beliefs, and level of acculturation.

1   2   3   4   5   6   7

9. I am aware some research indicates that minority clients are more likely to be diagnosed with mental illnesses than are majority clients.

1   2   3   4   5   6   7

10. I think that clients should perceive the nuclear family as the ideal social unit.

1   2   3   4   5   6   7

11. I think that being highly competitive and achievement oriented are traits that all clients should work toward.

1   2   3   4   5   6   7

12. I am aware of the differential interpretations of nonverbal communication (e.g., personal space, eye contact, handshakes) within various racial/ethnic groups.

1   2   3   4   5   6   7

13. I understand the impact and operations of oppression and the racist concepts that have permeated the mental health professions.

1   2   3   4   5   6   7

14. I realize that counselor-client incongruities in problem conceptualization and counseling goals may reduce counselor credibility.

1   2   3   4   5   6   7

15. I am aware that some racial/ethnic minorities see the profession of psychology as functioning to maintain and promote the status and power of the White Establishment.

1   2   3   4   5   6   7

16. I am knowledgeable of acculturation models for various ethnic minority groups.

1   2   3   4   5   6   7

17. I have an understanding of the role culture and racism play in the development of identity and worldviews among minority groups.

1   2   3   4   5   6   7

18. I believe that it is important to emphasize objective and rational thinking in minority clients.

1   2   3   4   5   6   7

19. I am aware of culture-specific, that is culturally indigenous, models of counseling for various racial/ethnic groups.

1   2   3   4   5   6   7

20. I believe that my clients should view a patriarchal structure as the ideal.

1   2   3   4   5   6   7

21. I am aware of both the initial barriers and benefits related to the cross-cultural counseling relationship.

1   2   3   4   5   6   7

22. I am comfortable with differences that exist between me and my clients in terms of race and beliefs.

1   2   3   4   5   6   7

23. I am aware of institutional barriers which may inhibit minorities from using mental health services.

1   2   3   4   5   6   7

24. I think that my clients should exhibit some degree of psychological mindedness and sophistication.

1   2   3   4   5   6   7

25. I believe that minority clients will benefit most from counseling with a majority counselor who endorses White middle-class values and norms.

1   2   3   4   5   6   7

26. I am aware that being born a White person in this society carries with it certain advantages.

1   2   3   4   5   6   7

27. I am aware of the value assumptions inherent in major schools of counseling and understand how these assumptions may conflict with values of culturally diverse clients.

1   2   3   4   5   6   7

28. I am aware that some minorities see the counseling process as contrary to their own life experiences and inappropriate or insufficient to their needs.

1   2   3   4   5   6   7

29. I am aware that being born a minority in this society brings with it certain challenges that White people do not have to face.

1   2   3   4   5   6   7

30. I believe that all clients must view themselves as their number one responsibility.

1   2   3   4   5   6   7

31. I am sensitive to circumstances (personal biases, language dominance, stage of ethnic identity development) that may dictate referral of the minority client to a member of his/her own racial/ethnic group.

1   2   3   4   5   6   7

32. I am aware that some minorities believe counselors lead minority students into non-academic programs regardless of student potential, preferences, or ambitions.

1   2   3   4   5   6   7

Thank you for completing this instrument. Please feel free to express in writing below any thoughts, concerns, or comments you have regarding this instrument:

Appendix III

Teacher Multicultural Attitude Survey (TMAS)

Utilization Request Form

In using the Teacher Multicultural Attitude Survey (TMAS) I agree to the following terms/conditions:

1. I understand that the TMAS is copyrighted by Joseph G. Ponterotto (Ph. D.) and colleagues at the Division of Psychological and Educational Services, Fordham University at Lincoln Center, 113 West 60th Street, New York, New York 10023-7478 (212-636-6480).

2. I am a trained professional in education, counseling, psychology, or a related field, having completed coursework (or training) in multicultural issues, psychometrics, and research ethics, or I am working under the supervision of such an individual.

3. In using the TMAS, all ethical standards of the American Educational Research Association, the American Psychological Association, the American Counseling Association, and/or related professional organizations will be adhered to. Furthermore, I will follow the "Research with Human Subjects" guidelines put forth by my school, university, institution, or professional setting. Ethical considerations include but are not limited to subject informed consent, confidentiality of records, adequate pre- and post-briefing of subjects, and subject opportunity to review a concise written summary of the study's purpose, method, results, and implications.

4. Consistent with accepted professional practice, I will save and protect my raw data for a minimum of five years; and if requested I will make the raw data available to Dr. Ponterotto (who is ethically responsible to monitor developments on the scale in terms of utility, reliability, and validity), and other students/scholars researching the multicultural counseling competency construct.

5. I will send a copy of my research results (for any study incorporating the TMAS) in manuscript form to Dr. Ponterotto, regardless of whether the study is published, presented, or fully completed.

Signature:_____   Date:_____

Name:_____   Phone:_____

Address:_____

_____

_____

If a student, supervisor/mentor's name and phone number, affiliation, and signature:

Name:_____   Phone:_____

Affiliation:_____

Signature:_____   Date:_____

Teacher Multicultural Attitude Survey (TMAS)

Copyrighted © by Joseph G. Ponterotto et al. (1995)

Scoring Directions as of 11/95

The TMAS gives one total score by summing (or averaging) all 20 items after reverse-scoring those items indicated.

The following items are scored as is (1 = 1, 2 = 2, 3 = 3, 4 = 4, 5 = 5)

Items 1, 2, 4, 5, 7, 8, 9, 10, 11, 13, 14, 17, 18

The following items are reverse-scored (1 = 5, 2 = 4, 3 = 3, 4 = 2, 5 = 1)

Items 3, 6, 12, 15, 16, 19, 20

Total scores can then range from 20 to 100 (or if dividing by the number of items [20] to get a Likert-type range mean, from 1 to 5).

Higher scores indicate more appreciation and awareness of multicultural teaching issues. The TMAS is only meant for large-scale mean research at this time, and should not be used in any evaluative way.

For recent validity information on the TMAS contact:

Joseph G. Ponterotto, Ph.D.
Division of Psychological & Educational Services
Room 1008
Fordham University—Lincoln Center
113 West 60th Street
New York, NY 10023-7478
(212) 636-6480

Teacher Multicultural Attitude Survey (TMAS)

Copyright © by Joseph G. Ponterotto et al. (1995)

Please respond to all items in the survey. Remember, there are no right or wrong answers. The survey is anonymous; do not put your name on the survey. Please circle the appropriate number below.

Use the following scale to rate each item.

1	2	3	4	5
Strongly Disagree	Disagree	Uncertain	Agree	Strongly Agree

---

1. I find teaching a culturally diverse student group rewarding.

1   2   3   4   5

2. Teaching methods need to be adapted to meet the needs of a culturally diverse student group.

1   2   3   4   5

3. Sometimes I think there is too much emphasis placed on multicultural awareness and training for teachers.

1   2   3   4   5

4. Teachers have the responsibility to be aware of their students' cultural backgrounds.

1   2   3   4   5

5. I frequently invite extended family members (cousins, grandparents, godparents, etc.) to attend parent-teacher conferences.

1   2   3   4   5

6. It is not the teacher's responsibility to encourage pride in one's culture.

1   2   3   4   5

7. As classrooms become more culturally diverse, the teacher's job becomes increasingly challenging.

1   2   3   4   5

8. I believe the teacher's role needs to be redefined to address the needs of students from culturally diverse backgrounds.

1   2   3   4   5

9. When dealing with bilingual students, some teachers may misinterpret different communication styles as behavioral problems.

1   2   3   4   5

10. As classrooms become more culturally diverse, the teacher's job becomes increasingly rewarding.

1   2   3   4   5

11. I can learn a great deal from students with culturally different backgrounds.

1   2   3   4   5

12. Multicultural training for teachers is not necessary.

1   2   3   4   5

13. In order to be an effective teacher, one needs to be aware of cultural differences present in the classroom.

1   2   3   4   5

14. Multicultural awareness training can help me work more effectively with a diverse student population.

1   2   3   4   5

15. Students should learn to communicate in English only.

1   2   3   4   5

16. Today's curriculum gives undue importance to multiculturalism and diversity.

1   2   3   4   5

17. I am aware of the diversity of cultural backgrounds in my classroom.

1   2   3   4   5

18. Regardless of the racial and ethnic makeup of my class, it is important for all students to be aware of multicultural diversity.

1   2   3   4   5

19. Being multiculturally aware is not relevant for the subject I teach.

1   2   3   4   5

20. Teaching students about cultural diversity will only create conflict in the classroom.

1   2   3   4   5

Do you have any thoughts or comments about this survey, or about the research topic?

_____

_____

_____

_____

_____

_____

Appendix IV

*Index of Race-Related
Stress–Brief Version (IRRS-B)*

IRRS–Brief Version

Copyrighted © 2000 by Shawn O. Utsey

1. **AGE** _____   2. **GENDER** (check) Male ___ Female ___

3. **MARITAL STATUS** (check)

Single ___ Married ___ Committed relationship ___ Separated ___
Divorced ___ Widowed ___

4. **OCCUPATIONAL STATUS** (check) Student ___ Unemployed ___
Employed ___ Homemaker ___

5. **YEARS OF EDUCATION** (please circle)

 1 2 3 4 5 6 7 8 9 10 11 12 13 14 15 16 17+

6. **ANNUAL INCOME** _____

7. **PLEASE INDICATE YOUR ETHNICITY** _____

Instructions

This survey questionnaire is intended to sample some of the experiences that Black people have in this country because of their "blackness." There are many experiences that a Black person can have in this country because of his/her race. Some events happen just once, some more often, while others may happen frequently. Below you will find listed some of these experiences, for which you are to indicate those that have happened to you or someone very close to you (i.e., a family member or loved one). It is important to note that a person can be affected by those events that happen to people close to them; this is why you are asked to consider such events as applying to your experiences when you complete this questionnaire. **Please circle the number on the scale (0 to 4) that indicates the reaction you had to the event at the time it happened. Do not leave any items blank**. If an event has happened more than once, refer to the first time it happened. *If an event did not happen, circle 0 and go on to the next item.*

0 = This never happened to me. 1 = This event happened but did not bother me. 2 = This event happened and I was slightly upset. 3 = This event happened and I was upset. 4 = This event happened and I was *extremely* **upset.**

1. You notice that crimes committed by White people tend to be romanticized, whereas the same crime committed by a Black person is portrayed as savagery, and the Black person who committed it, as an animal.
    0 1 2 3 4

2. Sales people/clerks did not say thank you or show other forms of courtesy and respect (e.g., put your things in a bag) when you shopped at some White-/non-Black-owned businesses.
    0 1 2 3 4

3. You notice that when Black people are killed by the police, the media inform the public of the victim's criminal record or negative information in their background, suggesting they got what they deserved.
    0 1 2 3 4

4. You have been threatened with physical violence by an individual or group of Whites/non-Blacks.
    0 1 2 3 4

5. You have observed that White kids who commit violent crimes are portrayed as "boys being boys," while Black kids who commit similar crimes are "wild animals."
    0 1 2 3 4

6. You seldom hear or read anything positive about Black people on the radio, TV, newspapers, or in history books.
    0 1 2 3 4

7. While shopping at a store, the sales clerk assumed that you couldn't afford certain items (e.g., you were directed toward the items on sale).
    0 1 2 3 4

8. You were the victim of a crime and the police treated you as if you should just accept it as part of being Black.
    0 1 2 3 4

9. You were treated with less respect and courtesy than Whites and other non-Blacks while in a store, restaurant, or other business establishment.
    0 1 2 3 4

10. You were passed over for an important project although you were more qualified and competent than the White/non-Black person given the task.
    0 1 2 3 4

11. Whites/non-Blacks have stared at you as if you didn't belong in the same place with them, whether it was a restaurant, theater, or other place of business.
    0 1 2 3 4

12. You have observed the police treat Whites/   0   1   2   3   4
non-Blacks with more respect and
dignity than they do Blacks.

13. You have been subjected to racist jokes   0   1   2   3   4
by Whites/non-Blacks in positions of
authority and you did not protest for fear
they might have held it against you.

14. While shopping at a store or when attempting   0   1   2   3   4
to make a purchase, you were ignored as
if you were not a serious customer or didn't
have any money.

15. You have observed situations where other   0   1   2   3   4
Blacks were treated harshly or unfairly by
Whites/non-Blacks due to their race.

16. You have heard reports of White people/   0   1   2   3   4
non-Blacks who have committed crimes,
and, in an effort to cover up their deeds,
falsely reported that a Black man was
responsible for the crime.

17. You notice that the media play up those stories   0   1   2   3   4
that cast Blacks in negative ways (child abusers,
rapists, muggers, etc. [or as savages] Wild Man
of 96th St., Wolf Pack, etc.), usually
accompanied by a large picture of a Black
person looking angry or disturbed.

18. You have heard racist remarks or comments   0   1   2   3   4
about Black people spoken with impunity by
White public officials or other influential
White people.

19. You have been given more work or the most   0   1   2   3   4
undesirable jobs at your place of employment
while White/non-Black employees of equal or
less seniority and credentials are given less
work and more desirable tasks.

20. You have heard or seen other Black people   0   1   2   3   4
express the desire to be White or to have
White physical characteristics because they
disliked being Black or thought it was ugly.

21. White people or other non-Blacks have   0   1   2   3   4
treated you as if you were unintelligent
and needed things explained to you
slowly or numerous times.

22. You were refused an apartment or other housing;   0   1   2   3   4
you suspect it was because you are Black.

SCORING FOR THE IRRS–BRIEF VERSION

In order to derive a race-related stress score for each of the IRRS-B racism domains, you must sum the raw scores for all items in each racism category. To obtain a global racism score, the summed scores for each racism category (i.e., each subscale score) should be transformed into z-scores and then summed.

FACTOR 1 CULTURAL RACISM	FACTOR 2 INSTITUTIONAL RACISM	FACTOR 3 INDIVIDUAL RACISM
Item #1	Item #4	Item #2
Item #3	Item #8	Item #7
Item #5	Item #10	Item #9
Item #6	Item #13	Item #11
Item #12	Item #19	Item #14
Item #15	Item #22	Item #21
Item #16		
Item #17		
Item #18		
Item #20		

References

Aboud, F. E. (1987). The development of ethnic self-identification and attitudes. In J. S. Phinney & M. J. Rotheram (Eds.), *Children's ethnic socialization: Pluralism and development* (pp. 32–55). Newbury Park, CA: Sage.

Aboud, F. E., & Levy, S. R. (2000). Interventions to reduce prejudice and discrimination in children and adolescents. In S. Oskamp (Ed.), *Reducing prejudice and discrimination* (pp. 269–293). Mahwah, NJ: Erlbaum.

Ackerman, N. W., & Jahoda, M. (1950). *Anti-Semitism and emotional disorder.* New York: Harper.

Akbar, N. (1984). *Chains and images of psychological slavery.* Jersey City, NJ: Mind Productions..

Akbar, N. (1996). *Breaking the chains of psychological slavery.* Tallahassee, FL: Mind Productions.

Ali, S. R., Liu, W. M., & Humedian, M. (2004). Islam 101: Understanding the religion and therapy implications. *Professional Psychology: Research and Practice, 35,* 635–642.

Allen, G. A. (2001, October 5). Is a new eugenics afoot? *Science Magazine, 294*(5540), 59–61. Retrieved October 19, 2005, from http://www.sciencemag.org/cgi/content/full/294/5540/59

Allport, G. W. (1954). *The nature of prejudice.* Reading, MA: Addison-Wesley.

Allport, G. W. (1979). *The nature of prejudice* (25th anniversary ed.). Reading, MA: Addison-Wesley.

Allport, G. W., & Odbert, H. S. (1936). Trait-names: A psycho-lexical study. *Psychological Monographs, 47*(211).

Altbach, P. (1991). The racial dilemma in American higher education. In P. G. Altbach & K. Lomotey (Eds.), *The racial crisis in American higher education* (pp. 3–29). Albany: State University of New York Press.

Altemeyer, B. (1996). *The authoritarian spector.* Cambridge, MA: Harvard University Press.

Altemeyer, B., & Hunsberger, B. (1992). Authoritarianism, religious fundamentalism, quest, and prejudice. *International Journal for the Psychology of Religion, 2,* 113–133.

American Heritage College Dictionary. (1993). Boston: Houghton-Mifflin.

American Psychological Association. (2003). Guidelines on multicultural education, training, research, practice, and organizational change for psychologists. *American Psychologist, 58,* 377–402.

American School Counselor Association. (1992). *Ethical standards for school counselors*. Alexandria, VA: Author.

American School Counselor Association. (1993). *Position statement: The professional school counselor and cross/multicultural counseling* (rev.). Alexandria, VA: Author.

Anderson, N. B., & Nickerson, K. J. (2005). Genes, race, and psychology in the genome era: An introduction. *American Psychologist, 60,* 5–8.

Andreasen, R. O. (2004). The cladistic race concept: A defense. *Biology and Philosophy, 19,* 425–442.

Andreasen, R. O. (2005). The meaning of "race": Folk conceptions and the new biology of race. *Journal of Philosophy, 102,* 94–106.

Ani, M. (1994). *Yurugu: An African-centered critique of European cultural thought and behavior.* Trenton, NJ: African World Press.

Arce, C. A. (1981). A reconsideration of Chicano culture and identity. *Daedalus, 110,* 177–192.

Armstead, C. A., Lawler, K. A., Gorden, G., Cross, J., & Gibbons, J. (1989). Relationship of racial stressors to blood pressure responses and anger expression in Black college students. *Health Psychology, 8,* 541–556.

Arthur, N., & Achenbach, K. (2002). Developing multicultural counseling competence through experimental learning. *Counselor Education and Supervision, 42,* 2–14.

Asante, M. K. (2000). *The Egyptian philosophers: Ancient African voices from Imhotep to Akhenaten.* Chicago: African American Images.

Ashton, M. C., Jackson, D. N., Paunonen, S. V., Helmes, E., & Rothstein, M. G. (1995). The criterion validity of broad factor scales versus specific trait scales. *Journal of Research in Personality, 29,* 432–442.

Atkinson, D. R., & Hackett, G. (2004). *Counseling diverse populations* (3rd ed.). Boston: McGraw-Hill.

Atkinson, D. R., Morten, G., & Sue, D. W. (Eds.). (1989). *Counseling American minorities* (3rd ed.). Boston: McGraw-Hill.

Atkinson, D. R., Morten, G., & Sue, D. W. (Eds.). (1998). *Counseling American minorities* (5th ed.). Boston: McGraw-Hill.

Atkinson, D. R., Thompson, C. E., & Grant, S. K. (1993). A three-dimensional model for counseling racial/ethnic minorities. *Counseling Psychologist, 21,* 257–277.

Baker, J. G., & Fishbein, H. D. (1998). The development of prejudice towards gays and lesbians by adolescents. *Journal of Homosexuality, 36,* 89–100.

Baldwin, J. A. (1981). Notes on an Africentric theory of Black personality. *Western Journal of Black Studies, 5,* 172–179.

Baldwin, J. A., & Bell, Y. R. (1985). The African Self-Consciousness Scale: An Africentric personality questionnaire. *Western Journal of Black Studies, 9,* 61–68.

Banks, J. A. (2001). Citizenship education and diversity: Implications for teacher education. *Journal of Teacher Education, 52,* 5–16.

Barbarin, O. A., & Gilbert, R. (1981). Institutional Racism Scale: Assessing self and organizational attributes. In O. A. Barbarin, P. R. Good, O. M. Pharr, & J. A. Siskind (Eds.), *Institutional racism and community competence* (DHSS Pub. No. ADM 81–907, pp. 147–171). Rockville, MD: National Institute of Mental Health, Center for Minority Group Mental Health Programs.

Barnett, R. C., & Hyde, J. S. (2001). Women, men, work, and family: An expansionist theory. *American Psychologist, 56,* 781–796.

Batson, C. D., & Burris, C. T. (1994). Personal religion: Depressant or stimulant of prejudice and discrimination? In M. P. Zanna & J. M. Olson (Eds.), *The psychology of prejudice: The Ontario Symposium* (Vol. 7, pp. 149–170). Hillsdale, NJ: Erlbaum.

Bell, L. A. (1997). Theoretical foundations for social justice education. In M. Adams, L. A. Bell, & P. Griffin (Eds.), *Teaching for diversity and social justice: A sourcebook* (pp. 3–15). New York: Routledge.

Bemak, F., & Chung, R. C. Y. (2003). Multicultural counseling with immigrant students in schools. In P. Pedersen & J. Carey (Eds.), *Multicultural counseling in schools: A practical handbook* (pp. 84–104). Boston: Allyn & Bacon.

Bennett, L. (1966). *Before the Mayflower: A history of the Negro in America, 1619–1966.* Chicago: Johnson.

Bergman, J. (2002). Evolution and the origins of the biological race theory. *Creation Ex Nihilo Technical Journal, 7,* 155–168.

Berry, J. W., & Kim, U. (1988). Acculturation and mental health. In P. R. Dasen, J. W. Berry, & N. Sartorius (Eds.), *Health and cross-cultural psychology: Toward applications* (pp. 207–236). Newbury Park, CA: Sage.

Bettelheim, B. (1964). *Social change and prejudice, including the dynamics of prejudice.* New York: Free Press of Glencoe.

Bicultural vision. (1994, Spring). *Teaching Tolerance, 3*(1), 6.

Bidell, M. P. (2005). The Sexual Orientation Counselor Competency Scale: Assessing attitudes, skills, and knowledge of counselors working with lesbian, gay, and bisexual clients. *Counselor Education and Supervision, 44,* 267–279.

Biernat, M., & Crandall, C. S. (1999). Racial attitudes. In J. P. Robinson, P. R. Shaver, & L. S. Wrightsman (Eds.), *Measures of political attitudes* (pp. 297–411). San Diego, CA: Academic Press.

Bigler, R. S. (1999). The use of multicultural curricula and materials to counter racism in children. *Journal of Social Issues, 55*(4), 667–766.

Bishop, R. S. (1992). Multicultural literature for children: Making informed choices. In V. Harris (Ed.), *Teaching multicultural literature in grades K-8* (pp. 37–53). Norwood, MA: Christopher-Gordon.

Bobo, L., Kluegel, J. R., & Smith, R. A. (1997). Laissez-faire racism: The crystallization of a kinder, gentler, antiblack ideology. In S. A. Tuch & J. K. Martin (Eds.), *Racial attitudes in the 1990s: Continuity and change* (pp. 15–42). Westport, CT: Prager.

Boeckmann, R. J., & Turpin-Petrosino, C. (2002). Understanding the harm of hate crimes. *Journal of Social Issues, 58*(2), 207–225.

Bonham, V. L., Warshauer-Baker, E., & Collins, F. S. (2005). Race and ethnicity in the genome era: The complexity of the constructs. *American Psychologist, 60,* 9–15.

Bowser, B. P., & Hunt, R. G. (1996). *Impacts of racism on White Americans* (2nd ed.). Thousand Oaks, CA: Sage.

Brabeck, M. M., Rogers, L. A., Sirin, S., Henderson, J., Benvenuto, M., Weaver, M., et al. (2000). Increasing ethical sensitivity to racial and gender intolerance in schools: Development of the Racial Ethical Sensitivity Test. *Ethics & Behavior, 10,* 119–137.

Bradby, D., & Helms, J. E. (1990). Black racial identity attitudes and white therapist cultural sensitivity in cross-racial therapy dyads: An exploratory study. In J. E. Helms (Ed.), *Black and white racial identity: Theory, research, and practice* (pp. 165–175). New York: Greenwood.

Braden, A. (1958). *The wall between.* New York: Monthly Review Press.

Bradley, M. (1991). *The iceman inheritance.* New York: Kayode.

Brislin, R. W., Cushner, K., Cherrie, C. & Young, M. (1986). *Intercultural interactions: A practical guide.* Beverly Hills, CA: Sage.

Brislin, R. W., & Yoshida, T. (1994). The content of cross-cultural training: An introduction. In R. W. Brislin & Y. Yoshida (Eds.), *Improving intercultural interaction* (pp. 1–14). Thousand Oaks, CA: Sage.

Brody, H. (1984). Growing up in interracial families: Suggestions for single parents. *Interracial Books for Children Bulletin, 15* (6), 12, 15.

Broman, C. L. (1997). Race-related factors and life satisfaction among African Americans. *Journal of Black Psychology, 23,* 36–49.

Brookins, C. C., Anyabwile, T. M., & Nacoste, R. E. (1996). Exploring the links between racial identity attitudes and psychological feelings of closeness in African American students. *Journal of Applied Social Psychology, 26,* 243–264.

Brown v. Board of Education, 347 U.S. 483 (1954).

Brown, T. N., Williams, D. R., Jackson, J. S., Neighbors, H., Torres, M., Sellers, S. L., et al. (2000). "Being Black and feeling blue": The mental health consequences of racial discrimination. *Race & Society, 2,* 117–131.

Brummett, B. R., Wade, J. C., Ponterotto, J. G., Thombs, B., & Lewis, C. (in press). Psychological well-being and a multicultural personality disposition. *Journal of Counseling and Development.*

Bulhan, H. A. (1985). *Frantz Fanon and the psychology of oppression.* New York: Plenum Press.

Burkard, A. W., Juarez-Huffaker, M., & Ajmere, K. (2003). White racial identity attitudes as a predictor of client perceptions of cross-cultural working alliances. *Journal of Multicultural Counseling and Development, 31,* 226–244.

Burkard, A. W., Medler, B. R., & Boticki, M. A. (2001). Prejudice and racism: Challenges and progress in measurement. Encountering nigrescence. In J. G. Ponterotto, J. M. Casas, L. A. Suzuki, & C. M. Alexander (Eds.), *Handbook of multicultural counseling* (2nd ed., pp. 457–481). Thousand Oaks, CA: Sage.

Burkard, A. W., Ponterotto, J. G., Reynolds, A. L., & Alfonso, V. C. (1999). White counselor trainees' racial identity and working alliance perceptions. *Journal of Counseling and Development, 77,* 324–329.

Bussey, K., & Bandura, A. (1999). Social cognitive theory of gender development and differentiation. *Psychological Review, 106,* 676–713.

Byrnes, D. A. (1988). Children and prejudice. *Social Education, 52,* 267–271.

California Postsecondary Education Commission. (1992). *Assessing campus climate: Feasibility of developing an educational equity assessment system* (Commission Report No. 92-2). Sacramento, CA: Author.

Carey, J. C., & Boscardin, M. L. (2003). Improving the multicultural effectiveness of your school in the context of state standards, accountability measures and high-stakes assessment. In P. Pedersen & J. Carey (Eds.), *Multicultural counseling in schools: A practical handbook* (pp. 270–289). Boston: Allyn & Bacon.

Carr, L. G. (1997). *Color-blind racism.* Thousand Oaks, CA: Sage.

Carter, R. T. (1990). The relationship between racism and racial identity among White Americans: An exploratory investigation. *Journal of Counseling and Development, 69,* 46–50.

Carter, R. T. (1991). Racial identity attitudes and psychological functioning. *Journal of Multicultural Counseling and Development, 19,* 105–114.

Carter, R. T., & Pieterse, A. L. (2005). Race: A social and psychological analysis of the term and its meaning. In R. T. Carter (Ed.), *Handbook of racial-cultural psychology and counseling: Theory and research* (Vol. 1, pp. 41–63). New York: Wiley.

Casas, J. M., Furlong, M. J., & de Esparza, C. R. (2003). Increasing Hispanic parent participation in schools: The role of the counselor. In P. B. Pedersen & J. C. Carey (Eds.), *Multicultural counseling in schools: A practical handbook* (2nd ed., pp. 105–130). Boston: Allyn & Bacon.

Cass, V. C. (1979). Homosexual identity formation: A theoretical model. *Journal of Homosexuality, 4,* 219–235.

Cass, V. C. (1984). Homosexual identity formation: Testing a theoretical model. *Journal of Sex Research, 20,* 143–167.

Cattell, R. B. (1943). The description of personality: Basic traits resolved into clusters. *Journal of Abnormal and Social Psychology, 38,* 476–506.

Cervantes, J. M., & Parham, T. A. (2005). Toward a meaningful spirituality for people of color: Lessons for the counseling practitioner. *Cultural Diversity and Ethnic Minority Psychology, 11,* 69–81.

Choi-Misailidis, S. (2003). *Multiracial-heritage awareness and personal affiliation: Development and validation of a new measure to assess identity in people of mixed race descent.* Unpublished doctoral dissertation, Fordham University, New York.

Choney, S. K., & Behrens, J. T. (1996). Development of the Oklahoma Racial Attitudes Scale–Preliminary Form (ORAS-P). In G. R. Sodowsky & J. C. Impara (Eds.), *Multicultural assessment in counseling and clinical psychology* (pp. 225–240). Lincoln, NE: Buros Institute of Mental Measurements.

Choney, S. K., & Rowe, W. (1994). Assessing White racial identity: The White Racial Consciousness Development Scale (WRCDS). *Journal of Counseling and Development, 73,* 102–104.

Claney, D., & Parker, W. M. (1989). Assessing White racial consciousness and perceived comfort with Black individuals: A preliminary study. *Journal of Counseling and Development, 67,* 449–451.

Clark, R. (2000). Perceptions of inter-ethnic group racism predict increased blood pressure responses to a laboratory challenge in college women. *Annals of Behavioral Medicine, 22,* 214–222.

Clark, R., Anderson, N. B., Clark, V. R., & Williams, D. R. (1999). Racism as a stressor for African Americans: A biopsychosocial model. *American Psychologist, 54,* 805–816.

Cokley, K. O. (2002). Testing Cross's revised racial identity model: An examination of the relationship between racial identity and internalized racism. *Journal of Counseling Psychology, 49,* 476–483.

Coleman, E. (1982). Developmental stages of the coming out process. In J. C. Gonsiorek (Ed.), *Homosexuality and psychotherapy: A practitioner's handbook on affirmative models* (pp. 31–43). New York: Haworth.

Coleman, H. L. K. (1995). Strategies for coping with cultural diversity. *Counseling Psychologist, 23,* 722–740.

Coleman, H. L. K., Casali, S. B., & Wampold, B. E. (2001). Adolescent strategies for coping with cultural diversity. *Journal of Counseling and Development, 79,* 356–364.

Constantine, M. G., Gloria, A. M., & Ladany, N. (2002). The factor structure underlying three self-report multicultural competence scales. *Cultural Diversity and Ethnic Minority Psychology, 8,* 334–345.

Constantine, M. G., & Ladany, N. (2001). New visions for defining and assessing multicultural counseling competence. In J. G. Ponterotto, J. M. Casas, L. A. Suzuki, & C. M. Alexander (Eds.), *Handbook of multicultural counseling* (2nd ed., pp. 482–498). Thousand Oaks, CA: Sage.

Constantine, M. G., & Ponterotto, J. G. (2005). Evaluating and selecting psychological measures for research purposes. In F. T. L. Leong & J. T. Austin (Eds.), *The psychology research handbook: A guide for graduate students and research assistants* (2nd ed., pp. 104–113). Thousand Oaks, CA: Sage.

Cook, S. W. (1978). Interpersonal and attitudinal outcomes in cooperating interracial groups. *Journal of Research and Development in Education, 12,* 97–113.

Corsini, R. J., & Wedding, D. (2004). *Current psychotherapies* (7th ed.). New York: Wadsworth.

Costa, P. T., Jr., & McCrae, R. R. (1992). *Revised NEO Personality Inventory (NEO-PI-R) and NEO Five Factor Inventory (NEO-FFI) professional manual.* Odessa, FL: Psychological Assessment Resources.

Coyne, R. K. (1987). *Primary preventive counseling: Empowering people and systems.* Munice, IN: Accelerated Development.

Cross, W. E., Jr. (1971, July). The Negro-to-Black conversion experience. *Black World,* pp. 13–27.

Cross, W. E., Jr. (1991). *Shades of Black: Diversity in African-American identity.* Philadelphia: Temple University Press.

Cross, W. E., Jr. (1995). The psychology of nigrescence: Revising the Cross model. In J. G. Ponterotto, J. M. Casas, L. A. Suzuki, & C. M. Alexander (Eds.), *Handbook of multicultural counseling* (pp. 93–122). Thousand Oaks, CA: Sage.

Cross, W. E., Jr. (2001). Encountering nigrescence. In J. G. Ponterotto, J. M. Casas, L. Suzuki, & C. M. Alexander (Eds.), *Handbook of multicultural counseling* (2nd ed., pp. 30–44). Thousand Oaks, CA: Sage.

Cross, W. E., Jr., & Fhagen-Smith, P. (1996). Nigrescence and ego identity development: Accounting for differential Black identity patterns. In P. B. Pedersen, J. G. Draguns, W. J. Lonner, & J. E. Trimble (Eds.), *Counseling across cultures* (4th ed., pp. 108–123). Thousand Oaks, CA: Sage.

Cross, W. E., Jr., Smith, L., & Payne, Y. (2002). Black identity: A repertoire of daily enactments. In P. B. Pedersen, J. G. Draguns, W. J. Lonner, & J. E. Trimble (Eds.), *Counseling across cultures* (5th ed., 93–108). Thousand Oaks, CA: Sage.

Cross, W. E., Jr., & Vandiver, B. J. (2001). Nigrescence theory and measurement: Introducing the Cross Racial Identity Scale (CRIS). In J. G. Ponterotto, J. M. Casas, L. A. Suzuki, & C. M. Alexander (Eds.), *Handbook of multicultural counseling* (2nd ed., pp. 371–393). Thousand Oaks, CA: Sage.

Crotcau, J. M., Lark, J. S., Lidderdale, M. A., & Chung, Y. B. (Eds.). (2005). *Deconstructing heterosexism in the counseling professions: A narrative approach.* Thousand Oaks, CA: Sage.

Cuellar, I., Arnold, B., & Maldonado, R. (1995). Acculturation Rating Scale for Mexican Americans–II: A revision of the original ARSMA scale. *Hispanic Journal of Behavioral Sciences, 17,* 275–304.

Cushner, K., & Brislin, R. W. (1997). *Improving intercultural interactions, Vol. 2. Modules for cross-cultural training programs.* Thousand Oaks, CA: Sage.

D'Andrea, M., & Daniels, J. (2001). Expanding our thinking about White racism: Facing the challenge of multicultural counseling. In J. Ponterotto, J. M. Casas, L. A. Suzuki, & C. M. Alexander (Eds.), *Handbook of multicultural counseling* (2nd ed., pp. 289–310). Thousand Oaks, CA: Sage.

D'Andrea, M., Daniels, J., Arredondo, P., Ivey, M. B., Ivey, A. E., Locke, D. C., et al. (2001). Fostering organizational changes to realize the revolutionary potential of the multicultural movement. In J. G. Ponterotto, J. M. Casas, L. A. Suzuki, & C. M. Alexander (Eds.), *Handbook of multicultural counseling* (2nd ed., pp. 222–253). Thousand Oaks, CA: Sage.

D'Andrea, M., Daniels, J., & Heck, R. (1991). Evaluating the impact of multicultural counseling training. *Journal of Counseling and Development, 70,* 143–150.

D'Andrea, M., Daniels, J., & Noonan, M. J. (2003). New developments in the assessment of multicultural competence: The Multicultural Awareness-Knowledge-Skills-Survey-Teacher Form. In D. B. Pope-Davis, H. L. K Coleman, W. M. Liu, & R. Toprek (Eds.), *Handbook of multicultural competencies* (pp. 154–167). Thousand Oaks, CA: Sage.

D'Angelo, E. (1971). *The teaching of critical thinking.* Amsterdam: B. R. Gruner.

Dashfsky, A. (Ed.). (1976). *Ethnic identity in society.* Chicago: Rand McNally.

Delphin, M. E., & Rollock, D. (1995). University alienation and African American ethnic identity as predictors of attitudes toward, knowledge about, and likely use of psychological services. *Journal of College Student Development, 36,* 337–346.

Denmark, F. L. (1994). Prejudice and discrimination. In R. J. Corsini (Ed.), *Encyclopedia of psychology* (2nd ed., pp.110–111). New York: Wiley.

DePorto, D. (2003). Battered women and separation abuse: A treatment approach based on "knowing." In M. Kopala & M. A. Keitel (Eds.), *Handbook of counseling women* (pp. 279–306). Thousand Oaks, CA: Sage.

Dillon, F., & Worthington, R. L. (2003). The Lesbian, Gay and Bisexual Affirmative Counseling Self-Efficacy Inventory (LGB-CSI): Development, validation, and training implications. *Journal of Counseling and Development, 50,* 235–251.

Dinsmore, B. D., & Mallinckrodt, B. (1996). Emotional self-awareness, eating disorders, and racial identity attitudes in African American women. *Journal of Multicultural Counseling and Development, 24,* 267–277.

Diop, C. A. (1981). Civilization or barbarism: An authentic anthropology. Brooklyn, NY: Lawrence Hill Books.

Dizard, J. E. (1970). Black identity, social class, and Black power. *Journal of Social Issues, 26,* 195–207.

Dobbins, J. E., & Skillings, J. H. (2000). Racism as a clinical syndrome. *American Journal of Orthopsychiatry, 70,* 14–27.

Dobbins, J. E., & Skillings, J. H. (2005). White racism and mental health: Treating the individual racist. In R. T. Carter (Ed.), *Handbook of racial-cultural psychology and counseling: Practice and training* (Vol. 2, pp. 427–446). New York: Wiley

DOEgenomes.org: Genome programs of the U.S. Department of Energy Office of Science [Home page]. (2003). Retrieved October 21, 2005, from http://www.doegenomes.org/

Dovidio, J. F., & Gaertner, S. L. (1986). Prejudice, discrimination, and racism: Historical trends and contemporary approaches. In J. F. Dovidio & S. L. Gaertner (Eds.), *Prejudice, discrimination, and racism* (pp. 1–34). Orlando, FL: Academic Press.

Dovidio, J. F., & Gaertner, S. L. (1998). On the nature of contemporary prejudice: The causes, consequences, and challenges of aversive racism. In J. L. Eberhardt & S. T. Fiske (Eds.), *Confronting racism* (pp. 3–32). Thousand Oaks, CA: Sage.

Dovidio, J. F., Gaertner, S. L., Niemann, Y. F., & Snider, K. (2001). Racial, ethnic and cultural differences in responding to distinctiveness and discrimination on campus: Stigma and common group identity. *Journal of Social Issues, 57*(1), 167–188.

Dovidio, J. F., Kawakami, K., & Gaertner, S. L. (2000). Reducing contemporary prejudice: Combating explicit and implicit bias at the individual and intergroup level. In S. Oskamp (Ed.), *Recuing prejudice and discrimination* (pp. 137–163). Hillsdale, NJ: Erlbaum.

Dowling, B. (1955). Some personality factors involved in tolerance and intolerance. *Journal of Social Psychology, 42,* 325–327.

Downing, N. E., & Roush, K. L. (1985). From passive acceptance to active commitment: A model of feminist identity development for women. *Counseling Psychologist, 13,* 695–709.

Driscoll, J. M., & Hoffman, M. A. (1997). Exploring attitudes of White dental students regarding willingness to treat people with HIV. *Journal of Dental Education, 61,* 717–726.

Duckitt, J. (1992). *The social psychology of prejudice.* New York: Praeger.

Dunton, B. C., & Fazio, R. H. (1997). An individual difference measure of motivation to control prejudiced reactions. *Personality and Social Psychology Bulletin, 23,* 316–326.

Eberhardt, J. L. (2005). Imaging race. *American Psychologist, 60,* 181–190.

Edler, J. M. (1974). *White on white: An anti-racism manual for white educators in the process of becoming.* Unpublished doctoral dissertation, University of Massachusetts, Amherst.

Ehrlich, H. J. (n.d.). *Understanding hate crimes.* Retrieved October 20, 2005, from http://www.prejudiceinstitute.org/understandinghatecrimes.html

Erikson, E. H. (1950). *Childhood and society.* New York: Norton.

Erikson, E. H. (1968). *Identity: Youth and crisis.* New York: Norton.

Essed, P. (1990). *Everyday racism: Reports from women of two cultures.* Claremont, CA: Hunter House.

Everett, S. (1991). *History of slavery.* Secaucus, NJ: Chartwell Books.

Fanon, F. (1963). *The wretched of the earth.* New York: Grove Press.

Fanon, F. (1964). *Toward the African revolution.* New York: Grove Press.

Fanon, F. (1967). *Black skin, White masks.* New York: Grove Press.

Fassinger, R. E. (1998). Lesbian, gay, and bisexual identity and student development theory. In R. L. Sanlo (Ed.), *Working with lesbian, gay, bisexual, and transgender college students: A handbook for faculty and administrators* (pp. 13–22). Westport, CT: Greenwood.

Fassinger, R. E., & Miller, B. A. (1997). Validation of an inclusive model of homosexual identity formation in a sample of gay men. *Journal of Homosexuality, 32,* 53–78.

Feagin, J. R. (1991). The continuing significance of race: Antiblack discrimination in public places. *American Sociological Review, 56,* 101–116.

Fernando, S. (1984). Racism as a cause of depression. *International Journal of Social Psychiatry, 30,* 41–49.

Festinger, L. (1954). A theory of social comparison processes. *Human Relations, 7,* 117–140.

Fischer, A. R., & Moradi, B. (2001). Racial and ethnic identity: Recent developments and needed directions. In J. G. Ponterotto, J. M. Casas, L. A. Suzuki, & C. M. Alexander (Eds.), *Handbook of multicultural counseling* (2nd ed., pp. 341–370). Thousand Oaks, CA: Sage.

Fischer, A. R., Tokar, D. M., Mergl, M. M., Good, G. E., Hill, M. S., & Blum, S. A. (2000). Assessing women's feminist identity development: Studies of convergent, discriminant, and structural validity. *Psychology of Women Quarterly, 24,* 15–29.

Fishbein, H. D. (2002). *Peer prejudice and discrimination: The origins of prejudice* (2nd ed.). Mahwah, NJ: Erlbaum.

Fisher, C. B., Wallace, S. A., & Fenton, R. E. (2000). Discrimination distress during adolescence. *Journal of Youth and Adolescence, 29,* 679–695.

Fontes, L. A. (2003). Reducing violence in multicultural schools. In P. Pedersen & J. Carey (Eds.), *Multicultural counseling in schools: A practical approach* (pp. 211–233). Boston: Allyn & Bacon.

Ford, M. E. (1992). *Motivating humans.* Thousand Oaks, CA: Sage.

Fox, R. (1992). Prejudice and the unfinished mind: A new look at an old failing. *Psychological Inquiry, 3,* 137–152.

Freire, P. (1970). *The pedagogy of the oppressed.* New York: Continuum.

Fuertes, J. N., Miville, M. L., Mohr, J. J., Sedlacek, W. E., & Gretchen, D. (2000). Factor structure and short form of the Miville-Guzman Universality-Diversity Scale. *Measurement and Evaluation in Counseling and Development, 33,* 157–169.

Fuertes, J. N., Sedlacek, W. E., Roger, P. R., & Mohr, J. J. (2000). Correlates of universal-diverse orientation among first-year university students. *Journal of the First-Year Experience, 12,* 45–59.

Fuller, N. (1969). *The united independent compensatory code/system/concept: A textbook/workbook for thought, speech and/or action for victims of racism (white supremacy).* Washington, DC: Library of Congress.

Funderburg, L. (1994). *Black, white, other: Biracial Americans talk about race and identity.* New York: William Morrow.

Gabelko, N. H. (1988). Prejudice reduction in secondary schools. *Social Education, 52,* 276–279.

Gaertner, S. L., & Dovidio, J. F. (1986). The aversive form of racism. In J. F. Dovidio & S. L. Gartner (Eds.), *Prejudice, discrimination, and racism* (pp. 61–89). Orlando, FL: Academic Press.

Gaertner, S. L., & Dovidio, J. F. (2000). *Reducing intergroup bias: The common ingroup identity model.* Philadelphia: Psychology Press.

Gamst, G., Dana, R. H., Der-Karabetian, A., Aragon, M., Arellano, L., Morrow, G., & Martenson, L. (2004). Cultural competency revised: The California Brief Multicultural Competence Scale. *Measurement and Evaluation in Counseling and Development, 37,* 163–183.

Gelso, C., & Fretz, B. (2001). *Counseling psychology* (2nd ed). Belmont, CA: Wadsworth.

Genesee, F., & Gandara, P. (1999). Improving intergroup relations: Lessons learned from Cooperative Learning Programs. *Journal of Social Issues, 55*(4), 665–686.

Gibbs, J. (1988). *Young, Black, and male in America: An endangered species.* Dover, MA: Auburn House.

Goldstein, S. (2000). *Cross-cultural explorations: Activities in culture and psychology.* Boston: Allyn & Bacon.

Goodstein, R., & Ponterotto, J. G. (1997). Racial and ethnic identity: Their relationship and their contribution to self-esteem. *Journal of Black Psychology, 23,* 275–292.

Gordon, M. M. (1964). *Assimilation in American life.* New York: Oxford University Press.

Graves, S. B. (1999). Television and prejudice reduction: When does television as a vicarious experience make a difference? *Journal of Social Issues, 55*(4), 707–728.

Gregory, S. (1970). *Hey, white girl.* New York: Norton.

Grieger, I. (1996). A multicultural organizational development checklist for student affairs. *Journal of College Student Development, 37,* 561–573.

Grieger, I., & Ponterotto, J. G. (1998). Challenging intolerance. In C. C. Lee & G. R. Walz (Eds.), *Social action: A mandate for counselors* (pp. 17–50). Alexandria, VA: American Counseling Association.

Grieger, I., & Toliver, S. (2001). Multiculturalism on predominantly white campuses: Multiple roles and functions for the counselor. In J. G. Ponterotto, J. M. Casas, L. A. Suzuki, & C. M. Alexander (Eds.), *Handbook of multicultural counseling* (2nd ed., pp. 825–848). Thousand Oaks, CA: Sage.

Grills, C., & Ajei, M. (2002). African-centered conceptualizations of self and consciousness: The Akan model. In T. A. Parham (Ed.), *Counseling persons of African descent: Raising the bar of practitioner competence* (pp. 75–99). Thousand Oaks, CA: Sage.

Grills, C., & Longshore, D. (1996). Africentrism: Psychometric analyses of a self-report. *Journal of Black Psychology, 22,* 86–106.

Gudykunst, W. B., Guzley, R. M., & Hammer, M. R. (1996). Designing intercultural training. In D. Landis & R. Bhagat (Eds.), *Handbook of intercultural training* (3rd ed., pp. 61–80). Thousand Oaks, CA: Sage.

Guthrie, R. V. (1998). *Even the rat was white: A historical view of psychology* (2nd ed.). Boston: Allyn & Bacon.

Haberman, M. (1994). Gentle teaching in an intolerant society. *Educational Horizons, 72,* 2–29.

Hansman, C. A., Spencer, L., Grant, D., & Jackson, M. (1999). Beyond diversity: Dismantling barriers in education. *Journal of Instructional Psychology, 26,* 16–22.

Hardiman, R. (1982). *White identity development: A process oriented model for describing the racial consciousness of White Americans.* Unpublished doctoral dissertation, University of Massachusetts, Amherst.

Harrell, S. P. (1994). *The Racism and Life Experience Scale.* Unpublished manuscript, Department of Psychology, Pepperdine University, Malibu, CA.

Harrell, S. P. (2000). A multidimensional conceptualization of racism-related stress: Implications for the well-being of people of color. *American Journal of Orthopsychiatry, 70,* 42–57.

Hashfield, G. A., Alpert, B. S., Willey, E., Somes, G. W., Murphy, J. K., & Dupaul, L. M. (1989). Race and gender influence ambulatory blood pressure patterns of adolescents. *American Journal of Hypertension, 14,* 598–603.

Hass, R. G., Katz, I., Rizzo, N., Bailey, J., & Moore, L. (1992). When racial ambivalence evokes negative affect, using a disguised measure of mood. *Personality and Social Psychology Bulletin, 18,* 786–797.

Haverkamp, B. E., Morrow, S. L., & Ponterotto, J. G. (Eds.). (2005). Knowledge in context: Qualitative methods in counseling psychology research. *Journal of Counseling Psychology, 52*(2, Special issue).

Hayes, S. A., & Lewis, A. C. (2002). School counselors: Professional origins in cross-cultural counseling. In P. Pedersen, J. Draguns, W. Lonner, & J. Trimble (Eds.), *Counseling across cultures* (5th ed., pp. 381–394). Thousand Oaks, CA: Sage.

Helms, J. E. (1984). Toward a theoretical explanation of the effects of race on counseling: A Black and White model. *Counseling Psychologist, 12,* 153–165.

Helms, J. E. (Ed.). (1990). *Black and White racial identity: Theory, research, and practice.* Westport, CT: Greenwood Press.

Helms, J. E. (1995). An update on Helms' White and people of color racial identity models. In J. G. Ponterotto, J. M. Casas, L. A. Suzuki, & C. M. Alexander (Eds.), *Handbook of multicultural counseling* (pp. 181–198). Thousand Oaks, CA: Sage.

Helms, J. E. (2001). Life questions. In J. G. Ponterotto, J. M. Casas, L. Suzuki, & C. M. Alexander (Eds.), *Handbook of multicultural counseling* (2nd ed., pp. 22–29). Thousand Oaks, CA: Sage.

Helms, J. E. (2003). Racial identity in the social environment. In P. Pedersen & J. Carey (Eds.), *Multicultural counseling in schools: A practical handbook* (2nd ed., pp. 44–58). Boston: Allyn & Bacon.

Helms, J. E. (2005). Challenging some misuses of reliability as reflected in the evaluations of the White Racial Identity Attitude Scale (WRIAS). In R. T. Carter (Ed.), *Handbook of racial-cultural psychology and counseling: Theory and research* (Vol. 1, pp. 360–390). New York: Wiley.

Helms, J. E., & Carter, R. T. (1990). Development of the White Racial Identity Inventory. In J. E. Helms (Ed.), *Black and White racial identity: Theory, research, and practice* (pp. 67–80). Westport, CT: Greenwood Press.

Helms, J. E., & Carter, R. T. (1991). Relationships of White and Black racial identity attitudes and demographic similarity to counselor preferences. *Journal of Counseling Psychology, 38,* 446–457.

Helms, J. E., & Cook, D. A. (1999). *Using race and culture in counseling and psychotherapy.* Boston: Allyn & Bacon.

Helms, J. E., & Parham, T. A. (1990). The relationship between Black racial identity attitudes and cognitive styles. In J. E. Helms (Ed.), *Black and White racial identity: Theory, research, and practice* (pp. 119–131). New York: Greenwood Press.

Helms, J. E., & Parham, T. A. (1996). The Racial Identity Attitudes Scale. In R. L. Jones (Ed.), *Handbook of tests and measurements for Black populations* (Vol. 1, pp. 167–174). Hampton, VA: Cobb & Henry.

Henry, G. B. (1986). *Cultural Diversity Awareness Inventory* (Rep. No. PS 016 636). East Lansing, MI: National Center for Research on Teacher Learning. (ERIC Document Reproduction Service No. ED 282 657)

Herring, R. D. (1999). *Counseling with Native American Indians and Alaska Natives: Strategies for helping professionals.* Thousand Oaks, CA: Sage.

Herrnstein, R., & Murray, C. (1994). *The bell curve: Intelligence and class structure in American life.* New York: Free Press.

Hines, A., & Pedersen, P. (1980). The cultural grid: Matching social system variables and cultural perspectives. *Asian Pacific Training Development Journal, 1*(1), 5–11.

Hofstede, G. J., Pedersen, P., & Hofstede, G. (2002). *Exploring culture: Exercises, stories and synthetic cultures.* Yarmouth, ME: Intercultural Press.

Holcomb-McCoy, C. C., & Day-Vines, N. (2004). Exploring school counselor multicultural competence: A multidimensional concept. *Measurement and Evaluation in Counseling and Development, 37,* 154–162.

Hoyle, F., & Wickramasinghe, C. (1999). Towards an understanding of the nature of racial prejudice. *Journal of Scientific Exploration, 13,* 681–684.

Hughes, M. (1999). Symbolic racism, old-fashioned racism, and Whites' opposition to affirmative action. In S. A. Tuch & J. K. Martin (Eds.), *Racial attitudes in the 1990s: Continuity and change* (pp. 45–75). Westport, CT: Prager.

Ichheiser, G. (1970). *Appearances and realities.* San Francisco: Jossey-Bass.

Ivey, A. E., Pedersen, P. B., & Ivey, M. (2001). *Intentional group counseling: A microskills approach.* Belmont, CA: Brooks/Cole.

Jackson, C. C., & Neville, H. A. (1998). Influence of racial identity attitudes on African American college students' vocational identity and hope. *Journal of Vocational Behavior, 53,* 97–113.

Jackson, J. S., Brown, T. N., Williams, D. R., Torres, M., Sellers, S. L., & Brown, K. (1992). *Racism and the physical and mental health status of African Americans: A thirteen year national panel study.* Ann Arbor: University of Michigan Institute for Social Research.

Jackson, J. S., Brown, K. T., & Kirby, D. C. (1998). International perspectives on prejudice and racism. In J. L. Eberhardt & S. T. Fiske (Eds.), *Confronting racism* (pp. 101–135). Thousand Oaks, CA: Sage.

Jackson, J. S., Williams, D. R., & Torres, M. (1995). *Racial discrimination, stress, action orientation and physical and psychological health.* Unpublished manuscript, University of Michigan.

Jacobs, J. H. (1977). Black/white interracial families: Marital process and identity development in young children. *Dissertation Abstracts International, 38,* 10-B (University Microfilms No. 78–3137).

Jacobs, J. H. (1992). Identity development in biracial children. In M. P. Root (Ed.), *Racially mixed people in America* (pp. 190–206). Thousand Oaks, CA: Sage.

Jahoda, G. (1999). Images of savages: Ancient roots of modern prejudice in Western culture. New York: Routledge.

Jensen, A. R. (1969). How much can we boost IQ and scholastic achievement? *Harvard Educational Review, 39,* 1–123.

John, O. P., & Srivastava, S. (1999). The Big Five trait taxonomy: History, measurement, and theoretical perspectives. In L. A. Pervin & O. P. John (Eds.), *Handbook of personality: Theory and research* (2nd ed., pp. 102–138). New York: Guilford Press.

Johnson, D. W., & Johnson, R. T. (1996). Conflict resolution and mediation programs in elementary and secondary schools: A review of the research. *Review of Educational Research, 66,* 459–506.

Johnson, P., Buboltz, W. C., Jr., & Seemann, E. (2003). Ego identity status: A step in the differentiation process. *Journal of Counseling & Development, 81,* 191–195.

Johnson, P. E., & Johnson, R. E. (1996). The role of concrete-abstract thinking levels in teachers' multiethnic beliefs. *Journal of Research and Development in Education, 29,* 134–140.

Jones, J. M. (1972). *Prejudice and racism.* Menlo Park, CA: Addison-Wesley.

Jones, J. M. (1997). *Prejudice and racism* (2nd ed.). New York: McGraw-Hill.

Jones, J. M. (2003). TRIOS: A psychological theory of the African legacy in American culture. *Journal of Social Issues, 59,* 217–242.

Jones, J. M., & Carter, R. T. (1996). Racism and white racial identity: Merging realities. In B. P. Bowser & R. G. Hunt (Eds.), *Impacts of racism on White Americans* (2nd ed., pp. 1–23). Thousand Oaks, CA: Sage.

Jones, M. (2002). *Social psychology of prejudice.* Upper Saddle River, NJ: Prentice Hall.

Jordan, W. D. (1968). *Black over white: American attitudes toward the Negro, 1550–1812.* New York: Norton.

Kambon, K. K. K. (1992). *The African personality in America: An African-centered framework.* Tallahassee, FL: Nubian Nation.

Kambon, K. K. K. (1998). *African/Black psychology in the American context.* Tallahassee, FL: Nubian Nation.

Karlsen, S., & Nazroo, J. Y. (2002). Relation between racial discrimination, social class, and health among ethnic minority groups. *American Journal of Public Health, 92,* 624–631.

Katz, I., & Hass, R. G. (1988). Racial ambivalence and American value conflict: Correlational and priming studies of dual cognitive structures. *Journal of Personality and Social Psychology, 55,* 893–905.

Katz, J. H. (1985). The sociopolitical nature of counseling. *Counseling Psychologist, 13,* 615–624.

Katz, P. A. (1987). Development and social processes in ethnic attitudes and self-identification. In J. S. Phinney & M. J. Rotheram (Eds.), *Children's ethnic socialization: Pluralism and development* (pp. 92–99). Newbury Park, CA: Sage.

Kerwin, C. (1991). Racial identity development in biracial children of Black/white racial heritage (Doctoral dissertation, Fordham University, 1991). *Dissertation Abstracts International, 52,* 2469-A.

Kerwin, C., & Ponterotto, J. G. (1995). Biracial identity development: Theory and research. In J. G. Ponterotto, J. M. Casas, L. A. Suzuki, & C. M. Alexander (Eds.), *Handbook of multicultural counseling* (pp. 199–217). Thousand Oaks, CA: Sage.

Kerwin, C., Ponterotto, J. G., Jackson, B. J., & Harris, A. (1993). Racial identity in biracial children: A qualitative investigation. *Journal of Counseling Psychology, 40,* 221–231.

Khmelkov, V. T., & Hallinan, M. T. (1999). Organizational effects on race relations in schools. *Journal of Social Issues, 55*(4), 627–645.

Kich, G. K. (1992). The developmental process of asserting a biracial, bicultural identity. In M. P. P. Root (Ed.), *Racially mixed people of America* (pp. 304–317). Newbury Park, CA: Sage.

Kim, B. S. K., & Abreu, J. M. (2001). Acculturation measurement: Theory, current instruments, and future directions. In J. G. Ponterotto, J. M. Casas, L. A. Suzuki, & C. M. Alexander (Eds.), *Handbook of multicultural counseling* (2nd ed., pp. 394–424). Thousand Oaks, CA: Sage.

Kim, B. S. K., Cartwright, B. Y., Asay, P. A., & D'Andrea, M. J. (2003). A revision of the Multicultural Awareness, Knowledge, and Skills Survey–Counselor Edition. *Measurement and Evaluation in Counseling and Development, 36,* 161–180.

Kim, J. (1981). *Process of Asian-American identity development: A study of Japanese American women's perceptions of their struggle to achieve positive identities.* Unpublished doctoral dissertation, University of Massachusetts, Amherst.

King, L. (1971). *Confessions of a white racist.* New York: Viking.

Kingsbury, W. L., Schiffner, T., Qin, X., & Cheng, S. J. (2005, February). *The development of the Racial Justice Action Scale.* Poster presented at the annual Winter Roundtable on Cross-Cultural Psychology and Education, Teachers College, Columbia University, New York.

Kiselica, M. S. (1999). *Prejudice and racism during multicultural training.* Alexandria, VA: American Counseling Association.

Kitcher, P. (1999). Race, ethnicity, biology, culture. In L. Harris (Ed.), *Racism* (pp. 87–120). Amherst, NY: Humanity.

Kobeisy, A. N. (2004). *Counseling American Muslims: Understanding the faith and helping the people.* Westport, CT: Praeger.

Kocarek, C. E., Talbot, D. M., Batka, J. C., & Anderson, M. Z. (2001). Reliability and validity of three measures of multicultural competency. *Journal of Counseling and Development, 79,* 486–496.

Kohut, H. (1971). *The analysis of the self.* New York: International Universities Press.

Kosciw, J. G. (2001). *The GLSEN 2001 national school climate survey: The school-related experiences of our nation's lesbian, gay, bisexual and transgendered youth.* New York: Gay Lesbian and Straight Education Network.

Kovel, J. (1970). *White racism: A psychohistory.* New York: Pantheon Press.

Krieger, N., & Sidney, S. (1996). Racial discrimination and blood pressure: The CARDIA study of young Black and White adults. *American Journal of Public Health, 86,* 1370–1378.

Krogman, W. M. (1945). The concept of race. In R. Linton (Ed.), *The science of man in world crisis* (pp. 38–61). New York: Columbia University Press.

Krosnick, J. A. (1999). Maximizing questionnaire quality. In J. P. Robinson, P. R. Shaver, & L. S. Wrightsman (Eds.), *Measures of political attitudes* (pp. 37–57). San Diego: Academic Press.

Ladany, N., Inman, A. G., Constantine, M. G., & Hofheinz, E. W. (1997). Supervisee multicultural case conceptualization ability and self-reported multicultural competence as a function of supervisee racial identity and supervisor focus. *Journal of Counseling Psychology, 44,* 284–293.

LaFleur, N. K., Rowe, W., & Leach, M. M. (2002). Reconceptualizing white racial consciousness. *Journal of Multicultural Counseling and Development, 30,* 148–152.

LaFromboise, T. D., Coleman, H. L. K., & Gerton, J. (1993). Psychological impact of biculturalism: Evidence and theory. *Psychological Bulletin, 114,* 395–412.

LaFromboise, T. D., Coleman, H. L. K., & Hernandez, A. (1991). Development and factor structure of the Cross-Cultural Counseling Inventory–Revised. *Professional Psychology: Research and Practice, 22,* 380–388.

Lalonde, R. N, Majunder, S., & Parris, R. D. (1995). Preferred responses to situations of housing and employment discrimination. *Journal of Applied Social Psychology, 25,* 1105–1119.

Landrine, H., & Klonoff, E. A. (1996). The Schedule of Racist Events: A measure of racial discrimination and a study of its negative physical and mental health consequences. *Journal of Black Psychology, 22,* 144–167.

Lattarulo, C. J. (2005). *Gay male identity development: A qualitative exploration.* Unpublished doctoral dissertation, Fordham University, New York.

Lazarus, R. S., & Folkman, S. (1984). *Stress, appraisal, and coping.* New York: Springer.

Leach, M. M., Behrens, J. T., & LaFleur, N. K. (2002). White racial identity and white racial consciousness: Similarities, differences, and recommendations. *Journal of Multicultural Counseling and Development, 30,* 66–80

Levy, S. R. (1999). Reducing prejudice: Lessons from social cognitive factors underlying perceiver differences in prejudice. *Journal of Social Issues, 55*(4), 745–766.

Lewis, J. A., Lewis, M. D., Daniels, J. A., & D'Andrea, M. J. (1998). *Community counseling.* Pacific Grove, CA: Brooks/Cole.

Liang, C. T. H., Li, L. C., & Kim, B. S. K. (2004). The Asian American Racism-Related Stress Inventory: Development, factor analysis, reliability, and validity. *Journal of Counseling Psychology, 51,* 103–114.

Lieber, E., Chin, D., Nihira, K., & Mink, I. T. (2001). Holding on and letting go: Identity and acculturation among Chinese immigrants. *Cultural Diversity and Ethnic Minority Psychology, 7,* 247–261.

Linton, R. (Ed.). (1945). *The science of man in world crisis.* New York: Columbia University Press.

Mann, M. (2005). *The dark side of democracy: Explaining ethnic cleansing.* Cambridge, UK: Cambridge University Press.

Marcia, J. (1966). Development and validation of ego-identity status. *Journal of Personality and Social Psychology, 3,* 551–558.

Marcia, J. (1980). Identity in adolescence. In J. Adelson (Ed.), *Handbook of adolescent psychology* (pp. 159–187). New York: Wiley.

Markides, K. S., & Mindel, C. H. (1987). *Aging and ethnicity.* Newbury Park, CA: Sage.

Marshall, P. L. (1996). Multicultural teaching concerns: New dimensions in the area of teacher concerns research. *Journal of Educational Research, 89,* 371–379.

Martin, J. K., & Hall, G. C. N. (1992), Thinking Black, thinking internal, thinking feminist. *Journal of Counseling Psychology, 39,* 509–514.

McCarn, S. R. (1991). *Validation of a model of sexual minority (lesbian) identity development.* Unpublished master's thesis, University of Maryland, College Park.

McCarn, S. R., & Fassinger, R. E. (1996). Revisioning sexual minority identity formation: A new model of lesbian identity and its implications for counseling and research. *Counseling Psychologist, 24,* 508–534.

McConahay, J. B. (1982). Self-interest versus racial attitudes as correlates of antibusing attitudes in Louisville: Is it the buses or is it the Blacks? *Journal of Politics, 44,* 692–720.

McConahay, J. B. (1986). Modern racism, ambivalence, and the Modern Racism Scale. In S. L. Gaertner & J. Dovidio (Eds.), *Prejudice, discrimination, and racism: Theory and research* (pp. 91–125). New York: Academic Press.

McCord, C., & Freeman, H. P. (1990). Excess mortality in Harlem. *New England Journal of Medicine, 322,* 173–177.

McCrae, R. R., & Costa, P. T., Jr. (1999). A five-factor theory of personality. In L. A. Pervin & O. P. John (Eds.), *Handbook of personality: Theory and research* (2nd ed., pp. 139–153). New York: Guilford Press.

McCrae, R. R., & Costa, P. T., Jr. (2003). *Personality in adulthood: A five-factor theory perspective.* New York: Guilford Press.

McIntosh, P. (1988). *White privilege and male privilege: A personal account of coming to see correspondences through work in women's studies* (Working Paper Series No. 189). Wellesley, MA: Wellesley Center for Research on Women.

McIntosh, P. (1998). White privilege: Unpacking the invisible knapsack. In M. McGoldrick (Ed.), *Re-visioning family therapy: Race, culture, and gender in clinical practice* (pp. 147–152). New York: Guilford Press.

McKenna, N., Roberts, J., & Woodfin, L. (2003). Working cross-culturally in family-school partnerships. In P. Pedersen & J. Carey (Eds.), *Multicultural counseling in schools: A practical handbook* (pp. 131–148). Boston: Allyn & Bacon.

McNeilly, M. D., Anderson, N. B., Armstead, C. A., Clark, R., Corbett, M., Robinson, E. L., et al. (1996). The Perceived Racism Scale: A multidimensional assessment of the experiences of White racism among African-Americans. *Health, Ethnicity, and Disease, 6,* 154–166.

Meerloo, J. A. M. (1961). *That difficult peace.* Great Neck, NY: Channel Press.

Merta, R. J., Wolfgang, L., & McNeil, K. (1993). Five models for using the experiential group in the preparation of group counselors. *Journal for Specialists in Group Work, 4,* 200–207.

Miles, R. (1989). *Racism.* New York: Routledge.

Mio, J. S., & Awakuni, G. I. (2000). *Resistance to multiculturalism: Issues and interventions.* Philadelphia: Brunner/Mazel.

Mitchell, S. L., & Dell, D. M. (1992). The relationship between Black students' racial identity attitude and participation in campus organizations. *Journal of College Student Development, 33,* 39–43.

Miville, M. L. (2005). Psychological functioning and identity development of biracial people: A review of current theory and research. In R. T. Carter (Ed.), *Handbook of racial-cultural psychology and counseling: Theory and research* (Vol. 1, pp. 295–319). New York: Wiley.

Miville, M. L., Constantine, M. G., Baysden, M. F., & So-Lloyd, G. (2005). Chameleon changes: An exploration of racial identity themes of multiracial people. *Journal of Counseling Psychology, 52,* 507–516.

Miville, M. L., Darlington, P., Whitlock, B., & Mulligan, T. (2005). Integrating identities: The relationships of racial, gender, and ego identities among white college students. *Journal of College Student Development, 46,* 157–175.

Miville, M. L., Gelso, C. J., Pannu, R., Liu, W., Touradji, P., Holloway, P., et al. (1999). Appreciating similarities and valuing differences: The Miville-Guzman Universality-Diversity Scale. *Journal of Counseling Psychology, 46,* 291–307.

Miville, M. L., Koonce, D., Darlington, P., & Whitlock, B. (2000). Exploring the relationships between racial/cultural identity and ego identity among African Americans and Mexican Americans. *Journal of Multicultural Counseling and Development, 28,* 208–224.

Miville, M. L., Rohrbacker, J. M., & Kim, A. (2004). Universal-diverse orientation: From prejudice and discrimination to awareness and acceptance. In J. L. Chin (Ed.), *The psychology of prejudice and discrimination* (Vol. 4, pp. 207–232). Westport, CT: Praeger.

Miville, M. L., Romans, J. S. C., Johnson, D., & Lone, R. (2004). Universal-diverse orientation: Linking wellness with social attitudes. *Journal of College Student Psychotherapy, 19*(2), 61–79.

Moradi, B., Subich, L. M., & Phillips, J. (2002). Revisiting feminist identity development: Theory, research, and practice. *Counseling Psychologist, 30,* 6–44.

Morgan, J. C. (1985). *Slavery in the United States: Four views.* Jefferson, NC: McFarland.

Myers, L. J. (1988). *Understanding an Afrocentric world view: Introduction to an optimal psychology.* Dubuque, IA: Kendall/Hunt.

Myers, L. J. (1993). *Understanding an Afrocentric world view: Introduction to an optimal psychology* (2nd ed.). Dubuque, IA: Kendall/Hunt.

Myrdal, G. (1944). *An American dilemma: The Negro problem and democracy.* New York: Harper & Row.

Myrick, R. D. (1997). *Developmental guidance and counseling.* Minneapolis, MN: Educational Media Corporation.

National Advisory Commission on Civil Disorders. (1968). *Report of the National Advisory Commission on Civil Disorders.* New York: Bantam Books.

Neville, H. A., Heppner, M. J., Louie, C. E., Thompson, C. E., Brooks, L., & Baker, C. E. (1996). The impact of multicultural training on White racial identity attitudes and therapy competencies. *Professional Psychology: Research and Practice, 27,* 83–89.

Neville, H. A., Heppner, P. P., & Wang, L. (1997). Relations among racial identity attitudes, perceived stressors, and coping styles in African American college students. *Journal of Counseling and Development, 75,* 303–311.

Neville, H. A., & Lilly, R. L. (2000). The relationship between racial identity cluster profiles and psychological distress among African American college students. *Journal of Multicultural Counseling and Development, 28,* 194–207.

Neville, H. A., Lilly, R. L., Duran, G., Lee, R., & Browne, L. (2000). Construction and initial validation of the Color-Blind Racial Attitude Scale (CoBRAS). *Journal of Counseling Psychology, 47,* 59–70.

Neville, H. A., Worthington, R. L., & Spanierman, L. B. (2001). Race, power, and multicultural counseling psychology: Understanding White privilege and color-blind racial attitudes. In J. G. Ponterotto, J. M. Casas, L. A. Suzuki, & C. M. Alexander (Eds.), *Handbook of multicultural counseling* (2nd ed., pp. 257–288). Thousand Oaks, CA: Sage.

Nieto, S. (2000). *Affirming diversity: The sociopolitical context of multicultural education* (3rd ed.). New York: Longman.

Nobles, W. W. (1986). *African psychology: Toward its reclamation, reascension, and revitalization.* Oakland, CA: Institute for the Advanced Study of Black Family Life and Culture.

Noh, S., Beiser, M., Kaspar, V., Hou, F., & Rummens, J. (1999). Perceived racial discrimination, depression, and coping: A study of Southeast Asian refugees in Canada. *Journal of Health and Social Behavior, 40,* 193–207.

Noyes, M. H. (2003). *Then there were none.* Honolulu, HI: Bess Press.

O'Bryan, M. C., Fishbein, H. D., & Ritchey, P. N. (1999, April). *Parental influences on adolescents' prejudicial attitudes.* Paper presented at the Society for Research on Child Development, Albuqerque, New Mexico.

O'Dougherty, W. M., & Littleford, L. N. (2002). Experiences and beliefs as predictors of ethnic identity and intergroup relations. *Journal of Multicultural Counseling and Development, 30,* 2–10.

Oetting, E. R., & Beauvais, F. (1991). Orthogonal cultural identification theory: The cultural identification of minority adolescents. *International Journal of Addictions, 25*(5A/6A), 655–685.

Omi, M., & Winant, H. (1986). *Racial formation in the United States: From the 1960s to the 1990s* (2nd ed.). New York: Routledge.

Ossana, S. M., Helms, J. E., & Leonard, M. M. (1992). Do "womanist" identity attitudes influence college women's self-esteem and perceptions of environmental bias? *Journal of Counseling and Development, 70,* 402–408.

Ottavi, T. M., Pope-Davis, D. B., & Dings, J. G. (1994). Relationship between White racial identity attitudes and self-reported multicultural counseling competencies. *Journal of Counseling Psychology, 41,* 149–154.

Outlaw, F. H. (1993). Stress and coping: The influence of racism on the cognitive appraisal processing of African Americans. *Issues in Mental Health Nursing, 14,* 399–409.

Pack-Brown, S. P., & Williams, C. B. (2003). *Ethics in a multicultural context.* Thousand Oaks, CA: Sage.

Parham, T. A. (1989). Cycles of psychological nigrescence. *Counseling Psychologist, 17,* 187–226.

Parham, T. A. (Ed.). (2002). *Counseling persons of African descent: Raising the bar of practitioner competence.* Thousand Oaks, CA: Sage.

Parker, W. M., Moore, M. A., & Neimeyer, G. J. (1998). Altering White racial identity and interracial comfort through multicultural training. *Journal of Counseling and Development, 76,* 302–312.

Parks, C. A. (1999). Bicultural competence: A mediating factor affecting alcohol use practices and problems among lesbian social drinkers. *Journal of Drug Issues, 29,* 135–154.

Parks, E. E., Carter, R. T., & Gushue, G. V. (1996). At the crossroads: Racial and womanist identity development in Black and white women. *Journal of Counseling and Development, 74,* 624–631.

Pate, G. S. (1988). Research on reducing prejudice. *Social Education, 52,* 287–289.

Paunonen, S. V. (1998). Hierarchical organization of personality and prediction of behavior. *Journal of Personality and Social Psychology, 74,* 538–556.

Paunonen, S. V., & Ashton, M. C. (2001). Big five predictors of academic achievement. *Journal of Research in Personality, 35,* 78–90.

Paunonen, S. V., & Gardner, R. C. (2001). Biases resulting from the use of aggregated variables in psychology. *Psychological Bulletin, 109,* 520–523.

Paunonen, S. V., & Jackson, D. N. (2000). What is beyond the big five? Plenty! *Journal of Personality, 68,* 821–835.

Paunonen, S. V., Rothstein, M. G., & Jackson, D. N. (1999). Narrow reasoning about the use of broad personality measures in personnel selection. *Journal of Organizational Behavior, 20,* 389–405.

Pedersen, P. B. (1991). Multiculturalism as a generic approach to counseling. *Journal of Counseling & Development, 70,* 6–12.

Pedersen, P. B. (1994). *A handbook for developing multicultural awareness.* Alexandria, VA: American Counseling Association.

Pedersen, P. (1995). *The five stages of culture shock: Critical incidents around the world.* Westport, CT: Greenwood.

Pedersen, P. (2000a). *A handbook for developing multicultural awareness.* Alexandria, VA: American Counseling Association.

Pedersen, P. (2000b). *Hidden messages in culture-centered counseling: A triad training model.* Thousand Oaks, CA: Sage.

Pedersen, P. B. (2001). The seamless cultural connections in my life: No beginning . . . no ending. In J. G. Ponterotto, J. M. Casas, L. A. Suzuki, & C. M. Alexander (Eds.), *Handbook of multicultural counseling* (2nd ed., pp. 96–102). Thousand Oaks, CA: Sage.

Pedersen, P. (2003). Multicultural training in schools as an expansion of the counselor's role. In P. Pedersen & J. Carey (Eds.), *Multicultural counseling in schools: A practical approach* (pp. 190–210). Boston: Allyn & Bacon.

Pedersen, P. B. (2004). *110 experiences for multicultural learning.* Washington, DC: American Psychological Association.

Pettigrew, T. F. (1981). The mental health impact. In B. P. Bowser & R. G. Hunt (Eds.), *Impacts of racism on White Americans* (pp. 97–118). Beverly Hills, CA: Sage.

Pettigrew, T. F. (1988). Integration and pluralism. In P. Katz & D. A. Taylor (Eds.), *Eliminating racism: Profiles in controversy* (pp. 19–30). New York: Plenum.

Pettigrew, T. F. (1996). Intergroup contact theory. *Annual Review of Psychology, 49,* 65–85.

Pettigrew, T. F., & Tropp, L. R. (2000). Does intergroup contact reduce prejudice? Recent meta-analytic findings. In S. Oskamp (Ed.), *Reducing prejudice and discrimination* (pp. 93–114). Mahwah, NJ: Erlbaum.

Phillips, S. T., & Ziller, R. C. (1997). Toward a theory and measure of the nature of nonprejudice. *Journal of Personality and Social Psychology, 72,* 420–434.

Phinney, J. S. (1989). Stages of ethnic identity in minority group adolescence. *Journal of Early Adolescence, 9,* 34–49.

Phinney, J. S. (1990). Ethnic identity in adolescents and adults: Review of research. *Psychological Bulletin, 108,* 499–514.

Phinney, J. S. (1992). The Multigroup Ethnic Identity Measure: A new scale for use with diverse groups. *Journal of Adolescent Research, 7,* 156–176.

Phinney, J. S., & Alipuria, L. (1990). Ethnic identity in older adolescents from four ethnic groups. *Journal of Adolescence, 13,* 171–183.

Phinney, J. S., Lochner, B. T., & Murphy, R. (1990). Ethnic identity development and psychological adjustment in adolescence. In A. R. Stiffman & L. E. Davis (Eds.), *Ethnic issues in adolescent mental health* (pp. 53–72). Newbury Park, CA: Sage.

Phinney, J. S., & Rotheram, M. J. (Eds.). (1987a). *Children's ethnic socialization: Pluralism and development.* Newbury Park, CA: Sage.

Phinney, J. S., & Rotheram, M. J. (1987b). Children's ethnic socialization: Themes and implications. In J. S. Phinney & M. J. Rotheram (Eds.), *Children's ethnic socialization: Pluralism and development* (pp. 274–292). Newbury Park, CA: Sage.

Phinney, J. S., & Tarver, S. (1988). Ethnic identity search and commitment in Black and white eighth graders. *Journal of Early Adolescence, 8,* 265–277.

Pinkney, A. (1993). *Black Americans* (4th ed.). Upper Saddle River, NJ: Prentice Hall.

Plomin, R., & Caspi, A. (1999). Behavioral genetics and personality. In L. A. Pervin & O. P. John (Eds.), *Handbook of personality: Theory and research* (2nd ed., pp. 252–276). New York: Guilford Press.

Plummer, D. L., & Slane, S. (1996). Patterns of coping in racially stressful situations. *Journal of Black Psychology, 22,* 302–315.

Pohan, C. (2000). Practical ideas for teaching children about prejudice, discrimination, and social justice through literature and a standards-based curriculum. *Multicultural Perspectives, 2,* 24–29.

Poindexter-Cameron, J. M., & Robinson, T. L. (1997). Relationships among racial identity attitudes, womanist identity attitudes, and self-esteem in African American college women. *Journal of College Student Development, 38,* 288–296.

Ponterotto, J. G. (1988). Racial consciousness development among White counselor trainees: A stage model. *Journal of Multicultural Counseling and Development, 16,* 146–156.

Ponterotto, J. G. (1991). The nature of prejudice revisited: Implications for counseling intervention. *Journal of Counseling and Development, 70,* 216–224.

Ponterotto, J. G. (2004, April). *The multicultural personality: An evolving construct for psychology.* Keynote address presented at the 14th Annual Diversity Conference, State University of New York, Albany.

Ponterotto, J. G. (in press). Multicultural personality. In Y. Jackson (Ed.), *Encyclopedia of multicultural psychology.* Thousand Oaks, CA: Sage.

Ponterotto, J. G., & Alexander, C. A. (1996). Assessing the multicultural competence of counselors and clinicians. In L. A. Suzuki, P. Meller, & J. G. Ponterotto (Eds.), *Handbook of multicultural assessment: Clinical, psychological, and educational implications* (pp. 651–672). San Francisco: Jossey-Bass.

Ponterotto, J. G., Baluch, S., Greig, T., & Rivera, L. (1998). Development and initial score validation of the Teacher Multicultural Attitude Survey. *Educational and Psychological Measurement, 58,* 1002–1016.

Ponterotto, J. G., Burkard, A. W., Rieger, B. P., Grieger, I., D'Onofrio, A., Dubuisson, A., et al. (1995). Development and initial validation of the Quick Discrimination Index (QDI). *Educational and Psychological Measurement, 55,* 1026–1031.

Ponterotto, J. G., & Casas, J. M. (1991). *Handbook of racial/ethnic minority counseling research.* Springfield, IL: Thomas.

Ponterotto, J. G., Casas, J. M., Suzuki, L. A., & Alexander, C. M. (Eds.). (1995). *Handbook of multicultural counseling.* Thousand Oaks, CA: Sage.

Ponterotto, J. G., Casas, J. M., Suzuki, L. A., & Alexander, C. M. (Eds.). (2001). *Handbook of multicultural counseling* (2nd ed.). Thousand Oaks, CA: Sage.

Ponterotto, J. G., Costa, C. I., Brobst, K., Kowalewska, D., Mendelsohn, J., Scheinholtz, J., et al. (2005). *Multicultural personality dispositions and psychological well-being.* Unpublished manuscript, Division of Psychological and Educational Services, Fordham University, New York.

Ponterotto, J. G., Costa, C. I., & Werner-Lin, A. (2002). Research perspectives in cross-cultural counseling. In P. B. Pedersen, J. G. Draguns, W. J. Lonner, & J. E. Trimble (Eds.), *Counseling across cultures* (5th ed., 395–420). Thousand Oaks, CA: Sage.

Ponterotto, J. G., Gretchen, D., Utsey, S. O., Rieger, B. P., & Austin, R. (2002). A revision of the Multicultural Counseling Awareness Scale. *Journal of Multicultural Counseling and Development, 30,* 153–180.

Ponterotto, J. G., Gretchen, D., Utsey, S. O., Stracuzzi, T., & Saya, R., Jr. (2003). The Multigroup Ethnic Identity Measure (MEIM): Psychometric review and further validity testing. *Educational and Psychological Measurement, 63,* 502–515.

Ponterotto, J. G., Mendelsohn, J., & Belizaire, L. (2003). Assessing teacher multicultural competence: Self-report scales, observer-report evaluations, and a portfolio assessment. In D. B. Pope-Davis, H. L. K Coleman, W. M. Liu, & R. Toporek (Eds.), *Handbook of multicultural competencies* (pp. 191–210). Thousand Oaks, CA: Sage.

Ponterotto, J. G., & Pedersen, P. B. (1993). *Preventing prejudice: A guide for counselors and educators.* Newbury Park, CA: Sage.

Ponterotto, J. G., & Potere, J. C. (2003). The Multicultural Counseling Knowledge and Awareness Scale (MCKAS): Validity, reliability, and user guidelines. In D. B. Pope-Davis, H. L. K Coleman, W. M. Liu, & R. Toporek (Eds.), *Handbook of multicultural competencies* (pp. 137–153). Thousand Oaks, CA: Sage.

Ponterotto, J. G., Potere, J. C., & Johansen, S. A. (2002). The Quick Discrimination Index: Normative data and user guidelines for counseling researchers. *Journal of Multicultural Counseling and Development, 30,* 192–207.

Ponterotto, J. G., Rieger, B. P., Barrett, A., Harris, G., Sparks, R., Sanchez, C., et al. (1996). Development and initial validation of the Multicultural Counseling Awareness Scale. In G. R. Sodowsky & J. C. Impara (Eds.), *Multicultural assessment in counseling and clinical psychology* (pp. 247–282). Lincoln, NE: Buros Institute of Mental Measurements.

Pope, R. L., & Mueller, J. A. (2000). Development and initial validation of the Multicultural Competence in Student Affairs–Version 2 (MCSA–2) Scale. *Journal of College Student Development, 41,* 599–608.

Pope, R. L., Reynolds, A. L., & Mueller, J. A. (2004). *Multicultural competence in student affairs.* San Francisco: Jossey-Bass.

Pope-Davis, D. B., Liu, W. M., Nevitt, J., & Toporek, R. L. (2000). The development and initial validation of the Multicultural Environment Inventory. *Cultural Diversity and Ethnic Minority Psychology, 6,* 57–64.

Pope-Davis, D. P., & Nielson, D. (1996). Assessing multicultural counseling competencies using the Multicultural Counseling Inventory: A review of research.

In G. R. Sodowsky & J. C. Impara (Eds.), *Multicultural assessment in counseling and clinical psychology* (pp. 325–343). Lincoln, NE: Buros Institute of Mental Measurements.

Pope-Davis, D. B., & Ottavi, T. M. (1992). The influence of white racial identity attitudes on racism among faculty members: A preliminary examination. *Journal of College Student Development, 33,* 389–394.

Pope-Davis, D. B., & Ottavi, T. M. (1994). Relationship between racism and racial identity among white Americans: A replication and extension. *Journal of Counseling and Development, 72,* 293–297.

Poston, W. S. C. (1990). The biracial identity development model: A needed addition. *Journal of Multicultural Counseling and Development, 18,* 152–155.

Pratkanis, A. R., & Turner, M. E. (1999). The significance of affirmative action for the souls of White folks: Further implications of a helping model. *Journal of Social Issues, 55*(4), 787–815.

The Prejudice Institute (n.d.). *What is ethnoviolence?* (Factsheet). Retrieved October 20, 2005, from http://www.prejudiceinstitute.org/ethnoviolenceFS.html

Purkey, W. (1992). Conflict resolution: An invitational approach. *Journal of Invitational Theory and Practice, 1,* 111–116.

Pyant, C. T., & Yanico, B. J. (1991). Relationship of racial identity and gender-role attitudes to Black women's psychological well-being. *Journal of Counseling Psychology, 38,* 315–322.

Raja, S., & Stokes, J. P. (1998). Assessing attitudes toward lesbians and gay men: The Modern Homophobia Scale. *Journal of Gay, Lesbian, and Bisexual Identity, 3,* 113–134.

Ramirez, M., III (1991). *Psychotherapy and counseling with minorities: A cognitive approach to individual and cultural differences.* New York: Pergamon Press.

Ramirez, M., III (1999). *Multicultural psychotherapy: An approach to individual and cultural differences* (2nd ed.). New York: Pergamon Press.

Reed, C. (1996). Overcoming prejudices: An invitational approach. *Urban Review, 28,* 81–93.

Ridley, C. R. (1989). Racism in counseling as an adverse behavioral process. In P. B. Pedersen, J. G. Draguns, W. J. Lonner, & J. E. Trimble (Eds.), *Counseling across cultures* (3rd ed., pp. 55–77). Honolulu: University of Hawai'i Press.

Ridley, C. R. (1995). *Overcoming unintentional racism in counseling and therapy: A practitioner's guide to intentional intervention.* Thousand Oaks, CA: Sage.

Ridley, C. R. (2005). *Overcoming unintentional racism in counseling and therapy: A practitioner's guide to intentional intervention* (2nd ed.). Thousand Oaks, CA: Sage.

Robbins, R. H. (1973). Identity, culture, and behavior. In J. J. Honigmann (Ed.), *Handbook of social and cultural anthropology* (pp. 97–124). Chicago: Rand McNally.

Rogler, L. H. (2002). Historical generations and psychology: The case of the Great Depression and World War II. *American Psychologist, 57,* 1013–1023.

Root, M. P .P. (1990). Resolving "other" status: Identity development of biracial individuals. In L. Brown & M. P. P. Root (Eds.), *Complexity and diversity in feminist theory and therapy* (pp. 185–205). New York: Haworth Press.

Root, M. P. P. (Ed.). (1992a). *Racially mixed people in America.* Newbury Park, CA: Sage.

Root, M. P .P. (1992b). Within, between, and beyond race. In M. P. P. Root (Ed.), *Racially mixed people in America* (pp. 3–11). Newbury Park, CA: Sage.

Root, M. P. P. (Ed.). (1996). *The multiracial experience: Racial borders as the new frontier.* Thousand Oaks, CA: Sage.

Root, M. P. P. (1998). Experiences and processes affecting racial identity development: Preliminary results from the Biracial Sibling Project. *Cultural Diversity and Mental Health, 4,* 237–247.

Root, M. P. P. (1999). The biracial baby boom: Understanding ecological constructions of racial identity in the 21st century. In R. Hernandez-Sheets & E. R. Hollins (Eds.), *Racial and ethnic identity in school practices: Aspects of human development* (pp. 67–90). Mahwah, NJ: Erlbaum.

Root, M. P. P. (2001). Negotiating the margins. In J. G. Ponterotto, J. M. Casas, L. A. Suzuki, & C. M. Alexander (Eds.), *Handbook of multicultural counseling* (2nd ed., pp. 113–121). Thousand Oaks, CA: Sage.

Rose, P. I. (1964). *They and we: Racial and ethnic relations in the United States.* New York: Random House.

Rosenbaum, R. (Ed.). (2004). Those who forget the past: The question of anti-semitism. New York: Random House.

Rowe, W., Behrens, J. T., & Leach, M. M. (1995). Racial/ethnic identity and racial consciousness: Looking back and looking forward. In J. G. Ponterotto, J. M. Casas, L. A. Suzuki, & C. M. Alexander (Eds.), *Handbook of multicultural counseling* (pp. 218–235). Thousand Oaks, CA: Sage.

Rowe, W., Bennett, S. K., & Atkinson, D. R. (1994). White racial identity models: A critique and alternate proposal. *Counseling Psychologist, 22,* 129–146.

Roysircar-Sodowsky, G., & Maestas, M. V. (2000). Acculturation, ethnic identity, and acculturation stress: Evidence and measurement. In R. H. Dana (Ed.), *Handbook of cross-cultural and multicultural personality assessment* (pp. 131–172). Mahwah, NJ: Erlbaum.

Ruiz, A. S. (1990). Ethnic identity: Crisis and resolution. *Journal of Multicultural Counseling and Development, 18,* 29–40.

Ryan, M. K., & Buirski, P. (2001). Prejudice as a function of self-organization. *Psychoanalytic Psychology, 18,* 21–36.

Sabnani, H. B., & Ponterotto, J. G. (1992). Racial/ethnic minority instrumentation in counseling research: A review, critique, and recommendations. *Measurement and Evaluation in Counseling and Development, 24,* 161–187.

Sabnani, H. B., Ponterotto, J. G., & Borodovsky, L. G. (1991). White racial identity development and cross-cultural counselor training: A stage model. *Counseling Psychologist, 19,* 76–102.

Sandhu, D. S., & Aspy, C. B. (1997). *Counseling for prejudice prevention and reduction.* Alexandria, VA: American Counseling Association.

Schaller, M. (2003). Ancestral environments and "motivated" social perception. In S. Spencer & S. Fein (Eds.), *Motivated social cognition: The Ninth Ontario Symposium.* Mahwah, NJ: Erlbaum.

Schaller, M., & Park, J. (in press). Prehistoric dangers and contemporary prejudices. In W. Stroebe & M. Hewstone (Eds.), *European Review of Social Psychology* (Vol. 14). Chichester UK: Wiley.

Schaller, M., Park, J. H., & Faulkner, J. (2003). Prehistoric dangers and contemporary prejudices. *European Review of Social Psychology, 14,* 105–137.

Schofield, J. S. (1995). Improving intergroup relations among students. In J. Banks & C. Banks (Eds.), *Handbook of research on multicultural education* (pp. 635–645). New York: Macmillan.

Schutz, H., & Six, B. (1996). How strong is the relationship between prejudice and discrimination? A meta-analytic answer. *International Journal of Intercultural Relations, 20,* 441–462.

Sears, D. O. (1988). Symbolic racism. In P. A. Katz & D. A. Taylor (Eds.), *Eliminating racism: Profiles in controversy* (pp. 53–84). New York: Plenum Press.

Sears, D. O. (1998). Racism and politics in the United States. In J. L. Eberhardt & S. T. Fiske (Eds.), *Confronting racism* (pp. 76–100). Thousand Oaks, CA: Sage.

Sedlacek, W. E., & Brooks, G. C., Jr. (1970). Measuring racial attitudes in a situational context. *Psychological Reports, 27,* 971–980.

Seligman, M. E. P., Steen, T. A., Park, N., & Peterson, C. (2005). Positive psychology progress: Empirical validation of interventions. *American Psychologist, 60,* 410–421.

Sellers, R. M., Rowley, S. A. J., Chavous, T. M., Shelton, J. N., & Smith, M. A. (1997). Multidimensional Inventory of Black Identity: A preliminary investigation of reliability and construct validity. *Journal of Personality and Social Psychology, 73,* 805–815.

Shelton, J. N., & Sellers, R. M. (2000). Situational stability and variability in African American racial identity. *Journal of Black Psychology, 26,* 27–50.

Sherif, M., Harvey, O. J., White, B. J., Hood, W. R., & Sherif, C. W. (1961). *Intergroup cooperation and competition: The Robbers Cave Experiment.* Norman, OK: University Book Exchange.

Sherif, M., & Sherif, C. (1953). *Groups in harmony and tension.* New York: Harper.

Short, G., & Carrington, B. (1991). Unfair discrimination: Teaching the principles to children of primary school age. *Journal of Moral Education, 20,* 157–177.

Sidanius, J., & Pratto, F. (1999). *Social dominance.* Cambridge, MA: Cambridge University Press.

Simpson, G. E., & Yinger, J. M. (1985). *Racial and cultural minorities: An analysis of prejudice and discrimination* (5th ed.). New York: Plenum Press.

Singelis, T. M. (Ed.). (1998). *Teaching about culture, ethnicity, and diversity: Exercises and planned activities.* Thousand Oaks, CA: Sage.

Singh, B. R. (1991). Teaching methods for reducing prejudice and enhancing academic achievement for all children. *Educational Studies, 17,* 157–172.

Skillings, J. H., & Dobbins, J. E. (1991). Racism as a disease: Etiology and treatment implications. *Journal of Counseling & Development, 70,* 206–212.

Slavin, R. E., & Cooper, R. (1999). Improving intergroup relations: Lessons learned from cooperative learning programs. *Journal of Social Issues, 55*(4), 647–664.

Smedley, A., & Smedley, B. D. (2005). Race as biology is fiction, racism as a social problem is real: Anthropological and historical perspectives on the social construction of race. *American Psychologist, 60,* 16–26.

Smith, G., Gerbick, G. L., Figueroa, M. A., Watkins, G. H., Levitan, T., Moore, L. C., et al. (1997). *Diversity works: The emerging picture of how students benefit.* Washington, DC: Association of American Colleges and Universities.

Smith, L. (1963). *Killers of the dream.* Garden City, NJ: Anchor Books.

Snowden, F. M., Jr. (1995). Europe's oldest chapter in the history of Black-White relations. In B. P. Bowser (Ed.), *Racism and anti-racism in world perspective* (pp. 3–26). Thousand Oaks, CA: Sage.

Sodowsky, G. R., Taffe, R. C., Gutkin, T., & Wise, S. L. (1994). Development of the Multicultural Counseling Inventory: A self-report measure of multicultural competencies. *Journal of Counseling Psychology, 41,* 137–148.

Southern Poverty Law Center. (2004, September). Hate among youth becomes widespread. *SPLC Report, 34*(3). Retrieved October 20, 2005, from http://www.splcenter.org/center/splcreport/article.jsp?aid=99

Southern Poverty Law Center. (2005, March). Hate group numbers up slightly in 2004. *SPLC Report, 35*(1), 3. Retrieved October 20, 2005, from http://www.splcenter.org/center/splcreport/article.jsp?aid=135

Spanierman, L. B., & Heppner, M. J. (2004). Psychosocial Costs of Racism to Whites Scale (PCRW): Construction and initial validation. *Journal of Counseling Psychology, 51,* 249–262.

Stalvey, L. M. (1970). *The education of a WASP.* New York: William Morrow.

Stampp, K. M. (1956). *The peculiar institution: Slavery in the ante-bellum south.* New York: Random House.

Stanley, P. H. (1991). Inviting things to do in the privacy of your own mind. In J. M. Novak (Ed.), *Advancing invitational thinking* (pp. 221–242). San Francisco: Caddo Gap Press.

Sternberg, R. J., & Kaufman, J.C. (1998). Human abilities. *Annual Review of Psychology, 49,* 479–502.

Steward, R. J., Boatwright, K. J., Sauer, E., Baden, A., & Jackson, J. D. (1998). The relationships among counselor-trainees' gender, cognitive development, and white racial identity: Implications for counselor training. *Journal of Multicultural Counseling and Development, 26,* 254–272.

Stonequist, E. V. (1935). The problem of marginal man. *American Journal of Sociology, 7,* 1–12.

Sue, D. W. (2003). *Overcoming our racism: The journey to liberation.* New York: Wiley.

Sue, D. W., Arredondo, P., & McDavis, R. J. (1992). Multicultural counseling competencies/standards: A call to the profession. *Journal of Multicultural Counseling and Development, 20,* 64–88.

Sue, D. W., Carter, R. T., Casas, J. M., Fouad, N. A., Ivey, A. E., Jensen, M., et al. (1998). *Multicultural counseling competencies: Individual and organizational development.* Thousand Oaks, CA: Sage.

Sutherland, M. (1993). *Black authenticity: A psychology for liberating people of African descent.* Chicago: Third World Press.

Sutherland, M. E., & Harrell, J. P. (1987). Individual differences in physiological responses to fearful, racially noxious, and neutral imagery. *Imagination, Cognition and Personality, 6,* 133–150.

Tajfel, H. (1970). Experiments in intergroup discrimination. *Scientific American, 223*(2), 96–102.

Tajfel, H. (1974). Social identity and intergroup behavior. *Social Science Information, 13*(2), 65–93.

Tajfel, H. (1978). *The social psychology of minorities.* New York: Minority Rights Group.

Tatum, B. D. (1997). *"Why are all the Black kids sitting together in the cafeteria?"* *and other conversations about race.* New York: Basic Books.

Taub, D. J., & McEwen, M. K. (1992). The relationship of racial identity attitudes to autonomy and mature interpersonal relationships in Black and White undergraduate women. *Journal of College Student Development, 33,* 439–446.

Taylor, C. M., & Howard-Hamilton, M. F. (1995). Student involvement and racial identity attitudes among African American males. *Journal of College Student Development, 36,* 330–336.

Terry, R. W. (1977). *For whites only.* Grand Rapids, MI: Erdmans.

Thomas, A., & Sillen, S. (1972). *Racism and psychiatry.* New York: Citadel Press.

Thompson, A. O. (1977). Race and color prejudice and the origin of the trans-Atlantic slave trade. *Caribbean Studies, 16,* 29–59.

Thompson, B. (Ed.). (2002). *Score reliability: Contemporary thinking on reliability issues.* Thousand Oaks, CA: Sage.

Thompson, R., Brossart, D., Carlozzi, A. F., & Miville, M. L. (2002). Five-factor model (Big Five) and universal-diverse orientation in counselor trainees. *Journal of Psychology, 136,* 561–572.

Timimi, S. B. (1996). Race and color in internal and external reality. *British Journal of Psychotherapy, 13,* 183–192.

Tokar, D. M., & Swanson, J. L. (1991). An investigation of the validity of Helms's (1984) model of White racial identity development. *Journal of Counseling Psychology, 38,* 296–301.

Toporek, R. L., Liu, W. M., & Poe-Davis, D. B. (2003). Assessing multicultural competence of the training environment: Further validation for the psychometric properties of the Multicultual Environment Inventory–Revised. In D. B. Pope-Davis, H. L. K Coleman, W. M. Liu, & R. Toporek (Eds.), *Handbook of multicultural competencies* (pp. 183–190). Thousand Oaks, CA: Sage.

Trask, H.-K. (1999). *From a native daughter: Colonialism and sovereignty in Hawai'i* (rev. ed.). Honolulu: University of Hawai'i Press.

Triandis, H. C., Vassiliou, V., Vassiliou, G., Tanaka, Y., & Shanmugam, A. V. (1972). *The analysis of subjective culture.* New York: Wiley.

Tupes, E. C., & Christal, R. C. (1961). *Recurrent personality factors based on trait ratings* (Technical report). Lackland Air Force Base, TX: United States Air Force.

Tyson, L., & Pedersen, P. (2000). *Critical incidents in school counseling* (2nd ed.). Alexandria, VA: American Counseling Association Reference.

U.S. Census Bureau. (2000). *Statistical abstract of the United States: 1999.* Washington, DC: U.S. Government Printing Office.

U.S. Census Bureau. (2005). *Statistical abstract of the United States: 2004–2005.* Washington, DC: U.S. Government Printing Office.

Utsey, S. O. (1998a). Assessing the stressful effects of racism: A review of instrumentation. *Journal of Black Psychology, 24,* 269–288.

Utsey, S. O. (1998b). Racism, discrimination, and the psychological well-being of African American men. *Journal of African American Men, 3,* 69–87.

Utsey, S. O. (1999). Development and validation of a short form of the Index of Race-Related Stress (IRRS–Brief Version). *Measurement and Evaluation in Counseling and Development, 32,* 149–167.

Utsey, S. O., Bolden, M. A., & Brown, A. L. (2001). Visions of revolution from the spirit of Franz Fanon: A psychology of liberation for counseling African Americans confronting societal racism and oppression. In J. G. Ponterotto, J. M. Casas, L. A. Suzuki, & C. M. Alexander (Eds.), *Handbook of multicultural counseling* (2nd ed., pp. 311–336). Thousand Oaks, CA: Sage.

Utsey, S. O., Bolden, M. A., Brown, C. F., & Chae, M. H. (2001). Assessing quality of life in a cultural context. In L. A. Suzuki, P. M. Meller, & J. G. Ponterotto (Eds.), *Handbook of multicultural assessment: Clinical, psychological, and educational applications* (2nd ed., pp. 191–212). San Francisco: Jossey-Bass.

Utsey, S. O., Chae, M. H., Brown, C. F., & Kelly, D. (2002). Effect of ethnic group membership on ethnic identity, race-related stress, and quality of life. *Cultural Diversity & Ethnic Minority Psychology, 8,* 366–377.

Utsey, S. O., & Gernat, C. A. (2002). White racial identity attitudes and the ego defense mechanisms used by White counselor trainees in racially provocative counseling situations. *Journal of Multicultural Counseling and Development, 80,* 474–483.

Utsey, S. O., Gernat, C., & Bolden, M. A. (2002). Teaching racial identity development and racism awareness: Training in professional psychology programs. In G. Bernal, J. E. Trimble, A. K. Burlew, & F. T. Leong (Eds.), *Handbook of racial and ethnic minority psychology* (pp. 147–166). Thousand Oaks, CA: Sage.

Utsey, S. O., & Ponterotto, J. G. (1996). Development and validation of the Index of Race Related Stress (IRRS). *Journal of Counseling Psychology, 43,* 490–501.

Utsey, S. O., & Ponterotto, J. G. (1999). Further factorial validity assessment of scores on the Quick Discrimination Index (QDI). *Educational and Psychological Measurement, 59,* 325–335.

Van Der Zee, K. I., & Van Oudenhoven, J. P. (2000). The Multicultural Personality Questionnaire: A multidimensional instrument of multicultural effectiveness. *European Journal of Personality, 14,* 291–309.

Van Der Zee, K. I., & Van Oudenhoven, J. P. (2001). The Multicultural Personality Questionnaire: Reliability and validity of self- and other ratings of multicultural effectiveness. *Journal of Research in Personality, 35,* 278–288.

Van der Zee, K. I., Zaal, J. N., & Piekstra, J. (2003). Validation of the Multicultural Personality Questionnaire in the context of personnel selection. *European Journal of Personality, 17,* 77–100.

Vandiver, B. J. (2001). Psychological nigrescence revisited: Introduction and overview. *Journal of Multicultural Counseling and Development, 29,* 165–173.

Vandiver, B. J., Cross, W. E., Jr., Worrell, F. C., & Fhagen-Smith, P. (2002). Validating the Cross Racial Identity Scale. *Journal of Counseling Psychology, 49,* 71–85.

Vandiver, B. J., Fhagen-Smith, P. E., Cokley, K. O., Cross, W. E., Jr., & Worrell, F. C. (2001). Cross's nigrescence model: From theory to scale to theory. *Journal of Multicultural Counseling and Development, 29,* 174–200.

Van Oudenhoven, J. P., Mol, S., & Van der Zee, K. I. (2003). Short note: Study of the adjustment of western expatriates in Taiwan ROC with the Multicultural Personality Questionnaire. *Asian Journal of Social Psychology, 6,* 159–170.

Vasquez, M.J.T. (2001). Reflections on unearned advantages, unearned disadvantages, and empowering experiences. In J. G. Ponterotto, J. M. Casas,

L. A. Suzuki, & C. M. Alexander (Eds.), *Handbook of multicultural counseling* (2nd ed., pp. 64–77). Thousand Oaks, CA: Sage.

Vera, E. M., & Speight, S. L. (2003). Multicultural competence, social justice, and counseling psychology: Expanding our roles. *Counseling Psychologist, 31,* 253–272.

Vinson, T., & Neimeyer, G. J. (2000). The relationship between racial identity development and multicultural counseling competency. *Journal of Multicultural Counseling and Development, 28,* 177–192.

Vinson, T., & Neimeyer, G. J. (2003). The relationship between racial identity development and multicultural counseling competency: A second look. *Journal of Multicultural Counseling and Development, 31,* 262–277.

Vontress, C. E. (1988). An existential approach to cross-cultural counseling. *Journal of Multicultural Counseling and Development, 16,* 78–83.

Vontress, C. E. (1996). A personal retrospective on cross-cultural counseling. *Journal of Multicultural Counseling and Development, 24,* 156–166.

Walker, I. (2001). The changing nature of racism: From old to new. In M. Augoustinos & K. J. Reynolds (Eds.), *Understanding prejudice, racism, and social conflict* (pp. 24–42). Thousand Oaks, CA: Sage.

Walsh, D. (1988). Critical thinking to reduce prejudice. *Social Education, 52,* 280–282.

Webster's New Collegiate Dictionary. (1977). Springfield, MA: Merriam.

Wehrly, B. (1996). *Counseling interracial individuals and families.* Alexandria, VA: American Counseling Association.

Wehrly, B., Kenney, K. R., & Kenney, M. E. (1999). *Counseling multiracial families.* Thousand Oaks, CA: Sage.

Wellman, D. (2000). From evil to illness: Medicalizing racism. *American Journal of Orthopsychiatry, 70,* 28–41.

Welsing, F. C. (1991). *The Isis Papers: The keys to the colors.* Chicago: Third World Press.

Westefeld, J. S., & Heckman-Stone, C. (2003). The integrated problem-solving model of crisis intervention: Overview and application. *Counseling Psychologist, 31,* 221–239.

Whatley, P. R., Allen, J., & Dana, R. H. (2003). Racial identity and the MMPI in African American male college students. *Cultural Diversity & Ethnic Minority Psychology, 9,* 345–353.

Willoughby, B. (2003). Hate on campus. Retrieved November 8, 2005, from the Southern Poverty Law Center Web site: http://www.tolerance.org/news/article_tol.jsp?id=780

Wilson, A. N. (1990). *Black-on-Black violence: The psychodynamics of Black self-annihilation in service of White domination.* New York: Afrikan World Infosystems.

Wilson, A. N. (1998). *Blueprint for Black power: A moral political and economic imperative for the twenty-first century.* New York: Afrikan World Infosystems.

Wilson, J. W., & Constantine, M. G. (1999). Racial identity attitudes, self-concept and perceived family cohesion in Black college students. *Journal of Black Psychology, 29,* 354–366.

Wirth, L. (1945). The problem of minority groups. In R. Linton (Ed.), *The science of man in world crisis* (pp. 347–372). New York: Columbia University Press.

Worrell, F. C., Cross, W. E., Jr., & Vandiver, B. J. (2001). Nigrescence theory: Current status and challenges for the future. *Journal of Multicultural Counseling and Development, 29,* 201–213.

Worthington, R. L., Dillon, F. R., & Becker-Schutte, A. M. (2005). Development, reliability, and validity of the Lesbian, Gay, and Bisexual Knowledge and Attitudes Scale for Heterosexuals (LGB-KASH). *Journal of Counseling Psychology, 52,* 104–118.

Wrenn, C. G. (1985). Afterword: The culturally encapsulated counselor revisited. In P. B. Pedersen (Ed.), *Handbook of cross-cultural counseling and therapy* (pp. 323–329). Westport, CT: Greenwood Press.

Wright, B. E. (1981). *The psychopathic racial personality and other essays.* Chicago: Third World Press.

Yeh, C. J., & Arora, A. K. (2003). Multicultural training and interdependent and independent self-construal as predictors of universal-diverse orientation among school counselors. *Journal of Counseling and Development, 81,* 73–83.

Yinger, J. M. (1976). Ethnicity in complex societies. In L. A. Coser & O. N. Larsen (Eds.), *The uses of controversy in sociology* (pp. 197–216). New York: Free Press.

Zarate, M. A., Garcia, B., Garza, A. A., & Hitlan, R. T. (2004). Cultural threat and perceived realistic group conflict as dual predictors of prejudice. *Journal of Experimental Social Psychology, 40,* 99–105.

Zimbardo, P. G. (2001). Opposing terrorism by understanding the human capacity for evil. *Monitor on Psychology, 32*(10), 48–50.

Author Index

Subject Index

About the Authors

Joseph G. Ponterotto, Ph.D., is Professor of Education in the Counseling Psychology Program at Fordham University, Lincoln Center campus, New York. He received his B.A. in Psychology (Magna Cum Laude) in 1980 from Iona College in New Rochelle, New York, and his M.A. (1981) and Ph.D. (1985) in Counseling Psychology from the University of California, Santa Barbara. His first academic position was at the University of Nebraska at Lincoln (1985–1987). Since 1987, he has been at Fordham University and has served as Director of its Doctoral Program in Counseling Psychology for 6 years. Dr. Ponterotto is a Fellow of the American Psychological Association and the American Association of Applied and Preventive Psychology.

Preventing Prejudice: A Guide for Counselors, Educators, and Parents (2nd ed.) is Dr. Ponterotto's 10th book. Among his other highly acclaimed coauthored or coedited books are the *Handbook of Multicultural Counseling* (also with Sage), the *Handbook of Multicultural Assessment: Clinical, Psychological, and Educational Applications,* and the *Handbook of Racial/Ethnic Minority Counseling Research.* In addition to his books, Dr. Ponterotto is the author of more than 80 peer-reviewed journal articles. He recently completed a term as Associate Editor of the *Journal of Counseling Psychology,* and he has served on the editorial boards of numerous journals in counseling and psychology. In 1994, he was a cowinner of the distinguished Early Career Scientist-Practitioner Award, given by the American Psychological Association's Division of Counseling Psychology.

Independent scholarly impact studies published in the *Journal of Counseling Psychology, The Counseling Psychologist,* the *Journal of Multicultural Counseling and Development,* the *Journal of Counseling and Development,* and *Cultural Diversity and Ethnic Minority Psychology* have identified Dr. Ponterotto as one of the most prolific, often-cited, and impactful multicultural psychology scholars in North America. Dr. Ponterotto is an active multicultural consultant to school districts, universities, hospitals, and mental health agencies nationwide.

 **Shawn O. Utsey** is Associate Professor of Counseling Psychology in the Department of Psychology at Virginia Commonwealth University and Licensed Clinical Psychologist in the state of Virginia. He is also the current Editor-in-Chief for the *Journal of Black Psychology.* Dr. Utsey received his B.A. in Psychology from North Carolina Agricultural and Technical State University in Greensboro, NC. He received his M.A. in Rehabilitation Counseling from New York University and his doctorate in Counseling Psychology from Fordham University. Dr. Utsey completed his clinical internship at Pace University in New York City. Prior academic appointments include Assistant Professor of Counseling Psychology at Seton Hall University (1997–2001) and Associate Professor of Counseling Psychology at Howard University (2001–2004).

Dr. Utsey's research interests are primarily in two areas, both of which are related to the psychology of the African American experience. First, he is interested in understanding how race-related stress affects the physical, psychological, and social well-being of African Americans. More recently, however, he has sought to examine how trauma is manifested in the victims of racial violence. Other areas of interest include examining the influence of African American culture (collective social orientation, spiritual centeredness, verve, etc.) on indicators of health and well-being. Dr. Utsey has published numerous journal articles and book chapters and has presented many papers at professional conferences. He was recently recognized at the 2004 conference of the American Psychological Association, Division 45 and APA Graduate Students, for his work in the area of ethnic minority psychology and for his dedication and commitment as a mentor to students of African descent.

**Paul B. Pedersen** is Visiting Professor in the Department of Psychology at the University of Hawai'i. He has taught at the University of Minnesota, Syracuse University, University of Alabama at Birmingham, and for 6 years at universities in Taiwan, Malaysia, and Indonesia. He was also on the Summer School Faculty at Harvard University (1984–1988) and the University of Pittsburgh Semester at Sea voyage around the world (spring 1992). His international experience includes numerous consulting appointments in Asia, Australia, Africa, South America, and Europe and a Senior Fulbright Award teaching at National Taiwan University (1999–2000).

He has authored, coauthored, or edited 40 books, 99 articles, and 72 chapters on aspects of multicultural counseling and international communication. He is a Fellow in Divisions 9, 17, 45, and 52 of the American Psychological Association. His research activities include Co-Director of Research in a 10-day intercultural communication laboratory for 60 Japanese and U.S. intercultural communication experts at Nihonmatsu, Japan, funded by the Lily Foundation; reentry research among LASPAU students from Brazil; Director of Higher Education Research on Sex-Role Stereotypes in Higher Education on a U.S. Department of Health, Education, and Welfare grant; Director of a 3-year National Institute of Mental Health mental health training program; National Science Foundation 6-year grant to study the reentry adjustment of engineers returning to Taiwan after study abroad; National Institute of Education grant to develop a measure of cross-cultural counseling skill; State of New York Department of Social Services grant to develop mental health training materials on unaccompanied refugee minors; a 2-year Harvard Institute for International Development project in Indonesia to evaluate and upgrade training at Bank Rakyat Training Centers; and an Asian Foundation grant to coorganize a conference in Penang, Malaysia, on constructive conflict management in a cultural context.

Professional activities have included 3 years as President of the 1800-member Society for Intercultural Education Training and Research; Senior Editor of the Sage Publications Multicultural Aspects of Counseling Series; Advising Editor for Education and for Psychology for Greenwood Press book series; Board Member of The Micronesian Institute, headquartered in Washington, D.C.; External Examiner for University Putra Malaysia,

University Kebangsaan, and University Malaysia Sabah in Psychology; Senior Fulbright Scholar teaching at National Taiwan University (1999–2000); Member of the Committee for International Relations in Psychology at the American Psychological Association (2001–2003); invited Master Lecturer at the American Psychological Association (August 1994); Senior Fellow at the East-West Center (1975–1976, 1978–1981); Senior Fulbright Award to teach at National Taiwan University (1999–2000); and election to APA's Committee for International Relations in Psychology.

Dr. Pedersen's Web site may be found at http://soeweb.syr.edu/chs/pedersen.